WHITE COLLAR

The American Middle Classes

WHITE COLLAR

The American Middle Classes

by C. Wright Mills

OXFORD UNIVERSITY PRESS

LONDON   OXFORD   NEW YORK

OXFORD UNIVERSITY PRESS
Oxford   London   Glasgow
New York   Toronto   Melbourne   Wellington
Nairobi   Dar es Salaam   Cape Town
Kuala Lumpur   Singapore   Jakarta   Hong Kong   Tokyo
Delhi   Bombay   Calcutta   Madras   Karachi

First published by Oxford University Press, New York, 1951

First issued as an Oxford University Press paperback, 1956

printing, last digit: 39 38 37

PRINTED IN THE UNITED STATES OF AMERICA

Contents

'No one could suspect that times were coming . . . when the man who did not gamble would lose all the time, even more surely than he who gambled.'

CHARLES PÉGUY

Introduction

THE white-collar people slipped quietly into modern society. Whatever history they have had is a history without events; whatever common interests they have do not lead to unity; whatever future they have will not be of their own making. If they aspire at all it is to a middle course, at a time when no middle course is available, and hence to an illusory course in an imaginary society. Internally, they are split, fragmented; externally, they are dependent on larger forces. Even if they gained the will to act, their actions, being unorganized, would be less a movement than a tangle of unconnected contests. As a group, they do not threaten anyone; as individuals, they do not practice an independent way of life. So before an adequate idea of them could be formed, they have been taken for granted as familiar actors of the urban mass.

Yet it is to this white-collar world that one must look for much that is characteristic of twentieth-century existence. By their rise to numerical importance, the white-collar people have upset the nineteenth-century expectation that society would be divided between entrepreneurs and wage workers. By their mass way of life, they have transformed the tang and feel of the American experience. They carry, in a most revealing way, many of those psychological themes that characterize our epoch, and, in one way or another, every general theory of the main drift has had to take account of them. For above all else they are a new cast of actors, performing the major routines of twentieth-century society:

At the top of the white-collar world, the old captain of industry hands over his tasks to the manager of the corporation. Alongside the politician, with his string tie and ready tongue, the salaried bureaucrat, with brief case and slide rule, rises into political view. These top managers now command hierarchies of anonymous middle managers, floorwalkers, salaried foremen, county agents, federal inspectors, and police investigators trained in the law.

In the established professions, the doctor, lawyer, engineer, once was free and named on his own shingle; in the new white-collar world, the salaried specialists of the clinic, the junior partners in the law factory, the captive engineers of the corporation have begun to challenge free professional leadership. The old professions of medicine and law are still at the top of the professional world, but now all around them are men and women of new skills. There are a dozen kinds of social engineers and mechanical technicians, a multitude of girl Fridays, laboratory assistants, registered and unregistered nurses, draftsmen, statisticians, social workers.

In the salesrooms, which sometimes seem to coincide with the new society as a whole, are the stationary salesgirls in the department store, the mobile salesmen of insurance, the absentee salesmen—ad-men helping others sell from a distance. At the top are the prima donnas, the vice presidents who say that they are 'merely salesmen, although perhaps a little more creative than others,' and at the bottom, the five-and-dime clerks, selling commodities at a fixed price, hoping soon to leave the job for marriage.

In the enormous file of the office, in all the calculating rooms, accountants and purchasing agents replace the man who did his own figuring. And in the lower reaches of the white-collar world, office operatives grind along, loading and emptying the filing system; there are private secretaries and typists, entry clerks, billing clerks, corresponding clerks—a thousand kinds of clerks; the operators of light machinery, comptometers, dictaphones, addressographs; and the receptionists to let you in or keep you out.

Images of white-collar types are now part of the literature of every major industrial nation: Hans Fallada presented the

Pinnebergs to pre-Hitler Germany. Johannes Pinneberg, a book-keeper trapped by inflation, depression, and wife with child, ends up in the economic gutter, with no answer to the question, 'Little Man, What Now?'—except support by a genuinely prole-tarian wife. J. B. Priestley created a gallery of tortured and in-secure creatures from the white-collar world of London in *Angel Pavement*. Here are people who have been stood up by life: what they most desire is forbidden them by reason of what they are. George Orwell's Mr. Bowling, a salesman in *Coming Up for Air,* speaks for them all, perhaps, when he says: 'There's a lot of rot talked about the sufferings of the working class. I'm not so sorry for the proles myself. . . The prole suffers physically, but he's a free man when he isn't working. But in every one of those little stucco boxes there's some poor bastard who's never free except when he's fast asleep and dreaming that he's got the boss down the bottom of a well and is bunging lumps of coal at him. Of course the basic trouble with people like us is that we all imagine we've got something to lose.'

Kitty Foyle is perhaps the closest American counterpart of these European novels. But how different its heroine is! In Amer-ica, unlike Europe, the fate of white-collar types is not yet clear. A modernized Horatio Alger heroine, Kitty Foyle (like Alice Adams before her) has aspirations up the Main Line. The book ends, in a depression year, with Kitty earning $3000 a year, about to buy stock in her firm, and hesitating over marrying a doctor who happens to be a Jew. While Herr Pinneberg in Ger-many was finding out, too late, that his proletarian wife was at once his life fate and his political chance, Kitty Foyle was busy pursuing an American career in the cosmetics business. But twenty-five years later, during the American postwar boom Willy Loman appears, the hero of *The Death of a Salesman,* the white-collar man who by the very virtue of his moderate success in business turns out to be a total failure in life. Frederic Wertham has written of Willy Loman's dream: 'He succeeds with it; he fails with it; he dies with it. But why did he have this dream? Isn't it true that he had to have a false dream in our society?'

The nineteenth-century farmer and businessman were gen-erally thought to be stalwart individuals—their own men, men who could quickly grow to be almost as big as anyone else. The twentieth-century white-collar man has never been independent as the farmer used to be, nor as hopeful of the main chance as the businessman. He is always somebody's man, the corporation's, the government's, the army's; and he is seen as the man who does not rise. The decline of the free entrepreneur and the rise of the dependent employee on the American scene has paralleled the decline of the independent individual and the rise of the little man in the American mind.

In a world crowded with big ugly forces, the white-collar man is readily assumed to possess all the supposed virtues of the small creature. He may be at the bottom of the social world, but he is, at the same time, gratifyingly middle class. It is easy as well as safe to sympathize with his troubles; he can do little or nothing about them. Other social actors threaten to become big and aggressive, to act out of selfish interests and deal in politics. The big businessman continues his big-business-as-usual through the normal rhythm of slump and war and boom; the big labor man, lifting his shaggy eyebrows, holds up the nation until his demands are met; the big farmer cultivates the Senate to see that big farmers get theirs. But not the white-collar man. He is more often pitiful than tragic, as he is seen collectively, fighting impersonal inflation, living out in slow misery his yearning for the quick American climb. He is pushed by forces beyond his control, pulled into movements he does not understand; he gets into situations in which his is the most helpless position. The white-collar man is the hero as victim, the small creature who is acted upon but who does not act, who works along unnoticed in somebody's office or store, never talking loud, never talking back, never taking a stand.

When the focus shifts from the generalized Little Man to specific white-collar types whom the public encounters, the images become diverse and often unsympathetic. Sympathy itself often carries a sharp patronizing edge; the word 'clerk,' for example, is likely to be preceded by 'merely.' Who talks willingly to the insurance agent, opens the door to the bill collector? 'Everybody knows how rude and nasty salesgirls can be.' Schoolteachers are standard subjects for businessmen's jokes. The housewife's opin ion of private secretaries is not often friendly—indeed, much of white-collar fiction capitalizes on her hostility to 'the office wife.'

These are images of specific white-collar types seen from above. But from below, for two generations sons and daughters of the poor have looked forward eagerly to becoming even 'mere' clerks. Parents have sacrificed to have even one child finish high school, business school, or college so that he could be the assistant to the executive, do the filing, type the letter, teach school, work in the government office, do something requiring technical skills: hold a white-collar job. In serious literature white-collar images are often subjects for lamentation; in popular writing they are often targets of aspiration.

Images of American types have not been built carefully by piecing together live experience. Here, as elsewhere, they have been made up out of tradition and schoolbook and the early, easy drift of the unalerted mind. And they have been reinforced and even created, especially in white-collar times, by the editorial machinery of popular amusement and mass communications.

Manipulations by professional image-makers are effective because their audiences do not or cannot know personally all the people they want to talk about or be like, and because they have an unconscious need to believe in certain types. In their need and inexperience, such audiences snatch and hold to the glimpses of types that are frozen into the language with which they see the world. Even when they meet the people behind the types face to face, previous images, linked deeply with feeling, blind them to what stands before them. Experience is trapped by false images, even as reality itself sometimes seems to imitate the soap opera and the publicity release.

Perhaps the most cherished national images are sentimental versions of historical types that no longer exist, if indeed they ever did. Underpinning many standard images of The American is the myth, in the words of the eminent historian, A. M. Schlesinger, Sr., of the 'long tutelage to the soil' which, as 'the chief formative influence,' results in 'courage, creative energy and resourcefulness. . .' According to this idea, which clearly bears a nineteenth-century trademark, The American possesses magical independence, homely ingenuity, great capacity for work, all of which virtues he attained while struggling to subdue the vast continent.

One hundred years ago, when three-fourths of the people were farmers, there may have been some justification for engraving such an image and calling it The American. But since then, farmers have declined to scarcely more than one-tenth of the occupied populace, and new classes of salaried employees and wage-workers have risen. Deep-going historic changes resulting in wide diversities have long challenged the nationalistic historian who would cling to The American as a single type of ingenious farmer-artisan. In so far as universals can be found in life and character in America, they are due less to any common tutelage of the soil than to the leveling influences of urban civilization, and above all, to the standardization of the big technology and of the media of mass communication.

America is neither the nation of horse-traders and master builders of economic theory, nor the nation of go-getting, claim-jumping, cattle-rustling pioneers of frontier mythology. Nor have the traits rightly or wrongly associated with such historic types carried over into the contemporary population to any noticeable degree. Only a fraction of this population consists of free private enterprisers in any economic sense; there are now four times as many wage-workers and salary workers as independent entrepreneurs. 'The struggle for life,' William Dean Howells wrote in the 'nineties, 'has changed from a free fight to an encounter of disciplined forces, and the free fighters that are left get ground to pieces. . .'

If it is assumed that white-collar employees represent some sort of continuity with the old middle class of entrepreneurs, then it may be said that for the last hundred years the middle classes have been facing the slow expropriation of their holdings, and that for the last twenty years they have faced the spectre of unemployment. Both assertions rest on facts, but the facts have not been experienced by the middle class as a *double* crisis. The property question is not an issue to the new middle class of the present generation. That was fought out, and lost, before World War I, by the old middle class. The centralization of small properties is a development that has affected each generation back to our great-grandfathers, reaching its climax in the Progressive Era.

It has been a secular trend of too slow a tempo to be felt as a continuing crisis by middle-class men and women, who often seem to have become more commodity-minded than property-minded. Yet history is not always enacted consciously; if expropriation is not felt as crisis, still it is a basic fact in the ways of life and the aspirations of the new middle class; and the facts of unemployment *are* felt as fears, hanging over the white-collar world.

By examining white-collar life, it is possible to learn something about what is becoming more typically 'American' than the frontier character probably ever was. What must be grasped is the picture of society as a great salesroom, an enormous file, an incorporated brain, a new universe of management and manipulation. By understanding these diverse white-collar worlds, one can also understand better the shape and meaning of modern society as a whole, as well as the simple hopes and complex anxieties that grip all the people who are sweating it out in the middle of the twentieth century.

The troubles that confront the white-collar people are the troubles of all men and women living in the twentieth century. If these troubles seem particularly bitter to the new middle strata, perhaps that is because for a brief time these people felt themselves immune to troubles.

Before the First World War there were fewer little men, and in their brief monopoly of high-school education they were in fact protected from many of the sharper edges of the workings of capitalist progress. They were free to entertain deep illusions about their individual abilities and about the collective trustworthiness of the system. As their number has grown, however, they have become increasingly subject to wage-worker conditions. Especially since the Great Depression have white-collar people come up against all the old problems of capitalist society. They have been racked by slump and war and even by boom. They have learned about impersonal unemployment in depressions and about impersonal death by technological violence in war. And in good times, as prices rose faster than salaries, the money they thought they were making was silently taken away from them.

The material hardship of nineteenth-century industrial workers finds its parallel on the psychological level among twentieth-century white-collar employees. The new Little Man seems to have no firm roots, no sure loyalties to sustain his life and give it a center. He is not aware of having any history, his past being as brief as it is unheroic; he has lived through no golden age he can recall in time of trouble. Perhaps because he does not know where he is going, he is in a frantic hurry; perhaps because he does not know what frightens him, he is paralyzed with fear. This is especially a feature of his political life, where the paralysis results in the most profound apathy of modern times.

The uneasiness, the malaise of our time, is due to this root fact: in our politics and economy, in family life and religion—in practically every sphere of our existence—the certainties of the eighteenth and nineteenth centuries have disintegrated or been destroyed and, at the same time, no new sanctions or justifications for the new routines we live, and must live, have taken hold. So there is no acceptance and there is no rejection, no sweeping hope and no sweeping rebellion. There is no plan of life. Among white-collar people, the malaise is deep-rooted; for the absence of any order of belief has left them morally defenseless as individuals and politically impotent as a group. Newly created in a harsh time of creation, white-collar man has no culture to lean upon except the contents of a mass society that has shaped him and seeks to manipulate him to its alien ends. For security's sake, he must strain to attach himself somewhere, but no communities or organizations seem to be thoroughly his. This isolated position makes him excellent material for synthetic molding at the hands of popular culture—print, film, radio, and television. As a metropolitan dweller, he is especially open to the focused onslaught of all the manufactured loyalties and distractions that are contrived and urgently pressed upon those who live in worlds they never made.

In the case of the white-collar man, the alienation of the wage-worker from the products of his work is carried one step nearer to its Kafka-like completion. The salaried employee does not make anything, although he may handle much that he greatly desires but cannot have. No product of craftsmanship can be his to contemplate with pleasure as it is being created and after it

is made. Being alienated from any product of his labor, and going year after year through the same paper routine, he turns his leisure all the more frenziedly to the *ersatz* diversion that is sold him, and partakes of the synthetic excitement that neither eases nor releases. He is bored at work and restless at play, and this terrible alternation wears him out.

In his work he often clashes with customer and superior, and must almost always be the standardized loser: he must smile and be personable, standing behind the counter, or waiting in the outer office. In many strata of white-collar employment, such traits as courtesy, helpfulness, and kindness, once intimate, are now part of the impersonal means of livelihood. Self-alienation is thus an accompaniment of his alienated labor.

When white-collar people get jobs, they sell not only their time and energy but their personalities as well. They sell by the week or month their smiles and their kindly gestures, and they must practice the prompt repression of resentment and aggression. For these intimate traits are of commercial relevance and required for the more efficient and profitable distribution of goods and services. Here are the new little Machiavellians, practicing their personable crafts for hire and for the profit of others, according to rules laid down by those above them.

In the eighteenth and nineteenth centuries, rationality was identified with freedom. The ideas of Freud about the individual, and of Marx about society, were strengthened by the assumption of the coincidence of freedom and rationality. Now rationality seems to have taken on a new form, to have its seat not in individual men, but in social institutions which by their bureaucratic planning and mathematical foresight usurp both freedom and rationality from the little individual men caught in them. The calculating hierarchies of department store and industrial corporation, of rationalized office and governmental bureau, lay out the gray ways of work and stereotype the permitted initiatives. And in all this bureaucratic usurpation of freedom and of rationality, the white-collar people are the interchangeable parts of the big chains of authority that bind the society together.

White-collar people, always visible but rarely seen, are politically voiceless. Stray politicians wandering in the political arena without party may put 'white collar' people alongside business-

men, farmers, and wage-workers in their broadside appeals, but no platform of either major party has yet referred to them directly. Who fears the clerk? Neither *Alice Adams* nor *Kitty Foyle* could be a *Grapes of Wrath* for the 'share-croppers in the dust bowl of business.'

But while practical politicians, still living in the ideological air of the nineteenth century, have paid little attention to the new middle class, theoreticians of the left have vigorously claimed the salaried employee as a potential proletarian, and theoreticians of the right and center have hailed him as a sign of the continuing bulk and vigor of the middle class. Stray heretics from both camps have even thought, from time to time, that the higher-ups of the white-collar world might form a center of initiative for new political beginnings. In Germany, the 'black-coated worker' was one of the harps that Hitler played on his way to power. In England, the party of labor is thought to have won electoral socialism by capturing the votes of the suburban salaried workers.

To the question, what political direction will the white-collar people take, there are as many answers as there are theorists. Yet to the observer of American materials, the political problem posed by these people is not so much what the direction may be as whether they will take any political direction at all.

Between the little man's consciousness and the issues of our epoch there seems to be a veil of indifference. His will seems numbed, his spirit meager. Other men of other strata are also politically indifferent, but electoral victories are imputed to them; they do have tireless pressure groups and excited captains who work in and around the hubs of power, to whom, it may be imagined, they have delegated their enthusiasm for public affairs. But white-collar people are scattered along the rims of all the wheels of power: no one is enthusiastic about them and, like political eunuchs, they themselves are without potency and without enthusiasm for the urgent political clash.

Estranged from community and society in a context of distrust and manipulation; alienated from work and, on the personality market, from self; expropriated of individual rationality, and politically apathetic—these are the new little people, the unwilling vanguard of modern society. These are some of the circum-

stances for the acceptance of which their hopeful training has quite unprepared them.

What men are interested in is not always what is to their interest; the troubles they are aware of are not always the ones that beset them. It would indeed be a fetish of 'democracy' to assume that men immediately know their interests and are clearly aware of the conditions within themselves and their society that frustrate them and make their efforts misfire. For interests involve not only values felt, but also something of the means by which these values might be attained. Merely by looking into himself, an individual can neither clarify his values nor set up ways for their attainment. Increased awareness is not enough, for it is not only that men can be unconscious of their situations; they are often falsely conscious of them. To become more truly conscious, white-collar people would have to become aware of themselves as members of new strata practicing new modes of work and life in modern America. To know what it is possible to know about their troubles, they would have to connect, within the going framework, what they are interested in with what is to their interest.

If only because of its growing numbers, the new middle class represents a considerable social and political potential, yet there is more systematic information available on the farmer, the wage-worker, the Negro, even on the criminal, than on the men and women of the variegated white-collar worlds. Even the United States census is now so arranged as to make very difficult a definitive count of these people. Meanwhile, theorizing about the middle class on the basis of old facts has run to seed, and no fresh plots of fact have been planted. Yet the human and political importance of the white-collar people continues to loom larger and larger.

Liberalism's ideal was set forth for the domain of small property; Marxism's projection, for that of unalienated labor. Now when labor is everywhere alienated and small property no longer an anchor of freedom or security, both these philosophies can characterize modern society only negatively; neither can articulate new developments in their own terms. We must accuse both John Stuart Mill and Karl Marx of having done their work a hundred years ago. What has happened since then cannot be adequately described as the destruction of the nineteenth-century world; by now, the outlines of a new society have arisen around us, a society anchored in institutions the nineteenth century did not know. The general idea of the new middle class, in all its vagueness but also in all its ramifications, is an attempt to grasp these new developments of social structure and human character.

In terms of social philosophy, this book is written on the assumption that the liberal ethos, as developed in the first two decades of this century by such men as Beard, Dewey, Holmes, is now often irrelevant, and that the Marxian view, popular in the American 'thirties, is now often inadequate. However important and suggestive they may be as beginning points, and both are that, they do not enable us to understand what is essential to our time.

We need to characterize American society of the mid-twentieth century in more psychological terms, for now the problems that concern us most border on the psychiatric. It is one great task of social studies today to describe the larger economic and political situation in terms of its meaning for the inner life and the external career of the individual, and in doing this to take into account how the individual often becomes falsely conscious and blinded. In the welter of the individual's daily experience the framework of modern society must be sought; within that framework the psychology of the little man must be formulated.

The first lesson of modern sociology is that the individual cannot understand his own experience or gauge his own fate without locating himself within the trends of his epoch and the life-chances of all the individuals of his social layer. To understand the white-collar people in detail, it is necessary to draw at least a rough sketch of the social structure of which they are a part. For the character of any stratum consists in large part of its relations, or lack of them, with the strata above and below it; its peculiarities can best be defined by noting its differences from other strata. The situation of the new middle class, reflecting conditions and styles of life that are borne by elements of both the new lower and the new upper classes, may be seen as symptom and symbol of modern society as a whole.

ONE

Old Middle Classes

'Whatever the future may contain, the past has shown no more excellent social order than that in which the mass of the people were the masters of the holdings which they plowed and of the tools with which they worked, and could boast . . . "it is a quietness to a man's mind to live upon his own and to know his heir certain." '

R. H. TAWNEY

1

The World
of the Small Entrepreneur

THE early history of the middle classes in America is a history
of how the small entrepreneur, the free man of the old middle
classes, came into his time of daylight, of how he fought against
enemies he could see, and of the world he built. The latter-day
history of these old middle classes is, in large part, the history
of how epochal changes on the farm and in the city have transformed him, and of how his world has been splintered and re-
fashioned into an alien shape.

The small entrepreneur built his world along the classic lines
of middle-class capitalism: a remarkable society with a self-balancing principle, requiring little or no authority at the center, but
only wide-flung traditions and a few safeguards for property.
Here the ideas of the political economist Adam Smith coincided
with those of the political moralist Thomas Jefferson; together
they form the ideology of the naturally harmonious world of the
small entrepreneur.

1. The Old Middle Classes

Unlike the European, the American middle classes enter modern history as a big stratum of small enterprisers. Here the bourgeoisie exists before and outside of the city. In rural Europe,
Max Weber has written, 'the producer is older than the market'; a
mass of peasants occupy the land, held to it by ancient tradition,

so firmly that even the force of law during later periods never turn them into rural entrepreneurs in the American sense. In America, the market is older than the rural producer.

The difference between a peasant mass and a scattering of farmers is one of the historic differences between the social structures of Europe and America, and is of signal consequence for the character of the middle classes on both continents. There they begin as a narrow stratum in the urban centers; here, as a broad stratum of free farmers. Throughout the whole of United States history, the farmer is the numerical ballast of the independent middle class.

In American society neither peasants nor aristocracy have ever existed in the European sense. The land was occupied by men whose absolute individualism involved an absence of traditional fetters, and who, unhampered by the heirlooms of feudal Europe, were ready and eager to realize the drive toward capitalism. They did not cluster together in villages but scattered into an open country. Even in the South men who held large acreages were usually of yeoman stock, and bore the economic and political marks of rural capitalists. After the American Revolution, many big northern estates were confiscated and some were sold on relatively easy terms in small lots to small farmers. Europe's five-hundred-year struggle out of feudalism has not absorbed the energies of the United States producer; a contractual society began here almost *de novo* as a capitalist order.

Capitalism requires private owners of property who direct economic activities for private profit. Toward this system and away from subsistence, the American farmers traveled by way of new transport systems on coastal waters, rivers, turnpikes, canals, and railroads. From the beginning those on the land needed cash for taxes, mortgage payments, and necessities they could not grow or build. The American farmer, always an enterpriser, labored to add to his capital plant; and, as Chevalier put it in 1835, 'everyone is speculating, and everything has become an object of speculation . . . cotton, land, city and town lots, banks, railroads.' The American farmer has always been a real-estate speculator as well as a husbandman, a 'cultivator,' as Veblen said, 'of the main chance as well as of the fertile soil,' riding the land-boom that characterized United States history up to 1920. Here, if anywhere, the small capitalist had his rural chance.

Before the Civil War, images of business were largely those conceived by farmers; business, in the American mind, was composed of moneylenders and bankers, controlled by powerful vested interests in eastern urban centers. Yet, as Guy Callender has observed, 'The stock of manufacturing companies was usually owned by the men directly interested in the enterprise, and was rarely bought and sold. . . Such capital as existed in 1830 was chiefly in the hand of small savers, who were naturally more interested in security than in the chance of large returns. . . The great majority of both banks and insurance companies were small concerns with less than $100,000 capital.' Manufacturing companies were even smaller.

The early businessman was a diversified economic type: merchant, moneylender, speculator, shipper, 'cottage' manufacturer. In the early nineteenth-century city, this undifferentiated merchant was at the top, the laborer in port, machine shop, and livery stable at the bottom of society; but the greatest numbers were handicrafters and tradesmen of small but independent means. The worker was no factory employee: he was a mechanic or journeyman who looked forward to owning his own shop, or a farmer to whom manufacturing was a sideline, carried on sometimes as a cottage industry. As the cities grew with industrialization, their entrepreneurs and workers formed larger markets for the farmers, and at the same time found their own expanding markets in the rural areas.

The industrialization of America, especially after the Civil War, gave rise not to a broad stratum of small businessmen, but to the captain of industry. He was our first national image of the middle-class man as businessman, and no one has ever supplanted him. In the classic image, the captain was at once a master builder and an astute financier, but above all a success. He was the active owner of what he had created and then managed. Nothing about the operation of his going concern failed to draw his alert attention or receive his loving care. In his role as employer, he provided opportunity for the best of the men he hired to learn from working under him; they might themselves save a portion of their wages, multiply this by a small private speculation, borrow more on their character, and start up on their own. Even as he had done before them, his employees could also become captains of industry.

The glory imputed to this urban hero of the old middle class has been due to his double-barrelled success, as technologist-in-dustrialist and as financier-businessman. In the nineteenth century these two distinct activities were closely enough centered in one type of man to give rise to the undivided image of the captain of industry as both master builder and organizer of all new beginnings.

The middle-class world was not inhabited entirely by ungraded, small entrepreneurs. Within it there was a division between small farmers and small producers on the one hand, and large landlords and merchants on the other. There were also those who not only owned no property but were themselves the property of others; yet slavery, the glaring exception to the more generous ideals of the American Revolution, did not loom so large as is often assumed. It was confined to one section, did not move very far west, and was abolished in mid-century. Even in the slave-holding states in 1850, only 30 per cent of the white families held slaves, and three-fourths of these held less than ten slaves; the average slave-holder was a small independent farmer who worked on his property in land alongside his property in men.

In the end, the development of the split between small and large property, rather than any sharp red line between those with property and those without it, destroyed the world of the small entrepreneur. Yet the historical fulfilment of the big enterpriser was hampered and delayed for long decades of the nineteenth century. The smaller world was sheltered by international distance, and if what was to destroy it already lay within it, the small entrepreneur in his heyday was not made anxious by this emerging fact about the society he was so confidently building. Between mercantilism and subsistence farming in the beginning, and monopoly and high finance at the end, the society of the small entrepreneur flourished and became the seedbed of middle-class ideal and aspiration and myth.

2. Property, Freedom & Security

The most important single fact about the society of small entrepreneurs was that a substantial proportion of the people owned
the property with which they worked. Here the middle class was
so broad a stratum and of such economic weight that even by
the standards of the statistician the society as a whole was a
middle-class society: perhaps four-fifths of the free people who
worked owned property. In 1830 Tocqueville wrote, 'Great
wealth tends to disappear, the number of small fortunes to increase.' Though he may well have exaggerated even for his own
time, the mood he reflects was that of the people about whom he
wrote.

This world did in reality contain propertyless people, but there
was so much movement in and out of the petty-bourgeois level
of farmers that it appeared that they need not remain propertyless for long. Among the generation of elite businessmen who
came to maturity during the first fifty years of the nineteenth century almost half were of lower-class origin; before that, under
mercantilism, and afterward, under monopoly capitalism, the
proportion was scarcely one-fifth. 'One could always begin again
in America,' John Krout and Dixon Ryan Fox pointed out; 'bankruptcy, which in the fixed society of Europe was the tragic end
of a career, might be merely a step in personal education.'

At the same time the rich could easily be tolerated—they were
so few. The ideal of universal small property held those without
property in collective check while it lured them on as individuals.
They would fight alongside those who already had it, joining
with them in destroying holdovers from the previous epoch which
hampered the way up for the small owner.

It seemed to the new citizens, as it has seemed to many after
them, that the road to success was purely economic. An individual established a farm or an urban business and this individual
expanded it, rising up the scale of success as he expanded his
property. That this was so could be plainly seen: you cleared a
farm or founded a business; you cultivated or operated; you expanded the business, the acreage, the profit. In the beginning of
the century necessary agricultural tools cost $15 or $20; by the

middle of the century they cost $400 or $500. Men rose along with the expansion of their property, the property became more valuable both because of their work and because of rising real-estate values in the long epoch of land boom. When Lincoln, in 1861, spoke the language of the small entrepreneur it had not yet lost its meaning: 'The prudent, penniless beginner in the world labors for wages a while; saves a surplus with which to buy tools or land for himself, then labors on his own account another while, and at length hires another beginner to help him.' Two years later he said: 'Property is the fruit of labor. . . That some should be rich shows that others may become rich, and hence is just encouragement to industry and enterprise.'

Under the pattern of individual success there were political and demographic conditions, notably the land policy, which opened economic routes to the masterless individual. The wide distribution of small property made freedom of a very literal sort seem, for a short time, an eternal principle. The relation of one man to another was a relation not of command and obedience but of man-to-man bargaining. Any one man's decisions, with reference to every other man, were decisions of freedom and of equality; no one man dominated the calculations affecting a market.

Small property meant security in so far as the market mechanism worked and slump and boom balanced each other into new and greater harmonies. The wide spread of rural property was especially important because small owners had one security that no other kind of holding could offer—the security, even if at low levels, of the shuttle between the market chance and subsistence. When the market was bad or cash crops failed, the farmer, if frugal and wise, could at least eat from his own garden.

Noah Webster, in 1787, asserted that tyranny was found in the power to oppress, freedom in the power to resist oppression; 'In what then, does *real* power consist? The answer is short, plain— in *property*. . . A general and tolerably equal distribution of landed property is the whole basis of national freedom. . . An equality of property, with the necessity of alienation constantly operating to destroy combinations of powerful families, is the very *soul of a Republic*. While this continues, the people will inevitably possess both *power* and *freedom;* when this is lost, power departs, liberty expires, and a commonwealth will inevitably assume some other form.'

In owning land the small entrepreneur owned not merely an 'investment': he owned the sphere of his own work, and because he owned it, he was independent. As A. Whitney Griswold has interpreted Jefferson's doctrine, 'Who would govern himself must own his own soul. To own his own soul he must own property, the means of economic security.' Self-management, work, and type of property coincided, and in this coincidence the psychological basis of original democracy was laid down. Work and property were closely joined into a single unit. Working skills were performed with and upon one's property; social status rested largely upon the amount and condition of the property that one owned; income was derived from profits made from working with one's property. There was thus a linkage of income, status, work, and property. And, as the power which property gave, like the distribution of property itself, was widespread, their coincidence was the source of personal character as well as of social balance.

Since few men owned more property than they could work, differences between men were due in large part to personal strength and ingenuity. The type of man presupposed and strengthened by this society was willingly economic, possessing the 'reasonable self-interest' needed to build and operate the market economy. He was, of course, more than an economic man, but the techniques and the economics of production shaped much of what he was and what he looked forward to becoming. He was an 'absolute individual,' linked into a system with no authoritarian center, but held together by countless, free, shrewd transactions.

3. The Self-Balancing Society

The world of small entrepreneurs was self-balancing. Within it no central authority allocated materials and ordered men to specified tasks, and the course of its history was the unintended consequence of many scattered wills each acting freely. It is no wonder that men thought this so remarkable they called it a piece of Divine Providence, each man's hand being guided as if by magic into a preordained and natural harmony. The science of economics, which sought to explain this extraordinary balance, which provided order through liberty without authority, has not yet entirely rid itself of the magic.

The providential society did have its economic troubles. Its normal rhythm of slump and boom alternately frightened and exhilarated whole sections and classes of men. Yet it was not seized by cycles of mania and melancholia. The rhythm never threw the economy into the lower depths known intimately to twentieth-century men, and for long years there were no fearful wars or threats of wars. The main lines of its history were linear, not cyclical; technical and economic processes were still expanding, and the cycles that did occur seemed seasonal matters which did not darken the whole outlook of the epoch. Through it all there ran the exhilaration of expansion across the gigantic continent.

In the building of his new world, the enterprising individual had also to build a government that would guard him from centralized authority. It is often said that he 'overthrew mercantilism,' and this is true in the narrower meaning of the term. He did throw off a king and enthrone in his place the free market. This market did not reign without support or without the exercise of political authority, but economic authority was dominant, and it was automatic, largely unseen, and, in fact, seldom experienced as authority at all. Political authority, the traditional mode of social integration, became a loose framework of protection rather than a centralized engine of domination; it too was largely unseen and for long periods very slight. The legal framework guaranteed and encouraged the order of small property, but the government was the guardian, not the manager, of this order. 'Let us be content with the results which have been achieved, and which as clearly indicate others, yet more brilliant, in the future,' wrote J. D. B. DeBow, the director of the 1850 census. 'The industry of our people needs no monitors, as to its best mode of application under every possible circumstance—and, least of all, monitors made out of stuff such as our politicians usually are. As intelligence is generally diffused throughout the masses, they will perceive and admit this, and the one cry everywhere heard, shall be, "*Let us alone.*"'

This decentralized and unguided economic life was paralleled by a decentralization of the military order. The state, erected by and for the small entrepreneurs, claimed to monopolize the means of accepted violence; yet, even in the field of military force, conditions conspired to limit government and to make for a political democracy of and for the small producer. For the means of violence, like those of production, were necessarily widely distributed; guns were locally and easily produced. Military technology did provide cannon and other artillery, but on the whole, one gun meant one man, and the basic law proclaimed: 'The right of the people to keep and bear arms shall not be infringed.' By technical necessity as well as by law, the possible means of coercion were thus scattered among the population; the scattering of economic power was paralleled by a scattering of military power. Order was often violently preserved without benefit of law: if there were cattle thieves, they were lynched; if there were claim jumpers, they were driven off.

To this basis of decentralized violence inside the country, there was added the fact of geographic isolation, not yet bridged by technology. Certainly no large standing army could easily be justified on grounds of national defense. A decentralized militia, relying on volunteers and long years of peace, a military college to which cadets were appointed by politicians, a thoroughgoing civilian control of military establishments and policies—these military foundations allowed for political democracy in the society of the self-balancing market.

Competition was the process by which men rose and fell and by which the economy as a whole was harmonized. But for men in the era of classic liberalism, competition was never merely an impersonal mechanism regulating the economy of capitalism, or only a guarantee of political freedom. Competition was a means of producing free individuals, a testing field for heroes; in its terms men lived the legend of the self-reliant individual. In every area of life, liberals have imagined independent individuals freely competing so that merit might win and character develop: in the free contractual marriage, the Protestant church, the voluntary

association, the democratic state with its competitive party system, as well as on the economic market. Competition was the
way liberalism would integrate its historic era; it was also a
central feature of the classic liberal's style of life.

With no feudal tradition and no bureaucratic state, the absolute individualist was exceptionally placed in this liberal society
that seemed to run itself and in which men seemed to make themselves. Individual freedom seemed the principle of social order,
and in itself entailed security. A free man, not a man exploited,
an independent man, not a man bound by tradition, here confronted a continent and, grappling with it, turned it into a million
commodities.

2

The Transformation of Property

W HAT happened to the world of the small entrepreneur is best seen by looking at what happened to its heroes: the independent farmers and the small businessmen. These men, the leading actors of the middle-class economy of the nineteenth century, are no longer at the center of the American scene; they are merely two layers between other more powerful or more populous strata. Above them are the men of large property, who through money and organization wield much power over other men; alongside and below them are the rank and file of propertyless employees and workers, who work for wages and salaries. Many former entrepreneurs and their children have joined these lower ranks, but only a few have become big entrepreneurs. Those who have persisted as small entrepreneurs are not much like their nineteenth-century prototypes, and must now operate in a world no longer organized in their image.

The free entrepreneurs of the old middle classes have diminished as a proportion of the gainfully occupied. They no longer enjoy the social position they once held. They no longer are models of aspiration for the population at large. They no longer fulfil their classic role as integrators of the social structure in which they live and work. These are the indices of their decline. The causes of that decline involve the whole push and shove of modern industrial society. Its consequences ramify deep into the world of twentieth-century America.

In the midst of the small entrepreneur's epoch, John Taylor had written: 'There are two modes of invading private property:

13

the first, by which the poor plunder the rich, is sudden and violent; the second, by which the rich plunder the poor, slow and legal. . . Whether the law shall gradually transfer the property of the many to the few, or insurrection shall rapidly divide the property of the few among the many, it is equally an invasion of private property, and equally contrary to our constitutions.' The course of U.S. history is a series of lessons in the second of these 'unconstitutional' modes of invading private property.

Changes in the spread and type of property have transformed the old middle class, changed the way its members live and what they dream about as political men, have pushed the free and independent man away from the property centers of the economic world. Democratic property, which the owner himself works, has given way to class property, which others are hired to work and manage. Rather than a condition of the owner's work, class property is a condition of his not having to work.

The individual who owns democratic property has power over his work; he can manage his self and his working day. The individual who owns class property has power over those who do not own, but who must work for him; the owner manages the working life of the non-owner. Democratic property means that man stands isolated from economic authority; class property means that, in order to live, man must submit to the authority which property lends its owner.

The right of man 'to be free and rooted in work that is his own' is denied by the transformation of property; he cannot realize himself in his work, for work is now a set of skills sold to another, rather than something mixed with his own property. His work, as Eduard Heiman puts it, is 'not his own, but an item in the business calculation of somebody else.'

The centralization of property has thus ended the union of property and work as a basis of man's essential freedom, and the severance of the individual from an independent means of livelihood has changed the basis of his life-plan and the psychological rhythm of that planning. For the entrepreneur's economic life, based upon property, embraced his entire lifetime and was set within a family heritage, while the employee's economic life is based upon the job contract and the pay period.

Secure in his world, the old entrepreneur could look upon his entire life as an economic unity, and neither his expectations nor his achievements were necessarily hurried. In his century, he had the chance to feel that his effort and initiative paid off, directly, securely, and freely. Some entrepreneurs no doubt continue to experience that old feeling, but the bourgeois rank and file is today locked in a contest against all of big capitalism's 'secondary modes of exploitation,' and many of them fail. For the population at large, the idea of going to work without an employer is an unserviceable myth. For those who nevertheless try it, it is frequently a disastrous illusion.

1. The Rural Debacle

The free man moving west did not, of course, know what his flight meant in the American phase of world capitalism's development. He did not understand that he was part of an economic arrangement, dependent for its well-being upon the structure of foreign markets and the paying off of the U.S. industrialists' debts to other countries. 'Great agricultural surpluses,' economic historians have shown, 'permitted American capitalism to grow to maturity behind high tariff walls, for our export of foodstuffs made possible the importation of the raw materials and capital needed for the development of American industry.'

By high tariffs, post-Civil War industrialists shut off foreign goods that might compete with their own products on the domestic market; whatever foreign goods and services they needed were bought by the production of surplus agricultural goods. In the last half of the nineteenth century, imports of raw materials for U.S. manufacture rose; imported manufactured goods for the consumer dropped, and the value of exported foodstuffs rose enormously—wheat, by the millions of bushels, pork, by the millions of pounds.

The American farmer, as Louis Hacker puts it, was both the tool and the victim of the rise of American capitalism; as a tool, his surpluses made possible the construction of industry behind high tariffs; as a victim, he paid higher prices for protected goods as well as high interest and freight rates.

For the American farmer the capitalist crisis began in the nine-teen-twenties, during which he experienced nine years of ruin-ously low prices; the general slump of the next decade only worsened his condition. During the 'twenties farm prices dropped, while those of other commodities rose, and, when all retail prices began to fall after 1929, farm prices fell faster. In the same period the average value of farm property dropped, and total farm income plummeted; cash crop receipts were cut to about one-fourth; and by 1929, the per capita income of the farm population was about two-thirds lower than that of the rest of the population.

This precipitous slump of agriculture coincided with long-term changes in farm ownership; the proportion of owners dropped, the proportion of tenants rose. Mortgage debt, as a percentage of total farm value, more than doubled. There were more debts and fewer owners to pay them. In the decade after 1925, almost one-third of all farms changed hands by forced sales of one kind or another. In 1930, only one-fourth of all farm operators, com-pared to over one-half in 1890, owned mortgage-free farms. With farm ownership thus forfeited by tenantry and restricted by mortgage, most American farmers were no longer free or independent.

Moreover, the total number of farmers, regardless of their con-dition, had long been declining. In 1820, almost three-quarters of the nation's labor force was engaged in agricultural produc-tion. In the century and a quarter since then, during most of which time frontier lands were still available, every census re-corded the numerical decline in the proportion of farmers; by 1880, they comprised one-half; by 1949 farmers of all sorts made up only one-eighth of the occupied populace.

The causes of such an epochal shift for an entire class lie deep within the total system; but since the farmer has been a creature of the free market, which tied his world together, the market is the central fact to consider:

1. With the opening of the twentieth-century, foreign markets contracted or disappeared; other grasslands of the world, in newer countries with lower costs and higher yield, came more and more into production. The hope of foreign outlets and high prices faded; between 1894 and 1898 nearly one-fifth of gross

farm income came from foreign exports; it dropped to less than one-tenth by the middle 'thirties. Europeans could not buy U.S. agricultural goods in the face of increased U.S. tariffs. Europe had no gold; America, who wanted to sell, not to buy, would not accept her goods. And in the subsequent epoch of permanent war economies, the nations of the world were doing their best to become self-sufficient.

II. The domestic market contracted. The rate of United States population growth had reached its peak and began a slow arc downward; there was no more big immigration; the population began to level off. Further, the diet of this market altered in such a way as to constrict the sales of the products of extensive agriculture. Even if income rose, the proportion spent for agricultural stuffs did not rise proportionately; demand for food is limited physiologically as demand for industrial products is not.

III. During the 'thirties, as monopoly features of the economy began to be more apparent, other mechanisms began to affect the farmer: his key economic concern has always been the ratio between the price he gets for his product and the price he must pay for the things he buys. During the depression of the 'thirties, when agricultural prices dropped about 70 per cent and utility rates did not drop at all, the farmer could afford only about one-fourth as much electricity as before the depression. The farmer's free market was being cut into by urban monopolists who practiced a new and more profitable kind of freedom—the freedom to hold prices up by cutting production. Thus a price squeeze was put on the farmer: as he entered the slump, Caroline Ware and Gardiner Means observed, the wholesale prices of farm equipment dropped only 15 per cent, while production was cut 80 per cent; but the prices for farm produce dropped 63 per cent while production was cut only 6 per cent. Such facts make clear the difference between the administered prices of the industrial corporation and the free market prices of the farmer.

IV. In no other area of the economy have the contradictions of U.S. capitalism been so apparent as in farming. Yet the technology back of such contradictions has only begun to have its way in the rural economy. In so far as the vision or classic economic liberalism was realized in America, it worked itself out on the family farm. But the technological revolution, which has dire consequences for old middle classes everywhere, largely by-passed the farmer; it may now be seen that, in its later period, the rural world of the small entrepreneur existed by virtue of technological backwardness. Even between 1900 and 1939, when manufacturing increased its output by 267 per cent, agricultural output was increased by only 60 per cent.

Yet, even so, agricultural production rose too much. For underlying the numerical decline of the rural populace is a constant increase in productivity; fewer men working shorter hours can produce more. This master trend, spurred by the First World War, got underway in earnest during World War II. If 1910 is assumed to equal 100, by 1945 farm employment had dropped to 82, while production per worker had increased to 209. Behind these figures two images loom: a thousand men each following a mule, and a big tractor driven by a single man. These are accurate images: during the generation before 1940, the number of tractors used on farms rose from 10,000 heavy, clumsy machines to 2,000,000 light, maneuverable, rubber-tired instruments of production; the number of mules and horses on farms was cut by about half.

In the second quarter of the twentieth century, for the first time in U.S. history, farm employment began an actual decline. World War II cut the farm population 15 per cent, drained off 40 per cent of the men under 45, but raised crop and livestock production 30 and 40 per cent. By 1950, four million farms were able to produce one-third more than did the six million farms of 1940. Thus, one underlying cause of the farm problem is simply that there are too many farmers. The demand for agricultural products is relatively inflexible; the techniques of production are constantly becoming more productive. As Griswold has indicated, the result has been 'the underemployment of agricultural labor shown up so vividly by the war, the price-depressing surpluses, the low income, and the correspondingly inferior cultural opportunities.'

Farming has thus moved in a full circle: what was once assumed to be a frontier outlet is now, in the dry words of a Department of Agriculture expert, 'a definite lack of employment opportunities in agricultural production.' Yet the consequences of the technological revolution for the American farmer go beyond the fact of numerical decline. This revolution emphasizes the fact that an 'overproduction crisis' like that of the 'thirties hangs as a constant threat over the farmers and over any plan that may be made for them.

Within the rural populace, the market mechanics and the technological motors of social change have been cutting down the proportion of free entrepreneurs. For at least fifty years the American ideal of the family-sized farm has been becoming more and more an ideal and less and less a reality. In 1945 full owners of farms made up only 6 per cent of the nation's civilian labor force.

The rural middle class has been slowly subjected to a polarization, which, if continued, will destroy the traditional character of farming, splitting it into subsistence cultivators, wage-workers, and sharecroppers on the one hand, and big commercial farmers and rural corporations on the other. By 1945, 2 per cent of all farms contained 40 per cent of all farm land.

Back of this drift to larger scale and increasing concentration is the machine, which has made farming a highly capitalized business. A tractor-operated farm requires from 30 to 50 per cent more capital than a horse-operated unit. According to a reputable business journal, a 'typical Iowa farmer' in 1946 would have around 160 acres, which might cost anywhere from $100 to $300 an acre—at a minimum, '$16,000 for land.' In addition, 'such a farmer would need about $33,000 of original investment in capital assets,' $30,000 for buildings and equipment, and $3000 in working capital.

The low rate at which farm machinery is normally used accelerates this trend. A manufacturer can expect a big lathe to be used two thousand hours a year; a farmer can expect only fifty hours from his hay baler. To make the baler pay the farmer buys more land on which to use it: average farm size has jumped from 138 acres in 1910 to 195 in 1945. If the ordinary small farmer mechanizes without expanding his holding, the overhead for repair and depreciation will get out of bounds. Either he must sell out, or try to hire out his machines to his neighbors.

The largest proportion of all agricultural commodities has always been produced by a comparatively few large farms; but over the last two or three decades this concentration has increased sharply. Farm prices rose greatly during World War II, but less than a tenth of the farmers received one-half of the total farm income. In such periods of farm prosperity the farmer as real-estate speculator increases the centralization; many marginal producers are thus eliminated, as farm land becomes even more concentrated, farmers fewer and richer.

Whether or not a tenant farmer or a rural wage-worker has an *easy* chance to climb the agricultural ladder from rural wage-worker to tenant to mortgaged owner to full owner is a question taken seriously only in popular fantasy. Just what the chance to climb may be and what the trend has been are difficult to show. But this much is certain: in the forty years after 1890, the absolute number of young farmers declined, and, among young men still on the farm, about 50 per cent more started as tenants than as owners. Many of them continued as tenants; many left for the city because they could not start as owners or did not see the chances to rise to full ownership. To many of these, the ladder has indeed seemed a treadmill: they have expressed their appreciation of rural life and of its chances by joining the rural exodus.

Farming is not yet rationalized, but the rural *world* of the small entrepreneur is already gone. The industrial revolution, only now getting under way on the farm, already has determined, in Griswold's words, that 'a self-sufficient farm in our time is more likely to be a haunt of illiteracy and malnutrition than a wellspring of democracy.' The industrial revolution tends to draw the family farm into its orbit, or leave it stranded in an archaic subsistence economy.

2. Business Dynamics

Nevertheless, as a broad American stratum, the small entrepreneurs are still mainly people on farms. Men entering the city seldom have acquired business properties and become free producers and traders; on the contrary, as members or potential members of the old middle class, they have been destroyed. The small urban entrepreneur has never formed a broad stratum which, like the rural, could enact a key role in the shaping of a free society. The city never matched the countryside: neat rows of independent shops never grew up to become the equivalents of sections of land. Industrial plants and retail stores were not given to smaller men as were farms, and the capital required to start new businesses became greater in rough proportion to technological progress. There was never any Homestead Act for the would-be urban entrepreneur, although for manufacturers the tariff was something of a Homestead Act. Industrialization does not necessarily develop a private centralization of enterprises, with resultant difficulties for small entrepreneurs, but that is the way it has worked out in America.

Even before the Civil War, as the new transportation network began to knit localities into a national market, local artisans began to work for merchant capitalists. The need for raw materials and capital and for outlets to the national market soon caused the independent producer to become dependent upon bigger men. The businessman of the city, who was tied to the technologist, considered it his role to organize technology and labor and become their profitable link with the protected market. And as the nation grew up, so did its heroes: not big farmers, but big businessmen, though often called by other names, rose to national eminence. By the 'nineties, William Dean Howells' Man Who Had Risen was supplementing Walt Whitman's Man in the Open Air.

In the twentieth century, technology continued rapidly to expand; but expansion of the market took place much more slowly. In the attempt to stabilize matters, the captains of industry began to draw together, and out of their epic competition there emerged impersonal monopoly. The freedom to compete—the main principle of order in the world of the small entrepreneur—became the freedom to shape the new society. As the concentration of private enterprise began to change the type of businessman that prevailed, the Captain of Industry gave way to the Rentier, the Absentee Owner, the Corporation Executive, and a type presently to be described, the New Entrepreneur.

Neither the Rentier nor the Absentee Owner, however, is, in the public mind, a productively competitive man. Each is a coupon clipper and a parasite, either a stealthy miser or a lavish consumer; theirs is not the business life of competition, and even liberal economists deplore their economic role. The Corporation Executive has never been a popular middle-class idol; as part of an impersonal corporation, he is too aloof to have a friendly reputation among smaller men. As an engineer he is part of inexorable science, and no economic hero; as a businessman he is part of the hidden world of finance, where all the big money mysteriously ends up.

None of these newer types of economic men has quite filled the heroic place of the old, undivided captain, who has gradually taken on a somewhat bloated, predatory, and overbearing shape. The more he became a big financier and the less an inventive organizer of the small factory—which everyone could see was producing things—the more sinister this predatory image became. The big businessman was generalized into the Financial Magnate, who, living in the lawful shade of society, uses other people's money for his own profit. Yet, as it has been often difficult to distinguish a dirt farmer from a real-estate operator, so has it been hard to distinguish a genuine captain of industry, even in the captain's heyday, from a generalissimo of high finance. Perhaps the urban American businessman has always been something of both.

If the old middle classes were to find a hero in the city, he would have to be from the small-business strata. And so the small businessman, especially with the general decline of the farmer, has come to be seen as the somewhat woebegone heir of the old captain's tradition, even if only by default. The harder his struggle becomes, the more sympathetic and heroic his image is drawn; and yet he can never live up to the heritage invented for him. More and more, it has become in his eyes a permanent burden rather than a glory to lean on in times of temporary trouble. As image he remains a prop to the captain-become-monopolist; as reality he persists more as a political than as a business force.

During the last several decades, the proportion of businessmen has stood at about 8 per cent of the nation's working force, and in the urban world has declined from 17 per cent in 1870 to 12 per cent in 1940. Their remarkable persistence as a stratum, however, should not be confused with the well-being of each individual enterprise and its owner-manager. While, as an aggregate, small businessmen persist and hold their own, the composition of this aggregate changes rapidly, and the economic well-being of its members undergoes shocking ups and downs.

In the four decades prior to World War II, the number of firms in existence rose from 1 to 2 million, but during the same period nearly 16 million firms began operation, and at least 14 million went out of business. There is a great flow of entrepreneurs and would-be entrepreneurs in and out of the small-business stratum, as each year hundreds of thousands fail and others, some new to the game, some previous failures, start out again on the brave venture.

The great bulk of businesses are small outfits, which do not last long. In fact, the turnover rate of one-man enterprises in 1940 was almost as high as the average annual separation rate for factory workers during the prewar decade. 'It is apparent,' as J. H. Cover the economist says, after examining the vital statistics of small business, 'that optimism exceeds understanding in the cases of possibly two-thirds of our new proprietors.'

It is an infant death rate in two senses: both the small and the new concerns typically fail. These two senses are related: in those industries where the capital involved in starting a new business is prohibitive to small entrepreneurs there often is stability; and in those industries where capital requirements do not stand in the way, the problems of survival are naturally greater.

It might be supposed that all these failures and new beginnings are only the unfit being eliminated by the fit in a normal competitive process. But such a view overlooks the fact that the *continuation* of bankruptcies and failures would seem to indicate that the unfit are often replaced by the unfit; and that, since the trend of bankruptcies is often upward, it might even be that the number of unfit often increases.

Back of the failures is the general fact that a larger number of small businesses are competing for a small share of the market. The stratum of urban entrepreneurs has been narrowing, and within it a concentration has been going on. Small business becomes smaller, big business becomes bigger.

The business world is less homogeneous now than seventy years ago: businessmen now work in a bewildering variety of types and sizes of enterprises, from the sidestreet laundry to the General Motors Corporation. At the bottom are a multitude of small firms, worth little financially, which do not produce or sell much of the nation's total goods and services, and do not employ many of the people at work. In 1939 the 1,500,000 one-man enterprises made up almost half of all non-farming businesses, but engaged only 6 per cent of all people at work in business. At the top are a handful of firms which employ the bulk of the people at work, produce or sell most of the goods and services handled, and hold most of the capital goods appropriated to private use. In 1939, 1 per cent of all the firms in the country—27,000 giants— engaged over half of all the people working in business. For about thirty years, now, three-fourths of U.S. corporations have got only about 5 per cent of the total corporate income.

No matter which year is studied, or what criteria are used, the fact of extreme business concentration is clear. Over-all measurements, however, conceal the crucial fact that concentration varies a great deal by line of business. Roughly speaking, the business world is polarized into two types: large industrial corporations and small retail or service firms.

In the generation before World War II, the number of proprietors of manufacturing establishments declined 34 per cent; the number of wage and salary workers employed in manufacturing rose 27 per cent. Manufacturing is no longer a small business world; it is increasingly dominated by large-scale bureaucratic structures. The war economy, built on top of this already extreme concentration, further concentrated American industry.

Retail trade, bottom of the business world in terms of persons engaged and value of business transacted, is still largely dominated by small business. The sales of the smallest three-quarters of retail stores represented 22 per cent of the total 1939 retail sales, nearly twice that of the smallest three-quarters of the manufacturing firms. As far as making up any dominant section of the total business world, the small businessman can now be seen to exist only in the retail and service industries, and to a lesser extent in finance and construction.

In the early nineteenth century the wholesaler was the big go-between of the business world: he was able to control the small manufacturer as well as the small retailer, for both, especially the retailer, were often dependent upon him for credit. But the manufacturer expanded and became independent of the wholesaler, often taking over many of his functions. In time, the retailer also moved in on the wholesaler's business. Then the manufacturer tried to eliminate both wholesaler and retailer by selling directly to the consumer.

As the volume of production rose in the later nineteenth century, the economic system was confronted with capitalism's peculiar and crucial problem: there is no profit to be made from huge volume unless a huge market exists. As technology pushed the manufacturer into higher productivity, he was confronted with an extremely inefficient and wasteful system of marketing. The smaller units in wholesaling and retailing—the bulk of the old urban middle class—had become a brake upon the technological wheels of capitalist progress, or so the big manufacturer thought.

At the same time, the retailer was also growing up. The department store is a stable member of the marketing community: the proportion of retail sales handled by department stores has not fluctuated very widely over the last fifteen years. The mail-order house now combines many of the features of the department store and the chain and, acting at a distance, reaches into the back eddies of the market. As this system of mass distributors began slowly to emerge, its units did their own wholesaling, from the mass producer to the consumer. As supermarkets mushroomed, outdoing the chain stores in the technique of mass distribution, the chains began to imitate their supermarket competitors, and the two giants of the retail trade battled with one another, competing far more than little businessmen ever could.

As wholesalers were displaced by retailers, the latter, from the central position of those close to the business at hand, began to bring pressure on the manufacturers, saying: 'Split up with us. Your low costs are due to your mass production, but what good would your mass production be without our mass distribution? Cut us in.' The manufacturer, having partly thrown off wholesaler control, being confronted now by another contender for his profits, replied with national advertising of his brand name and with retail outlets of his own. With these tools he has been trying to dominate both retailer and wholesaler.

Sears, Roebuck vice-president T. V. Houser sums up the present trend: on the one hand, there is 'the dominant large manufacturers with their own branded lines, distributing their products through thousands of independent dealers; on the other hand, the mass distributor with his many and various branded lines, buying each of these lines from smaller manufacturers . . . in one case, the manufacturer determines the . . . design, quality, price and production schedules [of the product]; while in the other case these functions are assumed by the mass distributor. . .' From both sides, the wholesaler takes the brunt of the competitive battle of the marketeers, and loses ground to both.

Not all domination by big business, however, results in outright mergers or bankruptcies or is revealed by the facts of concentration. The power of the larger businesses is such that, even though many small businesses remain independent, they become in reality agents of larger businesses. The important point is that the small businessman has been deprived of his old entrepreneurial function.

When banks demand managerial reforms before extending credit, they are centralizing the initiative and responsibility supposedly entailed in the entrepreneurial flair. Many small businessmen are now financed by supply houses, and large producers and suppliers not only set the prices which small businesses in the industry then follow, but often extend credit to small businesses; there are cases in which, if the big concern extending credit were to call it in, many small men would be ruined. Such dependency on trade credit tends to reduce the small businessman to an agent of the creditor.

The independence of small businessmen is also curtailed by 'exclusive dealing contracts' and 'full line forcing' by means of which manufacturers, who set retail prices and advertise nationally, turn small retailers into what amounts to salesmen on commission who take entrepreneurial risks. In manufacturing, subcontracting often turns the small subcontractor into what amounts to a risk-taking manager of a branch plant.

It might be thought that the small wholesaler, retailer, and manufacturer, each variously affected by the domination of large business, would get together against their common foe, but they have not done so on any scale. Instead, the small retailer, the largest element in small business, has sought refuge from competition in the national brands of big manufacturers and advertisers, and has demanded and got such stratagems as 'fair trade' legislation, under which all retailers of a product must sell at a uniform price. Legislation of this sort means that such competition as exists goes on among various manufacturers, in whose field monopoly is great, rather than among retailers, among whom monopoly is less well developed. Moreover, because the small manufacturer is largely cut off from the small retailer, he too comes under the domination of the big-scale operator, in this case the big retailer—the chain or department store, who as large-scale buyers can often dominate the price of the articles they buy.

Many smaller elements of the old middle class have slowly been ground to pieces. As the contest has shifted from production to salesmanship, many smaller manufacturers have continued to exist by becoming direct satellites of larger manufacturing concerns, and many retailers have become, in fact, maintenance agencies and distributors for big manufacturers. Thus, the small manufacturer and the small retailer, far from forming an alliance, are locked in struggle over the market, in the course of which both come under the domination of larger business.

Distribution is the home of small business, and distribution is one of the most wasteful features of the U.S. economy. In food retailing, for example, chains have definitely decreased the generous spread between farmer and consumer prices. A retail store cannot be run efficiently or cheaply unless there is an adequate turnover per store. Chains have this volume, and the additional advantage of being able to bring in salaried experts for every department of the business. They are more efficient and cheaper. In them the entrepreneurial flair is replaced by a standardized procedure. Buying, display, advertising, merchandising, attention to costs are each centralized and managed by salaried experts in chain, department store, and supermarket. 'We must,' says distribution authority A. C. Hoffman, 'either accept the ineptitude of the average person in order to preserve for him some measure of what is called economic individualism, or we must accept the change from enterpriser to employee status in order to achieve the advantages of centralized management.'

As the processor's influence and the engineer's ideas are taking over the functions of independent farmers, so the big manufacturer and the engineer of distribution are eyeing the marketing system, the home of the small businessmen. The old middle classes, on the farm and in the city, are clogging the wheels of progress as envisioned by the technologists and efficiency experts.

3. The Lumpen-Bourgeoisie

Examining the statistics that indicate the sad condition, the heavy rate of failure, and yet the curious survival of tiny businesses and farms, one is reminded of Balzac's unkind remark made in another connection: 'insignificant folk cannot be crushed, they lie too flat beneath the foot.' If we may speak of a 'lumpen-proletariat,' set off from other wage workers, we may also speak of a 'lumpen-bourgeoisie,' set off from other middle-class elements. For the bottom of the entrepreneurial world is so different from the top that it is doubtful whether the two should be classified together.

In the city the lumpen-bourgeoisie is composed of a multitude of firms with a high death rate, which do a fraction of the total business done in their lines and engage a considerably larger proportion of people than their quota of business. Thus, ten years ago over half of the retail stores did only 9 per cent of the business but engaged 21 per cent of all the people in retail trade. The true lumpen-bourgeoisie, however, *employ* no workers at all: the proprietors and their family members do the work, frequently sweating themselves night and day. At the bottom of the

depression, the 'proprietor's withdrawal' was liberally estimated
at $9.00 a week for stores with sales under $10,000. Here, at the
bottom of the twentieth-century business world, lies the owner-
operator who, in the classic image, is the independent man in
the city.

But it is on the farm with its dwarfish means of production
that the small entrepreneur has persisted as a large proportion
of the marginal victims of the old middle class. Twenty years
ago, at the 1929 peak of business prosperity, nearly half of the
nation's farms produced less than $1000 worth of products, in-
cluding those used by the family, but this least productive half
contributed only 11 per cent of all the products sold or traded by
farmers. By the middle 'forties, at the peak of the farm boom,
the relative figures had not changed much: 40 per cent of all
farms received less than $1000 a year; one-fourth yielded $600
or less. The rural malnutrition rate has been twice as high as the
urban, and it is on the farm that we find the national highest
birth and infant mortality rates. A full third of the farmers live
in rural slums, in houses virtually beyond repair; two-thirds are
'inadequately housed.' In 1945, only three out of ten U.S. farmers had mechanical refrigerators, only four had kitchen sinks with
drains. The small farmer and his family are caught up in an inefficient drudgery, and many are 'independent' only part of the
time, hiring themselves to large farmers the rest, and all the time
hovering above tenantry only by barbaric overwork and under-
consumption.

Engineers point out that 'one-fifth of our original area of till-
able land' has been ruined for further cultivation; 'a third of what
remains has already been badly damaged. Another third is highly
vulnerable.' Among the reasons for this, H. H. Bennett, chief of
a service in the Department of Agriculture, pointed out in 1946,
is the fact that 'too much of the land traditionally has been in
the hands of the untutored and the inept. . . Under the names
of peasant, farmer, rustic, and country fellow, these individuals
have been synonymous, for generations, with all that is naive,
uneducated, and backward. Possessed frequently of such virtues
as thrift and diligence, they have nevertheless often assumed a
scornful attitude toward education and the educated. And too

often, the farm has been the last resort to which men unsuccessful in other fields have turned.'

The midget entrepreneur, on the farm and in the city, is economically sensitive to the business cycle; his insecurities are
tightly geared to it. Slight shifts in the direction or volume of
business can be reflected sharply in his rate of profit. From
month to month, he may exist in acute anxiety; even slight economic forces, outside his control, may swing him off balance and
lower his level of psychic security. Once no individual could
direct the market, but now the small man feels, often correctly,
that it is fixed against him.

As owner, manager, and worker, the marginal victim typically
uses his family to help out in store, farm, or shop. Economic life
thus coincides with family life. In the hole-in-the-wall business,
also known as a Mom-and-Pop store, the parents can keep a constant eye on each other and on the children. Such economic freedom as the family enterprise may enjoy is often purchased by
lack of freedom within the family unit. It is, in fact, as Wilhelm
Reich has noted, a feature of such petty-bourgeois life that extreme repression is often exercised in its patriarchal orbit. Child
labor, often sweated child labor, has its home in the lumpen-
bourgeoisie. Of all industrial categories it is the farm and the
retail store that contain the highest proportion of free enterprisers—and the highest proportion of 'unpaid family workers.'
Business competition and economic anxiety thus come out in
family relations and in the iron discipline required to keep afloat.
Since there is little or no outlet for feelings beyond the confines
of the shop or farm, members of these families may grow greedy
for gain. The whole force of their nature is brought to bear upon
trivial affairs which absorb their attention and shape their character. They come to exercise, as Balzac has said, 'the power of
pettiness, the penetrating force of the grub that brings down
the elm tree by tracing a ring under the bark.'

The family circle is closed in and often withdrawn into itself,
thus encouraging strong intimacies and close-up hatreds. The
children of such families are often the objects upon which parental frustrations are projected. They are subjected alternately to
overindulgence, which springs from close parental competition

for their affection, and to strong discipline, which is based on the parents' urge to 'make the child amount to something.' In the meantime continual deprivations are justified in terms of the future success of the children, who must give up things now, but who, by doing so, may legitimately claim the rewards of great deference and gratification in the future. There is evidence that the coming to adolescence of the lumpen-bourgeois child is a painful juncture fraught with many perils for parent and child, and perhaps also for society.

Behind the colorless census category 'unpaid family worker,' there lie much misery and defeat in youth. That too was and is part of the old middle-class way. Perhaps in the nineteenth-century it paid off: the sons, or at least one of the sons, would take over his equipped station, and the daughter might better find a husband who would thus be set up. But the average life of these old middle-class, especially urban, units in the twentieth century is short; the coincidence of family-unit and work-situation among the old middle class is a pre-industrial fact. So even as the centralization of property contracts their 'independence,' it liberates the children of the old middle class's smaller entrepreneurs.

The difficulties of making a stable life-plan further augment the competitive anxieties and family tensions of the lumpen-bourgeoisie. On the one hand, the small man generally lives longer than the small business, so in many cases the business cannot provide income for a lifetime. On the other hand, the elderly proprietor of a small business frequently has difficulty replacing himself. He builds up a struggling enterprise over the years by hard work and fear, and then he wants to retire; but who could replace him? *He* has built up a little business and his impending retirement or death damages the credit standing of the enterprise with which he has been so personally identified.

The economic situation of the lumpen-bourgeoisie leads to insecurity, and often to petty aggressiveness. Their prestige is often considered by them to be low, in relation to those on whom their eyes are fixed—the larger, more successful entrepreneurs. And, over the last twenty years, they have felt a denial of deference in relation to workers organized in successful unions.

To these economic and social bases of insecurity and frustration may be added a more personal source, aptly noted by Harold D. Lasswell: running a business often involves a calculating posture toward other people which may cause a certain amount of guilt. The marginal victim is often economically compelled to calculate, plan, and evaluate his own actions and impulses, as well as those of his wife and children who help him in the business; he must do so in the cold light of his economic goal and often via sharp economic practices. So, the intensification of work, the deferral of consumption for his family and himself, is justified by the high premium on thrift and respectability.

During business hours at least, he must allow the customer always to be right. Subservient to any one above him, to whose level he may aspire and from whom he may suffer petty rebuffs, the lumpen-bourgeois often turns harshly against wage-workers in the abstract, although in so far as they are among his customers he may have to suppress such targets of aggression.

The capitalist spirit, Werner Sombart has written, combines a spirit of adventure, a desire for gain, and the middle-class virtues of the respectable citizen. Among those smaller bourgeois, the desire for gain now seems uppermost; it becomes the focus of virtue, and as the adventurous spirit is replaced by a search for the sure fix, the very norms of respectability become psychological traps and sources of guilt. The calculation for gain spreads into the whole social life, as the lumpen-bourgeois man thinks of his social universe, including the members of his family, as factors in his struggle, a struggle in which he is often as unsuccessful as he is ambitious.

The old bourgeois, the man of measure for whom wealth was not necessarily an end in itself but rather a means of continuing his unruffled way of life, the man who did not frenziedly reach out for customers but patiently expected, like a territorial prince, a fenced-off reserve of his share—that man is gone. Inner ease and wide range no longer derive from the business life of the old middle class on any level, and certainly not on its lumpen stratum; from the lumpen-bourgeoisie a sordid style and narrow ideas are more likely to come. No longer can the smallest entrepreneurs be characterized as among that middle class of which W. E. H. Lecky wrote, in 1896, that it was 'distinguished beyond all others for its political independence, its caution, its solid practical intelligence, its steady industry, its high moral average,' or which Georges Sorel characterized as a class of serious moral habits, filled with its own dignity, having the energy and will to govern a country without a centralized bureaucracy. No longer is there the effective will to power of the old middle class, but rather the tenacious will to fight off encircling competitive menaces. From this series of small-scale wretchedness, a fretful assertiveness is fed, human relations are poisoned, and a personality is formed with which it is not pleasant to exchange political greetings. The small entrepreneur is scared; so he embraces ideologies and struggles for prestige in ways not entirely befitting standard images of the free businessman and the independent farmer.

Yet despite their victimized elements and high turnover, the entrepreneurial strata as a whole persist, and, in certain phases of the economic cycle, some members do well enough. Most, however, no longer fulfil the entrepreneurial function; they are no longer independent operators. The character of their decline in this respect has primarily to do with the changed nature of competition in the twentieth-century economic order. Their economic anxieties have led many small entrepreneurs to a somewhat indignant search for some political means of security, and there have been many spokesmen to take up the search for them.

3

The Rhetoric of Competition

As an economic fact, the old independent entrepreneur lives on a small island in a big new world; yet, as an ideological figment and a political force he has persisted as if he inhabited an entire continent. He has become the man through whom the ideology of utopian capitalism is still attractively presented to many of our contemporaries. Over the last hundred years, the United States has been transformed from a nation of small capitalists into a nation of hired employees; but the ideology suitable for the nation of small capitalists persists, as if that small-propertied world were still a going concern. It has become the grab-bag of defenders and apologists, and so little is it challenged that in the minds of many it seems the very latest model of reality.

Nostalgia for the rural world of the small entrepreneur now so effectively hides the mechanics of industry that the farmer, the custodian of national life, is able to pursue his cash interests to the point of defying the head of the government in time of war. And while the small urban entrepreneur, as an examplar of the competitive way, suffers exhaustion, the officials of American opinion find more and more reason to proclaim his virtues. 'We realize . . .' Senator James Murray has said, 'that small business constitutes the very essence of free enterprise and that its preservation is fundamental to the American idea.' The logic of the small entrepreneurs is not the logic of our time; yet if the old middle classes have been transformed into often scared and always baffled defenders, they have not died easily; they persist

34

energetically, even if their energies sometimes seem to be those of cornered men.

Not the urgencies of democracy's problems, but the peculiar structure of American political representation; not the efficiency of small-scale enterprise, but the usefulness of its image to the political interests of larger business; not the swift rise of the huge city, but the myopia induced by small-town life of fifty years ago—these have kept alive the senator's fetish of the American entrepreneur.

1. The Competitive Way of Life

Official proclamations of the competitive ways of small entrepreneurs now labor under an enormous burden of fact which demonstrates in detail the accuracy of Thorstein Veblen's analysis. Competition, he held, is by no means dead, but it is chiefly 'competition between the business concerns that control production, on the one side, and the consuming public on the other side; the chief expedients in this businesslike competition being salesmanship and sabotage.' Competition has been curtailed by larger corporations; it has also been sabotaged by groups of smaller entrepreneurs acting collectively. Both groups have made clear the locus of the big competition and have revealed the mask-like character of liberalism's rhetoric of small business and family farm.

The character and ideology of the small entrepreneurs and the facts of the market are selling the idea of competition short. These liberal heroes, the small businessmen and the farmers, do not want to develop their characters by free and open competition; they do not believe in competition, and they have been doing their best to get away from it.

When small businessmen are asked whether they think free competition is, by and large, a good thing, they answer, with authority and vehemence, 'Yes, of course—what do you mean?' If they are then asked, 'Here in this, your town?' still they say, 'Yes,' but now they hesitate a little. Finally: 'How about here in this town in furniture?'—or groceries, whatever the man's line is. Their answers are of two sorts: 'Yes, if it's fair competition,' which turns out to mean: 'if it doesn't make me compete.' Their

second answer adds up to the same competition with the public:
'Well, you see, in certain lines, it's no good if there are too many
businesses. You ought to keep the other fellow's business in mind.'
The small businessman, as well as the farmer, wants to become
big, not directly by eating up others like himself in competition,
but by the indirect ways and means practiced by his own particular heroes—those already big. In the dream life of the small
entrepreneur, the sure fix is replacing the open market.

But if small men wish to close their ranks, why do they continue to talk, in abstract contexts, especially political ones, about
free competition? The answer is that the political function of
free competition is what really matters now, to small entrepreneurs, but especially to big-business spokesmen. This ideology
performs a crucial role in the competition between business on
the one hand and the electorate, labor in particular, on the other.
It is a means of justifying the social and economic position of
business in the community at large. For, if there is free competition and a constant coming and going of enterprises, the one who
remains established is 'the better man' and 'deserves to be where
he is.' But if instead of such competition, there is a rigid line between successful entrepreneurs and the employee community,
the man on top may be 'coasting on what his father did,' and not
really be worthy of his hard-won position. Nobody talks more
of free enterprise and competition and of the best man winning
than the man who inherited his father's store or farm. Thus the
principle of the self-made man, and the justification of his superior position by the competitive fire through which he has
come, require and in turn support the ideology of free competition. In the abstract political ranges, everyone can believe in
competition; in the concrete economic case, few small entrepreneurs can afford to do so.

Before the automobile was in wide use, the spread of the farming community over vast distances enabled the merchant of the
smaller town to effect a virtual monopoly over the small-town
population and the surrounding farming areas. The competition
between businessman and farmer was thus arranged by geog-
raphy and settlement in favor of the small-town businessman.
'The nearest thing we have ever had to monopoly in grocery

retailing,' remarks one T.N.E.C.* economist, '. . . was the old village grocery store. The prices which it charged were not elastic and usually not very competitive until the automobile made them so.'

It is ironic that this 'natural' monopoly of the small-town entrepreneur was broken, in large part, by precisely those agencies of mass distribution which small businessmen now denounce as 'unfair competitors.' The same forces that enlarged the market area and destroyed the old local monopoly—railroad and mail-order house, chain store, automobile, and supermarket—now appear as the very octopuses of monopoly. They might indeed become just that, but at the present time they are often the only active competitors in the retail field. In the end the choice is between types of monopolists.

It was during the 'thirties that the small entrepreneurs' opinion of competition became clear on a nation-wide scale. When the Depression hit, the independent businessmen, like the farmers, made their revealing shift in strategy: in an attempt to install a kept individualism, they moved the fight from the economic into the political field.

For the small entrepreneurs no ideological crash accompanied the economic crash; they went marching on ideologically. But they did not remain isolated economic men without any political front; they tried to tie themselves up in elaborate organizational networks. In Congress small-business committees clamored for legislation to save the weak backbone of the national economy. Their legislative efforts have been directed against their more efficient competitors. First they tried to kill off the low-priced chain stores by taxation; then they tried to eliminate the alleged buying advantages of mass distributors; finally they tried to freeze the profits of all distributors in order to protect their own profits from those who could and were selling goods cheaper to the consumer.

The independent retailer has been at the head of the movement for these adjuncts of free enterprise: in his fear of price competition and his desire for security, he has been pushing to

* Temporary National Economic Commission.

maintain a given margin under the guise of 'fair competition' and 'fair-trade' laws. He now regularly demands that the number of outlets controlled by chain stores be drastically limited and that production be divorced from distribution. This would, of course, kill the low prices charged consumers by the A&P, which makes very small retail profits, selling almost at cost, and whose real profits come from manufacturing and packaging.

The retailers in the small town need not foolishly compete with one another in terms of prices; they may as well co-operate with one another and thus compete more effectively with their mutual customers. In a well-organized little city, with a capable Chamber of Commerce, there is no reason why merchants should cut one another's throat, especially in view of chain stores and mail-order houses, good highways, and fast automobiles connecting smaller towns with larger cities. Why should the entrepreneur demand anything less than complete security in the risks he takes? Why shouldn't he exercise foresight by making sure he is 'in' on a deal before it becomes publicly known?

The competitive spirit, especially when embodied in an ethic which is conceived to be the source of all virtue, abounds only where there is consciousness of unlimited opportunity. Whenever there is consciousness of scarcity, of a limited, contracting world, then competition becomes a sin against one's fellows. The group tries to close its ranks, as in labor unions, to set up rules for insiders and rules against those who are closed out. This is what the small entrepreneur is in the process of doing. No longer filled with a consciousness of abundance, if he ever was, he now lives in a world of limited or scarce opportunities, and other people are seen as a competitive menace or as men to join up with.

Under the threat of 'ruinous competition,' laws are on the books of many states and cities legalizing the ruin of competition. Price-maintained items do sell for higher prices after the passage of such laws; and prices are higher for cities where the maintenance is legal than in cities where it is not. Such laws extend into small-enterprise fields the administered price that the large manufacturing corporations are able to fix among themselves. The small entrepreneur is thus only trying to have his government help him achieve what big business and big farmers have achieved before him. And the business world, a closed-in community of men with a consciousness of scarcity, is thus more co-operatively solidified.

The wholesaler, given his frequent dependence upon the good will of the independent merchant, strings along on resale price maintenance. He too would avoid 'competitive price cutting' in order to assure his profit margin. The manufacturer of trade-marked goods also likes it; like other people in the world of business, he has no love of low prices. Once 'destructive competition' begins, it will spread between manufacturers and distributors who will want higher margins and lower prices from manufacturers; also, the manufacturer needs the good will of the retailers so they will push his lines or brands, and finally the manufacturer spends money on advertising; and price cutting (competition) of any kind substitutes lower prices for the higher costs of advertising. National advertising and resale price maintenance thus supplement each other, and together further the competition between business and the consumer.

Today many small entrepreneurs are in no way competitive units steering independent courses in an open market; they are not centers of initiative or places of economic innovation; they operate within market channels and a tangled pile-up of restrictive legislation and trade practices firmly laid out by big business and firmly upheld by small business. The small entrepreneur tenders his ideological gifts to big business in return for a feudal-like protection. In the meantime, the fight between the two over the domain of the market goes on, although it increasingly becomes a fight between political spokesmen, who desire to exploit anxieties under the banner of free competition, and larger capitalists, who desire to rationalize the economics of distribution under the same banner.

In continuing to see competition as salvation from complicated trouble, the senators naturally fall into the small proprietor's old complaints; and the experts, perhaps for the record, fall in with the senators. From time to time they propose that the old captain of industry be given a rebirth with full benefit of governmental midwifery. Such proposals are the best that official liberals have to say about the economic facts of life. Their mood ought to be the mood of plight, but they have succeeded in setting up a

bright image of the small entrepreneur, who could be rehabili-
tated as the hero of their imagined system, if only competition
were once more to prevail.

2. The Independent Farmer

In making its terms with corporate business, farm entrepreneurship is in part becoming more like business management,
and in part meeting its problems with the help and support of
political power. All interests have come to look to government,
but the independent farmer has, in some respects, succeeded
more than others in turning the federal establishment into a
public means for his private economic ends. The world of the
farmer, especially its upper third, is now intricately related to
the world of big government, forming with it a combination of
private and public enterprise wherein private gains are insured
and propped by public funds. The independent farmer has become politically dependent; he no longer belongs to a world of
straightforward economic fact.

From on top, farming has recently been a good business proposition. Among the upper farm strata are included canners and
packers and other processors and distributors, as well as those
who look on the land as an investment only. For while the top-
level farmers do buy more land during prosperity, business interests buy land and move into farm profits in other ways, during
slumps as well as booms. Despite the great increase in productivity, the rapid increase in population, the vast expansion in
demand for farm products, the free land available for home-
steading—despite all this, the proportion of the rural real-estate
owned by working farmers has declined for over half a century.

Centralization has brought consolidated farming and farm
chains, run like corporate units by central management. In 1938,
one insurance company alone owned enough acreage to make a
mile-wide farm from New York to Los Angeles. Industrial and
finan ial interests that have invested in farm properties are active
agents for rational methods of production and management.
They have the money to buy the machines and employ the engineers. Even where they do not invest, own, or manage directly,
they take over processing and marketing. By the middle 'thirties,

five tobacco companies bought over half the total crop; four meat packers processed two-thirds of all meat animals slaughtered; thirteen flour mills processed 65 per cent of all the wheat marketed.

Thus the farmer must deal with the business interests closing in on the processing and the distributing of his product. He must also deal with those who sell him what he needs: he must buy most of his farm implements from one of the four industrial firms which in 1936 sold more than three-fourths of all important farm implements. His only recourse has been to keep prices as high as the traffic will bear. And he has attempted to do so by replacing the dictates of the free market by the edicts of political policy, to suspend the laws of supply and demand so as to guarantee a stable market and price bottoms. Only in so far as he was able to create an effective collusive control of the market by political tactics could the farmer hope to deal with modern business and with modern life on something like an equal footing.

In subsidizing free private enterprise, the New Deal paid special attention to the old rural middle class. In brief, the New Deal farm program attempted to transfer to the farm sector of the economy the well-known practices of the industrial sector; it taught the farmer the value of producing less in order not to break prevailing prices. To protect this 'race of free men in the open country' from the evils of free competition, it paid them subsidies or benefits to curtail their production. The Federal Government, one might say, became the farmer's executive committee.

Since the 'thirties, the government has tried to curtail production by paying benefits to farmers who raised less; it has bought up 'surplus' farm produce which threatened to break prices; it has paid direct subsidies in order to make up differences between market prices and established price minimums. And in the spring of 1949 it was proposed by the Secretary of Agriculture that, instead of keeping the prices of specific crops at parity, based on a previous 'good period,' the government should support the farmers' gross cash income in relation to total national income. It would work out in such a way as to guarantee the farmer an annual income comparable to his yearly income over the past ten boom years.

The latter-day history of the independent farmer is thus not a struggle of free producers loosely tied together by an impersonal market; it is a history of various attempts made by politicians and civil servants to raise and maintain agricultural prices. Failing in this, the farmers' political agents have arranged to compensate out of public funds the independent enterpriser who has become the victim of the free market.

The effectiveness of such measures, accompanied by war-time expansion, is amply attested. During World War II, land values went up more than during the First World War. Total farm income and cash receipts from crops in 1946 were five times higher than in 1932. The per-capita income of the farmers was almost tripled. By 1945, well over half of all farm operators were full owners of the land they worked and the proportion of farm tenants had dropped to about one-third; mortgage debt as a percentage of total farm value had declined from 23 per cent in 1935 to about 12 per cent.

Urban people helped pay for this rural prosperity, not only in taxes but directly in food costs, which make up about 40 per cent of the average family budget. In 1940, the budgeted cost of public money paid to agriculturists was about one-tenth of the nation's food bill. Given the lack of adequate price control, the war-born widening of markets acted during the 'forties to keep most farm prices well above government-supported levels. Just as the contraction of the foreign markets contributed to the farmer's collapse in the 'twenties, so in the 'forties its expansion aided in the farmer's rehabilitation. Between the middle 'thirties and the middle 'forties the average value of agricultural exports rose more than threefold. But this was a different kind of 'foreign market'; born of war, it was run, regulated, and price-controlled by a pro-farmer government. The domestic market also, after seven lean years of mass unemployment, was fattened by the war economy.

The farmer has been able to get governmental largesse because he enjoys three distinct political advantages. First, within the constitutional system the farmer is over-represented. By virtue of the geographical shape of the Senate, territorial rather than demographic, the farm bloc is one of the most powerful bodies in the formal government. New York's millions of employees and Nebraska's thousands of farmers each have two senators. Second, beginning in the early 'twenties, the farmer has built a set of pressure groups that has become perhaps the strongest single bloc in Washington; the American Farm Bureau is knit into the very structure of the governmental system. It speaks frankly not of 'one man alone individualism' but of 'powerful organized groups competing for economic advantage.' Third, the farmer has enjoyed an unusual degree of public moral support.

The farmers who are benefited by propped-up prices are more likely to be of the upper third who sell so much than the middle or lower third who sell so little. Even in the boom, the long-term trends of concentration remain evident. It is a narrowed upper stratum of businesslike, politically alert farmers who are flourishing, not a world of small entrepreneurs. And in this boom, based on political prices and increased productivity, the old forces, as well as many new ones, are still at work. And there is still the old contradiction: who will buy the flood of goods that the motors of technology are turning out? By the fall of 1948 agricultural planning was beginning to raise all the questions that beset it in the 'thirties. The Secretary of Commerce called for huge exports; the farm lobby and its Department of Agriculture called for more. 'What the Europeans thought and what they wanted was something else again,' wrote the editors of *Fortune*. 'It is a little silly . . . to preach the free market in one breath and in the next propound what amounts to a cartel system in agriculture.'

Farming may be seen (1) as a way of livelihood determining the life of its worker-owner; (2) as a real-estate investment from which owners, with the aid of others' work and political help, derive profit; or (3) in the efficient eyes of the state in a period of permanent war economy, as a natural resource and a piece of equipment that must be geared to the national usage.

Each of these three views entails different images of the farmer: land as livelihood means 'the farmer' as unalienated entrepreneur; land as productive real estate means 'the farmer' as big investor financially exploiting the landless worker; and there is this third image, which may be that of the future: land as equipment, and 'the farmer' as a salaried expert. Today the

American land is seen in all three ways, and there are, in fact, all three types of 'farmers.'

In the rhetoric of many farm spokesmen, farming as a business is disguised as farming as a way of life. The Second World War and its economic consequences saved the politically dependent farmer; the era of militarized economies may ruin him. The norm of rational efficiency, uppermost in war, is clearly violated by the system of present-day agriculture. Military and technological needs may take ascendance over economic greed and political fixing. Alongside the small independent farmer, a new breed of men might come onto the land, men who never were owners and do not expect to be, men who, like factory employees, manage and work the big machines. Then farming would take its place, not as the center of a social world as formerly, nor as a politically secured heirloom of free enterprise, but as one national industry among other intricate, rationalized departments of production.

In the meantime, farming is less a morally ascendant way of life than an industry; appreciation of the family farm as a special virtue-producing unit in a world of free men is today but a nostalgic mood among deluded metropolitan people. Moreover, it is an ideological veil for larger business layouts whose economic ally and ultimate victim the politically dependent farmer may well become.

3. The Small Business Front

Images of small men usually arise and persist widely only because big men find good use for them. Businessmen had not been taken as exemplars of the small individual, as were farmers, until in the twentieth century the small businessman arose as a counter-image to the big businessman. Then big business began to promulgate and use the image of the small businessman. Such spokesmen have been gravely concerned about the fate of small business because, in their rhetoric, small business is the last urban representative of free competition and thus of the competitive virtues of the private enterprise system.

In any well-conducted Senate hearing on economic issues, someone always says that the small entrepreneur is the backbone of the American economy, that he maintains the thousands of smaller cities, and that, especially in these cities, he is the very flower of the American way. 'It is the small businessman who has become so closely identified with the many hundreds of villages and cities of this land that he is the very foundation of the hometown's growth and development.' Perhaps giant monopolies do exist, the image runs, but, after all, they are of the big city; it is in the small towns, the locus of real Americans, that the small businessman thrives.

Quite apart from the larger interests the small-town small-business stratum serves and the nostalgia its existence taps, there is a solid reason why people hold so firmly to its image. In these towns the old urban middle class has been the historic carrier of what is called civic spirit, which in the American town has involved a widespread participation in local affairs on the part of those able to benefit a community by voluntary management of its public enterprises. These enterprises range from having the streets properly cleaned to improving the parks; as a matter of fact, they often seem to have something to do with real estate, in one way or another. The history of the civic spirit reveals that for the old middle class, especially the small merchants, it has meant a businesslike participation in civic matters.

For this role, the old middle-class individual was well fitted: he often had the necessary time and money; his success in his small business has, according to the prevailing idea, trained him for initiative and responsibility; he has been thrown into fairly continual contact with the administrative and political figures of the city; and, of course, he has often stood to benefit economically from civic endeavor and improvement. 'It is just good business to be somebody civically,' said a prosperous merchant, who was.

Yet economic self-interest has not been the whole motive; civic participation has also involved competition among small businessmen for prestige. They compete economically as businessmen, they compete civically as democratic citizens. Because of their local economic roots, they are truly local men; they wish to win standing in their city. If some are bigger businessmen than others, still the width of the stratum as a whole is not so great that those at the bottom could not see and aspire to the top.

Traditionally, the lower classes have also participated in civic euphoria, but only as an adjunct of businessmen. They have identified themselves with businessmen in such a way as to feel that this identification was with the town itself. This underside of civic spirit has been possible, first, because small plants and shops tended to make informal the relations between workers and businessmen; second, because the existence of many firms, graded in sizes, made it possible for the entrepreneurial system to extend, at least psychologically, to the working class; and third, because the population of small-business cities has grown rather slowly and, compared with cities subject to the booms of big business and rapid metropolitan mobility, has been the result more of natural increase than of migration. This rate and type of growth have meant that more of the people of the small city and its adjoining area 'grew up together,' and, in smaller towns, went to the same public schools. So the very pattern of city growth has made for an easier identification between classes and therefore for greater civic identification.

As the economic position and power of the small entrepreneur has declined, especially since the First World War, this old pattern of civic prestige, and hence civic spirit, has been grievously modified. In some smaller cities the mark of the big-business way is a bolder mark than in others, yet in all of them the new order is modifying the prestige and power of the small-business community.

The place of the small businessman in the class pattern of various smaller cities differs in accordance with the degree and type of industrialization, and with the extent to which one or two big firms dominate the city's labor market. But the over-all decline of small-business prestige is now fairly standard.

At the top of the occupational-income ranking are big-business people and executives. Next are small businessmen and free professionals, followed by higher salaried white-collar people, and then lower salaried office workers and foremen. At the bottom is labor of all grades. But no objective measure of stratification necessarily coincides with the social and civic prestige which various members of these strata enjoy. An examination of the images which the people of each level have of the people on all other levels reveals one major fact: small business (and white-collar) people occupy the most ambiguous social positions. It is as if the city's population were polarized into two groups, big business and labor, and everyone else were thrown together into a vague 'middle class.'

Wage-workers, to whom small businessmen are often the most visible element of the 'higher-ups,' do not readily distinguish between small business and the upper class in general. Wage-worker families ascribe prestige and power to the small business-man without really seeing the position he holds *vis-à-vis* the upper classes. 'Shopkeepers,' says a lower-class woman, 'they go in the higher brackets. Because they are on the higher level. They don't humble themselves to the poor.'

The upper-class person, on the other hand, places the small businessman, especially the retailer, much lower in the scale than he does the larger businessman, especially the industrialist. Both the size and the type of business are explicitly used as prestige criteria by the upper classes, among whom the socially new, larger, industrial entrepreneurs and their colleagues, the officials of absentee corporations, rank small business rather low because of the *local* nature of its activities. They gauge prestige mainly by the economic scope of a man's business and his social and business connections with members of nationally known firms. The old-family rentier, usually rich from real estate, ranks small businessmen low because of the way he feels about their background and education, 'the way they live.' Both of these upper-class elements more or less agree with the sentiment expressed by an old-family banker: 'Business ethics are higher, more broad-minded, more stable among industrialists, as over against retailers. We all know that.'

Small businessmen are of the generally upper ranks only in income, and then, usually, only during boom times; in terms of family origin, intermarriage, job history, and education, more of them than of any other higher income group are lower class. In these respects, a good proportion of the small businessmen have close biographical connections with the wage-worker strata. In the small city there is rigidity at the bottom and at the top—except as regards small businessmen who, compared with other income groups, have done a great deal of moving up the line.

These facts help to explain the different images of small businessmen held by members of upper and of lower strata. The old upper class judges more by status and 'background'; the lower class more by income and the appearances to which it readily leads.

When a big business moves into a town, the distribution of social prestige and civic effort changes; as big business enlarges its economic and political power, it creates a new social world in its image. Just as the labor markets of the smaller cities have been dominated, so also have their markets for prestige. The chief local executives of the corporations, the $10,000 to $25,000 a year men, gain the top social positions, displacing the former social leaders of the city. Local men begin to realize that their social standing depends upon association with the leading officials of the absentee firms; they struggle to follow the officials' style of living, to move into their suburbs, to be invited to their social affairs, and to marry their own children into these circles. Those whose incomes do not permit full realization of what has happened to the social world, or who refuse to recognize its dynamic, either become eccentric dwarfs of the new status system, or, perhaps without recognizing it, begin to imitate in curious miniature the new ways of the giants. When the big firm comes to the small city the wives of its officialdom become models for the local women of the old middle class. The often glamorous women of the firm's officials come and go between the metropolitan center and their exclusive suburb of the small city. In the eyes of the small businessman's wife who has Not Been Invited one sees the social meaning of the decline of the old middle class.

No matter how much or in what way the old middle class resists, the distribution of prestige follows in due course the distribution of economic and political power in the city. The ambiguous status of small business people in this new world of prestige has to do with their power position as well as their social background. In the polarization of the small city, both prestige and power become concentrated at the top: the big business people monopolize both.

Such power as the local business community has is organized in the Chamber of Commerce, to which most small businessmen belong. Yet everyone in the town who is politically literate feels that the larger firms 'run the town.' Many small businessmen will say so in semi-private contexts. 'If you live in this town,' a druggist says, 'you just know you're working for [the big plants], whether you're working *in* their plants or not.'

One of the most powerful weapons the large corporations possess is the threat to leave town; this veto is in effect the power of life or death over the economic life of the town, affecting the town's bank, the Chamber of Commerce, small businessmen, labor, and city officials alike. The history of its use in many smaller cities proves how effective it can be. To show their disapproval of a city project, big corporation officials may withdraw from the activities of the sponsoring organization, absenting themselves from meetings, or withholding financial support. But these methods, although they are used and are effective, are often too direct. Increasingly, large business mobilizes small-business-small-town sentiment, and uses it as a front. Where real power has consequences that many people do not like, there is need for the noisy appearance of power little business can provide. The old middle class is coming to serve a crucial purpose, as a concealing façade, in the psychology of civic prestige. 'They don't want it to appear that they control things,' an assistant manager of a Chamber of Commerce said. Nevertheless, 'they' do.

This use of small businessmen in big business towns can paralyze the civic will of the middle classes and confuse their efforts. Small business is out in front, busily accomplishing all sorts of minor civic projects, taking praise—and blame—from the rank-and-file citizenry. Among those in the lower classes who for one reason or another are anti-business, the small businessmen are often the target of aggression and blame; but from the lower-class individual who is pro-business or neutral, the small businessmen get high esteem because 'they are doing a lot for this city.'

The prestige often imputed to small businessmen by lower-class members is based largely on ascribed power, but neither this prestige nor this power is always claimed, and certainly it is not often cashed in among the upper classes. The upper-class businessman knows the actual power set-up; but if he or his clique is using small businessmen for some project, he may shower them with public prestige although he does not accept them or allow them more power than he can retain in his indirect control.

The political and economic composition of a well-run Chamber of Commerce enables it to borrow the prestige and power of the top strata; its committees include the 'leaders' of practically every voluntary association, including labor unions; within its organizations and through its contacts, it is able virtually to monopolize the organization and publicity talent of the city. Thus identifying its program with the unifying myth of the 'community interest,' big business, even in the home town, often toys with little business as a wilful courtesan treats an elderly adorer.

Yet the small businessman, in small city and in metropolitan area, clings stubbornly to the identity, 'business is business,' and his ideology rests upon his identification with business as such. The benefits derived from good relations with higher-ups, and the prestige-striving oriented toward the big men, tend to strengthen this identification; and this identification is energetically organized and actively promoted by the very organizations formed and supported by small businessmen.

A knowing business journal writes about the Fair Deal's wooing of small business: 'You can be pretty flexible in defining a "small business." Everyone outside the Big Three or Big Four you find at the top of most industries is small in Truman's eyes. And in the name of Small Business, you can do things to direct and stimulate the economy that would be politically difficult under any other label.'

Actually, small business is by no means unified in its outlook, nor agreed upon what it wants, as is evidenced by the disunity and weakness of the small-business national-trade associations. There are many such organizations but the largest probably has less than 5000 members; each is tied primarily to one line of business, which usually includes large as well as small firms. The small businessman sees first of all the conditions of his own industry in his local market, although the problem he has in common with all other small businessmen arises from the concentration process; to see that process for what it is requires an act of abstraction of which any significant number of small businessmen seem incapable.

The small-business wing of the old middle class stands in contrast to the farmer wing, whose political force is being used nationally and with great success. Nationally, the small businessman is overpowered, politically and economically, by big business; he therefore tries to ride with and benefit from the success of big business on the national political front, even as he fights the economic effects of big business on the local and state front. The local businessman is usually against only the unfair chain and the monster department store, and does not see the national movement. This is understandable: some 70 per cent of small businessmen are retail tradesmen; while they cannot see the big manufacturer so clearly, any new channel of distribution is right before their eyes, and evokes their resentment because they can immediately feel its competition.

There is reason in the small businessman's point that business, large or small, when contrasted with the consuming public, *is* after all business. The problem of small business is, in the end, a family quarrel, a quarrel between the big and the small capitalist over the distribution of available profits. The small capitalist desires profits to be more 'equally' divided within the 'business community'—that is what the restoration of free private competition means to him. Yet, at the same time that small firms are being driven to the wall, they are being used by the big firms with whom they publicly identify themselves. This fact underlies the ideology and the frustration of the small urban capitalist; it is the reason why his aggression is directed at labor and government.

Being closer to labor by social origin and business contact, small businessmen can the more easily magnify and develop resentments against labor's power. Being closer to them on economic levels, they are quick to observe any shifts in their relative economic positions. As an employer of labor the small business stratum, Rudolf Hilferding wrote in 1910, comes into 'more acute contradiction to the working class. . .' If the power of unions is not greater in small enterprises, still the exercise of that power seems more drastic; the small concern is less able than the large one to meet both the higher wages the union wins for its members and the costs of social security labor obtains from the state welfare coffers. As labor unions have organized and developed their political pressure, especially over the last fifteen years, and as wages went up during World War II, the small businessman readily developed a deep resentment, which fed his anti-labor ideology. He always says the working man is a fine fellow, but these unions are bad, and their leaders are still worse.

His attitude toward 'labor' magnifies its power, and his resentment takes a personal form: 'Think of the tremendous wages being paid to laboring men . . . all out of proportion to what they should be paid . . . a number of them have spoken to me, saying they are ashamed to be taking the wages.' And another one says: 'I had a young man cash a check at the store on Monday evening for $95.00. . . We would not class him as half as good as our clerks in our store. . .'

It is this feeling that makes it possible for big business to use small business as a shield. In any mêlée between big business and big labor, the small entrepreneurs seem to be more often on the side of business. It is as if the closer to bankruptcy they are, the more frantically they cling to their ideal. But much as they cling to big business, they do not look to it as the solver of their troubles; for this, strangely enough, they look to government. The little businessman believes, 'We are victims of circumstances. My only hope is in Senator Murray, who, I feel sure, will do all in his power to keep the little businessman who, he knows, has been the foundation of the country [etc.]. . . We all know no business can survive selling . . . at a loss, which is my case today, on the new cost of green coffee.'

Yet, while he looks to government for economic aid and political comfort, the independent businessman is, at the same time, resentful of its regulations and taxation, and he has vague feelings that larger powers are using government against him. And his attitude toward government is blended with estimates of his own virtue, for the criterion of man is success on Main Street: 'Another thing that I resent very much is the fact that most of these organizations are headed by men who are not able to make a success in private life and have squeezed into WPA [sic] and gotten over us and are telling us what to do, and it is to me very resentful. And all these men here know of people who head these organizations, who were not able to make a living on Main Street before.'

Small business's attitude toward government, as toward labor, plays into the hands of big-business ideology. In both connections, small businessmen are shock troops in the battle against labor unions and government controls.

Big government, organized labor, big business, as well as immediate competitors, prepare the soil of anxiety for small business; the ideological growth of this anxiety is thus deeply rooted in fears, which, though often misplaced, are not without foundation. Big business exploits in its own interests the very anxieties it has created for small business.

Many of the problems to which Nazism provided one kind of solution have by no means been solved in America. 'The ultimate success of national socialism,' A. R. L. Gurland, O. Kirchheimer, and F. Neumann have recalled, 'was due to a large extent to its ability to use the frustrations of [small-business] groups for its own purposes. Small business wanted to retain its independence and have an adequate income. But it was not allowed to do this. The Nazis directed the resentment of small businessmen against labor and against the Weimar Republic, which appeared to be, and to some extent was, the creation of the German labor movement . . . the frustrations of small businessmen, created primarily by the process of concentration, were not directed against the industrial and financial monopolists, but against those groups that appeared to have attained more security at the expense of small business. . . Thus, national socialism was able to organize small business by promising it the coming of a Golden Age. . . While victimized by the Government's tax policy and trade restrictions, small business was mortally hit by the spread of inflation which devoured its economies. This from the very beginning determined the political orientation which small business was to follow under the Republic. Assistance was expected from those parties which seemed able to resist labor and labor-influenced Government.' Policies that emphasized the middle-class aim of maintaining the *status quo* between the balance of social forces and promised legal measures to further and protect independent middle-class elements were welcomed by these elements. 'Small-business leaders did not mistrust the Nazi party. Did not many of the Nazi leaders come from the very social stratum to which they, the small businessmen, belonged? Had not many joined the party for the very reasons which had made life under the Republic unbearable for small businessmen?'

If the small businessman in America is going back on his spokesmen, he cannot really be blamed, for the spokesmen, without knowing it, have also been going back on the small businessman. These spokesmen would legally *guarantee* his chances. But once guaranteed, a chance becomes a sinecure. All the private and public virtues that self-help, manly competition, and cupidity are supposed to foster would be denied the little businessman. The government would expropriate the very basis of political freedom and of the free personality. If, as is so frequently insisted by senators, 'Democracy can exist only in a capitalistic system in which the life of the individual is controlled by supply and demand,' then democracy may be finished. It is now frequently added, however, that to save capitalism, the government 'must prevent small business from being shattered and destroyed.' The new way of salvation replaces the old faith in supply and demand with the hope of governmental aid and legalized comfort. By trying to persuade the government to ration out the main chance, large and small business alike are helping to destroy the meaning of competition in the style of life and the free society of the old middle classes.

4. Political Persistence

The old middle classes are still the chief anchors of the old American way, and the old way is still strong. Yet American history of the last century often seems to be a series of mishaps for the independent man. Whatever occasional victories he may have won, this man has been fighting against the main drift of a new society; even his victories have turned out to be illusory or temporary.

The economic tensions that developed in the world of the small entrepreneur and took political shape as this world was being destroyed were not between classes with and without property. That conflict was distracted by another, which has determined the course of U.S. politics: Until very recently, political issues have been fought between holders of small property, mainly rural, and holders of large property, mainly industrial and financial. While all the people were not owners, there were too many who thought they soon would be to fight politically against the institution of property itself. Politics was sidetracked into a fight between various sizes and types of property, while more and more of the population had no property of any size or type, and increasingly no chance to get any.

No U.S. political leader with following (with the possible exception of Debs with his 900,000 votes in 1912) has ventured even to discuss seriously the overturning of property relations. In American politics, those relations have been assumed, their strength rooted in the small entrepreneur's world, in which work created property before men's eyes, and in which pursuit of private gain seemed to be visibly in harmony with the public good. 'A nation consisting mainly of small capitalists and a government under their control is the outspoken ideal of American statesmen . . . from Jefferson and Lincoln to Roosevelt and Wilson,' wrote William Walling, one of the most penetrating analysts of the Progressive Era. Such a society is viewed in American political rhetoric as eternal; and no society is thought to be genuinely civilized until it has obtained the 'social maturity' of division into small holdings. 'The idea is that the small capitalist ought to be a privileged class and ought to rule the country, and that other classes ought to be prevented from growing too large, if possible, or at least should be kept from power. . .'

The old middle classes were perhaps at the height of their political consciousness when they made their last political stand in the Progressive Era. The fight against plutocracy was a fight in the name and in the interests of the small capitalist on farm and in city. Theodore Roosevelt and Woodrow Wilson were its leading rhetoricians. Wilson, who represented the *whole* system of business, regarded it as a system in which government should abolish private monopolies and hold any large interests which are not monopolies 'in their places.' Small businesses, he insisted, are to be provided for the whole population; each generation should look forward 'to becoming not employees but heads of small, it may be, but hopeful businesses.' Could Wilson imagine any U.S. government except a government of small capitalists? In Roosevelt's version, new classes, according to Walling, were 'to be admitted to power, but only as they become small capitalists: "Ultimately we desire to use the government to aid, as far as safely can be done, the industrial tool users 'to become in part tool-owners just as the farmers now are." ' 'The growth in the complexity of community life,' said Roosevelt, 'means the partial substitution of collectivism for individualism, not to destroy, but to save, individualism.'

The two general lines of strategy taken by liberal theorists and old middle-class politicians, led by these two men, were: (1) The view as expressed by Herbert Croly—and Theodore Roosevelt— that large concentrations of property should be fought indirectly. By bringing them under governmental control, through taxation and governmental guidance, he hoped to make monopolies function in the interest of public welfare, to make big business honest and respectable, in the manner of little business, and to give more little businesses the chance to become big. (2) Following the traditional Jeffersonian animus, the view of Louis D. Brandeis and Woodrow Wilson, the view that favored the outright breaking up of large monopolies and the restoration of the world of small free men. However the expedient details may have differed, American liberalism has based its main hope for democracy on the hope that the small capitalist, doing his own work, or working for others only until he sets up for himself, would control the wealth of the country.

'Progressive' political movements have thus been technologically reactionary, in the literal sense; they have been carried on by those who were defending small property by waging war against large concentrations of property. Breaks in the major parties have been breaks caused by conflicting tendencies among old middle-class politicians. In 1912, for example, when Theodore Roosevelt broke away from the Republican party with his Bull Moose campaign, he was on the one hand fighting those who wanted to give absolutely free reign to monopolies, and on the other restraining the nomination of LaFollette as a Republican candidate. As Matthew Josephson has shown, the small men

'who feared and hated monopolies,' who wished 'to make secure
the small property holder's way of life . . .' gave and received
support from LaFollette; it was primarily for such little men that
twelve years later, in 1924, the largest third-party vote in the
history of the United States was cast. But through the boom and
into the depression the monopolists continued to grow. The
New Deal—a shifting confusion of dominantly middle-class tendencies—did not materially lessen the concentration and the war
continued to facilitate it.

Yet the small entrepreneur has not quit easily. Increasingly his
weapons have become political: a tricky realm reflecting economic forces as much or more than political will. While spear-
heading the drive of technology, the enemies of the small entrepreneur have also fought with political as well as with economic weapons. These enemies have been winning without benefit of popular upsurges; their strength has not been people, but
technology and money and war. Their struggle has been hidden,
relentless, and successful.

'Middle-class radicalism' in the United States has been in truth
reactionary, for it could be realized and maintained only if production were kept small-scale. The small entrepreneur and his
champions have accepted the basic relations of capitalism, but
have hung back at an early stage, and have gained no leverage
outside the system with which they might resist its unfolding.
In their politics of desperation against large-scale property, small
businessmen and independent farmers have demanded that the
state guarantee the existence and profits of their small properties.

An economy dominated by small-scale factories, shops, and
farms may be integrated by a multitude of transactions between
individual men on free markets. The spread of large enterprises
has diminished the number and areas of those transactions.
Larger areas of modern society are integrated by bureaucratic
units of management, and such market freedom as persists is
more or less confined to higgling and conniving among bureaucratic agents, and to areas not yet in the grip of big management. The distribution of man's independence, in so far as it is
rooted in the ownership and control of his means of livelihood
and his equality of power in the market, is thus drastically narrowed. The free market which co-ordinated the world of the

small propertied producers is no longer the chief means of co-ordination.

No longer mechanisms of an impersonal adjustment, nor sovereign guides of the productive process, prices are now the object of powerful bargainings between the political blocs of big business, big farmers, and big labor. Price changes are signals of the relative powers of these interest blocs rather than signals of demand and supply on the part of scattered producers and consumers. War, slump, and boom increase this managed balance of power as against the self-balance of the old free market society. Other means of integration are indeed now needed to prop up what old market mechanisms still work. In three or four generations the United States has passed from a loose scatter of enterprisers to an increasingly bureaucratic co-ordination of specialized occupational structures. Its economy has become a bureaucratic cage.

Political freedom and economic security have different meanings and different bases in the social structure that has resulted from the centralization of property. When widely distributed properties are the dominant means of independent livelihood, men are free and secure within the limits of their abilities and the framework of the market. Their political freedom does not contradict their economic security; both are rooted in ownership. Political power, resting upon this ownership, is evenly enough distributed to secure political freedom; economic security, founded upon one man's property, is not the basis for another man's insecurity. Control over the property with which one works is the keystone of a classic democratic system which, for a while, united political freedom and economic security.

But the centralization of property has shifted the basis of economic security from property ownership to job holding; the power inherent in huge properties has jeopardized the old balance which gave political freedom. Now unlimited freedom to do as one wishes with one's property is at the same time freedom to do what one wishes to the freedom and the security of thousands of dependent employees. For the employees, freedom and security, both political and economic, can no longer rest upon individual independence in the old sense. To be free and to be secure is to have an effective control over that upon which one is dependent: the job within the centralized enterprise.

The broad linkage of enterprise and property, the cradle-condition of classic democracy, no longer exists in America. This is no society of small entrepreneurs—now they are one stratum among others: above them is the big money; below them, the alienated employee; before them, the fate of politically dependent relics; behind them, their world.

TWO

White Collar Worlds

4

The New Middle Class, I

In the early nineteenth century, although there are no exact figures, probably four-fifths of the occupied population were self-employed enterprisers; by 1870, only about one-third, and in 1940, only about one-fifth, were still in this old middle class. Many of the remaining four-fifths of the people who now earn a living do so by working for the 2 or 3 per cent of the population who now own 40 or 50 per cent of the private property in the United States. Among these workers are the members of the new middle class, white-collar people on salary. For them, as for wage-workers, America has become a nation of employees for whom independent property is out of range. Labor markets, not control of property, determine their chances to receive income, exercise power, enjoy prestige, learn and use skills.

1. Occupational Change

Of the three broad strata composing modern society, only the new middle class has steadily grown in proportion to the whole. Eighty years ago, there were three-quarters of a million middle-class employees; by 1940, there were over twelve and a half million. In that period the old middle class in-

THE LABOR FORCE	1870	1940
Old Middle Class	33%	20%
New Middle Class	6	25
Wage-Workers	61	55
Total	100%	100%

creased 135 per cent; wage-workers, 255 per cent; new middle class, 1600 per cent.*

The employees composing the new middle class do not make up one single compact stratum. They have not emerged on a single horizontal level, but have been shuffled out simultaneously on the several levels of modern society; they now form, as it were, a new pyramid within the old pyramid of society at large, rather than a horizontal layer. The great bulk of the new middle class are of the lower middle-income brackets, but regardless of how social stature is measured, types of white-collar men and women range from almost the top to almost the bottom of modern society.

The managerial stratum, subject to minor variations during these decades, has dropped slightly, from 14 to 10 per cent; the salaried professionals, displaying the same minor ups and downs, have dropped from 30 to 25 per cent of the new middle class. The major shifts in over-all composition have been in the relative

New Middle Class	1870	1940
Managers	14%	10%
Salaried Professionals	30	25
Salespeople	44	25
Office Workers	12	40
Total	100%	100%

decline of the sales group, occurring most sharply around 1900, from 44 to 25 per cent of the total new middle class; and the steady rise of the office workers, from 12 to 40 per cent. Today the three largest occupational groups in the white-collar stratum are schoolteachers, salespeople in and out of stores, and assorted office workers. These three form the white-collar mass.

White-collar occupations now engage well over half the members of the American middle class as a whole. Between 1870 and 1940, white-collar workers rose from 15 to 56 per cent of the middle brackets, while the old middle class declined from 85 to 44 per cent:

* For the sources of the figures in Part II, see Sources and Acknowledgments. In the tables in this section, figures for the intermediate years are appropriately graded; the change has been more or less steady.

Negatively, the transformation of the middle class is a shift from property to no-property; positively, it is a shift from property to a new axis of stratification, occupation. The nature and well-being of the old middle class can best be sought in the condition of entrepreneurial property; of

THE MIDDLE CLASSES	1870	1940
OLD MIDDLE CLASS	85%	44%
Farmers	62	23
Businessmen	21	19
Free Professionals	2	2
NEW MIDDLE CLASS	15%	56%
Managers	2	6
Salaried Professionals	4	14
Salespeople	7	14
Office Workers	2	22
Total Middle Classes	100%	100%

the new middle class, in the economics and sociology of occupations. The numerical decline of the older, independent sectors of the middle class is an incident in the centralization of property; the numerical rise of the newer salaried employees is due to the industrial mechanics by which the occupations composing the new middle class have arisen.

2. Industrial Mechanics

In modern society, occupations are specific functions within a social division of labor, as well as skills sold for income on a labor market. Contemporary divisions of labor involve a hitherto unknown specialization of skill: from arranging abstract symbols, at $1000 an hour, to working a shovel, for $1000 a year. The major shifts in occupations since the Civil War have assumed this industrial trend: as a proportion of the labor force, fewer individuals manipulate *things,* more handle *people* and *symbols.*

This shift in needed skills is another way of describing the rise of the white-collar workers, for their characteristic skills involve the handling of paper and money and people. They are expert at dealing with people transiently and impersonally; they are masters of the commercial, professional, and technical relationship. The one thing they do not do is live by making things; rather, they live off the social machineries that organize and coordinate the people who do make things. White-collar people help turn what someone else has made into profit for still another; some of them are closer to the means of production, supervising the work of actual manufacture and recording what is done. They are the people who keep track; they man the paper routines involved in distributing what is produced. They provide technical and personal services, and they teach others the skills which they themselves practice, as well as all other skills transmitted by teaching.

As the proportion of workers needed for the extraction and production of things declines, the proportion needed for servicing, distributing, and co-ordinating rises. In 1870, over three-fourths, and in 1940, slightly less than one-half of the total employed were engaged in producing things.

	1870	1940
Producing	77%	46%
Servicing	13	20
Distributing	7	23
Co-ordinating	3	11
Total employed	100%	100%

By 1940, the proportion of white-collar workers of those employed in industries primarily involved in the production of things was 11 per cent; in service industries, 32 per cent; in distribution, 44 per cent; and in co-ordination, 60 per cent. The white-collar industries themselves have grown, and within each industry the white-collar occupations have grown. Three trends lie back of the fact that the white-collar ranks have thus been the most rapidly growing of modern occupations: the increasing productivity of machinery used in manufacturing; the magnification of distribution; and the increasing scale of co-ordination.

The immense productivity of mass-production technique and the increased application of technologic rationality are the first open secrets of modern occupational change: fewer men turn out more things in less time. In the middle of the nineteenth century, as J. F. Dewhurst and his associates have calculated, some 17.6 billion horsepower hours were expended in American industry, only 6 per cent by mechanical energy; by the middle of the twentieth century, 410.4 billion horsepower hours will be expended, 94 per cent by mechanical energy. This industrial revolution seems to be permanent, seems to go on through war and boom and slump; thus 'a decline in production results in a more than proportional decline in employment; and an increase in production results in a less than proportional increase in employment.'

Technology has thus narrowed the stratum of workers needed for given volumes of output; it has also altered the types and proportions of skill needed in the production process. Know-how, once an attribute of the mass of workers, is now in the machine and the engineering elite who design it. Machines displace unskilled workmen, make craft skills unnecessary, push up front the automatic motions of the machine-operative. Workers composing the new lower class are predominantly semi-skilled: their proportion in the urban wage-worker stratum has risen from 31 per cent in 1910 to 41 per cent in 1940.

The manpower economies brought about by machinery and the large-scale rationalization of labor forces, so apparent in production and extraction, have not, as yet, been applied so extensively in distribution—transportation, communication, finance, and trade. Yet without an elaboration of these means of distribution, the wide-flung operations of multi-plant producers could not be integrated nor their products distributed. Therefore, the proportion of people engaged in distribution has enormously increased so that today about one-fourth of the labor force is so engaged. Distribution has expanded more than production because of the lag in technological application in this field, and because of the persistence of individual and small-scale entrepreneurial units at the same time that the market has been enlarged and the need to market has been deepened.

Behind this expansion of the distributive occupations lies the central problem of modern capitalism: to whom can the available goods be sold? As volume swells, the intensified search for markets draws more workers into the distributive occupations of trade, promotion, advertising. As far-flung and intricate markets come into being, and as the need to find and create even more markets becomes urgent, 'middle men' who move, store, finance, promote, and sell goods are knit into a vast network of enterprises and occupations.

The physical aspect of distribution involves wide and fast transportation networks; the co-ordination of marketing involves communication; the search for markets and the selling of goods involves trade, including wholesale and retail outlets as well as financial agencies for commodity and capital markets. Each of these activities engage more people, but the manual jobs among them do not increase so fast as the white-collar tasks.

Transportation, growing rapidly after the Civil War, began to decline in point of the numbers of people involved before 1930; but this decline took place among wage-workers; the proportion of white-collar workers employed in transportation continued to rise. By 1940, some 23 per cent of the people in transportation were white-collar employees. As a new industrial segment of the U.S. economy, the communication industry has never been run by large numbers of free enterprisers; at the outset it needed large numbers of technical and other white-collar workers. By 1940, some 77 per cent of its people were in new middle-class occupations.

Trade is now the third largest segment of the occupational structure, exceeded only by farming and manufacturing. A few years after the Civil War less than 5 out of every 100 workers were engaged in trade; by 1940 almost 12 out of every 100 workers were so employed. But, while 70 per cent of those in wholesaling and retailing were free enterprisers in 1870, and less than 3 per cent were white collar, by 1940, of the people engaged in retail trade 27 per cent were free enterprisers; 41 per cent white-collar employees.

Newer methods of merchandising, such as credit financing, have resulted in an even greater percentage increase in the 'financial' than in the 'commercial' agents of distribution. Branch banking has lowered the status of many banking employees to the clerical level, and reduced the number of executive positions. By 1940, of all employees in finance and real estate 70 per cent were white-collar workers of the new middle class.

The organizational reason for the expansion of the white-collar occupations is the rise of big business and big government, and the consequent trend of modern social structure, the steady growth of bureaucracy. In every branch of the economy, as firms merge and corporations become dominant, free entrepreneurs become employees, and the calculations of accountant, statistician, bookkeeper, and clerk in these corporations replace the free 'movement of prices' as the co-ordinating agent of the economic system. The rise of thousands of big and little bureaucracies and the elaborate specialization of the system as a whole create the need for many men and women to plan, co-ordinate, and administer new routines for others. In moving from smaller to larger and more elaborate units of economic activity, increased proportions of employees are drawn into co-ordinating and managing. Managerial and professional employees and office workers of varied sorts—floorwalkers, foremen, office managers—are needed; people to whom subordinates report, and who in turn report to superiors, are links in chains of power and obedience, co-ordinating and supervising other occupational experiences, functions, and skills. And all over the economy, the proportion of clerks of all sorts has increased: from 1 or 2 per cent in 1870 to 10 or 11 per cent of all gainful workers in 1940.

As the worlds of business undergo these changes, the increased tasks of government on all fronts draw still more people into occupations that regulate and service property and men. In response to the largeness and predatory complications of business, the crises of slump, the nationalization of the rural economy and small-town markets, the flood of immigrants, the urgencies of war and the march of technology disrupting social life, government increases its co-ordinating and regulating tasks. Public regulations, social services, and business taxes require more people to make mass records and to integrate people, firms, and goods, both within government and in the various segments of business and private life. All branches of government have grown, although the most startling increases are found in the executive branch of the Federal Government, where the needs for co-ordinating the economy have been most prevalent.

As marketable activities, occupations change (1) with shifts in the skills required, as technology and rationalization are unevenly applied across the economy; (2) with the enlargement and intensification of marketing operations in both the commodity and capital markets; and (3) with shifts in the organization of the division of work, as expanded organizations require co-ordination, management, and recording. The mechanics involved within and between these three trends have led to the numerical expansion of white-collar employees.

There are other less obvious ways in which the occupational structure is shaped: high agricultural tariffs, for example, delay the decline of farming as an occupation; were Argentine beef allowed to enter duty-free, the number of meat producers here might diminish. City ordinances and zoning laws abolish peddlers and affect the types of construction workers that prevail. Most states have bureaus of standards which limit entrance into professions and semi-professions; at the same time members of these occupations form associations in the attempt to control entrance into 'their' market. More successful than most trade unions, such professional associations as the American Medical Association have managed for several decades to level off the proportion of physicians and surgeons. Every phase of the slump-war-boom cycle influences the numerical importance of various occupations; for instance, the movement back and forth between 'construction worker' and small 'contractor' is geared to slumps and booms in building.

The pressures from these loosely organized parts of the occupational world draw conscious managerial agencies into the picture. The effects of attempts to manage occupational change, directly and indirectly, are not yet great, except of course during wars, when government freezes men in their jobs or offers incentives and compulsions to remain in old occupations or shift to new ones. Yet, increasingly the class levels and occupational composition of the nation are managed; the occupational structure of the United States is being slowly reshaped as a gigantic corporate group. It is subject not only to the pulling of autonomous markets and the pushing of technology but to an 'allocation of personnel' from central points of control. Occupational change thus becomes more conscious, at least to those who are coming to be in charge of it.

3. White-Collar Pyramids

Occupations, in terms of which we circumscribe the new middle class, involve several ways of ranking people. As specific activities, they entail various types and levels of *skill*, and their exercise fulfils certain *functions* within an industrial division of labor. These are the skills and functions we have been examining statistically. As sources of income, occupations are connected with *class* position; and since they normally carry an expected quota of prestige, on and off the job, they are relevant to *status* position. They also involve certain degrees of *power* over other people, directly in terms of the job, and indirectly in other social areas. Occupations are thus tied to class, status, and power as well as to skill and function; to understand the occupations composing the new middle class, we must consider them in terms of each of these dimensions.*

'Class situation' in its simplest objective sense has to do with the amount and source of income. Today, occupation rather than property is the source of income for most of those who receive any direct income: the possibilities of selling their services in the labor market, rather than of profitably buying and selling their property and its yields, now determine the life-chances of most of the middle class. All things money can buy and many that men dream about are theirs by virtue of occupational income. In new middle-class occupations men work for someone else on someone else's property. This is the clue to many differences between the old and new middle classes, as well as to the contrast between the older world of the small propertied entrepreneur and the occupational structure of the new society. If the old middle class once fought big property structures in the name of small, free properties, the new middle class, like the wage-workers in latter-day capitalism, has been, from the beginning, dependent upon large properties for job security.

Wage-workers in the factory and on the farm are on the propertyless bottom of the occupational structure, depending upon the equipment owned by others, earning wages for the time they spend at work. In terms of property, the white-collar people are *not* 'in between Capital and Labor'; they are in exactly the same property-class position as the wage-workers. They have no direct

---

* The following pages are not intended as a detailed discussion of the class, prestige, and power of the white-collar occupations, but as preliminary and definitional. See Chapter 11 for Status, 12 for Class, 15 for Power.

financial tie to the means of production, no prime claim upon the proceeds from property. Like factory workers—and day laborers, for that matter—they work for those who do own such means of livelihood.

Yet if bookkeepers and coal miners, insurance agents and farm laborers, doctors in a clinic and crane operators in an open pit have this condition in common, certainly their class situations are not the same. To understand their class positions, we must go beyond the common fact of source of income and consider as well the amount of income.

In 1890, the average income of white-collar occupational groups was about double that of wage-workers. Before World War I, salaries were not so adversely affected by slumps as wages were but, on the contrary, they rather steadily advanced. Since World War I, however, salaries have been reacting to turns in the economic cycles more and more like wages, although still to a lesser extent. If wars help wages more because of the greater flexibility of wages, slumps help salaries because of their greater inflexibility. Yet after each war era, salaries have never regained their previous advantage over wages. Each phase of the cycle, as well as the progressive rise of all income groups, has resulted in a narrowing of the income gap between wage-workers and white-collar employees.

In the middle 'thirties the three urban strata, entrepreneurs, white-collar, and wage-workers, formed a distinct scale with respect to median family income: the white-collar employees had a median income of $1,896; the entrepreneurs, $1,464; the urban wage-workers, $1,175. Although the median income of white-collar workers was higher than that of the entrepreneurs, larger proportions of the entrepreneurs received both high-level and low-level incomes. The distribution of their income was spread more than that of the white collar.

The wartime boom in incomes, in fact, spread the incomes of all occupational groups, but not evenly. The spread occurred mainly among urban entrepreneurs. As an income level, the old middle class in the city is becoming less an evenly graded income group, and more a collection of different strata, with a large proportion of lumpen-bourgeoisie who receive very low incomes, and a small, prosperous bourgeoisie with very high incomes.

In the late 'forties (1948, median family income) the income of all white-collar workers was $4000, that of all urban wage-workers, $3300. These averages, however, should not obscure the overlap of specific groups within each stratum: the lower white-collar people—sales-employees and office workers—earned almost the same as skilled workers and foremen,* but more than semi-skilled urban wage-workers.

In terms of property, white-collar people are in the same position as wage-workers; in terms of occupational income, they are 'somewhere in the middle.' Once they were considerably above the wage-workers; they have become less so; in the middle of the century they still have an edge but the over-all rise in incomes is making the new middle class a more homogeneous income group.

As with income, so with prestige: white-collar groups are differentiated socially, perhaps more decisively than wage-workers and entrepreneurs. Wage earners certainly do form an income pyramid and a prestige gradation, as do entrepreneurs and rentiers; but the new middle class, in terms of income and prestige, is a superimposed pyramid, reaching from almost the bottom of the first to almost the top of the second.

People in white-collar occupations claim higher prestige than wage-workers, and, as a general rule, can cash in their claims with wage-workers as well as with the anonymous public. This fact has been seized upon, with much justification, as the defining characteristic of the white-collar strata, and although there are definite indications in the United States of a decline in their prestige, still, on a nation-wide basis, the majority of even the lower white-collar employees—office workers and salespeople—enjoy a middling prestige.

The historic bases of the white-collar employees' prestige, apart from superior income, have included the similarity of their place and type of work to those of the old middle-classes' which has

---

* It is impossible to isolate the salaried foremen from the skilled urban wage-workers in these figures. If we could do so, the income of lower white-collar workers would be closer to that of semi-skilled workers.

permitted them to borrow prestige. As their relations with entrepreneur and with esteemed customer have become more impersonal, they have borrowed prestige from the firm itself. The
stylization of their appearance, in particular the fact that most
white-collar jobs have permitted the wearing of street clothes
on the job, has also figured in their prestige claims, as have the
skills required in most white-collar jobs, and in many of them
the variety of operations performed and the degree of autonomy
exercised in deciding work procedures. Furthermore, the time
taken to learn these skills and the way in which they have been
acquired by formal education and by close contact with the
higher-ups in charge has been important. White-collar employees
have monopolized high school education—even in 1940 they had
completed 12 grades to the 8 grades for wage-workers and entrepreneurs. They have also enjoyed status by descent: in terms of
race, Negro white-collar employees exist only in isolated instances—and, more importantly, in terms of nativity, in 1930 only
about 9 per cent of white-collar workers, but 16 per cent of free
enterprisers and 21 per cent of wage-workers, were foreign born.
Finally, as an underlying fact, the limited size of the white-
collar group, compared to wage-workers, has led to successful
claims to greater prestige.

The power position of groups and of individuals typically depends upon factors of class, status, and occupation, often in intricate interrelation. Given occupations involve specific powers
over other people in the actual course of work; but also outside
the job area, by virtue of their relations to institutions of property as well as the typical income they afford, occupations lend
power. Some white-collar occupations require the direct exercise of supervision over other white-collar and wage-workers,
and many more are closely attached to this managerial cadre.
White-collar employees are the assistants of authority; the power
they exercise is a derived power, but they do exercise it.

Moreover, within the white-collar pyramids there is a characteristic pattern of authority involving age and sex. The white-
collar ranks contain a good many women: some 41 per cent of
all white-collar employees, as compared with 10 per cent of free

enterprisers, and 21 per cent of wage-workers, are women.* As with sex, so with age: free enterprisers average (median) about 45 years of age, white-collar and wage-workers, about 34; but among free enterprisers and wage-workers, men are about 2 or 3 years older than women; among white-collar workers, there is a 6- or 7-year difference. In the white-collar pyramids, authority is roughly graded by age and sex: younger women tend to be subordinated to older men.

The occupational groups forming the white-collar pyramids, different as they may be from one another, have certain common characteristics, which are central to the character of the new middle class as a general pyramid overlapping the entrepreneurs and wage-workers. White-collar people cannot be adequately defined along any one possible dimension of stratification—skill, function, class, status, or power. They are generally in the middle ranges on each of these dimensions and on every descriptive attribute. Their position is more definable in terms of their relative differences from other strata than in any absolute terms.

On all points of definition, it must be remembered that white-collar people are not one compact horizontal stratum. They do not fulfil one central, positive *function* that can define them, although in general their functions are similar to those of the old middle class. They deal with symbols and with other people, co-ordinating, recording, and distributing; but they fulfil these functions as dependent employees, and the skills they thus employ are sometimes similar in form and required mentality to those of many wage-workers.

In terms of property, they are equal to wage-workers and different from the old middle class. Originating as propertyless dependents, they have no serious expectations of propertied independence. In terms of income, their class position is, on the average, somewhat higher than that of wage-workers. The overlap is large and the trend has been definitely toward less difference, but even today the differences are significant.

* According to our calculations, the proportions of women, 1940, in these groups are: farmers, 2.9%; businessmen, 20%; free professionals, 5.9%; managers, 7.1%; salaried professionals, 51.7%; salespeople, 27.5% office workers, 51%; skilled workers, 3.2%; semi-skilled and unskilled, 29.8%; rural workers, 9.1%.

Perhaps of more psychological importance is the fact that white-collar groups have successfully claimed more prestige than wage-workers and still generally continue to do so. The bases of their prestige may not be solid today, and certainly they show no signs of being permanent; but, however vague and fragile, they continue to mark off white-collar people from wage-workers.

Members of white-collar occupations exercise a derived authority in the course of their work; moreover, compared to older hierarchies, the white-collar pyramids are youthful and feminine bureaucracies, within which youth, education, and American birth are emphasized at the wide base, where millions of office workers most clearly typify these differences between the new middle class and other occupational groups. White-collar masses, in turn, are managed by people who are more like the old middle class, having many of the social characteristics, if not the independence, of free enterprisers.

5

The Managerial Demiurge

As the means of administration are enlarged and centralized, there are more managers in every sphere of modern society, and the managerial type of man becomes more important in the total social structure.

These new men at the top, products of a hundred-year shift in the upper brackets, operate within the new bureaucracies, which select them for their positions and then shape their characters. Their role within these bureaucracies, and the role of the bureaucracies within the social structure, set the scope and pace of the managerial demiurge. So pervasive and weighty are these bureaucratic forms of life that, in due course, older types of upper-bracket men shift their character and performance to join the managerial trend, or sink beneath the upper-bracket men.

In their common attempt to deal with the underlying population, the managers of business and government have become interlaced by committee and pressure group, by political party and trade association. Very slowly, reluctantly, the labor leader in his curious way, during certain phases of the business cycle and union history, joins them. The managerial demiurge means more than an increased proportion of people who work and live by the rules of business, government, and labor bureaucracy; it means that, at the top, society becomes an uneasy interlocking of private and public hierarchies, and at the bottom, more and more areas become objects of management and manipulation. Bureaucratization in the United States is by no means total; its spread is partial and segmental, and the individual is caught up in several

77

structures at once. Yet, over-all, the loose-jointed integration of
liberal society is being replaced, especially in its war phases, by
the more managed integration of a corporate-like society.

1. The Bureaucracies

As an epithet for governmental waste and red tape, the word
'bureaucracy' is a carry-over from the heroic age of capitalism,
when the middle-class entrepreneur was in revolt against mer-
cantile company and monarchist dynasty. That time is now long
past, but the epithet persists in the service of different aims.

In its present common meaning, 'bureaucracy' is inaccurate and
misleading for three major reasons: (1) When the corporation
official objects to 'bureaucracy' he means of course the programs
of the Federal Government, and then only in so far as they seem
to be against the interests of his own private business bureaucracy. (2) Most of the waste and inefficiency associated in popular imagery with 'bureaucracy' is, in fact, a lack of strict and complete bureaucratization. The 'mess,' and certainly the graft, of the
U.S. Army, are more often a result of a persistence of the entrepreneurial outlook among its personnel than of any bureaucratic tendencies as such. Descriptively, bureaucracy refers to
a hierarchy of offices or bureaus, each with an assigned area of
operation, each employing a staff having specialized qualifications. So defined, bureaucracy is the most efficient type of social
organization yet devised. (3) Government bureaucracies are, in
large part, a public consequence of private bureaucratic developments, which by centralizing property and equipment have been
the pace setter of the bureaucratic trend. The very size of modern business, housing the technological motors and financial
say-so, compels the rise of centralizing organizations of formal
rule and rational subdivisions in all sectors of society, most especially in government.

In business, as the manufacturing plant expands in size, it
draws more people into its administrative scope. A smaller proportion of plants employ a larger proportion of manufacturing
wage earners. Even before World War II concentration, 1 per
cent of all the plants employed over half the workers. These
enlarged plants are knit together in central-office or multi-plant

enterprises. Less than 6000 such enterprises control the plants
that employ about half of the workers; they have an output valued 760 per cent higher, and a production per wage-worker 19.5
per cent higher, than independent plants. Multi-plant as well as
independent-plant enterprises merge together in various forms
of corporation: by the time of the Great Depression, the 200
largest industrial corporations owned about half of the total industrial wealth of the country. These large corporations are
linked by their directorships and by trade associations. Administrative decisions merge into the check and balance of the interlocking directorships; in the middle 'thirties some 400 men held
a full third of the 3,544 top seats of the 250 largest corporations.
Supra-corporate trade associations, as Robert Brady has observed,
become 'funnels for the new monopoly,' stabilizing and rationalizing competing managements economically, and serving as the
political apparatus for the whole managerial demiurge of private
wealth.

The slump-war-boom rhythm makes business bureaucracy grow.
During the crises, the single business concern becomes tied to an
intercorporate world which manages the relations of large business and government. The larger and more bureaucratic business
becomes, the more the Federal Government elaborates itself for
purposes of attempted control, and the more business responds
with more rational organization. The bureaucracies of business
tend to duplicate the regulatory agencies of the federal hierarchy, to place their members within the governmental commissions and agencies, to hire officials away from government, and
to develop elaborate mazes within which are hidden the official
secrets of business operations. Across the bargaining tables of
power, the bureaucracies of business and government face one
another, and under the tables their myriad feet are interlocked
in wonderfully complex ways.

The American governing apparatus has been enlarged, centralized, and professionalized both in its means of administration
and the staff required. Presidents and governors, mayors and city
managers have gathered into their hands the means of administration and the power to appoint and supervise. These officials,
no longer simply political figures who deal mainly with legisla-
tures, have become general managerial chieftains who deal

mainly with the subordinates of a bureaucratic hierarchy. The executive branch of modern government has become dynamic, increasing its functions and enlarging its staff at the expense of the legislative and the judicial. In 1929, of all civilian governmental employees 18 per cent were employed in the executive branch of the Federal Government; in 1947, after the peak of World War II, the proportion was 37 per cent.

Who are the managers behind the managerial demiurge?

Seen from below, the management is not a Who but a series of Theys and even Its. Management is something one reports to in some office, maybe in all offices including that of the union; it is a printed instruction and a sign on a bulletin board; it is the voice coming through the loudspeakers; it is the name in the newspaper; it is the signature you can never make out, except it is printed underneath; it is a system that issues orders superior to anybody you know close-up; it blueprints, specifying in detail, your work-life and the boss-life of your foreman. Management is the centralized say-so.

Seen from the middle ranks, management is one-part people who give you the nod, one-part system, one-part yourself. White-collar people may be part of management, like they say, but management is a lot of things, not all of them managing. You carry authority, but you are not its source. As one of the managed, you are on view from above, and perhaps you are seen as a threat; as one of the managers, you are seen from below, perhaps as a tool. You are the cog and the beltline of the bureaucratic machinery itself; you are a link in the chains of commands, persuasions, notices, bills, which bind together the men who make decisions and the men who make things; without you the managerial demiurge could not be. But your authority is confined strictly within a prescribed orbit of occupational actions, and such power as you wield is a borrowed thing. Yours is the subordinate's mark, yours the canned talk. The money you handle is somebody else's money; the papers you sort and shuffle already bear somebody else's marks. You are the servant of decision, the assistant of authority, the minion of management. You are closer to management than the wage-workers are, but yours is seldom the last decision.

Seen from close to the top, management is the ethos of the higher circle: .concentrate power, but enlarge your staff. Down the line, make them feel a part of what you are a part. Set up a school for managers and manage what managers learn; open a channel of two-way communication: commands go down, information comes up. Keep a firm grip but don't boss them, boss their experience; don't <u>let them learn what you don't tell them</u>. Between decision and execution, between command and obedience, let there be reflex. Be calm, judicious, rational; groom your personality and control your appearance; make business a profession. Develop yourself. Write a memo; hold a conference with men like you. And in all this be yourself and be human: nod gravely to the girls in the office; say hello to the men; and always listen carefully to the ones above: 'Over last week end, I gave much thought to the information you kindly tendered me on Friday, especially . . .'

2. From the Top to the Bottom

According to Edwin G. Nourse, recently head of the President's Council of Economic Advisers, 'Responsibility for determining the direction of the nation's economic life today and of furnishing both opportunity and incentive to the masses centers upon some one or two per cent of the gainfully employed.' The managers, as the cadre of the enterprise, form a hierarchy, graded according to their authority to initiate tasks, to plan and execute their own work and freely to plan and order the work of others. Each level in the cadre's hierarchy is beholden to the levels above. Manager talks with manager and each manager talks with his assistant managers and to the employees, that is, those who do not plan work or make decisions, but perform assigned work. Contact with non-managerial employees probably increases down the managerial hierarchy: the top men rarely talk to anyone but secretaries and other managers; the bottom men may have 90 per cent of their contacts with managed employees. In employee parlance, The Boss is frequently the man who actually gives orders; the top men are The Higher Ups who are typically unapproachable except by the narrow circle directly around them.

Down the line, managers are typically split into two types: those who have to do with business decisions and those who have to do with the industrial run of work. Both are further subdivided into various grades of importance, often according to the number of people under them; both have assigned duties and fixed requirements; both as groups have been rationalized. The business managers range from top executives who hold power of attorney for the entire firm and act in its behalf, to the department managers and their assistants under whom the clerks and machine operators and others work. The industrial managers range from the production engineer and designer at the top to the foremen immediately above the workmen at the bottom. The engineering manager and technician are typically subordinated to the business and financial manager: in so far as technical and human skills are used in the modern corporation they serve the needs of the business side of the corporation as judged by the business manager. The engineering manager, recruited from upper middle-income groups, via the universities, is assisted by lower middle-income people with some technical training and long experience.

The men at the top of the managerial cadre in business are formally responsible to stockholders; in government, to the elected politicians and through them to the people. But neither are responsible to any other officials or managers; that is what being at the managerial top means. Often they are the least specialized men among the bosses; the 'general manager' is well named. Many a business firm is run by men whose knowledge is financial, and who could not hold down a job as factory superintendent, much less chief engineer.

Going from problem to problem and always deciding, like Tolstoy's generals, when there really is no basis for decision but only the machine's need for command, the need for no subordinate even to dream the chief is in doubt—that is different from working out some problem alone to its completion. For one thing, an appointment schedule, set more or less by the operation of the machine, determines the content and rhythm of the manager's time, and in fact of his life. For another, he hires and so must feel that the brains of others belong to him, because he knows how to use them. So Monroe Stahr, Scott Fitzgerald's hero in *The Last Tycoon*, first wanted to be chief clerk of the works, 'the one who knows where everything was,' but when he was chief, 'found out that no one knew where anything was.'

Relations between men in charge of the administrative branches of government and men who run the expanded corporations and unions are often close. Their collaboration may occur while each is an official of his respective hierarchy, or by means of personal shiftings of positions; the labor leader accepts a government job or becomes the personnel man of a corporation; the big-business official becomes a dollar-a-year man; the government expert accepts a position with the corporation his agency is attempting to regulate. Just how close the resemblance between governmental and business officials may be is shown by the ease and frequency with which men pass from one hierarchy to another. While such changes may seem mere incidents in an individual career, the meaning of such interpenetration of managerial elite goes beyond this, modifying the meaning of the upper brackets and the objective functions of the several big organizations.

Higher government officials, as Reinhard Bendix has suggested, probably come mostly from rural areas and medium-size towns, from middle-class and lower middle-class families; they have worked their way through college and often to higher educational degrees. Their occupational experience prior to government work is usually law, business, journalism, or college teaching. In line with general occupational shifts, the tendency over the last generation has been for fewer officials to come from farms and more from professional circles. Except perhaps on the very highest levels, these men do not suffer from lack of incentive, as compared with business officials. They do, however, tend to suffer from lack of those privileges of income, prestige, and security, which many of them believe comparable officials in large businesses enjoy.

The officials of business corporations are somewhat older than comparable government officials. The big companies do not yet have what experts in efficient bureaucracy would call an adequate system of recruiting for management. There may be even more 'politics' in appointments in the corporate hierarchies than in Federal Government bureaus. Among bureau heads in Washington, for instance, by 1938 only about 10 per cent were simple political appointees.

Seniority, of course, often plays a large part in promotions to managerial posts in both hierarchies. The tenure of one representative group of business bureaucrats was about 20 years; turnover among top executives of large corporations is typically small. But the average tenure for bureau heads in the federal service, as A. W. MacMahon and J. D. Millet have observed, is about 11 years. On the next level up the federal hierarchies, of course, the Secretaries and Under-secretaries of Departments average only from three to five years.

The upper management of U.S. business may be recruited from among (1) insiders in the administrative hierarchy; (2) insiders in the firm's financial or clique structure; (3) outsiders who have proved themselves able at managing smaller firms and are thus viewed as promising men on the management market; or (4) younger outsiders, fresh from technical or business training, who are usually taken in at lower levels with the expectation that their promotion will be unencumbered and rapid.

To the extent that the last three methods of recruitment are followed, the advancement chances of the upper middle brackets of the cadre are diminished; thus they typically desire the first alternative as a policy, in which they are joined by most personnel advisers. The upper middle brackets would further individual security and advancement in a collective way, by fair and equal chances' being guaranteed, which is to say by the strict bureaucratization of the management field.

Symptomatic of the shift from entrepreneurship to bureaucratic enterprise in business is the manner of executive compensation. In the world of the small entrepreneur, where owner and manager were one, net profit was the mode of compensation. In the white-collar worlds, the top manager is a salaried employee receiving $25,000 to $500,000 a year. With increasing bureaucratization, annuities, pensions, and retirement plans come into the picture and bonuses based on profit shares fade out.

In between the entrepreneurial and the bureaucratic mode of payment there are various intermediary forms, many of them designed to maximize incentive and to beat the federal tax. Over the last quarter of a century taxes have become big: in 1947, for instance, the $25,000-a-year-man took home about $17,000; the $50,000-a-year-man about $26,000, the $150,000-a-year-man about $45,000—this from salary, not counting returns from property. Above certain levels, money as such loses incentive value; its prestige value and the experience of success for which it is a token gain as incentives. The more one makes the more one needs, and if one did not continue to make money, one would experience failure. There is no limit to the game, and there is no way out. And its insecurities are unlimited. So heightened can they become on the upper income levels that one management consultant, after diligent research, has plainly stated that the high-paid executive, like the wage-worker and salaried employee, has security at the center of his dream-life. To the manager, according to an Elmo Roper survey, security means (1) a position with dignity; (2) a rich and prompt recognition of accomplishments; (3) a free hand to do as he wants with his job and company; and (4) plenty of leisure. These are the security contents of the Big Money, which combine, as is appropriate in the transition era of corporate business, entrepreneurial freedom with riskless bureaucratic tenure.

The recruitment of a loyal managerial staff is now a major concern of the larger businesses, which tend toward the development of 'civil service' systems for single large corporations and even for large parts of entire industries. The lag in putting such bureaucratic procedures into effect occasions much urging from more 'progressive' corporation officials.

The big management shortage, the consequent load of managerial work during the Second World War, and the boom led to many formal recruitment and training plans. Selected men are sent to courses in management at graduate schools of Business Administration. Rotation training systems for key managerial personnel are also frequently employed: by allowing managers to take up various tasks for scheduled brief periods of time, the system fits them for over-all as well as delimited spheres of management. In this way the managerial cadre rationally enlarges its opportunity for a secure chance by seeing the whole operation in detail; by definite schedules, the experience of individual members of the cadre can be guided and the grooming of men for advancement controlled. The management cadre itself is being rationalized into military-like shape; in fact, some of the very best ideas for business management have come from men of high military experience—the 'bureaucrats' about whom businessmen complained so during the war.

Yet this increased bureaucratic training, recruitment, and promotion does not extend to the very bottom or to the very top of the business hierarchies. At the top, especially, those who run corporations and governments are the least bureaucratic of personnel, for above a certain point 'political,' 'property,' and character' qualifications set in and determine who shapes policy for the entire hierarchy. It is in the middle brackets of managers that bureaucratic procedures and styles are most in evidence.

These middle managers can plan only limited spheres of work; they transmit orders from above, executing some with their staffs and passing on others to those below them for execution.

Although the middle management often contains the most technically specialized men in the enterprise, their skills have become less and less material techniques and more and more the management of people. This is true even though supervision has been both intensified and diversified, and has lost many of its tasks to newer specialists in personnel work. While engineers take over the maintenance of the plant's new machinery, the middle managers and foremen take on more 'personnel' controls over the workers, looking more often to the personnel office than to the engineering headquarters.

The existence of middle managers indicates a further separation of worker from owner or top manager. But even as their functions have been created, the middle managers have had their authority stripped from them. It is lost, from the one side, as management itself becomes rationalized and, from the other side, as lower-management men, such as foremen, take over more specialized, less authoritative roles.

The middle managers do not count for very much in the larger world beyond their individual bureaucracies. In so far as power in connection with social and economic change is concerned, the important group within the managerial strata is the top managers; in so far as numbers are concerned, the important group is the foremen, who are about half of all managers (although less than 1 per cent of the total labor force). As with any 'middle' group, what happens to the middle managers is largely dependent upon what happens to those above and below them—to top executives and to foremen. The pace and character of work in the middle management are coming increasingly to resemble those in the lower ranks of the management hierarchy.

3. The Case of the Foreman

Once the foreman, representing the bottom stratum of management, was everything to the worker, the holder of his 'life and future.' Industrial disputes often seemed disputes between disgruntled workmen and rawhiding foremen; and yet the foreman's position was aspired to by the workman. The close relations, favored by the smaller plant and town, helped make for contentment, even though the foreman held the first line of defense for management. Having a monopoly on job gratification, he often took for himself any feeling of achievement to which his gang's labor might lead; he solved problems and overcame obstacles for the men laboring below him. He was the master craftsman: he knew more about the work processes than any of the men he bossed. Before mass production, the foreman was works manager and supervisor, production planner and personnel executive, all in one.

He is still all of that in many small plants and in certain industries that have no technical staff and few office workers. But such plants may be seen historically as lags and their foremen as precursors of modern technical and supervisory personnel.

Of all occupational strata, in fact, none has been so grievously affected by the rationalization of equipment and organization as the industrial foreman. With the coming of the big industry, the foreman's functions have been diminished from above by the new technical and human agents and dictates of higher management; from below, his authority has been undermined by the growth of powerful labor unions.

Along with the host of supervisory assistants and new kinds of superiors there has been developed in many industries semi-automatic machinery that may require the service of highly trained technicians, but not master craftsmen. With such machinery, Hans Speier has observed, the foreman's sphere of technical competence diminishes and his skills become more those of the personnel agent and human whip than of the master craftsman and work guide. As engineers and college-trained technicians slowly took over, the foreman, up from the ranks, had to learn to take orders in technical matters. In many industries the man who could nurse semi-automatic machines, rather than boss gangs of workmen, became the big man in the shop.

The experience originally earned and carried by the foreman stratum is systematized, then centralized and rationally redistributed. The old functions of the foreman are no longer embodied in any one man's experience but in a team and in a rule book. Each staff innovation, of personnel specialist, safety expert, time-study engineer, diminishes the foreman's authority and weakens the respect and discipline of his subordinates. The foreman is no longer the only link between worker and higher management, although, in the eyes of both, he is still the most apparent link in the elaborate hierarchy of command and technique between front office and workshop.

Authority, Ernest Dale remarks, 'can now be exercised by many foremen only in consultation with numerous other authorities, and the resulting interrelationships are often ill-defined and disturbing.' The foremen exercise authority at the point of production but they are not its final source. Often they exercise an authority of social dominance without superior technical competence. Their sharing of authority, and thus being shorn of it, has gone far: in only 10 per cent of the companies in one sample study do foremen have the complete right to discharge; in only 14 per cent, the absolute right to make promotions within their departments; in only 10 per cent the complete right to discipline. Only 20 per cent of the companies hold foremen's meetings or practice any form of active consultation. 'The foreman,' concludes the Slichter panel of the National War Labor Board, 'is more managed than managing, more and more an executor of other men's decisions, less and less a maker of decisions himself.'

From below, the foreman has lost authority with the men, who are themselves often powerful in their union. Men who used to go to their foremen with grievances now go to their union. Foremen complain about union stewards, who frequently accomplish more for the subordinate than the foreman can. Stewards are said by foremen to be independent: 'We are unable to make the stewards do anything. . . They challenge even our limited authority.' The unions can do something about the rank-and-file's problems; in fact, the unions have in some shops got benefits for the men once enjoyed only by foremen, including increased security of the job. Originating typically in the working ranks, the foreman is no longer of them, socially or politically. He may be jealous of union picnics and parties, and he is socially isolated from higher management.

The foreman's anxiety springs from the fact that the union looks after the workmen; the employer is able to look after himself; but who will look after the foreman?

Having arisen from the ranks of labor, he often cannot expect to go higher because he is not college-trained. By 1910 it was being pointed out in management literature that if the manager, in his search for dependable subordinates, turns to a 'former subordinate or fellow worker, he finds that they are attached too much to the old regime and can't do the job well. In this dilemma, he will turn to the technically educated young man. The employer [not technically educated] sneers at and yet respects this man.' Today, only 21 per cent of the foremen under 40 years of age, and 17 per cent over 40, believe they will ever get above the foreman level. No longer belonging to labor, not 'one of the boys in the union,' the foreman is not secure in management either, not of it socially and educationally. 'The snobbery of executive management is his pet peeve and the chief cause of his complaining.' Foremen are older than the run-of-the-mill workers under them; they are more often settled and have larger families. These facts limit their mobility and perhaps to some extent their courage. Hans Speier has even asserted, on the basis of such factors, that 'political opportunism' is 'the outstanding characteristic of the foreman.'

During the late 'thirties and the war, standing thus in the middle, a traffic cop of industrial relations, with each side expect-

ing him to give its signals, the foreman became the object of
both union and management propaganda. Even though foremen
are no longer master craftsmen and work-guides as of old, they
are still seen by management as key men, not so much in their
technical roles in the work process as in their roles in the social
organization of the factory. It is in keeping with the managerial
demiurge and the changed nature of the foreman's role that he
is led into the ways of manipulation. He is to develop discipline
and loyalty among the workers by using his own personality as
the main tool of persuasion.

He must be trained as a loyal leader embodying managerially
approved opinions. 'Under present-day techniques the foreman
is chosen for his skillfulness in handling personnel—rather than
because of length-of-service or mastery of the particular operation in his charge. . . Getting along with people is 80 per cent
of the modern foreman's job.' Recruitment officers and personnel
directors are advised to consider the prospective foreman's family and social life along with his formal education and shop
ability. The prime requisite is a rounded, well-adjusted personality; foremen must 'always be the same' in their relations with
people—which means 'leaving your personal troubles at home,
and being just as approachable and amiable on a "bad day" as
on a good one.'

All manner of personal traits and behaviors are blandly suggested to foremen as indispensable. 'The essential quality of
friendliness is *sincerity*. . . They should memorize, from the personnel records, the following about all the members of their department: first name; if married, whether husband or wife works
in the plant; approximate ages and school grades of children . . .
etc.' From local newspapers 'he will learn such valuable items as:
accidents; births; deaths; children's activities; participation in
Red Cross, YMCA . . . wedding anniversaries; parties; recitals.'
'The orientation of new recruits offers a real opportunity to win
the friendship and loyalty of the new worker.' 'The manner of
speech of the foreman during even a minor conversation is perhaps more important than what he says. . . Good listening
habits are a must. . . He should fine himself 10 cents for every
fall from grace. . . He needs a pleasant, clear voice [test re-
cordings are recommended]. . . The words "definitely" and

"absolutely" are taboo. . . His own prejudices must be "parked" outside the plant.' Higher managers who cannot yet grasp the point should recognize that such human engineering is capable of reducing the 'hourly cost of 1.2 hours of direct labor cost per pound of fabricated aircraft to .7 hour per pound within an 18 month period.'

To secure the foreman's allegiance, management has showered attention upon him. In return, management has written into its rule book for foremen: 'Solidarity with his class, which is of course the middle management group, is owed to his fellows by every foreman.' 'What needs to be demonstrated is that executive and supervisory management are one. Their interests must not be divided and their only difference is that of function within management.'

Realizing management's exploitation of their developing insecurities, younger union-conscious foremen have attempted to rejoin the men, have tried to form unions. The unions that began under the Wagner Act, in the 'forties, soon found themselves caught between the antagonism of organized labor and the indifference of management. Probably not more than 100,000 foremen were directly committed to unions under the Wagner Act. During the Second World War, foreman unionization took on impetus, for foremen who had to train some 8 million green workers began to feel their mettle and to search for a means of asserting it. Yet out of an estimated one to one-and-a-half million foremen in the United States, the Foreman's Association, founded in Detroit in 1941, had at its peak only 50,000 or 5 per cent. Even these small beginnings were beset by legal confusion, and have certainly proved no solution.

4. The New Entrepreneur

Balzac called bureaucracy 'the giant power wielded by pygmies,' but actually not all the men who wield bureaucratic control are appropriately so termed. Modern observers without first-hand or sensitive experience in bureaucracies tend, first, to infer types of bureaucrats from the ideal-type definition of bureaucracy, rather than to examine the various executive adaptations to the enlarged enterprise and centralized bureau; and, second, to assume that big businesses are strictly bureaucratic in form. Such businesses are, in fact, usually mixtures, especially as regards personnel, of bureaucratic, patrimonial, and entrepreneurial forms of organization. This means, in brief, that 'politics' (as well as administration) is very much at work in selecting and forming types of managers.

There are in the modern enterprise men who fulfil the bureaucratic formula; in brief, here is how they look and act:

They follow clearly defined lines of authority, each of which is related to other lines, and all related to the understood purposes of the enterprise as a going concern. Their activities and feelings are within delimited spheres of action, set by the obligations and requirements of their own 'expertese.' Their power is neatly seated in the office they occupy and derived only from that office; all their relations within the enterprise are thus impersonal and set by the formal hierarchical structure. Their expectations are on a thoroughly calculable basis, and are enforced by the going rules and explicit sanctions; their appointment is by examination, or, at least, on the basis of trained-for competencies; and they are vocationally secure, with expected life tenure, and a regularized promotion scheme.

Such a description is, of course, a rational caricature, although useful as a guide to observation. There are, in fact, two sorts of managers whose personal adaptations most closely approximate the 'bureaucratic' type. At the top of some hierarchies, one often notices personalities who are calm and sober and unhurried, but who betray a lack of confidence. They are often glum men who display a great importance of manner, seemingly have little to do, and act with slow deliberation. They reduce the hazards of personal decision by carefully following the rules, and are heavily burdened by anxiety if decisions not covered by previous rule are forced upon them. They are carefully protected from the world-to-be-impressed by subordinates and secretaries who are working around them; they are men who have things done for them. Liking the accoutrements of authority, they are always in line with the aims of the employer or other higher ups; the ends of the organization become their private ends. For they are selected by and act for the owners or the political boss, as safe and sound men with moderate ambitions, carefully held within the feasible and calculable lines of the laid-out career. That is why they are at the top and that is the point to be made about them: they are cautiously selected to represent the formal interest of the enterprise and its organizational integrity: they serve that organization and, in doing so, they serve their own personal interests. Among all the apparatus, they sit cautiously, and after giving the appearance of weighty pondering usually say No.

Often identical with this bureaucratic type, but usually lower down the hierarchy of safety, are 'the old veterans.' They are men who say they started in the business when it was small, or in some other small business now a division of the big one. They follow instructions, feeling insecure outside the bounds of explicit orders, keeping out of the limelight and passing the buck. Usually they feel a disproportion between their abilities and their experience, and having come to feel that competition is without yield, often become pedantic in order to get a much-craved deference. Carefully attending to formalities with their co-workers and with the public, they strive for additional deference by obedience to rule. They sentimentalize the formal aspects of their office and feel that their personal security is threatened by anything that would detach them from their present setting.

But there are other types of managers who are adapted to bureaucratic life, but who are by no means bureaucrats in the accepted image. The bureaucratic ethos is not the only content of managerial personalities. In particular, bureaucracies today in America are vanguard forms of life in a culture still dominated by a more entrepreneurial ethos and ideology. Among the younger managers, two types display a blend of entrepreneurial and bureaucratic traits. One is the 'live-wire' who usually comes up from the sales or promotion side of the business, and who represents a threat to those above him in the hierarchy, especially the old veterans, although sometimes also to the glum men. It may be that in due course the live-wire will settle down; occasionally one does settle down, becomes somebody's 'bright boy,' somebody else's live-wire who is then liked

and favored by those whom he serves. If his loyalty is unques-
tionable, and he is careful not to arouse anxieties by his bright-
ness, he is on the road to the top.

Some live-wires, however, do not readily become somebody's
bright boy: they become what we may call New Entrepreneurs, a type that deserves detailed discussion.

The dominating fact of the new business setting is the business bureaucracy and the managerial supplementation, or even
replacement, of the owner-operator. But bureaucratization has
not completely replaced the spirit of competition. While the
agents of the new style of competition are not exactly old-fashioned heroes, neither are conditions old-fashioned. Initiative is
being put to an unexampled test.

In a society so recently emerged from the small-entrepreneur
epoch, still influenced by models of success congruent with that
epoch's ideology, it is not likely that the sober-bureaucratic
type can readily become dominant. Yet the structure of the
society will not permit the traditional way of amassing personal
wealth. The nineteenth-century scene of competition was one
of relatively equal powers and the competition was between
individual businessmen or firms. The twentieth-century scene
contains huge and powerful units which compete not so much
with one another but as a totality with the consuming public
and sometimes with certain segments of the government. The
new entrepreneur represents the old go-getting competition in
the new setting.

The general milieu of this new species of entrepreneur is
those areas that are still uncertain and unroutinized. The new
entrepreneur is very much at home in the less tangible of the
'business services'—commercial research and public relations,
advertising agencies, labor relations, and the mass communication and entertainment industries. His titles are likely to be
'special assistant to the president,' 'counsel for the general manager,' 'management counsellor and engineering adviser.' For
the bright, young, educated man, these fields offer limitless
opportunities, if he only has the initiative and the know-how,
and if only the anxieties of the bureaucratic chieftains hold up.

The new entrepreneur may in time routinize these fields, but, in the process of doing so, he operates in them.

The areas open to the new entrepreneur, usually overlapping in various ways, are those of great uncertainties and new beginnings: (1) adjustments between various business bureaucracies, and between business and government; (2) public relations, the interpretative justification of the new powers to the underlying outsiders; and (3) new industries that have arisen in the last quarter-century, especially those—for example, advertising —which involve selling somewhat intangible services.

The old entrepreneur succeeded by founding a new concern and expanding it. The bureaucrat gets a forward-looking job and climbs up the ladder within a pre-arranged hierarchy. The new entrepreneur makes a zig-zag pattern upward within and between established bureaucracies. In contrast to the classic small businessman, who operated in a world opening up like a row of oysters under steam, the new entrepreneur must operate in a world in which all the pearls have already been grabbed up and are carefully guarded. The only way in which he can express his initiative is by servicing the powers that be, in the hope of getting his cut. He serves them by 'fixing things,' between one big business and another, and between business as a whole and the public.

He gets ahead because (1) men in power do not expect that things can be done legitimately; (2) these men know fear and guilt; and (3) they are often personally not very bright. It is often hard to say, with any sureness, whether the new entrepreneur lives on his own wits, or upon the lack of wits in others. As for anxiety, however, it is certain that, although he may be prodded by his own, he could get nowhere without its ample presence in his powerful clients.

Like Balzac's des Lupeaulx, thrown up by the tide of political events in France in the first quarter of the nineteenth century, who had discovered that 'authority stood in need of a charwoman,' the American new entrepreneur is an 'adroit climber . . . to his professions of useful help and go-between he added a third—he gave gratuitous advice on the internal diseases of power. . . He bore the brunt of the first explosion of despair or anger; he laughed and mourned with his chief. . . It was his duty to flatter and advise, to give advice in the guise of flattery, and flattery in the form of advice.'

The talent and intelligence that go with the new entrepreneurship are often dangerous in the new society. He who has them but lacks power must act as if those in power have the same capacities. He must give credit for good ideas to his superiors and take the rap himself for bad ones. The split between the executive who judges and the intelligence that creates is sharp and finds a ready justification: 'So I write a show? Or produce one?' asks an account executive in one of the recent tales of unhappiness among the new entrepreneurs. 'And I take it down to [the] sponsor. And he asks me, in your judgment should I spend a million dollars a year on this show you've created? See, Artie? Actually, I'd have no judgment. I wouldn't be in a position to criticize. In short, I wouldn't be an executive.'

As a competitor, the new entrepreneur is an agent of the bureaucracy he serves, and what he competes for is the good will and favor of those who run the system; his chance exists because there are *several* bureaucracies, private and public, in complicated entanglements. Unlike the little white-collar man, he does not often stay within any one corporate bureaucracy; his path is within and between bureaucracies, in a kind of uneasy but calculated rhythm. He makes a well-worn path between big business and the regulatory agencies of the Federal Government, especially its military establishment and political parties.

On the higher managerial levels there is a delicate balance of power, security, and advancement resting upon a sensitive blend of loyalty to one's firm and knowledge of its intimately valuable secrets—secrets which other firms or governments would like to know. Not 'secrets' in any hush-hush sense, although there have been simple sell-outs, but secrets in the sense of what is inaccessible to those who have not operated in the context. In a bureaucratic world, the individual's experience is usually controlled; the clever executive squashes entrepreneurial tendencies by using his formal power position to monopolize contacts with important clients. It is a characteristic of the new entrepreneur that he manages to gain experience without being controlled.

There are many instances of men who learn the secrets and procedures of a regulatory agency of government to which they are not loyal in a career sense. Their loyalties are rather to the business hierarchy to which they intend to return. This is the structure of one type of twentieth-century opportunity. The curriculum of such 'businessmen in government' is familiar: they have been in and out of Washington since the NIRA days, serving on advisory boards, in commerce department committees and war production boards, retaining contact with a middle or large-scale business enterprise. In this interlinked world, there has been genuine opportunity for big success over the last fifteen years.

The openings have been on all levels. On the lower levels, a chief clerk of an OPA board may set up a business service—an OPA buffer—for firms dealing with OPA, and slowly grow into a management counselling service. At the center, however, operations have gone on in a big way during and after the war. Surplus-property disposal, for example, became so complicated that 'the government' wasn't sure just what it was doing. The surface has only been scratched, but evidence has been published of millions being made from investments of thousands; of expediters buying surplus tools from the government and selling them back again; of buying from the Navy and immediately selling to the Army, et cetera. A few smaller fry have been caught; the big fixers probably never will be, for they were only carrying on business as usual during wartime and with the government.

Perhaps the Number One figure in the short history of the new entrepreneur has been Thomas Gardner ('Tommy-the-Cork') Corcoran, who for two terms was one of President Roosevelt's 'principal advisers and . . . trouble shooters. . . He possessed that rare asset, either inside or outside of the Federal Government, of knowing the whole, intricate mechanism of the Washington establishment.' A free-ranging talent scout for the administration, he was, as John H. Crider of the *New York Times* puts it, 'personally responsible for putting literally scores of men in key positions throughout the Federal organization. . . He has more pipelines into the Government than probably any other individual on the outside. . . He always operated for the President behind the scenes, having had several titles during his government employment, including counsel . . . assistant . . . special

assistant.' Leaving the government service which paid him only
$10,000 a year, he earned as lawyer and expeditor $100,000 plus.

For the 'fixer,' who lives on the expectation that in the bureaucratic world things cannot be accomplished quickly through legitimate channels, bargaining power and sources of income consist
of intangible contacts and 'pipe-lines' rather than tangible assets.
Yet he is no less an entrepreneur in spirit and style of operation
than the man of small property; he is using his own initiative,
wile, and cunning to create something where nothing was before.
Of course, he does not have the security that property ownership
once provided; that is one thing that makes Sammy run. Yet, for
the successful, the risks are not incommensurate with the returns.

Sometimes, of course, the new entrepreneur does become a
member of the propertied rich. He can scatter his property in
various stocks in a sensible attempt to spread risks and concentrate chances of success. If he does not invest capital, his success
is all the greater measure of his inherent worth, for this means
that he is genuinely creative. Like the more heroic businessmen
of old, he manages to get something for very little or nothing.
And like them, he is a man who never misses a bet.

The power of the old captain of industry purportedly rested
upon his engineering ability and his financial sharp dealing. The
power of the ideal bureaucrat is derived from the authority
vested in the office he occupies. The power of the managerial
chieftain rests upon his control of the wealth piled up by the old
captain and is increased by a rational system of guaranteed
tributes. The power of the new entrepreneur, in the first instance
at least, rests upon his personality and upon his skill in using it
to manipulate the anxieties of the chieftain. The concentration
of power has thus modified the character and the larger meaning
of competition. The new entrepreneur's success or failure is decided not so much by the 'supply and demand' of the impersonal
market as by the personal anxieties and decisions of intimately
known chieftains of monopoly.

The careers of both the new entrepreneur and the ordinary
white-collar worker are administered by powerful others. But
there is this difference: the toadying of the white-collar employee
is small-scale and unimaginative; he is a member of the stable
corps of the bureaucracy, and initiative is regimented out of his

life. The new ulcered entrepreneur operates on the guileful edges of the several bureaucracies.

With his lavish expense account, the new entrepreneur sometimes gets into the public eye as a fixer—along with the respectable businessman whose work he does—or even as an upstart and a crook: for the same public that idolizes initiative becomes incensed when it finds a grand model of success based simply and purely upon it. For one Murray Garsson caught how many others were there? The Garssons ran a letterhead corporation title into a profit of 78 million dollars out of war contracts, and the same public that honors pluck and success and the Horatio Alger story became angry. In an expanding system, profits seem to coincide with the welfare of all; in a system already closed, profits are made by doing somebody in. The line between the legitimate and the illegitimate is difficult to draw because no one has set up the rules for the new situation. Moreover, such moral questions are decisively influenced by the size of the business and the firmness and reliability of contacts.

Part of the new entrepreneur's frenzy perhaps is due to apprehension that his function may disappear. Many of the jobs he has been doing for the chieftains are now a standardized part of business enterprise, no longer requiring the entrepreneurial flair, and can be handled by cheaper and more dependable white-collar men. Increasingly, big firms hire their own talent for those fields in which the new entrepreneurs pioneered. In so far as this is so, the new entrepreneurs become bright boys and, as salaried employees, are stable members of the managerial cadre.

In the more strictly bureaucratic setting, the value of contacts a given manager has and the secrets he learns are definitely lessened. Rationalization of the managerial hierarchy decreases the chance for any one man down the line to get a view of the whole. It is the Tommy Corcoran *without* a definite bureaucratic role who learns the whole, and serves his chief—and in due course himself—by telling selected others about it. In the General Somervell type of managership, the executive's control section monopolizes the chance to see things whole, and tells what it will once each month to all executives.

Rationalization prohibits a total view: by rationalizing the organization via rotation systems and control sections, top bureaucrats can guide the vision of underlings. The 'entrepreneurial type' who does not play ball can be excluded from inside information. Like the commodity market before it, the top level of the personality market may well become an object to be administered, rather than a play of free forces of crafty wile and unexampled initiative.

5. The Power of the Managers

There is no doubt that managers of big business have replaced captains of industry as the ostensibly central figures in modern capitalism. They are the economic elite of the new society; they are the men who have the most of whatever there is to have; the men in charge of things and of other men, who make the large-scale plans. They are the high bosses, the big money, the great say-so. But, in fact, the 'top' of modern business is complicated: alongside top corporation executives are scattered throngs of owners and, below them, the upper hierarchies of managerial employees.

As modern businesses have become larger, the ownership of any given enterprise has expanded and the power of 'the owners' in direct operation has declined.* The power of property within plant, firm, and political economy has often become indirect, and works through a host of new agents. The owners of property do not themselves give commands to their workmen: there are too many workmen and not enough concentrated owners. Moreover, even if personal command were technically possible, it is more convenient to hire others for this purpose. Adam Smith, writing even before the 'proprietor's liability' was limited, asserted: 'The greater part of the proprietors seldom pretend to understand anything of the business of the company . . . give themselves no trouble about it, but received contentedly each

* *Owners* are people who legally claim a share of profits and expect that those who operate the enterprise will act for their best interests. *Managers* are people who have operating control over the enterprise, the ones who run it.

half-yearly or yearly dividend as the directors think proper to make them.'

The facts of the split of manager and owner, and the indirect power of the owner, have long been known. Such facts, however, since at least the beginning of this century, have been widely and erroneously taken to mean that 'a managerial revolution' has been and is under way and that big management, replacing big property, is slated to be the next ruling class.

While owner and manager are no longer the same person, the manager has not expropriated the owner, nor has the power of the propertied enterprise over workers and markets declined. Power has not been split from property; rather the power of property is more concentrated than is its ownership. If this seems undemocratic, the lack of democracy is within the propertied classes. If the Van Sweringen brothers controlled 8 railroads worth $2 billion with only $20 million, still there was the $20 million, and the power they exercised was power made possible by the $2 billion.

The powers of property ownership are depersonalized, intermediate, and concealed. But they have not been minimized nor have they declined. Much less has any revolution occurred, managerial or otherwise, involving the legitimations of the institution of private property. Under the owners of property a huge and complex bureaucracy of business and industry has come into existence. But the right to this chain of command, the legitimate access to the position of authority from which these bureaucracies are directed, is the right of property ownership. The stockholder is neither willing nor able to exercise operating control of his ownership. That is true. And the power of the managers is not dependent upon their own personal ownership. That is also true. But it cannot be concluded that there is no functional relation between ownership and control of large corporations. Such an inference focuses upon personnel issues instead of legitimations and institutions.

Property as a going concern means that the owner may, if necessary, employ violent coercion against those who do not own but would use. With legal ownership, one may borrow the police force to oust and to punish anyone, including former owners and all their managers as well as non-owners, who tries to seize control of property. Even if it were true that the power of 'the owners' had been expropriated by the managers, this would not mean that their property has been expropriated. Any owner who can prove any case of 'expropriation' of property by any manager can have the managers prosecuted and put in jail.

Such changes in the distribution of power as have occurred between owners and their managers have certainly neither destroyed the propertied class nor diminished its power. All the structural changes upon which the notion of 'a managerial revolution' presumably rests are more accurately understood (1) as a modification of the distribution of operating power within the propertied class as a whole; and (2) as a general bureaucratization of property relations.

Changes have occurred within the industrial propertied class in such a way that the actual wielding of power is delegated to hierarchies; the entrepreneurial function has been bureaucratized. But the top man in the bureaucracy *is* a powerful member of the propertied class. He derives his right to act from the institution of property; he does act in so far as he possibly can in a manner he believes is to the interests of the private-property system; he does feel in unity, politically and status-wise as well as economically, with his class and its source of wealth.

Observers who are shocked by recognition of the fact that the immediate power which property gives may be delegated or, under certain circumstances, usurped by higher employees and cliques of minority owners, often overlook the source of power and the meaning of property, while looking at the huge and intricate form of bureaucratic big business. The division between 'ownership' and 'control' of property does not diminish the power of property: on the contrary, it may even increase it. It does, however, change the personnel, the apparatus, and the property status of the more immediate wielders of that power.

If the powerful officials of U.S. corporations do not act as old-fashioned owners within the plants and do not derive their power from personal ownership, their power is nevertheless contingent upon their control of property. They are managers *of* private properties, and if private property were 'abolished,' their power, if any, would rest upon some other basis, and they would have to look to other sources of authority. Many of these same men might continue as managers of factories and mines, but that is a new political question.

To say that managers are managers of private property means, first, that the principles they attempt to follow are not the budgetary considerations of those who manage public property, but rather that they use their power in the interest of maximizing profits. Secondly, it means that property institutions determine whom the managers are responsible to; 'they are responsible to the effective clique of owners,' conclude TNEC economists, and to the 'large property class in general.' Managers have not been known to act intentionally against the property interests of the large owners. Their actions are in the interests of property as they see them. This is the case whether they act in relation to the workman in the plant, toward competing firms, toward the government, or toward the consumers of their company's product. Of course many men who own stocks and bonds and other promises do now own enough productive facilities to make a difference in the distribution of power. But this only means that the managers are agents of big property owners and not of small ones. Managers of corporations are the agents of those owners who own the concentrated most; they derive such power as they have from the organizations which are based upon property as a going system.

'The Managers' are often thought of as scientific technologists or administrative experts having some autonomous aim. But they are not experts in charge of technology; they are executors of property. Their chief attention is to finance and profits, which are the major interests of owners. The managers who are supposed to have usurped the owners' function actually fulfil it with as much or more devotion as any owner could. The personal relations between big owners and their big managers are of course not necessarily 'authoritative,' except in so far as the owners and their boards of directors are interested in the profitable balance sheet, and accordingly judge their managers as, in fact, the managers judge themselves. External authority is not necessary when the agent has internalized it.

That the activities of the manager of industry and finance are in line with property interests, rather than with 'independent' aims, is revealed by the motives for the merging and building up of huge businesses. By the end of the nineteenth century, industrial consolidation in the United States had in many lines gone far enough to realize the major technical advantages of large-scale production. The pre-World War I trust movement was not primarily motivated by a desire for technical efficiency, but by 'financial and strategic advantages.' Creating size in business has often permitted the manipulation of funds and power by business insiders and financial outsiders for their own enrichment—and, of course, the suppression of competition and the gaining of promotional and underwriting profits. The kind of combinations of functions in industry which increases productivity occurs primarily within a physical plant, rather than between various plants.

The question is whether or not the managers fulfil the entrepreneurial function in such a way as to modify the way in which the owners would fulfil it. But how could they do so, when the institution of private property, the power of property, and the function of the entrepreneur remain? The manager, as Edwin Nourse observes, is still rated 'on evidence of the profitableness of the company's operations while under his management. . .' It is true that managers do not personally own the property they manage. But we may not jump from this fact to the assertion that they are not personally of the propertied class. On the contrary, compared to the population at large, they definitely form a segment of the small, much-propertied circle. At least two-thirds of the $75,000 a year and up incomes of corporation managers are derived from property holdings. Top-level managers (presumably the most 'powerful') are socially and politically in tune with other large property holders. Their image of ascent involves moving further into the big propertied circles. The old road to property was starting a firm and building it up, rising in class position with its expansion; that road is now closed to nearly all. The way into propertied circles, via management posts and/or suitable marriages, is more likely to be *within* the large propertied bureaucracies.

Intercorporate investments and multiple directorships among 'managers' give further unity to the propertied classes as a stratum. The handful of officers and directors of the A, T & T who hold 171 directorships or offices in other enterprises are not simply holding 'honorary degrees'; where the corporations whose directors interlock also have interlocking business, these men pay attention; in such ways a community of property interest, a resolution of sharp competitive conflicts, can arise. Consolidations have given further 'unity to the ownership, but not to the productive processes of subsidiary plants.' The aim has been further monopoly of national markets and the profitable consolidation of property.

The image of the big businessman as master-builder and profit-maker, as already noted of the old captain of industry, no longer holds. The top manager's relation to productive work and engineering is a financial one. His relations with the industrial manager, in terms of power, are not unlike those of the politician with the government official, or the elected labor leader with his appointed staff expert. The corporation official has the final say-so; for in the bureaucratization of the powers of property, he represents the big money and in his relations with major owners is treated as a status equal, belonging to their clubs, and acting in their behalf.

In the political sphere, no American manager has taken a stand that is against the interests of private property as an institution. As its chief defender, rhetorically and practically, the manager has a political mind similar to that of any large owner, from whom he derives his power; and in his present form he will last no longer than property as an institution. Thus, although the bureaucratization of property involves a distribution of power among large subordinate staffs, the executives of the modern corporation in America form an utterly reliable committee for managing the affairs and pushing for the common interests of the entire big-property class.

So far as men may do as they will with the property that they own or that they manage for owners, they have power over other men. Changes in the size and the distribution of property have brought with them an increased power for some and a corresponding powerlessness for many. The shift is from widespread entrepreneurial property to narrowed class property. The ownership of property now means much more than power over the

things that are owned; it means power over men who do not own
these things; it selects those who may command and those who
must obey.

6. Three Trends

The managerial demiurge has come to contain three trends
which increasingly give it meaning and shape. As it spreads (i),
its higher functions, as well as those lower in the hierarchy, are
rationalized; as this occurs (ii), the enterprise and the bureau
become fetishes, and (iii), the forms of power that are wielded,
all up and down the line, shift from explicit authority to manipulation.

i. The rationalization of the corporate structure, even at the
top, may not be lodged in the head of a single living man, but
buried in an accounting system served by dozens of managers,
clerks, and specialists, no one of whom knows what it is all about
or what it may mean. The man who started the enterprise, if
there ever was such a man, may long be gone. Franz Kafka has
written of '. . . a peculiar characteristic of our administrative
apparatus. Along with its precision it's extremely sensitive as
well . . . suddenly in a flash the decision comes in some unfore-
seen place, that moreover, can't be found any longer later on, a
decision that settles the matter, if in most cases justly, yet all the
same, arbitrarily. It's as if the administrative apparatus were unable any longer to bear the tension, the year-long irritation
caused by the same affair—probably trivial in itself—and had hit
upon the decision by itself, without the assistance of the officials.
Of course, a miracle didn't happen and certainly it was some
clerk who hit upon the solution or the unwritten decision, but in
any case it couldn't be discovered by us at least, by us here, or
even by the Head Bureau, which clerk had decided in this case
and on what grounds . . . we will never learn it; besides by this
time it would scarcely interest anybody.'

It seems increasingly that all managers are 'middle' managers,
who are not organized in such a manner as to allow them to assume collective responsibility. They form, as Edmund Wilson

has observed of 'capitalistic society in America,' 'a vast system for passing the buck.'

In trade, the department manager, floorman, and salesperson replace the merchant; in industry, the plant engineers and staffs of foremen replace the manufacturing proprietor; and in practically all brackets of the economy, middle managers become the routinized general staff without final responsibility and decision. Social and technical divisions of labor among executives cut the nerve of independent initiative. As decisions are split and shared and as the whole function of management expands, the filing case and its attendants come between the decision maker and his means of execution.

An 'inventory control' is set up for the management cadre and, as the U.S. Naval Institute has it, there is a 'detailed man-by-man analysis of all the people in a company who hold supervisory jobs'; classifying each man as 'promotable, satisfactory, unsatisfactory' on the basis of interviews 'with him, his superior, and his subordinates and perhaps some scientific testing'; working out a concrete time-schedule 'for each promotable man' and another 'for getting rid of the deadwood.' Since top managers cannot serve the market properly and at the same time manage their 'giant bureaucracy,' they rationalize the top, divide themselves into Boards, Commissions, Authorities, Committees, Departments; the organization expert thus becomes a key person in the managerial cadre, as it shifts from the open occupational market to managed selection and control. This administrative official, a sort of manager of managers, as well as of other personnel, is in turn rationalized and acquires a staff of industrial psychologists and researchers into human relations, whose domain includes personal traits and mannerisms, as well as technical skills. These officials and technicians embody the true meaning of the 'personal equation' in the mass life of modern organization: the rationalization of all its higher functions.

II. In the managerial demiurge, the capitalist spirit itself has been bureaucratized and the enterprise fetishized. 'There is,' Henry Ford said, 'something sacred about a big business.' 'The object of the businessman's work,' Walter Rathenau wrote in 1908, 'of his worries, his pride and his aspirations is just his enterprise . . . the enterprise seems to take on form and substance, and to be ever with him, having, as it were, by virtue of his bookkeeping, his organization, and his branches, an independent economic existence. The businessman is wholly devoted to making his business a flourishing, healthy, living organism.' This is the inner, fetish-like meaning of his activity.

The giant enterprise, Werner Sombart has shown, impersonally takes unto itself those sober virtues that in earlier phases of capitalism were personally cultivated by the entrepreneur. Thrift, frugality, honesty have ceased to be necessary to the managerial entrepreneur. Once these virtues were in the sphere wherein personal will-power was exercised; now they have become part of the mechanism of business; they 'have been transferred to the business concern.' They were 'characteristics of human beings'; now they are 'objective principles of business methods.' When 'the industrious tradesman went through his day's work in conscious self-mastery' it was necessary 'to implant a solid foundation of duties' in the consciousness of men. But now 'the businessman works at high pressure because the stress of economic activities carries him along in spite of himself.' When the private and business 'housekeeping' of the entrepreneur were identical, frugality was needed, but now the housekeeping is rigidly separated, and the frugal enterprise makes possible the lavish corporate manager, if he wants to be lavish. And so, 'the conduct of the entrepreneur as a man may differ widely from his conduct as a tradesman.' The name of the firm is all that matters, and this name does not rest upon the personal quality of the entrepreneurial flair of its head; it rests upon business routine and the careful administration of appropriate publicity.

No matter what the motives of individual owners and managers, clerks, and workers, may be, the Enterprise itself comes in time to seem autonomous, with a motive of its own: to manipulate the world in order to make a profit. But this motive is embodied in the rationalized enterprise, which is out for the secure and steady return rather than the deal with chance.

Just as the working man no longer owns the machine but is controlled by it, so the middle-class man no longer owns the enterprise but is controlled by it. The vices as well as the virtues of the old entrepreneur have been 'transferred to the business concern.' The aggressive business types, seen by Herman Melville as greedy, crooked creatures on the edges of an expanding nineteenth-century society are replaced in twentieth-century society by white-collar managers and clerks who may be neither greedy nor aggressive as persons, but who man the machines that often operate in a 'greedy and aggressive' manner. The men are cogs in a business machinery that has routinized greed and made aggression an impersonal principle of organization.

The bureaucratic enterprise itself sets the pace of decision and obedience for the business and governmental officialdom and the world of clerks and bookkeepers, even as the motions of the worker are geared to the jump of the machine and the command of the foreman. Since the aims of each of its activities must be related to master purposes within it, the purposes of the enterprise in time become men's motives, and vice versa. The manner of their action, held within rules, is the manner of the enterprise. Since their authority inheres not in their persons, but in its offices, their authority belongs to the enterprise. Their status, and hence their relations to others in the hierarchy, inhere in the titles on their doors: the enterprise with its Board of Directors is the source of all honor and authority. Their safety from those above and their authority over those below derive from its rules and regulations. In due course, their very self-images, what they do and what they are, are derived from the enterprise. They know some of its secrets, although not all of them, and their career proceeds according to its rule and within its graded channels. Only within those rules are they supposed, impersonally, to compete with others.

III. Coercion, the ultimate type of power, involves the use of physical force by the power-holder; those who cannot be otherwise influenced are handled physically or in some way used against their will. Authority involves the more or less voluntary obedience of the less powerful; the problem of authority is to find out who obeys whom, when, and for what reasons. Manipulation is a secret or impersonal exercise of power; the one who is influenced is not explicitly told what to do but is nevertheless subject to the will of another.

In modern society, coercion, monopolized by the democratic state, is rarely needed in any continuous way. But those who hold power have often come to exercise it in hidden ways: they have moved and they are moving from authority to manipulation. Not only the great bureaucratic structures of modern society, themselves means of manipulation as well as authority, but also the means of mass communication are involved in the shift. The managerial demiurge extends to opinion and emotion and even to the mood and atmosphere of given acts.

Under the system of explicit authority, in the round, solid nineteenth century, the victim knew he was being victimized, the misery and discontent of the powerless were explicit. In the amorphous twentieth-century world, where manipulation replaces authority, the victim does not recognize his status. The formal aim, implemented by the latest psychological equipment, is to have men internalize what the managerial cadres would have them do, without their knowing their own motives, but nevertheless having them. Many whips are inside men, who do not know how they got there, or indeed that they are there. In the movement from authority to manipulation, power shifts from the visible to the invisible, from the known to the anonymous. And with rising material standards, exploitation becomes less material and more psychological.

No longer can the problem of power be set forth as the simple one of changing the processes of coercion into those of consent. The engineering of consent to authority has moved into the realm of manipulation where the powerful are anonymous. Impersonal manipulation is more insidious than coercion precisely because it is hidden; one cannot locate the enemy and declare war upon him. Targets for aggression are unavailable, and certainty is taken from men.

In a world dominated by a vast system of abstractions, managers may become cold with principle and do what local and immediate masters of men could never do. Their social insulation results in deadened feelings in the face of the impoverishment of life in the lower orders and its stultification in the upper circles. We do not mean merely that there are managers of bureaucracies and of communication agencies who scheme (although, in fact, there are, and their explicit ideology is one of manipulation); but more, we mean that the social control of the system is such that irresponsibility is organized into it.

Organized irresponsibility, in this impersonal sense, is a leading characteristic of modern industrial societies everywhere. On every hand the individual is confronted with seemingly remote organizations; he feels dwarfed and helpless before the managerial cadres and their manipulated and manipulative minions.

That the power of property has been bureaucratized in the corporation does not diminish that power; indeed, bureaucracy increases the use and the protection of property power. The state purportedly contains a balance of power, but one must examine the recruitment of its leading personnel, and above all the actual effects of its policies on various classes, in order to understand the source of the power it wields.

Bureaucracies not only rest upon classes, they organize the power struggle of classes. Within the business firm, personnel administration regulates the terms of employment, just as would the labor union, should a union exist: these bureaucracies fight over who works at what and for how much. Their fight is increasingly picked up by governmental bureaus. More generally, government manages whole class levels by taxation, price, and wage control, administrating who gets what, when, and how. Rather than the traditional inheritance of son from father, or the free liberal choice of occupation on an open market, educational institutions and vocational guidance experts would train and fit individuals of various abilities and class levels into the levels of the pre-existing hierarchies. Within the firm, again, and as part of the bureaucratic management of mass democracy, the graded hierarchy fragments class situations, just as minute gradations replace more homogeneous masses at the base of the pyramids. The traditional and often patriarchal ties of the old enterprise are replaced by rational and planned linkages in the new, and the rational systems hide their power so that no one sees their sources of authority or understands their calculations. For the bureaucracy, Marx wrote in 1842, the world is an object to be manipulated.

6

Old Professions and New Skills

THE professional strata are the seat of such intellectual powers as are used for income in the United States. In and around these occupations, which require specialized, systematic, and often lengthy training, the highest skills of the arts and sciences are socially organized and applied. They most clearly exemplify the rationalist ethos that has been held to be the characteristic mark and the essential glory of western civilization itself. So any changes in their social basis and composition would, in one way or another, be reflected in western society's level of technique, art, and intellectual sensibility.

In no sphere of twentieth-century society has the shift from the old to the new middle-class condition been so apparent, and its ramification so wide and deep, as in the professions. Most professionals are now salaried employees; much professional work has become divided and standardized and fitted into the new hierarchical organizations of educated skill and service; intensive and narrow specialization has replaced self-cultivation and wide knowledge; assistants and sub-professionals perform routine, although often intricate, tasks, while successful professional men become more and more the managerial type. So decisive have such shifts been, in some areas, that it is as if rationality itself had been expropriated from the individual and been located, as a new form of brain power, in the ingenious bureaucracy itself.

Yet, the old professional middle class strongly persists. While many salaried professionals exemplify most sharply the bureaucratic manner of existence, many other professionals who remain free, especially in medicine and law, have in a curious way become a new seat of private-enterprise practice.

These two coexisting themes—of bureaucracy and of commercialization—guide our understanding of the U.S. professional world today.

1. The Professions and Bureaucracy

Most of the old professionals have long been free practitioners; most of the new ones have from their beginnings been salaried employees. But the old professions, such as medicine and law, have also been invaded by the managerial demiurge and surrounded by sub-professionals and assistants. The old practitioner's office is thus supplanted by the medical clinic and the law factory, while newer professions and skills, such as engineering and advertising, are directly involved in the new social organizations of salaried brain power.

Free professionals of the old middle class have not been so much replaced in the new society as surrounded and supplemented by the new groups. In fact, over the last two generations, free practitioners have remained a relatively constant proportion (about 1 per cent) of the labor force as a whole, and about 2 per cent of the middle class as a whole. In the meantime, however, salaried professionals have expanded from 1 to 6 per cent of all the people at work, and from about 4 to 14 per cent of the middle class. The expansion of the professional strata has definitely been an expansion of its new middle-class wing. Even in the old middle-class world of 1870, salaried professionals (mainly nurses and schoolteachers) made up a dominant section of the professional strata; only 35 per cent were free professionals. By 1940, however, only 16 per cent were.

The proliferation of new professional skills has been a result of the technological revolution and the involvement of science in wider areas of economic life; it has been a result of the demand for specialists to handle the complicated institutional machinery developed to cope with the complication of the technical environment. The new professional skills that have grown up thus center on the one hand around the machineries of business ad-

ministration and the mass media of communication, manipulation, and entertainment; and on the other hand, around the industrial process, the engineering firm, and the scientific laboratory. On both the technical and the human side, the rise of TV,
the motion picture, radio, mass-circulation magazine, and of
research organizations that marshal facts about every nook and
cranny of the social and technical organism has caused the rise
of many new professions and many more sub-professions.

The old professional middle class never needed to possess property, but whether its members owned their means of livelihood
or not, their working unit has been small and personally man-
ageable, and their working lives have involved a high degree of
independence in day-to-day decisions. They themselves set their
fees or other remuneration, regulate their own hours and conditions of work according to market conditions and personal incli-
nations.

As the old professions and the new skills have become involved in new middle-class conditions, professional men and
women have become dependent upon the new technical machinery and upon the great institutions within whose routines the
machines are located. They work in some department, under
some kind of manager; while their salaries are often high, they
are salaries, and the conditions of their work are laid down by
rule. What they work on is determined by others, even as they
determine how a host of sub-professional assistants will work.
Thus they themselves become part of the managerial demiurge.

As professional people of both old and new middle classes become attached to institutions, they acquire staffs of assistants,
who, in contrast to the old professional apprentices, are not
necessarily or even usually in training to become autonomous
professionals themselves. Thus physicians hand over some of their
work to trained nurses, laboratory technicians, physical thera-
pists. Ministers lose, sometimes willingly and sometimes not, several of their old functions to social workers and psychiatric welfare workers and teachers. Law partners give their less challeng-
ing tasks to clerks and salaried associates. Individual scholars
in the universities become directors of research, with staffs doing
specialized functions, while the remaining individual scholar
takes over some of the awe and receptiveness toward the expert

who manages his specialized and narrow domain. Alongside the graduate student apprentice there is now the research technician, who may have no thought of becoming an individual scholar; take her away from the machine and the organization and she ceases to work. Between the individual composer of music and his audience there is the big symphony orchestra, the radio-chain, the proprietors of the art world who manage the increasingly expensive means of execution and display. In practically every profession, the managerial demiurge works to build ingenious bureaucracies of intellectual skills.

Bureaucratic institutions invade all professions and many professionals now operate as part of the managerial demiurge. But this does not mean that professionals are no longer entrepreneurs. In fact, many among the new skill groups resemble new entrepreneurs more than bureaucratic managers, and many who work in the old free professions are still free practitioners. The bureaucratic manner has not replaced the entrepreneurial; rather the professional strata today represent various combinations of the two: at the bottom extreme, the staffs of lesser-skilled, newer members of the strata begin and remain bureaucratized; at the top, the free and the salaried professionals make their own curious adaptation to the new conditions prevailing in their work.

2. The Medical World

The white-collar world of medicine is still presided over by the physician as entrepreneur, and, as L. W. Jones has observed, 'his ideology remains dominant.' Yet the self-sufficiency of the entrepreneurial physician has been undermined in all but its economic and ideological aspects by his dependence, on the one hand, upon technical equipment that is formally centralized, and, on the other, upon informal organizations that secure and maintain his practice.

Medical technology has of necessity been centralized in hospital and clinic; the private practitioner must depend upon expensive equipment as well as upon specialists and technicians for diagnosis and treatment. He must also depend upon relations with other doctors, variously located in the medical hierarchy, to get started in practice and to keep up his clientele. For as medicine has become technically specialized, some way of getting those who are ill in contact with those who can help them is needed. In the absence of a formal means of referral, informal cliques of doctors, in and out of hospitals, have come to perform this function.

Tendencies toward bureaucratization in the world of medicine have expressed themselves in expansive and devious ways, but there is already something to be said for the idea that today the old general practitioner is either an old-fashioned family doctor in a small city, or a young doctor who has not yet got the money, skill, or connections for specializing successfully. The glorification of the old country doctor in the mass media suggests a nostalgic mood. This type, as well as all types of individual general practitioner, has been left behind by the progress of scientific medicine, in which the specialist also remains an entrepreneur in an institutional context he hasn't learned to accept and which he exploits economically.

The centralization in medicine does not concern individual partnerships or 'group practice' among physicians, but rather hospitals, to which there is a definite shift as the center of medical practice. Physicians and surgeons, who now comprise only one-fifth of medical and health workers, have come to represent a new sort of entrepreneur. For they are attached, as privileged entrepreneurs, to the otherwise bureaucratic hospital. Below the physician the shift to salaried positions of lesser skill is very marked; the sub-professions in medicine are attached to the institution.

The hospital, as Bernhard Stern and others have made clear, is now 'the strategic factor' in medical care and education; scientific and technological developments are making it more so. Here the specialists have access to the funded equipment for diagnosis and experiment and to contacts with other specialists, so important for scientific advancement and learning. Economically, the coming of the hospital into a focal position has 'increased the medical bill of the population and put adequate medical care, as now organized, beyond the reach of the low income groups.'

The old general practitioner, whom scientific advances and team-work in hospital and clinic have made technologically obsolete, fights the hospital as any old middle-class entrepreneur fights large-scale technical superiority. The new specialist, if he is 'in,' exploits his position economically, or, if he is 'out,' often has a trained incapacity to practice general medicine.

In the medical world as a whole an increased proportion of physicians are specialists who enjoy greater prestige and income than the general practitioner and are necessarily relied upon by him. These specialists are concentrated in the cities and tend to work among the wealthy classes, making about twice as much money as general practitioners. They form, in most cities, what Oswald Hall has aptly called 'the inner fraternity' of the medical profession and, as Professor Hall has indicated, they control appointments to medical institutions, discipline intruders, distribute patients among themselves and other doctors—in short, seek to control competition and the medical career at each of its stages. They form a tightly organized in-group, with a technical division of labor and a firmly instituted way of organizing the sick market. As young doctors see the way the pyramid is shaped, they tend to bypass the experience of the old general practitioner altogether.

But specialized or not, the proportion of physicians has narrowed, while that of all other medical personnel has expanded; and all medical personnel other than doctors tend to become salaried employees of one sort or another, whereas most physicians are still independent practitioners. The proportionately narrowed stratum of physicians has, in fact, been made possible precisely by the enormous increase of specialized and general assistants. In 1900 there were 11 physicians to every 1 graduate nurse; in 1940 there were 2 graduate nurses for every physician. Above the general practitioner is the specialist, informally organized with reference to the inner fraternity; below him are the increasing number of assistants and sub-professionals, at the first call of the inner fraternity and usually attached to the hospital.

The nurse is most curiously involved in this complicated institution. Most 'training schools' are owned and operated by hospitals; 'in return for classroom education, apprenticeship training in hospital, room, board, laundry, and free medical attention, the student nurse is expected to give her services willingly to the hospital; in many of these hospital schools, it has been asserted, most recently by Eli Ginzberg, director of the New York State Hospital Study, the primary purpose is not so much 'education' as simply a means of getting cheap labor, for they find it less expensive to train students than to hire graduate nurses.

The persistence of its independent practitioners is one of the most decisive facts about the medical world today. Of all professions, those of physicians, surgeons, osteopaths, and dentists contain the highest proportion of independent practitioners: from 80 to 90 per cent. They are still a scatter of individual practices, but they are clustered around the large-scale institutional developments. Only 46 per cent of the pharmacists and only 8 per cent of the nurses—the largest single group in medicine—are free practitioners, and the many fledgling sub-professionals and technicians of medicine are without notable exception in salaried positions. The sub-professions and assistants are concentrated in institutional centers, which the physicians use—as individual practitioners.

A hospital is a bureaucracy with many traditional hangovers from its less bureaucratic past; it is a bureaucracy that trains many of its own staff and, while it may set some free again, they still depend upon it. As hospitals replace the doctor's office as the center of the medical world, the young doctor himself is no longer apprenticed to another physician, as was the case up to the 1840's, but becomes an intern, an apprentice to the institution of the hospital. Later, as a private practitioner, if he is fortunate, he uses its facilities for his patients. Moreover, throughout his career, his appointments to hospital posts are crucial to his medical practice. 'The more important hospital posts,' Oswald Hall has concluded, 'are associated with the highly specialized practices and usually with the most lucrative types. The two form an interrelated system.' This system narrows the general practitioner's market and implies (correctly) that he is incompetent to handle many types of illness.

The large-scale medical institution, with its specialization and salaried staff, is controlled by an inner corps of physicians cooperating with one another as entrepreneurs. In this situation, a selection of those with managerial abilities, who are in with the clique, undoubtedly goes on. Who becomes the hospital head, the clinic chieftain, the head of a medical office of a great industry? The medical bureaucrat and the scientific laboratory-oriented specialist, and above all, the man with entrepreneurial talent working through medical bureaucracies, now surround the old general practitioner who once was all these things on a small scale. But what seems important about the specialization of medicine is that it has *not* occurred in a strictly bureaucratic way; these trends, as well as others, have all been limited and even shaped by commercial motives.

The relative lack of expansion of the medical profession, despite two world wars with their enormous medical demands and a general increase in medical needs, is one of the most remarkable facts of U.S. occupational structure. In 1900 there was 1 licensed physician for every 578 persons in the United States; in 1940 there was 1 for every 750 persons. Moreover, not all licensed physicians were practicing; in 1940 there was 1 active physician to every 935 persons. This closing up of the medical ranks has been made possible by (1) the expansion of medical assistants and sub-professions in medical organizations, to which the entrepreneurial physician has had access; (2) the increased difficulty of ascent possible through expensive educational processes; (3) the deliberate policies of the American Medical Association and the heads of some of the leading medical schools.

The AMA, the trade association of the physician as a small businessman, represents him—to federal and state governments, medical schools and hospital boards, as well as to the lay public. It has great weight within the leading medical schools. Physicians may differ about the public problems of medicine and health, many individuals among them may even be confused, but the point of view of the AMA is that of the NAM applied to medicine in a complicated and needful world. It cries aloud against the 'evils of regimentation' and national health bills. While the fact, agreed to by the majority of scholars in the field, is that 'where the need is greatest, there satisfaction is least,' the principle expounded by the AMA is liberty for all physicians, which, profession or no profession, means exactly what it means for all old middle-class elements. The profession as a whole is politically uninterested or ignorant; its members are easy victims and ready exponents ot the U.S. businessman's psychology of individualism, in which liberty means no state interference, except a rigid state licensing system.

The professional ethics in which this interest group clothes its business drive is an obsolete mythology, but it has been of great use to those who would adapt themselves to predatory ways, attempting to close the ranks and to freeze the inequality of status among physicians and the inequality of medical care among the population at large. Even in the middle of the Second World War, the dean of a leading medical school held 'the supply of doctors adequate' and bewailed the 'alarm over the alleged shortage . . .' of doctors.

Other occupations in medicine have followed the AMA lead. The entrepreneurial policy of business unionism in medicine has been implemented by the fact that medical education has become increasingly expensive at a time when upward mobility has been generally tightening up. It has been correctly charged that there are quotas for minorities in medical schools; in addition to skin color, religion, and national origin, the quota system rests on the class and professional status of the would-be doctor's parents.

Once through the medical school, the young doctors face the hospital, which they find also contains departments, hierarchies, and grades. One hospital administrator in an eastern city told Oswald Hall how interns are selected: 'The main qualification as far as I can see is "personality." Now that is an intangible sort of thing. It means partly the ability to mix well, to be humble to older doctors in the correct degree, and to be able to assume the proper degree of superiority toward the patient. Since all medical schools now are Grade A there is no point in holding competitive examinations. . . Another reason for not holding competitive examinations for internships is that there are a lot of Jews in medicine. Did you know that?' Another hospital administrator said: 'There are good specialists among the older doctors who cannot pass examinations but they deserve to be protected in their positions in the hospitals.' After discussing various changes that have lengthened the period of training and prohibited the poor from working their way into medicine, this physician spoke of the ethics of his profession: 'It means that the specialists are selected from the old established families in the community, and family and community bonds are pretty important in making a person abide by a code.'

The inner core that abides by this code not only controls the key posts in the hospital, but virtually the practice of medicine in a city, much more effectively it often seems than boilermakers or auto-workers control the work and pay in their fields. It is with reference to these highly co-operative enterprisers that the individual practitioner must find his medical role and practice it. He cannot now successfully do so as a free-lance man in an old middle-class world, in which the talented, openly competitive, come to the top.

3. Lawyers

Both Tocqueville, near the beginning of the nineteenth century, and Bryce, near the end, thought the American lawyers' prestige was very high; in fact, they believed lawyers, as Willard Hurst puts it, to be a sort of ersatz aristocracy. Yet there has always been an ambiguity about the popular image of lawyers—they are honorable but they are also sharp. A code of professional ethics, it should be recalled, was not adopted by the American Bar Association until 1908, and even then did not really deal with the Bar's social responsibility.

Before the ascendancy of the large corporation, skill and eloquence in advocacy selected nineteenth-century leaders of the bar; reputations and wealth were created and maintained in the courts, of which the lawyer was an officer. He was an agent of the law, handling the general interests of society, as fixed and allowed in the law; his day's tasks were as varied as human activity and experience itself. An opinion leader, a man whose recommendations to the community counted, who handled obligations and rights of intimate family and life problems, the liberty and property of all who had them, the lawyer personally pointed out the course of the law and counseled his client against the pitfalls of illegality. Deferred to by his client, he carefully displayed the dignity he claimed to embody. Rewarded for apparent honesty, carrying an ethical halo, held to be fit material for high statesmanship, the lawyer upheld public service and was professionally above business motives.

But the skills and character of a profession shift, externally, as the function of the profession changes with the nature of its clients' interests, and internally, as the rewards of the profession are given to new kinds of success. The function of the law has been to shape the legal framework for the new economy of the big corporation, with the split of ownership and control and the increased monopoly of economic power. The framework for this new business system has been shaped out of a legal system rooted in the landed property of the small entrepreneur, and has been adapted to commercial, industrial, and then investment economies. In the shift, the public has become for the lawyer what the public has been for the lawyer's chief client—an object of profit rather than of obligation.

There is one lawyer for approximately every 750 persons in the United States but this lawyer does not serve equally each of these 750. In rural districts and small cities, there is one lawyer for approximately every 1200, in big cities one for every 400 or 500. More directly, people with little or no money are largely unable to hire lawyers. Not persons, not unorganized publics of small investors, propertyless workers, consumers, but a thin upper crust and financial interests are what lawyers serve. Their income, a better income today than that received by any other professional group except doctors, comes from a very small upper income level of the population and from institutions.

In fulfilling his function the successful lawyer has created his office in the image of the corporations he has come to serve and defend. Because of the increased load of the law business and the concentration of successful practice, the law office has grown in size beyond anything dreamed of by the nineteenth-century solicitor. Such centralization of legal talent, in order that it may bear more closely upon the central functions of the law, means that many individual practitioners are kept on the fringes, while others become salaried agents of those who are at the top. As the new business system becomes specialized, with distinct sections and particular legal problems of its own, so do lawyers become experts in distinct sections and particular problems, pushing the interests of these sections rather than standing outside the business system and serving a law which co-ordinates the parts of a society.

In the shadow of the large corporation, the leading lawyer is selected for skill in the sure fix and the easy out-of-court settlement. He has become a groomed personality whose professional success is linked to a law office, the success of which in turn is linked to the troubles of the big corporation and contact with those outside the office. He is a high legal strategist for high finance and its profitable reorganizations, handling the affairs of a cluster of banks and the companies in their sphere in the cheapest way possible, making the most of his outside opportunities as an aide to big management that whistles him up by telephone; impersonally teaching the financiers how to do what they want within the law, advising on the chances they are taking and how best to cover themselves. The complications of modern corporate business and its dominance in modern society, A. A. Berle Jr. has brilliantly shown, have made the lawyer 'an intellectual jobber and contractor in business matters,' of all sorts. More than a consultant and counselor to large business, the lawyer is its servant, its champion, its ready apologist, and is full of its sensitivity. Around the modern corporation, the lawyer has erected the legal framework for the managerial demiurge.

As big capitalist enterprise came into social and economic dominance the chance to climb to the top ranks without initial large capital declined. But the law 'remained one of the careers through which a man could attain influence and wealth even without having capital at the start.' With law as background, the lawyer has often become a businessman himself, a proprietor of high acumen, good training, many contacts, and sound judgment. In his own right, he has also become the proprietor and general manager of a factory of law, with forty lawyers trained by Harvard, Yale, Columbia, and two hundred clerks, secretaries, and investigators to assist him. He competes with other law factories in pecuniary skills and impersonal loyalties, in turning out the standardized document and the subtle fix on a mass production basis. Such offices must carry a huge overhead; they must, therefore, obtain a steady flow of business; they therefore become adjuncts 'to the great commercial and investment banks.' They appear less in court than as 'financial experts and draftsmen of financial papers.'

The big money in law goes to some three or four hundred metropolitan law factories specializing in corporation law and constituting the brains of the corporate system. These law factories, as Ferdinand Lundberg has called them, are bureaucracies of middle size. Perhaps the largest has about seventy-five lawyers, with an appropriate staff of office workers.

The top men are chosen as are film stars, for their glamour. Behind them, the front men, stand men with technical abilities, as in Hollywood, looking out for the main chance and sometimes finding it, but working for a small salary. Below the partners are associates who are salaried lawyers, each usually working in a specialized department: general practice, litigation, trusts, probate, real estate, taxation. Below them are the clerk-apprentices in the law, then the investigators, bookkeepers, stenographers, and clerks. In special instances there are certified accountants and investment consultants, tax experts, engineers, lobbyists, also ranged in rank. For every partner there may be two salaried lawyer assistants, for every lawyer two or three office workers. A partnership of 20 lawyers may thus have some 40 associates and 120 office workers. Such offices, geared to quantity and speed of advice, must be highly organized and impersonally administered. High overhead—including oriental rugs and antique desks, panelled walls and huge leather libraries—often accounts for 30 per cent of the fees charged; the office must earn steadily, and the work be systematically ordered in the way of the managerial demiurge everywhere. Under the supervision of one of the partners, the office manager, sometimes a lawyer who seldom practices law, must see that production lines and organization run smoothly. Efficiency experts are called in to check up on the most effective operations for given tasks. In some offices each salaried lawyer, like a mechanic in a big auto repair shop, is required to account for his time, in order that fees may be assigned to given cases and the practice kept moving.

Each department, in turn, has its subdivisions: specialization is often intense. Teams of three lawyers or so, usually including one partner, work for only one important client or on one type of problem. Some lawyers spend all their time writing briefs, others answer only constitutional questions; some deal in Federal

Trade Commission actions, others only with the rulings of the Interstate Commerce Commission.

Much of the work is impersonal, vitiating the professional precept that lawyer and client should maintain a personal relationship. Personal intercourse between the members of the profession and between lawyers and clients, calls upon each other on matters of business, have been replaced by hurried telephone conversations, limited to the business at hand, entirely eliminating the personal quality. An opponent may be absolutely unknown, except over the telephone: you know the sound of his voice, but if you were to meet him on the street, you would be unable to recognize him. In the earlier days, a comparatively intimate acquaintance might have been formed even with an opponent. Once a meeting in a lawyer's office with a client not only was agreeable, but had a tendency to begin and cement a personal relationship. It now frequently happens that, although a lawyer may be actively employed for a client, personal intercourse does not occur.

Under this specialization, the young salaried lawyer does not by his experience round out into a man adept at all branches of law; indeed, his experience may specifically unfit him for general practice. The big office, it is said within the bar, often draws its ideas from the young men fresh from the preferred law schools, whom the big offices 'rush,' like fraternity men seeking pledges. Certainly the mass of the work is done by these able young men, while their product goes out under the names of the senior partners.

The young lawyer, just out of law school, fresh from matching wits with law professors and bar examiners, lacks one thing important for successful practice—contacts. Not only knowledge of trade secrets, but the number of contacts, is the fruit of what is called experience in modern business professions. The young men may labor and provide many of the ideas for the produce that goes out under the older man's name, but the older man is the business-getter: through his contacts, Karl Llewellyn has observed, he can attract more orders than he or twenty like him can supply. The measure of such a man is the volume of business he can produce; he creates the job for the young salaried lawyers, then puts his label on the product. He accumulates his reputation outside the office from the success of the young men, themselves striving for admittance to partnership, which comes after each has picked up enough contacts that are too large and dangerous to allow him to be kept within the salaried brackets. In the meantime he sweats, and in the meantime, the new law-school graduates are available every year, making a market with depressed salaries, further shut out by those new young men who have already inherited through their families a name that is of front-office caliber. The powerful connection, the strategic marriage, the gilt-edged social life, these are the obvious means of success.

Not only does the law factory serve the corporate system, but the lawyers of the factory infiltrate that system. At the top they sit on the Boards of Directors of banks and railroads, manufacturing concerns, and leading educational institutions. The firm of Sullivan and Cromwell, one of the largest law factories, holds 65 directorships. Below the directors, staff lawyers may be vice presidents of the corporation, other lawyers may be on annual retainers, giving the corporation a proprietary right to the lawyer as a moral agent. Of the corporation, for the corporation, by the corporation. Listening in on every major directors' meeting, phrasing public statements on all problems, the omnipresent legal mind, an officer of the court, assists the corporation, protects it, cares for its interests.

As annex to the big finance, the law factory is in politics on a national scale, but its interest in politics is usually only a means of realizing its clients' economic interests. Yet the lawyer who is successful in politics in his own right is all the more important and useful to his former clients, to whose fold he often returns after a political interlude. In corporation law firms one finds former senators and representatives, cabinet officers, federal prosecutors, state and federal tax officials, ambassadors and ministers, and others who have been acquainted with the inside workings of the upper levels of the government. High government officials, cabinet officers, ambassadors, and judges are often drawn directly from the corporation law offices, the partners of which welcome the opportunity to be of national service. Since the Civil War, the corporation law firms have contributed many justices to the United States Supreme Court; at present the majority of its members are former corporation lawyers. Lawyers have been in politics since the constitutional period but today the lawyers from law factories work less as political heroes in the sunlight than as fixers and lobbyists in the shade. When the TNEC investigations were going on, lawyers for the big corporations took up one entire hotel in Washington, D.C.

There are also, of course, political law firms, smaller than the law factories, which draw their clients from the political world and regularly enter that world themselves. For it is through politics that the lawyer may attain a position on the bench. Usually these political law offices have only local political interests. Whereas corporate law factories are usually headed by men of Anglo-Scotch stock, these political offices, mainly in the northeast and in big cities, where politics often centers on immigrant levels, are frequently staffed by Irish, Polish, Jewish, Italian Americans. The opportunism of these smaller firms may make them appear tolerant and liberal, and certainly many of the partners in them are up from the ranks.

The lawyer uses political office as a link in a legal career, and the politician uses legal training and law practice as links in a political career. Skills of pleading and bargaining are transferable to politics; moreover, in exercising them as a lawyer, there is a chance to obtain politically relevant publicity. The lawyer is occupationally and financially mobile: more easily than most men, he can earn a living and still give time to politics. So it is not surprising that 42 per cent of the members of Congress in 1914, 1920, and 1926 and of state governors in 1920 and 1924 had been prosecuting attorneys; and of these, Raymond Moley has calculated, 94 per cent had held this office first or second in their political careers. Between 1790 and 1930, Willard Hurst has computed, two-thirds of the Presidents and of the U.S. Senate, and about half of the House of Representatives were lawyers.

Below the corporation law offices and the political firms are middle-sized law offices, containing from 3 to 20 partners and few, if any, associates. These offices, especially in small towns, are rooted in the local affairs of their business communities, dividing their time between local politics and the practice of local litigations. Finally, at the bottom of the legal pyramid is the genuine entrepreneur of law, the individual practitioner who handles the legal affairs of individuals and small businesses. At the lower fringe of this stratum, in the big cities especially, are those lawyers who live 'dangerously close to the criminal class.' The hierarchical structure of the legal profession is thus not confined inside the big offices; it is characteristic of the profession as a whole, within various cities as well as nationally.

In most cities, the legal work of banks and local industries, of large estates and well-to-do families, is divided among a few leading law firms, whose members sit on the boards of local banks and companies, who lead church, college, and charity affairs. They perpetuate themselves by carefully selecting the most likely young men available and by nepotism, sons of relatives, of partners, and of big clients being given marked preference over strangers, local graduates of local law schools over outside ones. In St. Paul, Minnesota, for example, graduates of Princeton or Yale often take their law work in St. Paul Law School, rather than in the University of Minnesota, in order to become acquainted with members of the local bar who act as instructors. Below these leading firms, the small firms and individual practitioners get the business that is left over: occasional cases for well-to-do citizens, the plaintiff's damage suit, criminal defense cases, divorce work. Below all these groups are the lumpen-bourgeoisie of the law profession. Usually products of local schools, they haunt the courts for pickups; large in number, small in income, living in the interstices of the legal-business system, besieging the larger office for jobs, competing among themselves, from time to time making irritating inroads into the middle-sized firms, lowering the dignity of the profession's higher members by competing for retainers instead of conferring a favor by accepting a case. Even as top men toady to big corporation chieftains, men on the bottom assiduously chase ambulances and cajole the injured.

Among the difficulties that have arisen for lawyers since 1929 is the fact that laymen are invading many fields that were long considered the lawyers' domain. Drafting of deeds and mortgages has been taken over by real-estate men; various service organizations have taken over taxation difficulties, automobile accidents, and conditional sales; workmen's compensation now takes care of many industrial accidents. There has also been a declining use of courts and litigation methods of settling controversies, caused by the public desire for speedy settlements. Traditional litigation is giving way to a system of administrative adjudication in which the lawyer has an equal footing with the layman. Members of the legal profession are slowly losing their monopoly of political careers, as men trained in such disciplines as economics increasingly find their way into higher government offices.

Yet, despite the displacement of individual practitioner by legal factory, law has remained enticing to many young men. Thousands every year graduate from law schools. The war temporarily solved the problem of 'crowding'; for the first time since the early 'twenties, law schools were capable of finding jobs for each graduate as enrollment was severely cut down by the draft. But the bases of the problem for young, unconnected lawyers, and for American society, still remain.

4. The Professors

Schoolteachers, especially those in grammar and high schools, are the economic proletarians of the professions. These outlying servants of learning form the largest occupational group of the professional pyramid; some 31 per cent of all professional people are schoolteachers of one sort or another. Like other white-collar groups, their number has expanded enormously; they have, in addition, been instrumental, through education, in the birth and growth of many other white-collar groups.

The increase in enrollment and the consequent mass-production methods of instruction have made the position of the college professor less distinctive than it once was. Although its prestige, especially in the larger centers, is considerably higher than that of the public-school teacher, it does not usually attract sons of cultivated upper-class families. The type of man who is recruited for college teaching and shaped for this end by graduate school training is very likely to have a strong plebeian strain. His culture is typically narrow, his imagination often limited. Men can achieve position in this field although they are recruited from the lower-middle class, a milieu not remarkable for grace of mind, flexibility or breadth of culture, or scope of imagination. The profession thus includes many persons who have experienced a definite rise in class and status position, and who in making the climb are more likely, as Logan Wilson has put it, to have acquired 'the intellectual than the social graces.' It also includes people of 'typically plebeian cultural interests outside the field of specialization, and a generally philistine style of life.'

Men of brilliance, energy, and imagination are not often attracted to college teaching. The Arts and Sciences graduate schools, as the president of Harvard has indicated, do not receive 'their fair share of the best brains and well-developed, forceful personalities.' Law and medical schools have done much better. It is easier to become a professor, and it is easier to continue out of inertia. Professions such as law and medicine offer few financial aids by way of fellowships, while that of teaching the higher learning offers many.

The graduate school is often organized as a 'feudal' system: the student trades his loyalty to one professor for protection against other professors. The personable young man, willing to learn quickly the thought-ways of others, may succeed as readily or even more readily than the truly original mind in intensive contact with the world of learning. The man who is willing to be apprenticed to some professor is more useful to him.

Under the mass demand for higher degrees, the graduate schools have expanded enormously, often developing a mechanically given doctoral degree. Departmental barriers are accentuated as given departments become larger in personnel and budget. Given over mainly to preparing college teachers, the graduate schools equip their students to fulfil one special niche. This is part of the whole vocationalizing of education—the preparation of people to fulfil technical requirements and skills for immediate adjustment to a job.

The specialization that is required for successful operation as a college professor is often deadening to the mind that would grasp for higher culture in the modern world. There now is, as Whitehead has indicated, a celibacy of the intellect. Often the only 'generalization' the professor permits himself is the textbook he writes in the field of his work. Such serious thought as he engages in is thought within one specialty, one groove; the remainder of life is treated superficially. The professor of social science, for example, is not very likely to have as balanced an intellect as a top-flight journalist, and it is usually considered poor taste, inside the academies, to write a book outside of one's own field. The professionalization of knowledge has thus narrowed the grasp of the individual professor; the means of his success further this trend; and in the social studies and the humanities, the attempt to imitate exact science narrows the mind to microscopic fields of inquiry, rather than expanding it to embrace man and society as a whole. To make his mark he must specialize, or so he is encouraged to believe; so a college faculty of 150 members is split into 30 or 40 departments, each autonomous, each guarded by the established or, even worse, the almost-established man who fears encroachment or consolidation of his specialty.

After he is established in a college, it is unlikely that the professor's milieu and resources are the kind that will facilitate, much less create, independence of mind. He is a member of a petty hierarchy, almost completely closed in by its middle-class environment and its segregation of intellectual from social life. In such a hierarchy, mediocrity makes its own rules and sets its own image of success. And the path of ascent itself is as likely to be administrative duty as creative work.

But the shaping of the professor by forces inside the academy is only part of the story. The U.S. educational system is not autonomous; what happens in it is quite dependent upon changes in other areas of society. Schools are often less centers of initiative than adaptive organisms; teachers are often less independent minds than low-paid employees.

External circumstances and demands have affected the enrollment and curriculum of high schools and colleges, as well as the types of teachers, and the roles they play within and out of the academy. By making an analogy between the world of knowledge and the economic system, we can get a fuller picture of the types of academic men who people U.S. centers of higher learning.

The *producer* is the man who creates ideas, first sets them forth, possibly tests them, or at any rate makes them available in writing to those portions of the market capable of understanding them. Among producers there are individual entrepreneurs— still the predominant type—and corporation executives in research institutions of various kinds who are in fact administrators over production units. Then there are the *wholesalers,* who while they do not produce ideas do distribute them in textbooks to other academic men, who in turn sell them directly to student consumers. In so far as men teach, and only teach, they are *retailers* of ideas and materials, the better of them being serviced by original producers, the lesser, by wholesalers. All academic men, regardless of type, are also *consumers* of the products of others, of producers and wholesalers through books, and of retailers to some extent through personal conversation on local markets. But it is possible for some to specialize in consumption: these become great *comprehenders,* rather than *users,* of books, and they are great on bibliographies.

In most colleges and universities, all these types are represented, all may flourish; but the producer (perhaps along with the textbook wholesaler) has been honored the most.

The general hierarchy of academic standing runs from the full professor in a graduate school, who teaches very little and does much research, to the instructor of undergraduates, who teaches a great deal and does little or no research. Getting ahead academically means attracting students, but at the same time pursuing research work—and in the end, especially for the younger man, publication may weigh more heavily than teaching success. The normal academic career has involved a hierarchy *within* an institution, but success within this institution draws heavily upon outside success. There is a close interaction between local teaching, research publication, and offers from other institutions.

In the twentieth century, academic life in America has by and large failed to make ambitious men contented with simple academic careers. The profession carries little status in relation to the pecuniary sacrifices often involved; the pay and hence the style of life is often relatively meager; and the discontent of some scholars is heightened by their awareness that their intelligence far exceeds that of men who have attained power and prestige in other fields. For such unhappy professors, new developments in research and administration offer gratifying opportunities to become, so to speak, Executives without having to become Deans.

As internal academic forces turn some professors into retailers or administrators, external forces draw others, especially in the big universities, toward careers of a new entrepreneurial type.

War experience has indicated that the professor can be useful in government programs, as well as in the armed forces. But it is research that is most likely to get him out of the academy and into other life-situations. It is also in connection with research, and the money it entails, that professors become more directly an appendage of the larger managerial demiurge, which their professional positions allow them to sanctify as well as to serve in more technical ways. Since knowledge is a commodity that may be sold directly, perhaps it is inevitable that some professors specialize in selling knowledge after others have created it, and that still others shape their intellectual work to meet the market directly. Like the pharmacist who sells packaged drugs with more authority than the ordinary storekeeper, the professor sells packaged knowledge with better effect than laymen. He brings to the market the prestige of his university position and of the ancient academic tradition of disinterestedness. This halo of disinterestedness has more than once been turned to the interests of companies who purchase the professor's knowledge and the name of his university.

It has long been known, of course, that economics has been the 'Swiss guard of the vested interests'—but usually from some distance. Now, however, many top professional economists are direct agents of business. Engineers and lawyers, the most frequent professionals found in the service of advising business, are being joined by academicians, who associate with management in the solution of policy problems, who gauge the market for products, and who assay opinions about the firm or about business in general. These needs have increased as business and trade associations have become larger and have taken up the role of economic statesmen for the entire economy. For these organizations have felt the need of spokesmen for their new roles, and as public relations has become a top management concern, simple hot air has lost ground to research, carefully prepared for internal and external uses. This has meant that researchers of some talent have to be retained, as well as professors from various universities, who set the seal of their universities upon the research findings.

The new academic practicality, in the social studies, for instance, is not concerned with the broken-up human results of the social process: the bad boy, the loose woman, the un-Americanized immigrant. On the contrary, it is tied in with the top levels of society, in particular with enlightened circles of business executives. For the first time in the history of their discipline, for example, sociologists have become linked by professional tasks and social contacts with private and public powers well above the level of the social-work agency. Now, alongside the old, there are the new practitioners who study workers who are restless and lack morale, and managers who do not understand the art of managing human relations.

Among social science and business professors in three or four large universities, the new entrepreneurial pattern of success is well under way. One often hears in these centers that 'the professor does everything but teach.' He is a consultant to large corporations, real-estate bodies, labor-management committees; he has built his own research shop, from which he sells research services and the prestige of his university's traditional impartiality. He becomes a man with a staff—and with overhead. It is high overhead with a system of fees for given jobs that causes his business-like frenzy. The fact that such an academic entrepreneur is not usually out after money often gives the outsider the impression that the professor is play-acting at business, gaining prestige because of his own eccentricity and low personal income. But regardless of motives or consequences, some academic careers are becoming dependent upon the traits of the go-getter in business and the manager in the corporation.

It must be understood that all this is still exceptional, certainly so in terms of the number of professors involved. It may well be seen as an interlude, for on the one side, as the professorial entrepreneur succeeds, his university takes over what he has built, turning it into a department of the endowed plant, and using its reputation to get more respectable, steady money. And on the

other side, the orientation and technical skills taught to apprentices enable them to enter the corporations and government bureaus as professional employees.

In contrast with businessmen and other laymen, the professors
are probably not primarily concerned with the pecuniary, the
managerial, or the political uses of their practicality. Such results
are to them primarily means to other ends which center around
their 'careers.' It is true that professors certainly welcome the
small increases to their salaries that may come with research
activity: they may or may not feel gratified to be helping managers administer their plant more profitably and with less trouble;
they may or may not be powerfully lifted by building new and
more intellectually acceptable ideologies for established powers.
But in so far as they remain scholars, their extra-intellectual aims
center around furthering their careers.

From this point of view, the professor's participation in the
new ideological and practical studies is, in part, a response to the
new job opportunities arising from the increased scale and intensified bureaucratic character of modern business and government, and from the institutionalization of the relations between
business corporations and the rest of the community. Bureaucratization brings with it an increased demand for experts and the
formation of new career patterns: social scientists responding to
this demand, more or less happily, become business and government officials, on higher or lower levels. The centers of higher
learning themselves reflect this outside demand for scholars by
tending increasingly to produce supposedly apolitical technicians, as against free intellectuals. Thus college-trained labor-
relations scholars become 'experts' and serve on the War Labor
Board, rather than write and fight for radical and/or conservative publics and for the public dissemination of theoretical ideas.
In this connection, modern war is the health of the expert and,
particularly, the expert in the rhetoric of liberal justification.

For those who remain in academic life the career of the new
entrepreneur has become available. This type of man is able to
further his career in the university by securing prestige and small-
scale powers outside of it. Above all, he is able to set up on the
campus a respectably financed institute that brings the academic
community into contact with men of affairs, thus often becoming

the envy of his more cloistered colleagues and looked to by them for leadership in university affairs.

Yet there is evidence, here and there, even among the youngest men in the greatest hurry, that these new careers, while lifting them out of the academic rut, may have dropped them into something which in its way is at least as unsatisfactory. At any rate, the new academic entrepreneurs often seem unaware just what their goals may be: indeed, they do not seem to have firmly in mind even the terms in which possible success may be defined.

As a group, American professors have seldom if ever been politically engaged: the trend toward a technician's role has, by strengthening their apolitical professional ideology, reduced whatever political involvement they may have had and often, by sheer atrophy, their ability even to grasp political problems. That is why one often encounters middle-rank journalists who are more politically alert than top sociologists, economists, or political scientists.

The American university system seldom provides political training—that is, how to gauge what is going on in the general struggle for power in modern society. Social scientists have had little or no real contact with such insurgent sections of the community as exist; there is no left-wing press with which the average academic man in the course of his career would come into live contact; there is no movement which would support or give prestige, not to speak of jobs, to the political intellectual; the academic community has few roots in labor circles. This vacuum means that the American scholar's situation allows him to take up the new practicality—in effect to become a political tool—without any shift of political ideology and with little political guilt.

5. Business and the Professions

United States society esteems the exercise of educated skill, and honors those who are professionally trained; it also esteems money as fact and as symbol, and honors those who have a lot of it. Many professional men are thus at the intersection of these two systems of value and many businessmen strive to add the professional to the pecuniary. When we speak of the commercialization of the professions, or of the professionalization of business, we point to the conflict or the merging of skill and money. Out of this merging, professions have become more like businesses, and businesses have become more like professions. The line between them has in many places become obscured, especially as businesses have become big and have hired men of the established professions.

Yet, in so far as both business and the professions are organized in bureaucratic structures, the present differences between their individual practitioners are not great. The managerial demiurge involves both business and the professions, and, as it does so, individuals perform duties within specific offices, making money for the organization perhaps, but themselves receiving a salary. For the salaried agent the consequences of a businesslike decision react not directly upon his own bank account, but upon the profit position of the firm for which he works.

If more and more businesses and occupations in America are called professions, or their practitioners try to behave like professionals, this is certainly not, as has been claimed by Harold Laski, because of any 'equalitarian' urge, either on the part of the country as a whole or on the part of the established professions. It is most crucially a result of the fact that as business has become enlarged and complicated, the skills needed to operate it become more difficult to acquire through an apprenticeship. People have had to be more highly trained, and often very specialized. Business has thus become a market for educated labor; including both the established as well as the newer professions, it has itself come to educate in the process of its own work.

When, as is happening today, special training for selected managers of business is instituted, and when such training becomes a prerequisite to being hired, then we can speak of business as a profession, like medicine or law. Today the situation is quite mixed, but large businesses are moving in this direction.

Increasingly both business and the professions are being rationally organized, so that the 'science of business' arises in the schools even as do courses in 'business practice' for doctors and lawyers. Both businessmen and professionals strive for rationality of the social machineries in which they work, and are honored if they achieve it. Both strive to become looked upon as experts and to be so judged, within a narrowed area of specific competence. Both are masters of abstracted human relations, whether as in business they see a customer, or in the professions a client or case.

The main trend is for the bureaucratic organization of businessmen and of professionals to turn both into bureaucrats, professionalized occupants of specified offices and specialized tasks. It is certainly not in terms of 'pecuniary vs. service,' or in any terms of motivation, that business and the professions can be distinguished.

The businessman, it has been thought, egotistically pursues his self-interest, whereas the professional man altruistically serves the interest of others. Such distinctions do prevail, but, as Talcott Parsons has correctly observed, the difference is not between egotistic self-interest and altruism. It is, rather, a difference in the entrance requirement, as this bears upon specialized training; a difference in the way the professional and business groups are socially organized and controlled; and a difference in the rules that govern the internal and external relations of the members of each group.

If professional men are not expected to advertise (although some of them do), if they are expected, as in medicine or law, to take cases in need regardless of credit rating (although there is wide variation on this point), if they are forbidden to compete with one another for clients in terms of costs (although some do)—this is not because they are less self-interested than businessmen; it is because they are organized, in a guild-like system, so as best to promote long-run self-interest. It does not matter whether as individuals they are aware of this as a social fact or understand it only as an ethical matter.

So effective is the professional ideology of altruistic service that businessmen, especially certain types of small traders, are eagerly engaged in setting up the same practices of non-competition and guild-like closure. Even among businessmen who are not directly involved in the technicalities of modern business bureaucracy, there is the urge to seem professional and to enjoy professional privileges. This, first of all, rests upon their aspirations for status: the 'professional' wears a badge of prestige. Any position that is 'responsible and steady' and, above all, that carries prestige may become known, or at least promoted by its members, as a profession. Real-estate men become realtors; undertakers become morticians; advertising men and public-relations counsels, radio commentators and gag men, interior decorators and special-effects experts all try to look and act 'professional.' This trend is allowed and encouraged, if not implemented, by the fact that business functions, and so businessmen, are often accorded so high a status that they can 'borrow' the status adhering to other pursuits. If the professions are honorific, the businessman reasons, then business should be a profession.

One method of achieving this status, as well as of increasing income and warding off competition, is to close up the ranks without forming labor unions, to form professional associations which limit entrance to the fields of profits and fees. It was not until the 'seventies that the first state bar examinations were installed and medical licensing was begun; accountants, architects, and engineers were licensed at the beginning of the twentieth century. But by the 1930's, according to Willard Hurst's count in 18 representative states, some 210 occupations or businesses had come under some sort of legal closure.

The chief stock in trade, for example, of pharmacists as small businessmen is their status, however anomalous, as professional men. Their professional claims and prestige encourage the consumer's confidence in the goods they sell; and, as one business journal asserts, 'their legal franchise as professional dispensers of health products enables them to stay open and sell non-drug products at odd times—Sundays, holidays, at night—when other stores are closed.' The professional basis of pharmacists, however, has been slipping, because packaged drug sales have increased, while prescription sales have declined.

The economic meaning of the pharmacists' claims to professional status lies in the fact that they will lose many drug sales unless restrictive laws limit such sales to registered pharmacists. In part at least, the professional cry of the pharmacist is the economic cry of a small businessman against drug manufacturers who desire broader outlets. Small druggists often consider it highly unethical, even as do doctors, to compete in terms of the prices of retail price-maintained goods. They, too, would like a professional closure and 'professional standing.' In the extreme case, ostracism and expulsion are used to uphold the rules of the guild in a society dominated by the acquisition and guarantee of profit. The balance between wise restraint and commercial advantage is uneasy, the line between them difficult to draw.

The merging type of professional-and-businessman seeks to be and often is an entrepreneur who can exploit special privileges. Among these is the use of both business and professional bureaucracies. The professor sells the prestige of his university to secure market-research jobs in order to build a research unit; he is privileged over commercial agencies because of his connection with the university. The doctor who is connected with the hospital secures patients as well as the use of equipment because of his connection. The lawyer, in his shuttles between one business and another, and between business and government, borrows prestige from both.

Like other privileged groups, the professional entrepreneurs and the entrepreneurial professionals seek to monopolize their positions by closing up their ranks; they seek to do so by law and by stringent rules of education and entrance. Whenever there is a feeling of declining opportunity, occupational groups will seek such closure. That strategy is now back of many of the rules and policies adopted by professional associations as well as by businessmen who seek to claim professional status.

The ingenious bureaucracies among professionals, the increased volumes of work demanded of them, the coincidence of the managerial demiurge with commercial zeal, and all the policies and attempts on the part of professional and business groups to close up their ranks—these developments are alienating the individual, free intelligence from many white-collared professionals. Individual reflection is being centralized, sometimes at the top, more often just next to the top, as there are jobs requiring and monopolizing more of it, and, down the white-collar line, jobs requiring or allowing less of it.

The centralization of planful reflection and the consequent expropriation of individual rationality parallel the rationalization of the white-collar hierarchy as a whole. What a single individual used to do is now broken up into functions of decision and research, direction and checking up, each performed by a separate group of individuals. Many executive functions are thus becoming less autonomous and permitting less initiative. The centralization of reflection entails for many the deprivation of initiative: for them, decision becomes the application of fixed rules. Yet these developments do not necessarily mean that the *top men* have less intellectual tasks to perform; they mean rather, as Henri de Man has observed, that the *less* intellectual tasks are broken up and transferred down the hierarchy to the semi-skilled white-collar employees, while the managerial top becomes even more intellectualized, and the unit of its intellectuality becomes a set of specialized staffs. The more those down the line are deprived of intellectual content in their work, the more those on top need to be intellectualized, or at least the more dependent they become upon the intellectually skilled.

If in this process some professionals are forced down the line, more of those who take on the new subaltern intellectual tasks come from lower down the social scale. For the centralization of professional skills and the industrialization of many intellectual functions have not narrowed the full professional stratum so much as proliferated the semi-professions and the quasi-intellectual, and between these and the fully professional, created a more marked separation. So great has the expansion been that children of the wage-worker and the clerk are often raised into semi-professional status, while top men of the professional world merge with business and become professional entrepreneurs of the managerial demiurge.

7

Brains, Inc.

Oғ all middle-class groups, intellectuals are the most far-flung and heterogeneous. Unlike small businessmen, factory workers, or filing clerks, intellectuals have been relatively classless. They have no common origin and share no common social destiny. They differ widely in income and in status; some live, residentially and intellectually, in suburban slums; others, in propaganda bureaus of continent-wide nations. Many intellectuals are members of the old middle class; they work a specialized market made up of editors and business managers, as entrepreneurs using their education and their verbal skills as capital. Others are primarily new middle class: their styles of life and of work are set by their position as salaried employees in various white-collar pyramids.

Many professional people, by virtue of their education and leisure, have a good chance to become intellectuals, and many intellectuals earn their living by practicing some profession. Moreover, people of professional skills form a substantial proportion of the intellectuals' public. So what happens to professional and technical groups also affects the intellectuals' conditions of work and life.

Intellectuals cannot be defined as a single social unit, but rather as a scattered set of grouplets. They must be defined in terms of their function and their subjective characteristics rather than in terms of their social position: as people who specialize in symbols, the intellectuals produce, distribute, and preserve distinct forms of consciousness. They are the immediate carriers of art and of ideas. They may have no direct responsibility for any practice; or, being engaged in institutional roles, they may be firmly attached to going institutions. They may be onlookers and outsiders, or overseers and insiders; but however that may be, *as* intellectuals they are people who live *for* and not *off* ideas.

Seeking to cultivate a sense of individual mind, they have been, in their self-images, detached from popular values and stereotypes, and they have not been consciously beholden to anyone for the fixing of their beliefs. A remark William Phillips made of modern literature applies equally well to intellectuals: they have been in 'recoil from the practices and values of society toward some form of self-sufficiency, be it moral, or physical, or merely historical, with repeated fresh starts from the bohemian underground as each new movement runs itself out. . .' They are thus 'in a kind of permanent mutiny against the regime of utility and conformity. . .' All these elements of 'freedom' hold for political as well as artistic intellectuals. All intellectual work is, in fact, relevant in so far as it is focused upon symbols that justify, debunk, or divert attention from authority and its exercise. Political intellectuals are specialized dealers in such symbols and states of political consciousness; they create, facilitate, and criticize the beliefs and ideas that support or attack ruling classes, institutions and policies; or they divert attention from these structures of power and from those who command and benefit from them as going concerns.

For a brief liberal period in western history, many intellectuals were free in the sense mentioned. They were in a somewhat unique historical situation, even as the situation of the small entrepreneur was unique: one historic phase sandwiched between two more highly organized phases. The eighteenth-century intellectual stood on common ground with the bourgeois entrepreneur; both were fighting, each in his own way, against the remnants of feudal control, the writer seeking to free himself from the highly placed patron, the businessman breaking the bonds of the chartered enterprise. Both were fighting for a new kind of freedom, the writer for an anonymous public, the businessman for an anonymous and unbounded market. It was their victory which Philip Rahv describes when he says that 'during the greater part of the bourgeois epoch . . . [the artist] preferred alienation from the community to alienation from himself.' But no longer are such conditions of freedom available for the entrepreneur or the intellectual, and nowhere has its collapse for intellectuals been more apparent than in twentieth-century America.

1. Four Phases

The practice of a free intellectual life has in the course of this century undergone several transformations and come up against several rather distinct sets of circumstance. To follow these changes it is necessary to examine shifting models of thought and mood and to track down intangible influences. Throughout this century there has arisen a new kind of patronage system for free intellectuals, which at mid-century seems to have effected a loss of political will and even of moral hope.

An over-simplified history of free, political intellectuals in the United States falls into four broad phases, outlined according to their major areas of attention and their pivotal values.

I. Before World War I, the liberalism of pragmatic thought was widespread among muckrakers, who individually sought out the facts of injustice and corruption and reported them to the middle class. In the first decade and a half of the century, these intellectuals as muckrakers had a firm base in a mass public; in magazines like *McClure's* they could operate as free-lance journalists, focusing on specific cities and specific businesses. In that expanding society, with new routines and groups arising, these intellectuals were sometimes overwhelmed by the need for sheer description, but they were critical journalists, having a vested interest in attack on established corruption, in a kind of ethical bookkeeping for the old middle-class world.

In fact, muckraking attacks were thought or were feared to be so effective that, in reflex fashion, men of power hired publicity agents to defend their authority and their public images. Some of these publicity agents were at least in the beginning intellectuals: it is, in fact, characteristic of intellectuals that they are able to attach themselves to the defense and elaboration of almost any social interest. By World War I, many who had been muckrakers took up the defense of a new synthetic faith that was being created for the vested interests. The very magazines for which the muckrakers wrote, William Miller has shown, were in due course transformed into carefully guarded advertising media of enormous circulation.

The muckrakers did not, of course, monopolize the intellectual scene. Centered in Henry Adams' house in Washington, D.C., and in the circles of strenuous idea-men like Theodore Roosevelt, there was a conservative elite who also were critical of crass capitalism, but in a gentlemanly manner, from the standpoint of the patrician rentier. The muckrakers and conservatives did not long remain free or retain any unity: precisely because of their multiplicity of origin and interests, and their social heterogeneity, it was not difficult for them to take the different directions and join the different classes or parties that they did.

II. The range of styles for intellectuals available in the 'twenties, as they 'attempted to reconcile themselves to the brokers' world,' has been well-described by Edmund Wilson: 'the attitude of the Menckenian gentleman, ironic, beer-loving and "civilized," living principally on the satisfaction of feeling superior to the broker and enjoying the debauchment of American life as a burlesque show; the attitude of the old-American-stock smugness . . . the liberal attitude that American capitalism was going to show a new wonder to the world by gradually and comfortably socializing itself and that we should just have to respect and like it in the meantime, taking a great interest in Dwight Morrow and Owen D. Young; the attitude of trying to get a kick out of the sheer energy and size of American enterprises, irrespective of what they were aiming at; the attitude of proudly withdrawing and cultivating a refined sensibility; the attitude of letting one's self be carried along by the mad hilarity and tragedy of jazz, of living only for the excitement of the night.'

What all these attitudes have in common is an apolitical tone, or a cultivated relaxation into a soft kind of liberalism, which relieved political tension and dulled political perception. The intellectuals diverted public attention from major political symbols, even as they broke cultural and social idols. Many rejected middle-western America for the eastern cities and, in fact, all America for Europe, but their revolt was esthetic and literary rather than explicitly political. It was an enthusiastic revolt against 'provincial' regional hankerings, against social and ideological proprieties, against gentility in all forms.

III. For a while, during the 'thirties, there was a widespread model of the intellectual as political agent. Some of the most talented free intellectuals played at being Leninist men. They joined or traveled with splinter parties, with first the Third and then the Fourth International; they wrote in support of the general ideas and policies current in these circles.

For the first several decades of this century, pragmatism was the nerve of leftward thinking. By the nineteen-thirties, as pragmatism as such began to decline as a common denominator of liberalism, its major theme was given new life by a fashionable Marxism. One idea ran through both ideologies: the optimistic faith in man's rationality. In pragmatism this rationality was formally located in the individual; in Marxism in a class of men; but in both it was a motif so dominant as to set the general mood.

In Marx's theory of historical change, as modified by Lenin, the intellectual supplemented the proletariat. Only if these gadflies, bearing the idea, joined the movement as its heroic vanguard would the workers make a new world—or at least so did many U.S. intellectuals interpret Leninism.

Some few joined the organizing staffs of unions, becoming journalists and publicity agents, to gauge when the time was ripe—although none became firmly attached to the labor movement without ceasing to be intellectuals. But also novelists, critics, and poets, historians, both academic and free-lance—the leading intellectuals—became political, went left. If they broke away from the Communist party, as members or as fellow travelers, still they remained radical, as Trotskyist intellectuals or as independent leftists. For a time, all live intellectual work was derived from leftward circles or spent its energy defending itself against left views.

IV. With the war came a period of deliberation. Intellectuals broke with the old radicalism and became in one way or another liberals and patriots, or gave up politics altogether. Dwight Macdonald has observed how 'religious obscurantists,' who returned to precapitalist values, and 'totalitarian liberals,' who accepted the process of rationalization, trying to make of it a positive thing, came forth, bringing with them a strong effort to de-politicize the war in every respect. And, as James Farrell has pointed out, a 'metaphysics of the war' was necessary: in the name of the American past such men as Brooks, MacLeish, and Mumford, official spokesmen of the war ideology, provided it. Intellectuals who remained free, who scorned the new metaphysics, were still much affected by it because it had the initiative, even as big business gained the initiative inside the war agencies: WPA became WPB for many businessmen and for many intellectuals.

In the effort to discuss but not face up to the irresponsibilities and sustaining deceptions of modern society at war, the publicists called upon images of the Future. But even the production of utopias seemed to be controlled, monopolized by adjuncts of big business, who set the technological trap by dangling baubles before the public without telling how those goods might be widely distributed. Political writers focused attention away from the present and into the several planful models of the future, drawn up as sources of unity and morale. 'Post-war planning,' with emphasis upon the coming technological marvels, was the chief intellectual form of war propaganda in America.

Few intellectuals arose to protest against the war on political or moral grounds, and the prosperity after the war, in which intellectuals shared, was for them a time of moral slump. They have not returned to politics, much less turned left again, and no new generation has yet moved into their old stations. With this disintegration has gone political will; in its place there is hopelessness. Among U.S. intelligentsia, as all over the world, Lionel Trilling has remarked, the 'political mind lies passive before action and the event . . . we are in the hands of the commentator.'

Since the war years, the optimistic, rational faith has obviously been losing out in competition with more tragic views of political and personal life. Many who not long ago read Dewey or Marx with apparent satisfaction have become more vitally interested in such analysts of personal tragedy as Soren Kierkegaard or such mirrors of hopeless bafflement as Kafka. Attempts to reinstate the old emphasis on the power of man's intelligence to control his destiny have not been taken up by American intellectuals, spurred as they are by new worries, seeking as they are for new gods. Suffering the tremors of men who face defeat, they are worried and distraught, some only half aware of their condition, others so painfully aware that they must obscure their knowledge by rationalistic busy-work and many forms of self-deception.

No longer can they read, without smirking or without bitterness, Dewey's brave words, 'Every thinker puts some portion of an apparently stable world in peril,' or Bertrand Russell's 'Thought looks into the face of hell and is not afraid,' much less Marx's notion that the role of the philosopher was not to interpret but to change the world. Now they hear Charles Péguy: 'No need to conceal this from ourselves: we are defeated. For ten years, for fifteen years, we have done nothing but lose ground. Today, in the decline, in the decay of political and private morals, literally we are beleaguered. We are in a place which is in a state of siege and more than blockaded and all the flat country is in the hands of the enemy.' What has happened is that the terms of acceptance of American life have been made bleak and superficial at the same time that the terms of revolt have been made vulgar and irrelevant. The malaise of the American intellectual is thus the malaise of a spiritual void.

The political failure of intellectual nerve is no simple retreat from reason. The ideas current among intellectuals are not merely fads of an epoch of world wars and slumps. The creation and diffusion of ideas and moods must be understood as social and historical phenomena. What is happening is not entirely explained, however, by the political defeat and internal decay of radical parties. The loss of will and even of ideas among intellectuals must in the first instance be seen in terms of their self-images, which have in turn been anchored in social movements and political trends. To understand what has been happening to American intellectual life we have to go beyond the decline of radical movements and of Marxism as a packaged intellectual option, and realize the effects upon the carriers of intellectual life of certain deep-lying, long-term trends of modern social and ideological organization.

2. The Bureaucratic Context

Bureaucracy increasingly sets the conditions of intellectual life and controls the major market for its products. The new bureaucracies of state and business, of party and voluntary association, become the major employers of intellectuals and the main customers for their work. So strong has this demand for technical and ideological intelligentsia of all sorts become that it might even be said that a new patronage system of a complicated and sometimes indirect kind has arisen. Not only the New Deal, Hollywood, and the Luce enterprises, but business concerns of the most varied types, as well as that curious set of institutions clustering around Stalinism, have come to play an important role in the cultural and marketing life of the intellectual. The Young & Rubicam mentality is not confined to Young and Rubicam; there are wider groupings which have become adjuncts of the marketeers and which display the managing mentality and style of those who sell systematically.

The 'opinion-molding profession,' Elliot Cohen has observed, 'is a tight little community, inhabiting a small territory four blocks wide and ten or so blocks long centering around Radio City, with business suburbs of the same narrow geographical dimensions in Hollywood and Chicago. . .' But its reach is wide: at the top, the communications intellectuals (idea men, technicians, administrators) blend with the managerial demiurge in more concrete businesses. Indeed, the styles of work and life of intellectuals and managers, as well as their dominating interests, coincide at many points. In and around these managed structures are intellectuals who, given the modern dominance, must now be considered as hold-outs. And between the two there is much traffic.

For the intellectual who would remain free yet still seek a public, this general trend is sharpened by the fact that, in a bureaucratic world of organized irresponsibility, the difficulty of speaking one's mind in dissent has increased. Between the intellectual and his potential public stand technical, economic, and social structures which are owned and operated by others. The medium of pamphlets offered to Tom Paine a direct channel to readers that the world of mass advertising-supported publications clearly cannot afford to provide the dissenter. If the intellectual becomes the hired man of an information industry, his general aims must, of course, be set by the decisions of others rather than by his own integrity. If he is working for such industries on a 'putting-out' basis, he is of course only one short step from the hired-man status, although in his case manipulation rather than authority may be exercised. The freedom of the freelance is minimized when he goes to market, and if he does go, his freedom is without public value.

Even craftsmanship, so central to intellectual and artistic gratification, is thwarted for an increasing number of intellectual workers who find themselves in the predicament of the Hollywood writer. Unlike the Broadway playwright who retains at least some command over his play when the manager, director, and cast take it over, the Hollywood script writer has no assurance that what he writes will be produced in even recognizable form. His work is bent to the ends of mass effects to sell a mass market; and his major complaint, as Robert E. Sherwood has said, is not that he is underpaid, but that while he has responsibility for his work he has no real authority over it.

The themes of mass literature and entertainment, of pulps and slicks, of radio drama and television script, are thus set by the editor or director. The writer merely fills an order, and often he will not write at all until he has an order, specifying content, slant, and space limits. Even the editor of the mass magazine, the director of the radio drama, has not escaped the depersonalization of publishing and entertainment; he is also the employee of a business enterprise, not a personality in his own right. Mass magazines and radio shows are not so much edited by a personality as regulated by an adroit formula.

With the general speed-up of the literary industry and the advent of go-getters in publishing, the character of book publishing has changed. Writers have always been somewhat limited by the taste and mentality of their readers, but the variety and levels to which the publishing industry was geared made possible a large amount of freedom. Recent changes in the mass distribution of books may very well require, as do the production and distribution of films, a more cautious, standardized product. It is likely that fewer and fewer publishers will handle more and more of those manuscripts which reach mass publics through large-scale channels of distribution.

The rationalization of literature and the commercialization of the arts began in the sphere of distribution. Now it reaches deeper and deeper into the productive aspects. 'We seldom stop to think,' wrote Henry Seidel Canby, in 1933, 'how strange it is that literature has become an industry. . . Everything is taken care of . . . in the widely ramified organizations [of] the publishing houses and the agencies . . . [the author's] name is down . . . and the diplomacy department dispatches bright young envoys to them at brisk intervals. They are part of the organization now.' So also the book editors, who increasingly become members of a semi-anonymous staff governed by formula, rather than devoted, professional men.

Editors seek out prominent names, and men with such names crave even more prominence; given go-getting editors and craving notables, it is inevitable in our specialized age that reliance on the expert should bring about a large expansion of ghost-writing. The chance is probably fifty-fifty that the book of a prominent but non-literary man is actually written by someone else. Yet perhaps the ghost-writer is among the honest literary men; in him alienation from work reaches the final point of complete lack of public responsibility.

Although the large universities are still relatively free places in which to work, the trends that limit independence of intellect are not absent there. The professor is, after all, an employee, subject to what this fact involves, and institutional factors select men and have some influence upon how, when, and upon what they will work. Yet the deepest problem of freedom for teachers is not the occasional ousting of a professor, but a vague general fear—sometimes called 'discretion' and 'good judgment'—which leads to self-intimidation and finally becomes so habitual that the scholar is unaware of it. The real restraints are not so much external prohibitions as manipulative control of the insurgent by the agreements of academic gentlemen. Such control is, of course, furthered by Hatch Acts, by political and business attacks upon professors, by the restraints necessarily involved in Army programs for colleges, and by the setting up of committees by trade associations, which attempt to standardize the content and effects of teaching in given disciplines. Research in social science is increasingly dependent upon funds from foundations, which are notably averse to scholars who develop unpopular, 'unconstructive,' theses.

The United States' growing international entanglements have still other, subtle effects upon American intellectuals: for the young man who teaches and writes on Latin America, Asia, or Europe, and who does not deviate from acceptable facts and policies, these entanglements lead to a kind of voluntary censorship. He hopes for opportunities of research, travel, and foundation subsidies. Tacitly, by his silence, or explicitly in his work, the academic intellectual often sanctions illusions that uphold authority, rather than speak out against them. In his teaching, he may censor himself by carefully selecting safe problems in the name of pure science, or by selling such prestige as his scholarship may have for ends other than his own.

More and more people, and among them the intellectuals, are becoming dependent salaried workers who spend the most alert hours of their lives being told what to do. In our time, dominated by the need for swift action, the individual, including the free intellectual, feels dangerously lost; such are the general frustrations of contemporary life. But they are reflected very acutely, in direct and many indirect ways, into the world of the intellectual. For he lives by communication, and the means of effective communication are being expropriated from the intellectual worker.

Knowledge that is not communicated has a way of turning the mind sour, of being obscured, and finally of being forgotten. For the sake of the integrity of the discoverer, his discovery must be effectively communicated. Such communication is also a necessary element in the very search for clear understanding, including the understanding of one's self. Only through social confirmation by others whom he believes adequately equipped can a man earn the right of feeling secure in his knowledge. The basis of integrity can be gained or renewed only by activity, including communication, in which there is a minimum of repression. When a man sells the lies of others he is also selling himself. To sell himself is to turn himself into a commodity. A commodity does not control the market; its nominal worth is determined by what the market will offer.

3. The Ideological Demand

The market, though it is undoubtedly a buyer's market, has been paying off well. The demand of the bureaucracies has been not only for intellectual personnel to run the new technical, editorial, and communication machinery, but for the creation and diffusion of new symbolic fortifications for the new and largely private powers these bureaucracies represent. In our time, every interest, hatred, or passion is likely to be intellectually organized, no matter how low the level of that organization may be. There is a great 'increase of conscious formulation,' Lionel Trilling remarks, and an 'increase of a certain kind of consciousness by formulation.' Around each interest a system is made up, a system founded on Science. A research cartel must be engaged or, if none yet exists, created, in which careful researchers must turn out elaborate studies and accurately timed releases, buttressing the interest, competing with other hatreds, turning pieties into theologies, passions into ideologies. In all these attempts to secure attention and credulity, in all this justifying and denying, intellectuals are required. The great demand for new justifications has been facilitated by four interrelated and cumulative processes:

1. Traditional sanctifications have in the course of modern times been broken up; no longer are underlying meanings tacitly accepted. With the new, diverse, and enlarged means of communication, traditional symbols have been uprooted and exposed to competition. In this breakup, the intellectual has played a major role; and as urban society has demanded new heroes and meanings, it has been the intellectual who has found them and spread them to mass publics.

II. As every interest has come to have its ideological apparatus, and new means of communication have become available, symbols of justification and diversion have multiplied and competed with one another for the attention of various publics. Continuously in demand as new devices to attract attention and hold it, symbols become banalized shortly after their release, and the turnover of appealing symbols must be speeded up. An elaborate study is outdated when a new one is made the next month. Thus the continual demand for new ideas—that is, acceptable ideas, attractive modes of statement of interests, passions, and hatreds.

III. The very size of the private powers that have emerged has made it necessary to work out new justifications for their exercise. Clearly the power of the modern corporation is not easily justifiable in terms of the simple democratic theory of sovereignty inherited from the eighteenth and nineteenth centuries. Many an intellectual earns a good income because of that fact. The whole growth of ideological work is based on the need for the vested interests lodged in the new power centers to be softened, whitened, blurred, misinterpreted to those who serve the interests of the bureaucracies inside, and to those in its sphere outside. Because of the funded wealth and centralized power, opinions must be funded and centralized into good will, which must be continually managed and sustained. The men at the helm of the managerial apparatus derive their self-esteem from their bureaucracies and hence need intellectuals to compose suitable myths, about them and it. In their relation to managers new entrepreneurs of various types have had their main chance; among these are many former intellectuals who have seen and taken that chance.

In the world of the small entrepreneur, power was decentralized and anonymous; it did not require a systematic ideological cement. In the new managed society, power is centralized and only anonymous when it is manipulative; one of the major tasks of its managers is ideological. Their problem is not easy; their search for new and compelling justifications might well be frenzied.

IV. Along with the break up of traditional sanctions, the speed-up in the competition of symbols, and the rise of new unsanctified powers, from the recurrent crises of war and slump which have beset modern society, deep fears and anxieties have spread. These have put new urgency into the search for adequate explanations for everyone directly involved. The middle classes, both old and new, seen as a bulwark of the new powers, are filled with anxieties and the need for new opinions of the new world in which they find themselves, or for diversion from it. It has been the intellectual's part to divert these intermediary strata and to keep them oriented in an appropriate manner despite their anxieties.

When irresponsible decisions prevail and values are not proportionately distributed, universal deception must be practiced by and for those who make the decisions and who have the most of what values there are to have. An increasing number of intellectually equipped men and women work within powerful bureaucracies and for the relatively few who do the deciding. If the intellectual is not directly hired by such an organization, he seeks by little steps and in self-deceptive as well as conscious ways, to have his published opinions conform to the limits set by the organizations and by those who are directly hired. In either case, the intellectual becomes a mouthpiece. There often seems to be no areas left between 'outright rebellion and grovelling sycophancy.'

Perhaps, in due course, intellectuals have at all times been drawn into line with either popular mentality or ruling class, and away from the urge to be detached; but now in the middle of the twentieth century, the recoil from detachment and the falling into line seem more organized, more solidly rooted in the centralization of power and its rationalization of modern society as a whole. If, as never before, intellectuals find it difficult to locate their masters in the impersonal machineries of authority in which they work, this, despite the anxieties it may at times cause them, makes more possible the postures of objectivity and integrity they continue to fancy.

4. The Rise of the Technician

The social developments centered upon the rise of bureaucracies and the ideological developments centered upon the continual demands for new justifications have coincided: together they increasingly determine the social position and ideological posture of the intellectual.

Busy with the ideological speed-up, the intellectual has readily taken on the responsibilities of the citizen. In many cases, having ceased to be in any sense a free intellectual, he has joined the expanding world of those who live off ideas, as administrator, idea-man, and good-will technician. In class, status, and self-image, he has become more solidly middle class, a man at a desk, married, with children, living in a respectable suburb, his career pivoting on the selling of ideas, his life a tight little routine, substituting middle-brow and mass culture for direct experience of his life and his world, and, above all, becoming a man with a job in a society where money is supreme.

In such an atmosphere, intellectual activity that does not have relevance to established money and power is not likely to be highly valued. In the 'capitalization of the spirit,' as George Lukács has remarked, talent and ideology become commodities. The writing of memoranda, telling others what to do, replaces the writing of books, telling others how it is. Cultural and intellectual products may be valued as ornaments but do not bring even ornamental value to their producers. The new pattern sets the anxious standards of economic value and social honor, making it increasingly difficult for such a man to escape the routine ideological panic of the managerial demiurge.

The scope and energy of these new developments, the spread of managed communications, and the clutch of bureaucracies have changed the social position of many intellectuals in America. Unlike some European countries, especially central and eastern Europe, the United States has not produced a sizable stratum of intellectuals, or even professionals, who have been unemployed long enough or under such conditions as to cause frustration among them. Unemployment among American intellectuals has been experienced as a cyclical phenomenon, not, as in some parts of Europe, as a seemingly permanent condition. The administrative expansion of the liberal state and the enormous growth of private-interest and communications bureaucracies have in fact multiplied opportunities for careers. It cannot be said that the intellectuals have cause for economic alarm, as yet. In fact, amazing careers have become legends among them. Having little or none of that resentment and hostility that arose in many European intellectual circles between the wars, American intellectuals have not, as an articulate group, become leaders for such discontented mass strata as may have become politically aware of their discontent. Perhaps they have become disoriented and estranged, from time to time, but they have not felt disinherited.

The ascendency of the technician over the intellectual in America is becoming more and more apparent, and seems to be taking place without many jolts. The U.S. novelist, artist, political writer is very good indeed at the jobs for which he is hired. 'What is fatal to the American writer,' Edmund Wilson has written, 'is to be brilliant at disgraceful or second-rate jobs . . . with the kind of American writer who has had no education to speak of, you are unable to talk at all once Hollywood or Luce has got him.' No longer, in Matthew Josephson's language, 'detached from the spirit of immediate gain,' no longer having a 'sense of being disinterested,' the intellectual is becoming a technician, an idea-man, rather than one who resists the environment, preserves the individual type, and defends himself from death-by-adaptation.

The intellectual who remains free may continue to learn more and more about modern society, but he finds the centers of political initiative less and less accessible. This generates a malady that is particularly acute in the intellectual who believed his thinking would make a difference. In the world of today the more his knowledge of affairs grows, the less impact his thinking seems to have. If he grows more frustrated as his knowledge increases, it seems that knowledge leads to powerlessness. He comes to feel helpless in the fundamental sense that he cannot control what he is able to foresee. This is not only true of his own attempts to act; it is true of the acts of powerful men whom he observes.

Such frustration arises, of course, only in the man who feels compelled to act. The 'detached spectator' does not feel his helplessness because he never tries to surmount it. But the political man is always aware that while events are not in his hands he must bear their consequences. He finds it increasingly difficult even to express himself. If he states public issues as he sees them, he cannot take seriously the slogans and confusions used by parties with a chance to win power. He therefore feels politically irrelevant. Yet if he approaches public issues 'realistically,' that is, in terms of the major parties, he inevitably so compromises their initial statement that he is not able to sustain any enthusiasm for political action and thought.

The political failure of nerve thus has a personal counterpart in the development of a tragic sense of life, which may be experienced as a personal discovery and a personal burden, but is also a reflection of objective circumstances. It arises from the fact that at the fountainheads of public decision there are powerful men who do not themselves suffer the violent results of their own decisions. In a world of big organizations the lines between powerful decisions and grass-roots democratic controls become blurred and tenuous, and seemingly irresponsible actions by individuals at the top are encouraged. The need for action prompts them to take decisions into their own hands, while the fact that they act as parts of large corporations or other organizations blurs the identification of personal responsibility. Their public views and political actions are, in this objective meaning of the word, irresponsible: the social corollary of their irresponsibility is the fact that others are dependent upon them and must suffer the consequence of their ignorance and mistakes, their self-deceptions and biased motives. The sense of tragedy in the intellectual who watches this scene is a personal reaction to the politics and economics of collective irresponsibility.

The shaping of the society he lives in and the manner in which he lives in it are increasingly political. That shaping has come to include the realms of intellect and of personal morality, which are now also subject to organization. Because of the expanded reach of politics, it is his own personal style of life and reflections he is thinking about when he thinks about politics.

The independent artist and intellectual are among the few remaining personalities presumably equipped to resist and to fight the stereotyping and consequent death of genuinely lively things. Fresh perception now involves the capacity to unmask and smash the stereotypes of vision and intellect with which modern communications swamp us. The worlds of mass-art and mass-thought are increasingly geared to the demands of power. That is why it is in politics that some intellectuals feel the need for solidarity and for a fulcrum. If the thinker does not relate himself to the value of truth in political struggle, he cannot responsibly cope with the whole of live experience.

As the channels of communication become more and more monopolized, and party machines and economic pressures, based on vested shams, continue to monopolize the chances of effective political organization, the opportunities to act and to communicate politically are minimized. The political intellectual is, increasingly, an employee living off the communication machineries which are based on the very opposite of what he would like to stand for.

Just as the bright young technicians and editors cannot face politics except as news and entertainment, so the remaining free intellectuals increasingly withdraw; the simple fact is that they lack the will. The external and internal forces that move them away from politics are too strong; they are pulled into the technical machinery, the explicit rationalization of intellect, or they go the way of personal lament.

Today there are many forms of escape for the free intellectuals from the essential facts of defeat and powerlessness, among them the cult of alienation and the fetish of objectivity. Both hide the fact of powerlessness and at the same time attempt to make that fact more palatable.

'Alienation,' as used in middle-brow circles, is not the old detachment of the intellectual from the popular tone of life and its structure of domination; it does not mean estrangement from the ruling powers; nor is it a phase necessary to the pursuit of truth. It is a lament and a form of collapse into self-indulgence.

It is a personal excuse for lack of political will. It is a fashionable way of being overwhelmed. In function, it is the literary counterpart to the cult of objectivity in the social sciences.

Objectivity or Scientism is often an academic cult of the narrowed attention, the pose of the technician, or the aspiring technician, who assumes as given the big framework and the political meaning of his operation within it. Often an unimaginative use of already plotted routines of life and work, 'objectivity' may satisfy those who are not interested in politics; but it is a specialized form of retreat rather than the intellectual orientation of a political man.

Both alienation and objectivity fall in line with the victory of the technician over the intellectual. They are fit moods and ideologies for intellectuals caught up in and overwhelmed by the managerial demiurge in an age of organized irresponsibility; signals that 'the job,' as sanction and as censorship, has come to embrace the intellectual; and that the political psychology of the scared employee has become relevant to understanding his work. Simply to understand, or to lament alienation—these are the ideals of the technician who is powerless and estranged but not disinherited. These are the ideals of men who have the capacity to know the truth but not the chance, the skill, or the fortitude, as the case may be, to communicate it with political effectiveness.

The defeat of the free intellectuals and the rationalization of the free intellect have been at the hands of an enemy who cannot be clearly defined. Even given the power, the free intellectuals could not easily find the way to work their will upon their situation, nor could they succeed in destroying its effect upon what they are, what they do, and what they want to become. They find it harder to locate their external enemies than to grapple with their internal conditions. Their seemingly impersonal defeat has spun a personally tragic plot and they are betrayed by what is false within them.

8

The Great Salesroom

In the world of the small entrepreneur, selling was one activity among many, limited in scope, technique, and manner. In the new society, selling is a pervasive activity, unlimited in scope and ruthless in its choice of technique and manner.

The salesman's world has now become everybody's world, and, in some part, everybody has become a salesman. The enlarged market has become at once more impersonal and more intimate. What is there that does not pass through the market? Science and love, virtue and conscience, friendliness, carefully nurtured skills and animosities? This is a time of venality. The market now reaches into every institution and every relation. The bargaining manner, the huckstering animus, the memorized theology of pep, the commercialized evaluation of personal traits—they are all around us; in public and in private there is the tang and feel of salesmanship.

1. Types of Salesmen

The American Salesman has gone through several major phases, each of which corresponds to a phase in the organization of the business system. This system is a vast and intricate network of institutions, each strand of which is a salesman of one sort or another. Any change in this system and of its relations to society as a whole will be reflected in the development of types of salesmen and of the kind of salesmanship that prevails.

When demand was generally greater than production, selling

occurred largely in a seller's market, and was in the main a more or less effortless matter of being in a certain place at a certain time in order to take an order. When demands balanced supplies the salesman as a means of distribution merely provided information. But when the pressure from the producer to sell became much greater than the capacity of the consumer to buy, the role of the salesman shifted into high gear. In the twentieth century, as surpluses piled up, the need has been for distribution to national markets; and with the spread of national advertising, co-extensive sales organizations have been needed to cash in on its effects.

When business firms were able to increase their output in an enlarging market, they could conveniently underbid one another; but in a contracted or closed market, they prefer not to compete in terms of price. It may be that lower prices, as many economists hold, are 'more effective . . . than the . . . methods of "aggressive"—and cost-increasing—salesmanship.' But in its way high-pressure selling is a substitute stimulator of demand, not by lowering prices but by creating new wants and more urgent desires. 'The business,' wrote Veblen, 'reduces itself to a traffic in salesmanship, running wholly on the comparative merit of . . . the rival salesmen.' Salesmanship in the United States has been made into a virtually autonomous force dependent only upon will, which keeps the economy in high-gear operation.

In the older world of the small entrepreneur there were storekeepers but few salesmen. After the Revolutionary War, there began to be traveling peddlers, whose markets were thin but widespread. By the middle of the nineteenth century the wholesaler—then the dominant type of entrepreneur—began to hire drummers or greeters, whose job it was to meet retailers and jobbers in hotels or saloons in the market centers of the city. Later, these men began to travel to the local markets. Then, as manufacturers replaced wholesalers as dominant powers in the world of business, their traveling agents joined the wholesalers.

Goods produced in the factory are transported to urban centers of consumption; there they pile up, and are unpiled into the market radius of the city. Without mass production, commodities cannot be accumulated to fill great stores. Without big cities there are no markets large enough and concentrated enough to support such stores. Without a transportation net, the goods produced cannot be picked up at scattered points and placed in the middle of the urban mass. Each of these is a center of the modern web-work of business and society.

On the other hand, the same conditions also make possible the smaller specialty shop—shops that sell only gloves or ties. In the history of modern trade, N. S. B. Gras observes, there seems to be a sort of oscillation between specialization and integration. An enterprise may specialize in terms of the lines of commodities that it handles, or in terms of the junctures of the economic circuit that it serves. It may handle many lines of merchandise or few; it may retail, wholesale, and manufacture, or it may perform only one of these functions. The oscillation of modern enterprise between specialization and integration involves lines of merchandise as well as economic functions. With some simplification, the historical rhythm of enterprise, as it involves the American store, may be outlined in this way: (1) In the eighteenth century, the market was small-scale and the ways of reaching it were primitive. There was little specialization and the small general store prevailed. (2) In the first half of the nineteenth century, specialization proceeded; by the mid years of the century the cities were full of specialty shops, each focusing on a narrow area of the enlarging market. They were mainly retail, and were advised, in the business lore of the time, to stick each to its own economic function. (3) For the last hundred years, the amalgamating, integrating tendency, of which the department store is a prime exemplar, has been on the upswing.

There are still trading posts in outlying areas, and general merchandise stores. Single-line or specialty shops still numerically dominate U.S. retailing. But the department store, the chain store, the mail order house—all principally types of this century—are most in tune with the new society.

Dependent as the economy is upon replacement markets and rapid turnover, obsolescence must be planned into the commodities produced, speeded up by the technique of marketing. The needs of salesmanship are thus geared even to the design of commodities; the chief concern of the industrial designers, the great packagers, is the appearance of commodities, changing colors, shapes, and names. The whole of fashion, not only in clothing, automobiles, and furniture, but in virtually all commodities, is deliberately managed to the end of greater sales volume. Fashion has become a rational attempt to exploit the status market for a greater turnover of goods. Behind the $126.3 billion worth of goods U.S. consumers bought in 1948 there lie not only the economic facts of need and exchange, but the social fact that U.S. society has in crucial aspects become a continuous fashion show.

The shift in economic emphasis from production to distribution has meant both the persistence of the old urban middle class, which is now located in distribution, and the expansion of considerable portions of the new middle class. Of the old middle class 19 per cent are directly involved in retail and wholesale selling. They are not captains of industry, but corporals of retailing. In the meantime, the era of big retailing has brought forth over 3 million white-collar people who are now directly involved in selling; in 1940, they were 6 per cent of the labor force, 14 per cent of the total middle class, 25 per cent of all white-collar people.

In terms of skills involved, sales personnel range from the salesmen who create and satisfy new desires, through salespeople who do not create desires or customers but wait for them, to the order-fillers who merely receive payment, make change, and wrap up what is bought. Some salesmen must know the technical details of complex commodities and their maintenance; others need know nothing about the simple commodities they sell.

In terms of social level, at the top of the sales hierarchy are the Prima Donna Vice-Presidents of corporations, who boast that they are merely salesmen, and at the bottom, the five-and-ten-cent-store girls who work for half days several months before they leave the job market for marriage. Near the top of the hierarchy are the Distribution Executives who design, organize, and direct the selling techniques of salesforces. Close to them are the absentee salesmen who create the slogans and images that spur sales from a distance by mass media.

In terms of where the sale is made, salespeople may be classified as stationary, mobile, or absentee. Stationary salespeople—
now about 60 per cent of the white-collar people involved in
selling—sell in stores, behind the counters. Mobile salesmen—now
about 38 per cent—make the rounds to the houses and offices of
the customers. They range from peddlers walking from door-to-
door, to 'commercial travelers' who fly to their formal appointments expertly made weeks in advance. Absentee salesmen—ad
men, now 2 per cent of all salespeople—manage the machineries
of promotion and advertising and are not personally present at
the point of the sale, but act as all-pervasive adjuncts to those
who are.

The national market has become an object upon which many
white-collar skills focus: the professional market researcher examines it intensively and extensively; the personnel man selects
and trains salesmen of a thousand different types for its exploitation; the manager studies the fine art of prompting men to 'go
get 'em.' As competition for restricted markets builds up, and
buyers' markets become more frequent, the pressure mounts in
the salesman's immediate domain. Psychologists bend their minds
to improving the technique of persuading people to commercial
decisions. Before high-pressure salesmanship, emphasis was upon
the salesmen's knowledge of the product, a sales knowledge
grounded in apprenticeship; after it, the focus is upon hypnotiz-
ing the prospect, an art provided by psychology.

The salesmen link up one unit of business society with another;
salesmanship is coextensive with the cash nexus of the modern
world. It is not only a marketing device, it is a pervasive apparatus of persuasion that sets a people's style of life. For all
types of marketing-entrepreneurs and white-collar salespeople,
in and out of stores, on the roads and in the air, are only the concentration points in the cadre of salesmanship. So deeply have
they infiltrated, so potent is their influence, that they may be
seen as a sort of official personnel of an all-pervasive atmosphere.
That is why we cannot understand salesmanship by studying
only salesmen. The American premium, we learn in *Babbitt*, is
not upon 'selling anything in particular for or to anybody in particular, but pure selling.' Now, salesmanship has become an
abstracted value, a science, an ideology and a style of life for a

society that has turned itself into a fabulous salesroom and be-become the biggest bazaar in the world.

2. The Biggest Bazaar in the World *

Fifty years ago, the Big Bazaar moved uptown to become one of the hubs of the megalopolis. When it moved, thirty-two build-ings, housing smaller and less independent establishments, had to be knocked down. Everybody said it was the biggest and the best bazaar in the world.

Its twenty-three acres of floor, each a square block, were built for ups and downs as well as for cross-floor movement. The esca-lators alone could lift and sink 40,000 people every hour. And all day long, folded money and slips of paper were shot through eighteen miles of brass tubing to end in the cartellized brain, the office center of the big bazaar.

Then, alongside the first square block, they built again and still again, the additions rearing up to dwarf the old beginning. Now there are almost fifty acres of floor, and off the island of Manhattan, there are thirty more acres where men and commodi-ties wait to move in on the biggest bazaar in the world.

Now there are 58 escalators, 29 elevators, and 105 conveyer belts; 26 freight lifts whisk loaded trucks from floor to floor; 75 miles of tubing carry the records of who bought it, who sold it, what it was, how much was paid, when did all this happen.

Still it cannot be contained: it reaches out to Ohio and San Francisco, to Alabama, Chicago, Rochester; it is a chain of chains of departments. And deep in its heart, they have a professional staff and ten clerks who sit every day figuring out the portentous question: Where will the next one be planted?

One hundred and eighty incoming telephones keep one hun-dred operators politely tired. If you can't come, phone; we also deliver. Out from the bazaar for fifty miles, our four hundred and ten vans carry the bazaar into your very home, leaving a little part of itself, making it a part of you.

* The typological statement in sections 2 and 3, which is modeled on large middle-class department stores in big cities, draws heavily upon Ralph M. Hower's excellent *History of Macy's of New York*, 1859-1919 (Cambridge: Harvard University Press, 1943).

Do you think the family is important to society? But the Big Bazaar feeds, clothes, amuses; it replaces families, in every respect but the single one of biological reproduction. From womb to grave, it watches over you, supplying the necessities and creating the unmet need. Back in the 'nineties, the Bazaar had begun to speak as the Universal Provider: 'Follow the crowd and it will always take/you to/ (The Big Bazaar). . . /The All Around Store. . . /Ride our bicycles,/ read our books, cook in our saucepans,/ dine off our china, wear our silks,/ get under our blankets, smoke our cigars,/ drink our wines . . . / and life will Cost You Less and Yield You More/Than You Dreamed Possible.'

Do you think factories are something to know about? But the Bazaar is a factory: it has taken unto itself the several phases of the economic circuit, and now contains them all. And it is also a factory of smiles and visions, of faces and dreams of life, surrounding people with the commodities for which they live, holding out to them the goals for which they struggle. What factory is geared so deep and direct with what people want and what they are becoming? Measured by space or measured by money, it is the greatest emporium in the world: it *is* a world—dedicated to commodities, run by committees and paced by floor-walkers.

It is hard to say who owns the Bazaar. It began when a petty capitalist left whaling ships for retail trade. Then it became a family business; some partners appeared, and they took over; now it is a corporation, and nobody owns more than 10 per cent. From a single proprietor to what, in the curious lingo of finance, is called the public. The eldest son of an eldest son has a lot of say-so about its workings, but if he went away, nobody doubts that it would go on: it is self-creative and self-perpetuating and nobody owns it.

But who runs it? Someone has to run it. At first one person did —knew all about it and owned it and ran it. Once a week this merchant stood in the middle of his store and read impressively and out loud the name of the clerk who had sold the most during the past week. From where he stood, he could see all the operations in each department of his store. But now there is no merchant and no place for such a merchant to stand, now a hundred people do what that man did. What one of them does is often secret to the others. It has become so impersonal at the top and bottom that a major problem is how to make it personal again, and still smooth-running and continuous.

There are managers of this and managers of that, and there are managers of managers, but when any one of them dies or disappears, it doesn't make any difference. The store goes on. It was created by people who did not know what they were creating; and now it creates people, who in turn do not know what they are creating. Every hour of the day it creates and destroys and re-creates itself, nobody knowing about it all but somebody knowing about every single part of it.

So the chaos you see is only apparent: nothing haphazard happens here. Things are under control; everything is accounted for; it is all in the files, and the committees know about the files, and other committees know about those committees.

In the cathedral, worship is organized; this is the cathedral of commodities, whispering and shouting for its 394,000 assorted gods (not including colors and sizes). In organizing the congregation, the Big Bazaar has been training it for faster and more efficient worship. Its most effective prayers have been formed in the ritual of the Great Repetition, a curious blending of piety and the barking of the circus.

The gods men worship determine how they live. Gods have always changed, but never before has their change been so well or so widely organized; never before has their worship been so universal and so devout. In organizing the fetishism of commodities, the Big Bazaar has made gods out of flux itself. Fashion used to be something for uptown aristocrats, and had mainly to do with deities of dress. But the Big Bazaar has democratized the idea of fashion to all orders of commodities and for all classes of worshipers. Fashion means faster turnover, because if you worship the new, you will be ashamed of the old. In its benevolence, the Big Bazaar has built the rhythmic worship of fashion into the habits and looks and feelings of the urban mass: it has organized the imagination itself. In dressing people up and changing the scenery of their lives, on the street and in the bedroom, it has cultivated a great faith in the Religion of Appearance.

Before the age of the Big Bazaar, these gods had no large-scale evangelist. The old fair and the little shop sat passive and still. Before there were quiet little notices, like those for birth or death, in close lines, somberly announcing what was available. But the Big Bazaar is the continuous evangelist for 394,000 commodities; every day it tempts 137,000 women; while 11,000 employees fill their ears with incantations, their innermost eyes with visions.

3. Buyers and Floorwalkers

The department store is not a continuation of the old general store, but a synthesis of general store and specialty shop. Fairs in the medieval West and bazaars in the Orient were many little shops under one roof, each under its own management and the total but a passing combination. The old general store was small and not organized by departments; peddlers grew up to become Woolworths, not Macy's. None of these quasi-prototypes provided the 'liberal services' that the department store often provides: free delivery, charge account, the return privilege, free rest room, information service.

The modern department store is a congeries of little hierarchies, which in turn sum up to the store as a whole. It is a curious blend of decentralized organs and intricate centralizing nerves. Departments are organized along commodity lines, each with its own managers, all knit firmly together by a financial and personnel network. By watching the running balance of outgo and yield, the accounting system keeps alert to the work of each department. The big store is departmentalized by commodities and centralized by accounting.

In the last quarter of the nineteenth century the owners or their top managers worked through a superintendent, who was in charge of the placement of employees, the movement of goods, and general maintenance. Below him and his office's circle, managerial responsibility ran along merchandise lines, each department keeping its own accounts.

At the head of each department was a buyer, who was responsible for what was for sale at any given time, the manner in which it was sold, the terms and the turnover of goods, and the resultant profits.

Alongside the buyer, who handled merchandise and money, was the floorwalker, who handled customers and salesclerks. His language was the language of service, his aim the union for profit of customer and clerk. The floorwalker-manager, now often known as a service or section manager, watched the clerks and the cash girls, served as timekeeper, checked the employees in and out of the store, enforced a disciplined politeness, and, as an expert at softening complaints, approved or rejected refunds and exchanges.

Relations between buyers and floorwalkers were not always cordial. It was the floorwalker's consistent 'care not to displease the all-powerful and often crotchety buyers.' Formally, the top superintendent was supposed to hire and fire salespeople, the floorwalker 'to keep them in order.' But actually, 'the buyer's voice was usually the deciding one.' Since he was responsible for the turnover of goods at a profit, he directed the selling operations of his department. The buyer was the point of intersection between the rules of the bureaucracy and the chance calculation of the unrationalized market.

By 1900, with many departments in the store, the firm began to bring in a new type of personnel, men and women trained in colleges rather than in little retail shops; bookkeeping became a tool for the systematic analysis of operations, rather than mere historical record. Committees began to co-ordinate, operations were standardized, all under a control from above. In this centralization, the authority of the buyer, although not his responsibility, has been minimized. As a result, the buyer often becomes a pocket of anxiety, often being blamed 'if the departmental operations were considered unsatisfactory, even if the trouble was actually beyond his control.'

By World War I, the department store was almost entirely run by central plan, the execution of which was watched and checked by central agents. Buyers were managed through a social club, the 'Managers' Association'; a 'Board of Operations' and an 'Advisory Council,' containing all top people, further completed the bureaucratic reorganization, 'so that it would function continuously without depending upon the presence of any one person.' By a series of small developments, the Controller's Office began to allocate expenses, direct and indirect, to each buyer and his department, to take over more and more decisions. The buyer was watched, coached, and ordered by committees and boards; his decisions about the merchandise were expropriated. No longer the lord of a small domain in feudalism, the buyer became a higher-salaried employee in a bureaucracy.

The floorwalker, too, like the industrial foreman, began to lose many of his functions, in particular the training of new salespeople. By 1915 a separate training organization, which taught the rules of the store and the merchandise to be handled, was set up. No longer did the floorwalker preside over small weekly staff meetings in each department, where 'matters of store discipline, courtesy to customer, and related topics' were discussed. In 1911, the Board of Operations, analyzing its statistics, 'offered clerks ten cents for every error they detected in credit slips made out by floorwalkers. . .'

In the 'nineties, the middle management of buyers and floorwalkers and other minor executives often seemed to be 'poorly educated and hardened by failure and adversity,' and according to some contemporary observers, even 'never wholly reliable, constantly shifting from one store to another in search of a "real opportunity" which could never materialize for them, they often sought consolation in the bottle. Indeed, one of the management's problems in this period was the buyer or floorwalker who went out to lunch and failed to return or came back too drunk to be tolerated on the selling floor. At least one young clerk won promotion through his ability to act as substitute on such occasions,' thus confirming the linkage of virtue and success.

But in the twentieth century, the 'scientific selection and training of personnel' replaced haphazard hiring as the store began systematically 'to seek college graduates as material for the organization they were building'; and to expand the training program for these employees, so as to draw from their own carefully selected ranks people for higher positions. After World War I, this new personnel program replaced the old pattern of employing executives from other, usually smaller, establishments, where they had acquired merchandising experience. Before, the 'primary qualification for the job was merchandise experience'; now, the prerequisites were 'formal training and general cultural background.' College people, entering the store when relatively young, can be provided with the experience necessary for higher posts. Today, 'A large proportion of the executives . . . are persons who were selected and trained 15 or 20 years ago for the very positions they now hold.'

The department store has thus built into itself a career pattern; it selects applicants carefully on each level; then its own elevators grind slowly upward with them, ascent being made possible by death and turnover and being impelled by individual ambition. The files of the personnel manager and the accounts of the controller's office have replaced the store-to-store jumping and the chances on the open market.

4. The Salesgirls

One of the most crucial changes in the work-life of salesgirls over the last decades is the shift in their relation to customers. What has occurred may be gauged by comparing the outlook of (i) salespeople in small and middle-sized cities, with (ii) salesgirls in big metropolitan stores.

i. Salespeople, as well as small merchants in the small city, are often proud to say that they know well most of the people they serve. Their work satisfactions spring directly from this experience of the personally known market, from a communalization not with their superiors or bosses, but with the customers.

In the small towns, salespeople feel they are learning human nature at a gossip center. 'I like meeting the public; it broadens your views on life,' one saleslady in her late fifties in a medium-sized jewelry store says. 'I would not take anything for the knowledge I have gained of human nature through my contacts as a saleslady.' This theme of 'learning about human nature' is explicitly connected with the small, personally known character of the market. Again, the comments of a forty-year-old clerk in a small grocery store: 'Meeting the people, I actually make friends in a neighborhood store, because I know their family problems as well as their likes and dislikes,' and, 'I gain from my customers . . . confidences which brings a certain satisfaction in being of help.'

Both salesladies in department stores and women owners of small stores borrow prestige from customers. One saleslady in a medium-sized department store says: 'I like most meeting the public and being associated with the type of customer with whom I come in contact. The majority of my customers are very high type; they are refined and cultured.' A few of the salespeople also borrow prestige from the stores in which they work, some even from handling the merchandise itself. 'I like the displays and the connection with fine china and silverware.'

The power to change people, an attitude that may be considered the opposite of borrowing prestige from the customer, also permits satisfaction. 'I like the satisfaction I secure in my work in improving my customer's appearance,' says a cosmetic-counter woman of about forty. 'I have some very homely customers, as far as physical features are concerned, whom I have transformed into very attractive women.'

Many salespeople try to bring out the human aspect of their work by expressing an ideology of 'service.' This ideology is often anchored (1) in the feeling of being worth while: 'It is a pleasure to serve them. It makes you feel you are necessary and doing something worth while'; (2) in the borrowing of prestige from customers; (3) in the feeling of gaining knowledge of human nature; (4) in the tacit though positive identification with the store itself or with its owner. Such elements form the occupational ideology of salespeople in smaller cities; each rests upon and assumes a small and personally known market—the aspect of their work that is primarily responsible for the main features of their ideology. For the emphasis upon the 'handling of people' brings to the fore precisely the experience that wage and factory workers do not have.

II. Salesgirls in large department stores of big cities often attempt to borrow prestige from customers, but in the big store of strangers, the attempt often fails, and, in fact, sometimes boomerangs into a feeling of powerless depression. The hatred of customers, often found in an intense form, is one result; the customer becomes the chief target of hostility; for she is an ostensible source of irritation, and usually a safe target.

Salesgirls in the big city store may be possessive of their own 'regular customers' and jealous of other's, but still when wealthier customers leave the store there is often much 'pulldown' talk about them, and obvious envy. 'The main thing we talk about,' says a salesgirl, 'is the customers. After the customers go we mimic them.' Salesgirls often attempt identification with customers but often are frustrated. One must say 'attempt' identification because: (1) Most customers are strangers, so that contact is brief. (2) Class differences are frequently accentuated by the sharp and depressing contrast between home and store, customer, or commodity. 'You work among lovely things which you can't buy, you see prosperous, comfortable people who can buy it. When you go home with your [low pay] you do not feel genteel or anything but humiliated. You either half starve on your own or go home to mama, as I do, to be supported.' (3) Being 'at their service,' 'waiting on them,' is not conducive to easy and gratifying identification. Caught at the point of intersection between big store and urban mass, the salesgirl is typically engrossed in seeing the customer as her psychological enemy, rather than the store as her economic enemy.

Today salesgirls for big stores are selected from hundreds of thousands of applicants, who are chiefly women between 18 and 30 years of age. Some are merely waiting to marry; others are older women without marriage prospects; some are permanent full-time employees; others are temporary or part-time. As a mobile labor market, the department store is not very secure for the full-time regular worker, broken as it is by the vacationing college girl, the housewife, and the girl just out of high school still living at home, none of whom must make a regular living.

Out of this variety of women, and the interplay of individual with the store and the flow of customers, a range of sales personalities develops. Here is one such typology, based upon James B. Gale's prolonged and intensive observations in big stores.

The Wolf prowls about and pounces upon potential customers: 'I go for the customer. . . Why should I wait for them

to come to me when I can step out in the aisles and grab them?
The customers seem to like it; it gives them a feeling of importance. I like it; it keeps me on my toes, builds up my salesbook
. . . the buyer likes it too. . . Every well-dressed customer,
cranky or not, looks like a five-dollar bill to me.'

Intensified, the wolf becomes *The Elbower,* who is bent upon
monopolizing all the customers. While attending to one, she
answers the questions of a second, urges a third to be patient,
and beckons to a fourth from the distance. Sometimes she will
literally elbow her sales colleagues out of the way. Often she is
expert in distinguishing the looker or small purchaser from the
big purchaser. 'I had to develop a rough-house technique here
in order to make the necessary commissions. I just couldn't waste
time with people who didn't want to buy but who were just kill-
ing time. And, after all, why waste time? Why should I bother
with the pikers? Let the new clerks cut their teeth on them. Why
waste good selling time with the folks who can't make up their
mind, the ones who want to tell you their life-history, the bargain
wolves, the advice-seekers, and the "I'm just looking" boobs? I
want the women who buy three pairs of shoes at a time, stock-
ings to go with them, and maybe slippers, too. I believe I can
satisfactorily wait on five at a time, and keep them happy, so
I wait on five! Look at my salesbook and note the total for the
first five hours today. Traffic is good. . .'

The Charmer focuses the customer less upon her stock of
goods than upon herself. She attracts the customer with modu-
lated voice, artful attire, and stance. 'It's really marvelous what
you can do in this world with a streamlined torso and a brilliant
smile. People do things for me, especially men when I give them
that slow smile and look up through my lashes. I found that out
long ago, so why should I bother about a variety of selling techniques when one technique will do the trick? I spend most of my
salary on dresses which accentuate all my good points. After all,
a girl should capitalize on what she has, shouldn't she? And you'll
find the answer in my commission total each week.'

The Ingénue Salesgirl is often not noticed; it is part of her
manner to be self-effacing. Still ill at ease and often homesick,
still confused by trying to apply just-learned rules to apparent
chaos, she finds a way out by attaching herself like a child

to whoever will provide support. 'Everything here is so big. There are so many confusing rules. . . A lot of customers scare me. They expect too much for their money. If it wasn't for Miss B. I'd have to quit. . . When I make errors, she laughs and straightens me out; she shows me how the cash register runs; and yesterday she spoke severely to a customer who was bullying me . . . Handling so much money and so many sales-checks and remembering so many rules; and not being able to wear any pretty dresses, just blue, grey, black, brown—all this gets me down. At the end of the day I'm mostly a nervous wreck. Oh, for those easy days at high school. . .'

The Collegiate, usually on a part-time basis from a local campus, makes up in her impulsive amateurishness for what she lacks in professional restraint. Usually she is eager to work and fresh for the job, a more self-confident type of ingénue.

The Drifter may be found almost anywhere in the big store except at her assigned post; she is a circulating gossip, concerned less with customers and commodities than with her colleagues. When criticized for her style of floor behavior, she replies: 'I'm different from a lot of the clerks here, and I have a restless energy driving me all the time. I just can't stay here at my counter like an elephant chained to a post, day in and day out. I like people; I have friends all around the floor; and I want to tell them occasionally what I do and think and feel, and listen to their ideas too. I sell my share, don't I? I have good sales volume, don't I? I have to move around or I'll go crazy.'

The Social Pretender, well known among salesgirls, attempts to create an image of herself not in line with her job, usually inventing a social and family background. She says she is selling temporarily for the experience, and soon will take up a more glittering career. This may merely amuse her older sales colleagues, but it often pleases the buyer, who may notice that the social pretender sometimes attracts wealthy customers to her counter. A plain-clothes man in a big store said: 'That gal S—— O—— amuses me because she's so cute and such a phony too. . . She poses here as a girl from a well-to-do family who wants to sell just long enough to catch the selling spirit, then become an assistant buyer long enough to get a good flair for style, and then flutter back to her family's gold-plated bosom and on to a wealthy marriage. She was telling one of her side-kicks there this morning that she "didn't need the money; this was just an exciting proletariat experience" for her. Experience, my eye! She needs the dough and needs it badly or I miss my guess. At that, though, she gives a damn good imitation of one of those spoiled Park Avenue darlings . . .. keep your eye open for these phonies; you'll see a couple in every department.'

The Old-Timer, with a decade or more of experience in the store, becomes either a disgruntled rebel or a completely accommodated saleswoman. In either case, she is the backbone of the salesforce, the cornerstone around which it is built. As a rebel, the old-timer seems to focus upon neither herself nor her merchandise, but upon the store: she is against its policies, other personnel, and often she turns her sarcasm and rancor upon the customer. Many salesgirls claim to hate the store and the customers; the rebel enjoys hating them, in fact, she lives off her hatred, although she can be quick to defend the store to a customer. Older women, who have transferred from one department to another, make up the majority of this type. 'In those days the customers were nearly all ladies and gentlemen, really different from these phonies that come in here today from all around. They scream about the merchandise and scream about the service, and I just give 'em a deadpan face and a chilly stare, and ignore them. When I get good and ready I wait on them. I get sick of listening to them. I also get tired of hearing talk about the rules and the regulations; I even get tired of eating the half-cooked food they toss at me in the cafeteria after standing in line twenty minutes while [some people] try to decide whether to have kale or alfalfa for their noon roughage. Yes, there is a lot of change here, but nothing really new: just the same old rules and same old stuff about selling approaches and customer types —old stuff, I say, with different words, more angles, new bosses. Every boss I ever had here pushed me around until now I take it almost as a matter of course.' 'The buyer just hates me but I've been here so long there isn't much he can do about it. As long as my sales volume keeps up—and it's always been very good—he can only criticize me on small stuff. Buyers and I never did get along very well, and I've seen a lot of them come and go. They want this and then they want that and after that it's something else, always carping around about one thing or another. I often wonder if they believe it themselves. . . They burn me up with their "new selling techniques" and all the rest of that crap. After seventeen years here I don't need advice or instruction in selling ways. They aren't kidding me; I've had their number for years. The present buyer isn't kidding me either. He goes for youth and the stream-lined torso. . . To hell with all of them—I work for me first, last, always; and the customers and the store can take it and like it. You ask me then why I stay here. I'm not sure I could do anything else. I get up, I wash and dress and eat, and I put on my things and come to Macy's. It's almost automatic; in fact several times I did all that on Sundays, once actually getting as far as the train before I came to and realized it was Sunday. Just an old fire-horse listening for the bell, that's me.'

The accommodated old-timer has become gentle and complacent. 'I came here, as part-time help, one November in the Christmas season. I have been very happy here and have never wanted to leave here or to work in any other store. . . Last year I got my Twenty-Five-Year-Club pin; it makes me feel like someone and it looks nice with this blue dress, doesn't it? . . . That's not bad, is it, for an old lady putting her daughter through school. This store and my daughter are my whole life. See that young girl over there. . . She's a new girl, and she reminds me of my Jennie. I am sponsoring her; you know, teaching her the ropes, showing her how to get started correctly. I like that; I sponsor nearly all the new people in the department. I teach them that we have a fine department in a fine store, and that the customer is important, because, after all, if it wasn't for the customers, none of us would have our nice jobs here.'

5. The Centralization of Salesmanship

Salesmanship seems a frenzied affair of flexibility and pep; the managerial demiurge, a cold machinery of calculation and planning. Yet the conflict between them is only on the surface: in the new society, salesmanship is much too important to be left to pep alone or to the personal flair of detached salesmen. Since the first decade of the century, much bureaucratic attention has been given to the gap between mass production and individual consumption. Salesmanship is an attempt to fill that gap. In it, as in material fabrication, large-scale production has been instituted, in the form of reliable salespeople and willing customers. The dominant motive has been to lower the costs of selling per head; the dominant technique, to standardize and rationalize the processes of salesmanship, not only in the obvious sense of mass retailing in department stores, but in the technique and organization of selling everywhere.

In selling, as elsewhere, centralization has meant the expropriation of certain traits previously found in creative salesmen, by a machinery that codifies these traits and controls their acquisition and display by individual salesmen. The rise of absentee selling, rooted in the mass media, has done much to spur these centralizing and rationalizing trends. From the very beginning, absentee selling, being expensive, has been in the hands of top management, which has had its use studied, probably more carefully than any other activity in modern society.

In the 1850's, one large store in Philadelphia began to letter all departments, and to number each row on each shelf. From the proprietor's desk tubes ran to every department: from each department, pages ran with parcels and money and bills to the cashier's cage and back to the seller's counter. No salesperson needed to leave his station; from his position at the center, the proprietor could, at any time, a contemporary observer states, 'form a just estimate of the relative value of the services of each, in proportion to his salary,' and thus 'to speak understandingly of the capabilities and business qualities of any of his employees.' In New York, at about the same time, a proprietor wrote: 'There is but one mark on the Goods, and that is the selling mark, and no clerk in my store knows any other mark but that.' This meant that both clerk and customer were expropriated of higgling and bargaining.

All along the line, the entrepreneurial aspects of the salesclerk's role have been expropriated by the rationalized division of labor. If the entrepreneur himself does not sell, he has to have one price; he cannot trust clerks to bargain successfully. One-price is part of the bureaucratization of salesmanship. It also is fair to the customer, who is also bureaucratized and cannot higgle. All are equal before the machine of salesmanship, and things are under control.

The detached creative salesman is disappearing and the man who is taking his place is neither detached nor so creative in the old sense. Small-scale retailing, of course, continues with its handicraft methods of creating and maintaining the customer, but in the big store, and on the road, the role of the individual salesperson has been circumscribed and standardized in every possible feature, and thus the salesperson has been made highly replaceable. The old 'manufacturer's representative,' who sold to retailers and wholesalers, was supervised very little; he was on his own in manner and even in territory. The new commercial traveler is one unit in an elaborate marketing organization. What he says and what he can't say is put down for him in his sales manual. Even though he feels that he is a man with a proposition looking for someone to tie it to, his very presentation of proposition, product, and self is increasingly given to him, increasingly standardized and tested. Sales executives, representing the force that is centralizing and rationalizing salesmanship, have moved to the top levels of the big companies. The brains in salesmanship, the personal flair, have been centralized from scattered individuals and are now managed by those who standardize and test the presentation which the salesmen memorize and adapt.

It used to be, and still is in many cases, that the man on the road could become a virtual prima donna of the organization: in the end the success of the business depended on him and if he could capture a given set of important customers he might high-jack his company with the threat of taking himself and these customers to another company. Rationalization is in part an attempt to meet this threat. The vice president of one large company, in speaking of the status and power of such salesmen and the threat they may come to have over a company, says: 'The first thing I'm going to do is to make up a presentation, with clear charts and telling slogans. Maybe it will be a turnover booklet, maybe even a sound film. Then I'm going to hire me a bunch of salaried men and teach them how to show this presentation. They can still get in the personal adaptation of it to different clients they're handling, but they will damn well give that presentation the way I want it given and there's not going to be any high-priced prima-donna stuff about that. I'll pay plenty to have the presentation made and tested; I'll get experts and pay them expert's salaries on that, but every salesman isn't going to be paid like an expert.'

It is, of course, precisely with such 'presentations' that advertising crosses the personal arts of salesmanship. But advertising of every sort is also an adjunct of the salesman, which at times threatens to displace many of his skills. Selling becomes a pervasive process, of which the personal salesman, crucial though he may be, is only one link.

If selling is broken down into its component steps, it becomes clear that the first three—contacting, arousing interest, creating preference—are now done by advertising. Two final steps are left to the salesman: making the specific proposal, and closing the order. The better the first three jobs are done by the absentee salesman, the more the salesman can concentrate on the two pay-off jobs. But as the presentation and the visual aids move in they displace the personal flair of the salesman even in the pay-off jobs. Moreover, the salesman himself becomes an object of standardization in the way he is selected and trained, so that his personal development as a salesman becomes subject to centralized control.

Selling was once an aspect of the artisan's or farmer's role; the sale was an integral but not very important aspect of the whole craft or job. With specialization some men began to do nothing but sell, although they were still related by ownership to the commodities they handled. They judged the market and higgled over the price, selling or not selling as they themselves decided.

As the organization of the market becomes tighter, the salesman loses autonomy. He sells the goods of others, and has nothing to do with the pricing. He is alienated from price fixing and product selection. Finally, the last autonomous feature of selling, the art of persuasion and the sales personality involved, becomes expropriated from the individual salesman. Such has been the general tendency and drift, in the store as well as on the road.

6. The Personality Market

In the world of the small entrepreneur, men sold goods to one another; in the new society of employees, they first of all sell their services. The employer of manual services buys the workers' labor, energy, and skill; the employer of many white-collar services, especially salesmanship, also buys the employees' social personalities. Working for wages with another's industrial property involves a sacrifice of time, power, and energy to the employer; working as a salaried employee often involves in addition the sacrifice of one's self to a multitude of 'consumers' or clients or managers. The relevance of personality traits to the often monotonous tasks at hand is a major source of 'occupational disability,' and requires that in any theory of 'increasing misery' attention be paid to the psychological aspects of white-collar work.

In a society of employees, dominated by the marketing mentality, it is inevitable that a personality market should arise. For in the great shift from manual skills to the art of 'handling,' selling, and servicing people, personal or even intimate traits of the employee are drawn into the sphere of exchange and become of commercial relevance, become commodities in the labor market. Whenever there is a transfer of control over one individual's personal traits to another for a price, a sale of those traits which affect one's impressions upon others, a personality market arises.

The shift from skills with things to skills with persons; from small, informal, to large, organized firms; and from the intimate local markets to the large anonymous market of the metropolitan area—these have had profound psychological results in the white-collar ranks.

One knows the salesclerk not as a person but as a commercial mask, a stereotyped greeting and appreciation for patronage; one need not be kind to the modern laundryman, one need only pay him; he, in turn, needs only to be cheerful and efficient. Kindness and friendliness become aspects of personalized service or of public relations of big firms, rationalized to further the sale of something. With anonymous insincerity the Successful Person thus makes an instrument of his own appearance and personality.

There are three conditions for a stabilized personality market: First, an employee must be part of a bureaucratic enterprise, selected, trained, and supervised by a higher authority. Second, from within this bureaucracy, his regular business must be to contact the public so as to present the firm's good name before all comers. Third, a large portion of this public must be anonymous, a mass of urban strangers.

The expansion of distribution, the declining proportion of small independent merchants, and the rise of anonymous urban markets mean that more and more people are in this position. Salespeople in large stores are of course under rules and regulations that stereotype their relations with the customer. The salesperson can only display pre-priced goods and persuade the acceptance of them. In this task she uses her 'personality.' She must remember that she 'represents' the 'management'; and loyalty to that anonymous organization requires that she be friendly, helpful, tactful, and courteous at all times. One of the floorwalker's tasks is to keep the clerks friendly, and most large stores employ 'personnel shoppers' who check up and make reports on clerks' 'personality.'

Many salesgirls are quite aware of the 'difference between what they really think of the customer and how they must act toward her. The smile behind the counter is a commercialized lure. Neglect of personal appearance on the part of the employee is a form of carelessness on the part of the business management. 'Self-control' pays off. 'Sincerity' is detrimental to one's job, until the rules of salesmanship and business become a 'genuine' aspect of oneself. Tact is a series of little lies about one's feelings, until one is emptied of such feelings. 'Dignity' may be used only to make a customer feel that she shouldn't ask the price too soon or fail to buy the wares. Dixon Wector, who writes that 'It has justly been remarked that the filling station attendant has done more to raise the standard of courtesy en masse in the United States than all the manuals of etiquette,' does not see that this is an impersonal ceremonial, having little to do psychologically with old-fashioned 'feeling for another.'

In the formulas of 'personnel experts,' men and women are to be shaped into the 'well-rounded, acceptable, effective personality.' Just like small proprietors, the model sales employees com-

pete with one another in terms of services and 'personality';
but unlike proprietors, they cannot higgle over prices, which
are fixed, or 'judge the market' and accordingly buy wisely. Experts judge the market and specialists buy the commodities. The
salesgirl cannot form her character by promotional calculations
and self-management, like the classic heroes of liberalism or the
new entrepreneurs. The one area of her occupational life in which
she might be 'free to act,' the area of her own personality, must
now also be managed, must become the alert yet obsequious instrument by which goods are distributed.

In the normal course of her work, because her personality becomes the instrument of an alien purpose, the salesgirl becomes
self-alienated. In one large department store, a planted observer
said of one girl: 'I have been watching her for three days now.
She wears a fixed smile on her made-up face, and it never varies,
no matter to whom she speaks. I never heard her laugh spontaneously or naturally. Either she is frowning or her face is
devoid of any expression. When a customer approaches, she immediately assumes her hard, forced smile. It amazes me because,
although I know that the smiles of most salesgirls are unreal,
I've never seen such calculation given to the timing of a smile.
I myself tried to copy such an expression, but I am unable to
keep such a smile on my face if it is not sincerely and genuinely
motivated.'

The personality market is subject to the laws of supply and
demand: when a 'seller's market' exists and labor is hard to buy,
the well-earned aggressions of the salespeople come out and
jeopardize the good will of the buying public. When there is a
'buyer's market' and jobs are hard to get, the salespeople must
again practice politeness. Thus, as in an older epoch of capitalism, the laws of supply and demand continue to regulate the
intimate life-fate of the individual and the kind of personality
he may develop and display.

Near the top of the personality markets are the new entrepreneurs and the bureaucratic fixers; at the bottom are the people
in the selling ranks. Both the new entrepreneurs and the sales
personalities serve the bureaucracies, and each, in his own way,
practices the creative art of selling himself. In a restricted market

economy, salesmanship is truly praised as a creative act, but, as more alert chieftains have long been aware, it is entirely too serious a matter to be trusted to mere creativity. The real opportunities for rationalization and expropriation are in the field of the human personality. The fate of competition and the character it will assume depend upon the success or failure of the adventures of monopolists in this field.

Mass production standardizes the merchandise to be sold; mass distribution standardizes the prices at which it is to be sold. But the consumers are not yet altogether standardized. There must be a link between mass production and individual consumption. It is this link that the salesman tries to connect. On the one hand, his selling techniques are mapped out for him, but on the other, he must sell to individuals. Since the consumer is usually a stranger, the salesman must be a quick 'character analyst.' And he is instructed in human types and how to approach each: If a man is phlegmatic, handle him with deliberation; if sensitive, handle him with directness; if opinionated, with deference; if open-minded, with frankness; if cautious, handle him with proof. But there are some traits common to all mankind, and hence certain general methods of handling any type: 'we refer now to a certain spirit of fraternity, courtesy, and altruism.'

The area left open for the salesman's own creativity, his own personality, is now the area into which the sales executives and psychologists have begun to move. This personal equation is stressed by them, but as it is stressed it is rationalized into the high-powered sales-personality itself: 'The time has come,' it was written in the middle 'twenties, 'when the salesman himself must be more efficiently developed.' Men must be developed who have the positive mental attitude. Their thoughts must 'explode into action.' 'The mind of the quitter always has a negative taint.' The high-powered sales-personality is a man 'who sees himself doing it.' 'Never harbor a thought unless you wish to generate motor impulses toward carrying it out. . . No one can prevent such thoughts from arising in the mind. They spring up automatically. But we need not entertain them. . . Reject them absolutely. . .' 'It means simply a quiet, persistent choice to think affirmatively and act accordingly. . . Fritz Kreisler practices six hours each day to maintain his technique upon the violin. Is it not worth while for the salesman to practice every day upon that most marvelous instrument, the mind, in order that he may achieve success?' The high-powered personality gets that way by fixing healthy positive ideas in his consciousness and then manipulating himself so that they sink into his subconscious mind: '. . . when one is alone amid quiet and restful surroundings . . . preferably just before going to sleep . . . the doorway . . . into the subconscious seems to be more nearly ajar than at any other time. If at that time one will repeat over and over again an affirmation of health, vigor, vital energy, and success, the idea will eventually obtain lodgement in the subconscious mind. . .'

Employers again and again demand the selection of men with personality. A survey of employment offices made by a university indicated that 'the college graduate with a good personality . . . will have the best chance of being hired by business. . . Moreover, personality will be more important than high grades for all positions except those in technical and scientific fields.' The traits considered most important in the personnel literature are: 'ability to get along with people and to work co-operatively with them, ability to meet and talk to people easily, and attractiveness in appearance.'

In the literature of vocational guidance, personality often actually replaces skill as a requirement: a personable appearance is emphasized as being more important in success and advancement than experience or skill or intelligence. 'In hiring girls to sell neckwear, personal appearance is considered to outweigh previous experience.' 'Personality pays dividends that neither hard work nor sheer intelligence alone can earn for the average man.' In a recent study of graduates of Purdue University, 'better intelligence paid only $150.00 a year bonuses, while personality paid more than six times that much in return for the same period and with the same men.'

The business with a personality market becomes a training place for people with more effective personalities. Hundreds of white-collar people in the Schenley Distillers Corporation, for example, took a personality course in order to learn 'greater friendliness . . . and warmer courtesy . . . and genuine interest in helping the caller at the reception desk.' As demand increases, public schools add courses that attempt to meet the business demand 'for workers with a pleasant manner.' Since business leaders hold that 'a far greater percentage of personnel lose their jobs because of personality difficulties than because of ineffi- ciency,' the course features 'training in attitudes of courtesy, thoughtfulness and friendliness; skills of voice control . . .' et cetera. In Milwaukee, a 'Charm School' was recently set up for city employees to teach them in eight one-hour classes 'the art of pleasant, courteous, prompt and efficient service.' Every 'step in every public contact' is gone into and the employees are taught how to greet and listen to people.

Elaborate institutional sets-ups thus rationally attempt to pre- pare people for the personality market and sustain them in their attempt to compete on it successfully. And from the areas of salesmanship proper, the requirements of the personality market have diffused as a style of life. What began as the public and commercial relations of business have become deeply personal: there is a public-relations aspect to private relations of all sorts, including even relations with oneself. The new ways are diffused by charm and success schools and by best-seller literature. The sales personality, built and maintained for operation on the per- sonality market, has become a dominating type, a pervasive model for imitation for masses of people, in and out of selling. The literature of self-improvement has generalized the traits and tactics of salesmanship for the population at large. In this litera- ture all men can be leaders. The poor and the unsuccessful simply do not exist, except by an untoward act of their own will.

'A new aristocracy is springing up in the world today, an aris- tocracy of personal charm,' each of whose members treats every- one else as his superior, while repeating to himself that he is the biggest and most important man in the world. It is a magnetic society where every man is not only his own executive but secretly, everyone else's too.*

The personality market, the most decisive effect and symptom of the great salesroom, underlies the all-pervasive distrust and

* These statements are based on a thematic examination of seven or eight inspirational books, including Dale Carnegie's classic, *How to Win Friends and Influence People*.

self-alienation so characteristic of metropolitan people. Without common values and mutual trust, the cash nexus that links one man to another in transient contact has been made subtle in a dozen ways and made to bite deeper into all areas of life and relations. People are required by the salesman ethic and convention to pretend interest in others in order to manipulate them. In the course of time, and as this ethic spreads, it is got on to. Still, it is conformed to as part of one's job and one's style of life, but now with a winking eye, for one knows that manipulation is inherent in every human contact. Men are estranged from one another as each secretly tries to make an instrument of the other, and in time a full circle is made: one makes an instrument of himself, and is estranged from It also.

9

The Enormous File

As skyscrapers replace rows of small shops, so offices replace free markets. Each office within the skyscraper is a segment of the enormous file, a part of the symbol factory that produces the billion slips of paper that gear modern society into its daily shape. From the executive's suite to the factory yard, the paper webwork is spun; a thousand rules you never made and don't know about are applied to you by a thousand people you have not met and never will. The office is the Unseen Hand become visible as a row of clerks and a set of IBM equipment, a pool of dictaphone transcribers, and sixty receptionists confronting the elevators, one above the other, on each floor.

The office is also a place of work. In the morning irregular rows of people enter the skyscraper monument to the office culture. During the day they do their little part of the business system, the government system, the war-system, the money-system, co-ordinating the machinery, commanding each other, persuading the people of other worlds, recording the activities that make up the nation's day of work. They transmit the printed culture to the next day's generation. And at night, after the people leave the skyscrapers, the streets are empty and inert, and the hand is unseen again.

The office may be only a bundle of papers in a satchel in the back of somebody's car; or it may be a block square, each floor a set of glass rabbit warrens, the whole a headquarters for a nation-wide organization of other offices, as well as plants and mines and even farms. It may be attached to one department, division, or unit, tying it to another office which acts as the command post for all the offices in the enterprise as a whole. And some enterprises, near the administrative centers of the economic file, are nothing more than offices.

But, however big or little and whatever the shape, the minimum function of an office is to direct and co-ordinate the activities of an enterprise. For every business enterprise, every factory, is tied to some office and, by virtue of what happens there, is linked to other businesses and to the rest of the people. Scattered throughout the political economy, each office is the peak of a pyramid of work and money and decision.

'When we picture in our minds,' says an earnest assistant general manager, 'the possibility for absolute control over the multitude of individual clerical operations through a control of forms . . . the most important items . . . arteries through which the life blood flows. . . Every function of every man or woman in every department takes place by means of, or is ultimately recorded on, an office or plant form.'

1. The Old Office

Just the other day the first typist in the city of Philadelphia, who had served one firm 60 years, died at the age of 80. During her last days she recalled how it was in the earlier days. She had come into the office from her employer's Sunday school class in 1882. She remembered when the office was one rather dark room, the windows always streaked with dust from the outside, and often fogged with smoke from the potbellied stove in the middle of the room. She remembered the green eyeshade and the cash book, the leather-bound ledger and the iron spike on the desk top, the day book and the quill pen, the letter press and the box file.

At first there were only three in the office: at the high roll-top desk, dominating the room, sat the owner; on a stool before a high desk with a slanted top and thin legs hunched the bookkeeper; and near the door, before a table that held the new machine, sat the white-collar girl.

The bookkeeper, A. B. Nordin, Jr. recently told the National Association of Office Managers, was an 'old-young man, slightly stoop-shouldered, with a sallow complexion, usually dyspeptic-looking, with black sleeves and a green eyeshade. . . Regardless of the kind of business, regardless of their ages, they all looked alike. . .' He seemed tired, and 'he was never quite happy, because . . . his face betrayed the strain of working toward that climax of his month's labors. He was usually a neat penman, but his real pride was in his ability to add a column of figures rapidly and accurately. In spite of this accomplishment, however, he seldom, if ever, left his ledger for a more promising position. His mind was atrophied by that destroying, hopeless influence of drudgery and routine work. He was little more than a figuring machine with an endless number of figure combinations learned by heart. His feat was a feat of memory.'

Of course there had been bookkeepers long before the 'eighties; Dickens wrote about just such men; and, as Thomas Cochran and William Miller have observed, as early as the 1820's fear was expressed in New York State that this new alpaca-clad man would join with factory owners and even factory workers to rout the landed aristocracy.

But the office girl in the 'eighties and 'nineties saw the bookkeeper at the very center of the office world. He recorded all transactions in the day book, the journal, the cash book, or the ledger; all the current orders and memoranda were speared on his iron spike; on his desk and in the squat iron safe or inside two open shelves or drawers with box files were all the papers which the office and its staff served.

The girl in the office struggling with the early typewriters spent at least 15 minutes every morning cleaning and oiling her massive but awkwardly delicate machine. At first typing was tedious because she could not see what she was typing on the double-keyboard machine without moving it up three spaces, but after a while she seldom had to see. She also whittled pencils, and worked the letter press, a curious device at which people had gazed during the 1893 Chicago World's Fair, which made a dim copy from the ink of the original letter.

The man at the big roll-top desk was often absent during the day, although his cigar smoke hung in the air. Later there was an office boy who went on many errands, but in the pre-telephone office, the owner had often to make personal calls to transact business. This personal contact with the outside world was paralleled by relations inside the office; the center was in personal contact with the circumference and received 'its impetus therefrom.' As Balzac wrote of early offices, 'there was devotion on one side and trust on the other.' As those on the circumference were being trained, some could look to gaining a rounded view of the business and in due course to moving to more responsible positions.

2. Forces and Developments

The era of this old office was a long one; in the United States it did not really begin to change shape until the 'nineties. Since then, many and drastic changes have occurred, but unevenly: offices still exist that are basically not different from the old office, but other offices seemingly have little resemblance to the nineteenth-century structure. The unevenness is due to the fact that offices are attached to all forms of enterprise, many of which are small, many big. It is especially in the big offices of the 'office industries' that the new type has emerged—the insurance, banking, and financial lines, for example. The later history of the office, as adapted from W. H. Leffingwell, may be described in terms of the following developments:

i. Under the impetus of concentrated enterprise and finance, when the office was enlarged during the first decade of the twentieth century, a need was felt for a systematic arrangement of business facts. The numerical file, with an alphabetical index, was devised and came into broad use. Alongside the bookkeeper and the stenographer, the clerk came to man often complicated 'systems.' As the army of clerks grew, they were divided into departments, specialized in function, and thus, before machines were introduced on any scale, socially rationalized. The work was reorganized in a systematic and divided manner.

ii. It was this social reorganization, under the impetus of work load, higher cost, and the need for files and figures, that made possible wide application of office machines. Machines did not begin to be used widely until the second decade of the century. A practical typewriter existed in 1874 but it was 1900 before any considerable use of it was made; a non-listing adding machine was invented in the late 'eighties, but only in the early twentieth century was it used widely. Thus, machines did not impel the development, but rather the development demanded machines, many of which were actually developed especially for tasks already socially created.

Office machines became important during the World War I era. Already convinced of the need for a systematic approach, and pressed by the need for more and more statistics, managers began to use the machine more and more to handle the existing systems. In 1919, the National Association of Office Managers was formed under the aegis of Frederick Taylor's ideas of scientific management. In the six or seven years before 1921, at least a hundred new office machines a year were put on the market. By the latter half of the 'twenties, most offices of any size were equipped with many types; by 1930, according to one government survey, some 30 per cent of the women in offices were, in the course of at least part of their work, using machines other than typewriters. Eight years later, well over a million office workers were. Today it is repeatedly asserted that at least 80 per cent of office jobs can be mechanized.

Yet, it has to be recognized that in the twenty years before World War II, there was a lag in the office's industrial revolution: office employment rose faster than office machines were introduced. The number of office people rose steadily since 1900, but office-machine sales remained at relatively low levels. World War II gave the real impetus to office technology: the prewar rate of office-machine sales was about 270 million dollars; by 1948 it was grossing one billion. Before the war there was serious talk of office decentralization in order to lower office costs; now new office machines, as one business journal puts it, make bigness workable.

In the later 'forties there were 3000 machines on display each year at business shows. There is a mechanical collator whose metal fingers snatch sheets of paper from five piles in proper sequence, and staple them for distribution. There are ticket and

money counters, mechanical erasers and automatic signature
machines, which promise to increase office production from 25
to 300 per cent. Gadgets can add, subtract, multiply, divide and
duplicate—all at once; can type in 51 languages, open and seal
envelopes, stamp and address them. There is a billing machine
that takes raw paper in at one end, cuts it to size, perforates it,
prints two-color forms on it, prints the amounts of the bills,
addresses them, and neatly piles them up for the postman. There
is a television set-up through which a man can flick a switch and
observe a worker in any part of his office or plant. There is an
incredibly dextrous machine into which cards are slipped, which
sends out tailor-made replies to every imaginable complaint and
inquiry.

Most startling perhaps are the new electronic calculators,
which store up one thousand units of information on a quarter
of an inch of magnetic tape. In one insurance company, such
machines 'take in the data in regard to a policy being surren-
dered, look up the cash value, interpolate for the premium paid
to date, multiply by the amount of insurance, total any loans,
compute the interest on each loan and total that, credit the value
of any dividend accumulations and any premiums paid in advance, and type out the check in payment of the net value of the
policy.'

Of course, such machines are practical only in big offices. But
there are incredible savings in time and cost and accuracy from
even simple, inexpensive gadgets: for example, a speed-feed for
a single typewriter which inserts and removes carbons automatically—by hand, 25 bills an hour; by speed-feed, 75 an hour. A
table especially constructed for opening letters increases output
some 30 per cent. With a standard typewriter one girl can turn
out 600 premium-due notices a day; with electric typewriters
and continuous forms, the same girl can do 700. Dictating machines can cut a secretary's letter time in half. The small businessman can also draw upon one of the 80 IBM service stations
throughout the nation, which will handle his whole payroll by
machine on punch cards.

The industrial revolution now comes to the office much faster
than it did to the factory, for it has been able to draw upon the
factory as a model. The very size of U.S. industry has brought

an incredible increase in paper work, and the enlargement and complication of the U.S. office. Machines in the office were needed to keep up with the effects and management of machines in the plant. The sweep of increased corporation mergers, especially in the 'twenties, further enlarged the unit of the business structure and entailed more extensive co-ordination. Then the government demanded more business records: in the First World War, national income taxes were instituted; the New Deal brought the volume of paper work to new heights by social security, wage-hour laws, deductions of taxes, et cetera, from payrolls; the Second World War not only added to the paper burden but, as the labor market tightened, made it more difficult to get college-level people to do cabinet filing jobs. The income of office workers rose also; trade unions threatened continuously, and office productivity was considered low. The answer was clear: machinery in the office.

Yet we are still only in the beginning of the office-machine age. Only when the machinery and the social organization of the office are fully integrated in terms of maximum efficiency per dollar spent will that age be full blown. Today, the machine investment per industrial worker varies from $19,375 in the chemical industry to $2,659 in textiles; the average per office worker is not more than $1000.

III. As machines spread, they began to prompt newer divisions of labor to add to those they had originally merely implemented. The new machines, especially the more complex and costly ones, require central control of offices previously scattered throughout the enterprise. This centralization, which prompts more new divisions of labor, is again facilitated by each new depression, through the urge to cut costs, and each new war, through the increased volume of office work. The present extent of office centralization has not been precisely measured, although the tendency has been clear enough since the early 'twenties: by then machines and social organizations had begun to interact, and that is the true mark of the 'era of scientific management in the office.' That era is still in its late infancy, but it is clearly the model of the future.

Neither machines nor other factory-type techniques could be efficiently applied until 'small groups of uncontrolled stenographers throughout the office' were brought into 'one central stenographic section.' Detached office units, often duplicating one another's work, must be drawn into a central office. New work and job routines are invented in order to get maximum use from the costly machines. Like manufacturing equipment, they are not to remain idle if it can possibly be avoided. Therefore, the work the machines do must be centralized into one pool.

Machines and centralization go together in company after company: and together they increase output and lower unit costs. They also open the way to the full range of factory organization and techniques: work can be simplified and specialized; work standards for each operation can be set up and applied to individual workers. 'We believe firmly,' says one office manager, 'in getting a proper record of individual production in order . . . [to] determine a definite cost unit of work. . .' By 'measuring the work of individual employees . . . we have a firm basis on which . . . to effect economy of operation.'

Any work that is measurable can be standardized, and often broken down into simple operations. Then it can proceed at a standard pace, which 'scientific investigation has determined can be performed by a first class worker in a stated time.' The very computation of such standards prompts new splitting of more complex tasks and increased specialization. For specialization and control from the top, along with standards, interact. When a gauge can be provided for the abilities of each person, the establishment of standards gives the office a new, more even tempo.

Time and motion studies are, of course, well known in many insurance companies and banks. In the 'twenties, some 16 per cent of one group of companies, and in 1942, some 28 per cent, were making time and motion measurements. One company, for example, which sets its standards this way, decreased its personnel by one-third; another decreased its personnel 39 per cent, while increasing its volume of work 40 per cent.

Cost reduction proceeds by eliminating some work and simplifying the rest. To do this, a functional breakdown of job operations is made, and a functional breakdown of human abilities;

then the two breakdowns are mated in a new, simplified set of routinized tasks. Along with this, machines are introduced for all possible features of the work process that cost factors allow. Then the effects of these factory-like procedures upon the office workers are rationalized and compulsory rest periods set up to relieve fatigue.

The process is extended even to the worker's life before he enters the office. Crack office men have known for some time that training for rationalization must start in the schools: 'The office manager should contact local schools, explain his require-ments and solicit school aid in training students of commercial subjects to meet office requirements. School courses can easily be designed to qualify graduates for the work requirements in our offices.'

Even the physical layout and appearance of the office become more factory-like. Office architecture and layout move toward two goals: the abolition of private offices and the arrange-ment of a straight-line flow of work. One office moved to new quarters where 200 former private offices were reduced to 17. This shift provided more light and better supervision. 'People really do keep busier when the officer in charge can look at them occasionally.' In this same office, 'the various activities have been placed to facilitate the flow of work. Work flows vertically from one floor to another, as well as horizontally on the same floor. That departments may be near each other vertically is usually taken into consideration when planning factories; this vertical "nearness" is not always considered in planning clerical working quarters.' Merely re-shuffling the desk plan can effect a saving of 15 per cent in standard hour units.

The next step is clear: a moving 'belt' replaces desks. As early as 1929, Grace Coyle observed in one large firm: 'orders are passed along by means of a belt and lights from a chief clerk to a series of checkers and typists, each of whom does one opera-tion. The girl at the head of the line interprets the order, puts down the number and indicates the trade discount; the second girl prices the order, takes off the discount, adds carriage charges and totals; the third girl gives the order a number and makes a daily record; the fourth girl puts this information on an alphabetical index; the fifth girl time-stamps it: it next goes along the belt to one of several typists, who makes a copy in sextuplicate and puts on address labels; the seventh girl checks it and sends it to the storeroom.'

Today one machine can do what this belt-line of girls did twenty-five years ago. But even with machines—'In any production process the importance of good tools is no greater than the relationship that exists between them,' Albert H. Stricker has observed. 'Before a production line can attain maximum effectiveness, the machines must be arranged to permit the unimpeded flow of parts or products from one end of the line to the other. In their proper position as the vital tools of paper-work production, typewriters and calculating machines, tabulators and book-keeping machines, furniture and all forms of office equipment can be arranged and combined to create an effective office-production line.'

These techniques and ways of reasoning have been long established in office-management circles and are identical with the reasoning found in factory-management circles. Their advance in offices, however, is still uneven, being perhaps, in the first instance, limited by the size of the office. Only about half of U.S. clerical workers in 1930 were in offices of over 50 workers; but offices continually become larger and, as they do, changes occur: personal telephone calls, smoking during office hours, visits from personal friends, and handling of personal mail are restricted, while mechanization and social rationalization—including rest periods, rest rooms, and hospital plans—increase.

3. The White-Collar Girl

Between the still-remaining old office and the vanguard, fully-rationalized office, there is a widespread, intermediate type. Just before World War I, Sinclair Lewis in *The Job* described such an office, which, although caricatured, is not untypical:

At the top, the chiefs, department heads and officers of the company, 'big, florid, shaven, large-chinned men, talking easily . . . able in a moment's conference at lunch to "shift the policy." . . . When they jovially entered the elevator together, some high-strung stenographer would rush over to one of the older women to weep and be comforted. . .'

Below them there was 'the caste of bright young men who would some day have the chance to be beatified into chiefs,' who looked loyally to the chiefs, 'worshipped the house policy,' and sat, 'in silk shirts and new ties, at shiny, flat-topped desks in rows' answering the telephone 'with an air.'

Intermingled with them were the petty chiefs, the office managers and bookkeepers, who were 'velvety' to those above them, but 'twangily nagging' to those under them. 'Failures themselves, they eyed sourly the stenographers who desired two dollars more a week, and assured them that while, personally, they would be very glad to obtain the advance for them, it would be "unfair to the other girls." '

Somewhat outside the main hierarchy was the small corps of private secretaries, each the 'daily confidante to one of the gods.' Nevertheless, these confidantes were not able 'to associate' with the gods, or 'be friendly, in coat-room or rest-room or elevator, with the unrecognized horde of girls who merely copied or took the bright young men's dictation.'

'These girls of the common herd were expected to call the secretaries "Miss," no matter what street corner impertinences they used to one another.' Factional rivalry split them. 'They were expected to keep clean and be quick-moving; beyond that they were as unimportant to the larger phases of office politics as frogs to a summer hotel. Only the cashier's card index could remember their names.' Their several types included 'the white-haired, fair-handed women of fifty and sixty . . . spinsters and widows, for whom life was nothing but a desk and a job of petty pickings —mailing circulars or assorting letters or checking up lists.' And also, 'the girls of twenty-two getting tired, the women of twenty-eight getting dried and stringy, the women of thirty-five in a solid maturity of large-bosomed and widowed spinster-hood, the old women purring and catty and tragic. . .'

It is from this kind of office, rather than the dusty, midget office of old or the new factory-like lay-out, that the common stereotypes of the office world and its inhabitants, particularly the white-collar girl, are drawn. Probably the major image is that the office is full of women. Of course, American women work elsewhere; they have had two generations of experience in factories and in service industries. But this experience has not been so generalized and diffused, except briefly during wars, as has the experience of the white-collar girl.

It is as a secretary or clerk, a business woman or career girl, that the white-collar girl dominates our idea of the office. She *is* the office, write the editors of *Fortune:* 'The male is the name on the door, the hat on the coat rack, and the smoke in the corner room. But the male is not the office. The office is the competent woman at the other end of his buzzer, the two young ladies chanting his name monotonously into the mouthpieces of a kind of gutta-percha halter, the four girls in the glass coop pecking out his initials with pink fingernails on the keyboards of four voluble machines, the half dozen assorted skirts whisking through the filing cases of his correspondence, and the elegant miss in the reception room recognizing his friends and disposing of his antipathies with the pleased voice and impersonal eye of a presidential consort.'

Novels about white-collar girls, appearing mainly in the 'twenties, were very popular. Kitty Foyle's time is from 1911 through the middle 'thirties; Minnie Hutzler, another Morley character in *Human Beings,* is followed from 1889 to 1929; the story of Janey Williams of Dos Passos' *USA* runs from 1900 to 1920; Tarkington's Alice Adams and Sinclair Lewis's Una Golden lived before World War I. Ten years on either side of the First World War—that was the time of the greatest literary interest in the white-collar girl. The images are tied to the scenes of that period of white-collar work, and many of the images presented are strikingly similar.

Sinclair Lewis's Una Golden, Booth Tarkington's Alice Adams, and Christopher Morley's Kitty Foyle—each was thrown into white-collar work after the death or failure of her father and in each case the father was an old middle-class man who had not been doing well.

The small-town Goldens were 'too respectable to permit her to have a job, and too poor to permit her to go to college.' Her father, 'a petty small town' lawyer, died when she was 24, and she and her mother were left with no inheritance. They began to enact the standard pattern of widowed mother, 'pawing at culture,' and the unemployed daughter. For such mother-daughter teams there were three small-town possibilities: 'If they were wealthy, daughter collected rents and saw lawyers and belonged to a club and tried to keep youthful at parties. If middle class, daughter taught school, almost invariably. If poor, mother did the washing and daughter collected it. So it was marked down for Una that she would be a teacher.' But she didn't want to teach; the only other job available was in a dry-goods store, which would have meant loss of caste; and all the energetic young men had gone to the big cities; so she gambled and went with her mother to New York, where she attended a 'college of commerce' and became an 'office woman.'

The story of Alice Adams—sociologically the most acute of these novels—is a story of aspirations being whittled down to white-collar size. It opens with Alice going to a party at the home of an upper-class family; it ends with her climbing the darkened stairway of a business college, like a girl taking the nun's veil, after frustration in love and social aspiration. Throughout the book, lurking in the background like a slum by a gold coast, the 'begrimed stairway' of the business college is seen by Alice, with 'a glance of vague misgiving,' as a road to 'hideous obscurity.' When Alice thinks of it, she thinks of 'pretty girls turning into withered creatures as they worked at typing machines'; old maids 'taking dictation' from men with double chins, a dozen different kinds of old maids 'taking dictation.' The office is a production plant for old maids, a modern nunnery. The contrast is between the business college and the glamorous stage, or the profitable, early, lovely marriage.

Yet the business college has 'an unpleasant fascination for her, and a mysterious reproach, which she did not seek to fathom.' At the end, her ascent of the begrimed stairway is 'the end of youth and the end of hope.' When she goes to the business college, she does not wear any 'color' (rouge) even though her ambitious mother, not knowing where she is going, tells her to get up gay when she goes out.

Alice Adams is a novel of Alice's father's occupational fate as well as of Alice's. The father is the head of the 'sundries department' of a wholesale drug house; he displays an intense loyalty to the firm and the man who owns and runs it. But the little

motor of his wife's ambition drives him to quit the salaried employee's meager dole and go on the market with a business of his
own. He fails. Both Alice and her father finally face modern
realities; at the end, the father moves from clerk to entrepreneur-
failure to 'the landlady's husband around a boarding-house';
Alice becomes the white-collar girl.

In American folklore, the white-collar girl is usually born of
small-town lower middle-class parents. High school plays an
important part in the creation of her rather tense personality.
She may take a commercial course in high school, and possibly
a year or two of business college. Upon graduation, being smart
and pretty, she gets a job in her own town. But she yearns for
independence from family and other local ties; she wants to go
to the big city, most of all, New York. She leaves home, and the
family becomes of secondary importance, for it represents a
status restriction on independence. Going home to see the folks
is a reluctantly done chore, and she can't wait to get back to
the big city. To get started in New York she may even borrow
money from a bank, rather than ask her parents for it.

The white-collar girl in the big city often looks back on her
high-school period in the small town as the dress rehearsal for
something that never came off. The personal clique of the high
school is not replaced by the impersonal unity of the office; the
adolescent status equality is not replaced by the hierarchy of the
city; the close-up thrill of the high-school date is not replaced
by the vicarious distances of the darkened movie; the high-
school camaraderie of anticipations is not fulfilled by the realization of life-fate in the white-collar world.

The white-collar girl has a close friend, sometimes from the
same home town, and usually a girl more experienced in the big
city. They commonly share an apartment, a wardrobe and a
budget, their dates and their troubles. The close friend is an
essential psychological need in the big city, and the white-collar
girl's only salvation from loneliness and boredom.

The first job is a continuation of her education as a stenographer or typist. Her pay check is small, but she does learn
office routine with its clean, brisk, new, efficient bustle. She also
learns how to handle the male element in the office, begins to

believe that all men are after only one thing. She laughs about small, funny incidents with the other girls, especially last night's date and tonight's. She is given her first cocktail by a salesman who is an expert on the psychology of girl stenographers.

The first job is usually the toughest, and she goes through several jobs before she gets the one she settles down in, if she can be said to settle down. In between jobs, of course, she has the most difficult time. The office is at first not a pleasant place, but she gets to know it and can soon classify all its people. There is the boss in the front, whose private secretary she hopes some day to become. There are minor executives and salesmen, who are eligible for marriage or dates or at least good for dinners. 'When you're working on $18-a-week like those kids you don't go out evenings unless someone takes you. You sit home with a lemon coke and wash stockings and iron a slip and buy the evening papers in turns and set the alarm clock so there'll be time to walk to work in the morning.' Finally there is the old man who is either a clerk or an accountant, and there are the 'fresh' office boys.

The love story of the white-collar girl often involves frustrating experiences with some boy-friend. For Kitty Foyle, there was Wyn; for Minnie, there was Richard Roe; for Janey, there was Jerry. When the white-collar girl does not get her man, the experience hardens her, turns her from the simple, small-town girl to the cool, polished, and urbane career woman or bachelor girl. She has no objection to love affairs 'if she cares enough' about the fellow, but she cannot get over her interest in marriage.

After her first frustrating experience, however, love becomes secondary to her career. For she has begun to enjoy her position and is promoted; after the first level stretch she is always on the slight upgrade. As she becomes a successful career woman, her idea of getting an upper-class man increases, and she is 'too mature to interest the average male of her acquaintance.' Usually she prefers men who are older than she. After 30, she looks back, somewhat maternally, upon the casual love life of the happy-go-lucky younger girls. Now she is the mature woman, efficient in her job, suppressing her love for her married boss, to whom she makes herself indispensable, doing the housework of his business. This relieves the impersonal business atmosphere and the tension between superior and employee, but it is also complicated by the fact that she may feel threatened by the eroticism of younger women.

Between the first two wars she talks like this: 'Molly and me had a talk one time about the white-collar woman—there's millions of them, getting maybe 15 to 30 a week—they've got to dress themselves right up to the hilt, naturally they have a yen for social pleasure, need to be a complete woman with all woman's satisfaction and they need a chance to be creating and doing. And the men their own age can't do much for them, also the girls grow up too damn fast because they absorb the point of view of older people they work for. Their own private life gets to be a rat-race. Jesusgod, I read about the guts of the pioneer woman and the woman of the dust bowl and the gingham goddess of the covered wagon. What about the woman of the covered typewriter! What has she got, poor kid, when she leaves the office. . . Do you know what we are? We're sharecroppers. We work like nigger hands in a cotton field and give Palmer's more brainwork than they know what to do with, what do we get for it? Eight hours' sleep, I guess, because that's about all we're fit for. . . I guess nobody minds so much being a sharecropper if he's damn sure that the crop's worth raising. But it must be nice to feel some of that ground you sweat belongs to yourself.'

In time she yearns for a family future, but settles down for longer stretches into the loveless routine of the office. Somehow it sustains her. Minnie, in fact, is against the institution of marriage; Kitty has an abortion in order that a child will not interfere with her position. Career has been substituted for marriage; the conflict of the white-collar girl is resolved; she has climbed the stairway; she is in the nunnery.

4. The New Office

The modern office with its tens of thousands of square feet and its factory-like flow of work is not an informal, friendly place. The drag and beat of work, the 'production unit' tempo, require that time consumed by anything but business at hand be explained and apologized for. Dictation was once a private meeting of executive and secretary. Now the executive phones a pool of dictaphone transcribers whom he never sees and who know him merely as a voice. Many old types of personnel have become machine operators, many new types began as machine operators.

I. The rise of the office manager, from a 'chief clerk' to a responsible executive reporting directly to the company treasurer or vice president, is an obvious index to the enlargement of offices and to the rise of the office as a centralized service division of the entire enterprise. It is under him that the factory-like office has been developing. Specializing as he does in the rational and efficient design and service of office functions, the office manager can obviously do a better job than a detached minor supervisor.

The office manager had begun to appear in the larger companies by the late 'twenties. Many early office managers were 'detail men' holding other positions, perhaps in the accounting department, but at the same time 'handling' the office force. But as the office increased in importance and in costs, it grew into an autonomous unit and the office manager grew with it. He had to know the clerical work and the routing of all departments; he had to be able to design and to adapt to new administrative schemes and set-ups; he had to train new employees and re-train old ones. The all-company scope of his domain gave room for his knowledge and prestige to increase, or at least his claims for prestige *vis à vis* 'other department heads.' By 1929, about one-third of one large group of office managers came from non-office executive positions, whereas half worked up through the office, and some 17 per cent came up through other offices, so that one may assume the position already had a recognized status.

II. As office machinery is introduced, the number of routine jobs is increased, and consequently the proportion of 'positions requiring initiative' is decreased. 'Mechanization is resulting in a much clearer distinction between the managing staff and the operating staff,' observed the War Manpower Commission. 'Finger dexterity is often more important than creative thinking. Promotions consequently become relatively rare. . . Some large office managers actually prefer to hire girls who are content to remain simply clerks, who will attempt to rise no higher than their initial level.'

As we compare the personnel of the new office with that of the old, it is the mass of clerical machine-operatives that immediately strikes us. They are the most factory-like operatives in the white-collar worlds. The period of time required to learn their skills seems steadily to decline; it must, in fact, if the expense of introducing machines and new standardized specializations is to be justified. For the key advantages of most mechanical and centralizing office devices are that, while they permit greater speed and accuracy, they also require cheaper labor per unit, less training, simpler specialization, and thus replaceable employees.

These interchangeable clerks often punch a time clock, are not allowed to talk during working hours, and have no tenure of employment beyond a week or sometimes a month. They typically have no contact with supervisors except in the course of being supervised. In large offices these people are the major links in the system, but in their minds and in those of their managers, there is rarely any serious thought of learning the whole system and rising within it. Even in the middle 'twenties 88 per cent of the office managers questioned in one survey indicated that they definitely needed people 'who give little promise of rising to an executive status,' and 60 per cent stated that there was 'very little opportunity' in their offices to learn, and hence rise, by apprenticeship.

The rationalization of the office, on the one hand, attracts and creates a new mass of clerks and machine operators, and their work increasingly approximates the factory operative in light manufacturing. On the other hand, this new office requires the office manager, a specialized manager who operates the human machinery.

III. The bookkeeper has been grievously affected by the last half century of office change: his old central position is usurped by the office manager, and even the most experienced bookkeeper with pen and ink cannot compete with a high-school girl trained in three or four months to use a machine. It is like a pick and shovel against a power scoop.

The bookkeeping or billing machine posts, enters, totals, and balances; from the accumulated postings control accounts are made up. And such a machine is a simple sort of apparatus, although it is still second only to the typewriter in offices today. Other new machines displace ten of the old, and their operatives, at one stroke. Just as the high-school girl with her machine has displaced the pen-and-ink bookkeeper, so the big new machines promise, in due course, to displace the high-school girl. At the top of the new 'bookkeeping' world are the professional account-ants and electronic technicians. But their predominance on any practical scale is still largely to come. In the meantime, the stratum of older bookkeepers is demoted to the level of the clerical mass.

'When recruiting new employees for this operation,' says the manager of a bookkeeping operation in a large company, 'we seek girls about seventeen years minimum age, at least two years' high school or its equivalent, with no previous business experience and good personal qualifications. We prefer inexperi-enced girls and those who have some economic incentive to work as we have found they make the steadiest workers; so we select from our recruits what we classify as the semi-dependent or wholly dependent applicant. . .'

IV. The secretary has been the model of aspiration for most office girls. The typewriter has, of course, been the woman's machine, and in itself it has not led to factory-like effects. In and out of the office world, it has been a highly respectable ma-chine. Its operator, equipped with stenographer's pad, has man-aged to borrow prestige from her close and private contact with the executive.

The standard girl-hierarchy in offices has been formed around the typewriter in the following way: (1) The private secretary, as someone's confidential assistant, in many cases can actually act for him on many not always routine matters. She takes care of his appointments, his daily schedule, his check book—is, in short, justifiably called his office wife. If her boss's office warrants it, she may even have stenographers and typists working for her. (2) The stenographer is a typist who also takes dictation. (3) The typist works only with the machine; because her work is a straight copying matter, her most important traits are speed and accuracy at the keyboard. Unlike the secretary, and to a lesser extent the stenographer, she is usually closely supervised.

In the new, rationalized office, this hierarchy—graded in income, skill, degree of supervision, and access to important persons—has begun to break down. There is now a strong tendency to limit the number of secretaries; many $15,000-a-year executives do not have private secretaries and never see a shorthand stenographer. Instead they dictate to a machine, whose cylinders go to a pool of typists. Although this pooling of stenographic services took place in many big offices before dictaphone equipment was installed, usually the two went together. Systematic studies clearly revealed the wastefulness of individually assigned stenographers, the alternate periods of slack and of frenzy rather than a smooth and efficient flow.

Since its beginnings in the 'twenties, the centralization of the stenographic operation has spread continuously, being limited only by size of office and inertia. The trend is for only the senior executives to have private secretaries and for both stenographers and typists to become pooled as transcribing typists. In one large insurance company's home office less than 2 per cent of the employees are assigned as secretaries to persons above the rank of Division Manager. The junior executive has his stenographer on his desk in a metal box, or may even dictate directly to the transcribing pool via inter-office telephone.

The centralized transcribing pool has further advantages: for the 'poor dictator,' the machines allow adjustments in audibility; they eliminate over-time imposed by late afternoon dictation, and also the strain of reading hurriedly written notes. 'They hear it automatically and have only to punch the keys to get the results,' the managerial literature states. 'Girls with speed and accuracy' are what are wanted in the new office.

The skill of shorthand becomes obsolete; the white-collar girl becomes almost immediately replaceable; work in offices becomes increasingly a blind-alley. The new white-collar girl cannot know intimately some segment of the office or business, and has lost the private contact that gave status to the secretary and even the stenographer. The work is regulated so that it can be speeded up and effectively supervised by non-executive personnel. In short, the prized white-collar spot for women is becoming more and more the job of a factory-like operative. By the early 'thirties, Amy Hewes was observing, 'The shadowy line between many . . . clerical tasks and *unskilled* factory occupations is becoming more and more imperceptible.'

The new office is rationalized: machines are used, employees become machine attendants; the work, as in the factory, is collective, not individualized; it is standardized for interchangeable, quickly replaceable clerks; it is specialized to the point of automatization. The employee group is transformed into a uniform mass in a soundless place, and the day itself is regulated by an impersonal time schedule. Seeing the big stretch of office space, with rows of identical desks, one is reminded of Herman Melville's description of a nineteenth-century factory: 'At rows of blank-looking counters sat rows of blank-looking girls, with blank, white folders in their blank hands, all blankly folding blank paper.'

5. The White-Collar Hierarchy

The new office at once raises a hierarchy and levels out personnel. The hierarchy is based upon the power and authority held by the managerial cadre, rather than upon the levels of skill. The individual employee is a unit in an administrative hierarchy of authority and discipline, but he is also equal before it with many other employees. Within this hierarchy and mass, he is classified by the function he performs, but sometimes there are also 'artificial' distinctions of status, position, and above all title. These distinctions, to which Carl Dreyfuss has called attention, arise on the one hand from the employee's need to personalize a little area for himself, and on the other, they may be encouraged by management to improve morale and to discourage employee 'solidarity.'

In the enormous file, smaller hierarchies fit into larger ones and are interlinked in a dozen ways. There is a formal line-up expressed by titles, and beneath these, further gradations in status and rank. Rank does not always correspond to skill or salary level; in general, it is expressed in the authority to give orders. The managerial cadre, infiltrating all divisions and units, is the backbone of the hierarchy. Where one stands depends, first upon the extent to which one participates in the cadre's authority, and second, the closeness of one's association with its members. The private secretary of the top manager of a division may thus be superior in rank and status to the assistant manager of a division further down. Educational level and experience naturally lend status, but only secondarily. It is from the managerial cadre that esteem is derived and status borrowed.

If the white-collar hierarchy were purely bureaucratic it would be based upon sheer formal authority, as in an army; but actually, nowhere are bureaucratic principles of organization strictly carried through. Within and between offices, there is usually a system of cliques, which often cut across the formal line of authority and work. Through them 'the man in the know' can cut red tape, and secretaries of top men, 'administrative assistants' as they are called in Washington, can call other secretaries to expedite matters that would take much longer through the regular channels.

Status inside the hierarchy is not always in line with formal participation in management; a fictitious closeness to authority may bring prestige. Private secretaries, as well as other confidential assistants to managers, thus often stand out. Only in rare cases do they actively show or have authority, but their position requires close contact with authority and they handle and even help to shape its secrets. By inner identification, they often have a strong illusion of authority and, by outward manner, impress it on others. This is by no means discouraged by the managers, for the gap between the confidential employee and 'the girls' is a guarantee of loyalty, and moreover a reciprocal influence in the increased prestige of the managers themselves. The scale of available beauty, for instance, may influence the selection as well as class factors—the Anglo-Saxon, upper middle-class girl having a better chance.

Those in intimate contact with authority form a sort of screen around the persons who carry it, insuring its privacy and hence heightening its prestige. In a great many offices and stores today the rank and file never see 'the higher ups,' but only their immediate supervisors, who are known as 'the boss.' Grievances and resentments are aimed at 'the boss'; the 'higher-ups' come within psychological view, if at all, only in fantasy: 'If I could only get in contact with them, I know I'd be given my chance.'

Titles and appurtenances, which are related in intricate ways to formal authority, are outward and crucial signs of status. To have a telephone on one's desk, to use one lavatory or another, to have one's name on the door or even on a placard on a desk— all such items can and do form the content of the employee's conscious striving and hope. A great deal has been made of such distinctions. Carl Dreyfuss alleged that they form 'an artificial hierarchy' which is encouraged and exploited by the employer who does not wish solidarity. When many small gradations in status exist, the employee can more often experience the illusion of 'being somebody' and of ascending the scale. Often 'there are more rank than salary gradations but even the latter exceed the number of groupings actually required from a technical point of view.'

But such distinctions, in so far as they are not based on work performed, fall, in time, before the cost-reduction drives of management and the egalitarian push of trade unions, which strive to classify jobs more systematically. According to this view, the norm of the 'genuine' hierarchy is technical and economic, that is, strictly bureaucratic; but actually status elements are no more 'artificial' than technical and economic ones. Differentiations do, of course, develop on status factors alone, and they are often of crucial, even overpowering importance in white-collar hierarchies. But the over-all trend is against them. Even though employers may try to exploit them to discourage solidarity, once a union tries to break the job divisions down and then to fight for corresponding income gradations, employers are usually ready to level out status differences in order to lower costs.

Only a sophisticated employer strongly beleaguered by attempted unionization might see reasons to make conscious use of prestige gradations. It would not, however, seem the most rational choice he might make and, in fact, the employer has been the leader of job descriptions and personnel work that reduce the number of complex functions and break down the work and hence lower pay. Machines implement and prompt such strict technical and bureaucratic gradation. And certainly, even if the artificial hierarchy has been used as a manner of control, ration-alization and mechanization are now well on their way to destroy such schemes.

Mechanized and standardized work, the decline of any chance for the employee to see and understand the whole operation, the loss of any chance, save for a very few, for private contact with those in authority—these form the model of the future. At present, status complications inside office and store are still often quite important in the psychology of the employee; but, in the main drift, technical and economic factors and the authoritative line-up will gain ascendency over such status factors as now interfere with the rationalization of the white-collar hierarchy.

THREE

Styles of Life

'My active life, if I ever had one, ended when I was sixteen,' says Mr. Bowling of George Orwell's *Coming Up for Air.* 'I got the job and . . . the job got me. . . Everything that really matters to me had happened before that date. . . Well, they say that happy people have no histories, and neither do the blokes who work in insurance offices.'

10

Work

Work may be a mere source of livelihood, or the most significant part of one's inner life; it may be experienced as expiation, or as exuberant expression of self; as bounden duty, or as the development of man's universal nature. Neither love nor hatred of work is inherent in man, or inherent in any given line of work. For work has no intrinsic meaning.

No adequate history of the meanings of work has been written. One can, however, trace the influences of various philosophies of work, which have filtered down to modern workers and which deeply modify their work as well as their leisure.

While the modern white-collar worker has no articulate philosophy of work, his feelings about it and his experiences of it influence his satisfactions and frustrations, the whole tone of his life. Whatever the effects of his work, known to him or not, they are the net result of the work as an activity, plus the meanings he brings to it, plus the views that others hold of it.

1. Meanings of Work

To the ancient Greeks, in whose society mechanical labor was done by slaves, work brutalized the mind, made man unfit for the practice of virtue.* It was a necessary material evil, which the elite, in their search for changeless vision, should avoid. The

* In this historical sketch of philosophies of work I have drawn upon Adriano Tilgher's *Work: What It Has Meant to Men through the Ages* (New York: Harcourt, Brace, 1930).

Hebrews also looked upon work as 'painful drudgery,' to which, they added, man is condemned by sin. In so far as work atoned for sin, however, it was worth while, yet Ecclesiastes, for example, asserts that 'The labor of man does not satisfy the soul.' Later, Rabbinism dignified work somewhat, viewing it as worthy exercise rather than scourge of the soul, but still said that the kingdom to come would be a kingdom of blessed idleness.

In primitive Christianity, work was seen as punishment for sin but also as serving the ulterior ends of charity, health of body and soul, warding off the evil thoughts of idleness. But work, being of this world, was of no worth in itself. St. Augustine, when pressed by organizational problems of the church, carried the issue further: for monks, work is obligatory, although it should alternate with prayer, and should engage them only enough to supply the real needs of the establishment. The church fathers placed pure meditation on divine matters above even the intellectual work of reading and copying in the monastery. The heretical sects that roved around Europe from the eleventh to the fourteenth century demanded work of man, but again for an ulterior reason: work, being painful and humiliating, should be pursued zealously as a 'scourge for the pride of the flesh.'

With Luther, work was first established in the modern mind as 'the base and key to life.' While continuing to say that work is natural to fallen man, Luther, echoing Paul, added that all who can work should do so. Idleness is an unnatural and evil evasion. To maintain oneself by work is a way of serving God. With this, the great split between religious piety and worldly activity is resolved; profession becomes 'calling,' and work is valued as a religious path to salvation.

Calvin's idea of predestination, far from leading in practice to idle apathy, prodded man further into the rhythm of modern work. It was necessary to act in the world rationally and methodically and continuously and hard, as if one were certain of being among those elected. It is God's will that everyone must work, but it is not God's will that one should lust after the fruits even of one's own labor; they must be reinvested to allow and to spur still more labor. Not contemplation, but strong-willed, austere, untiring work, based on religious conviction, will ease guilt and lead to the good and pious life.

The 'this-worldly asceticism' of early Protestantism placed a premium upon and justified the styles of conduct and feeling required in its agents by modern capitalism. The Protestant sects encouraged and justified the social development of a type of man capable of ceaseless, methodical labor. The psychology of the religious man and of the economic man thus coincided, as Max Weber has shown, and at their point of coincidence the sober bourgeois entrepreneur lived in and through his work.

Locke's notion that labor was the origin of individual ownership and the source of all economic value, as elaborated by Adam Smith, became a keystone of the liberal economic system: work was now a controlling factor in the wealth of nations, but it was a soulless business, a harsh justification for the toiling grind of nineteenth-century populations, and for the economic man, who was motivated in work by the money he earned.

But there was another concept of work which evolved in the Renaissance; some men of that exuberant time saw work as a spur rather than a drag on man's development as man. By his own activity, man could accomplish anything; through work, man became creator. How better could he fill his hours? Leonardo da Vinci rejoiced in creative labor; Bruno glorified work as an arm against adversity and a tool of conquest.

During the nineteenth century there began to be reactions against the Utilitarian meaning assigned to work by classical economics, reactions that drew upon this Renaissance exuberance. Men, such as Tolstoy, Carlyle, Ruskin, and William Morris, turned backward; others, such as Marx and Engels, looked forward. But both groups drew upon the Renaissance view of man as tool user. The division of labor and the distribution of its product, as well as the intrinsic meaning of work as purposive human activity, are at issue in these nineteenth-century speculations. Ruskin's ideal, set against the capitalist organization of work, rested on a pre-capitalist society of free artisans whose work is at once a necessity for livelihood and an act of art that brings inner calm. He glorified what he supposed was in the work of the medieval artisan; he believed that the total product of work should go to the worker. Profit on capital is an injustice and, moreover, to strive for profit for its own sake blights the soul and puts man into a frenzy.

In Marx we encounter a full-scale analysis of the meaning of work in human development as well as of the distortions of this development in capitalist society. Here the essence of the human being rests upon his work: 'What [individuals] . . . are . . . co-incides with their production, both with *what* they produce and with *how* they produce. The nature of individuals thus depends on the material conditions determining their production.' Capitalist production, thought Marx, who accepted the humanist ideal of classic German idealism of the all-round personality, has twisted men into alien and specialized animal-like and deperson-alized creatures.

Historically, most views of work have ascribed to it an extrinsic meaning. R. H. Tawney refers to 'the distinction made by the philosophers of classical antiquity between liberal and servile occupations, the medieval insistence that riches exist for man, not man for riches. Ruskin's famous outburst, "there is no wealth but life," the argument of the Socialist who urges that production should be organized for service, not for profit, are but different attempts to emphasize the instrumental character of economic activities by reference to an ideal which is held to express the true nature of man.' But there are also those who ascribe to work an intrinsic worth. All philosophies of work may be divided into these two views, although in a curious way Carlyle managed to combine the two.

I. The various forms of Protestantism, which (along with classical economics) have been the most influential doctrines in modern times, see work activity as ulterior to religious sanctions; gratifications from work are not intrinsic to the activity and experience, but are religious rewards. By work one gains a religious status and assures oneself of being among the elect. If work is compulsive it is due to the painful guilt that arises when one does not work.

II. The Renaissance view of work, which sees it as intrinsically meaningful, is centered in the technical craftsmanship—the manual and mental operations—of the work process itself; it sees the

reasons for work in the work itself and not in any ulterior realm
or consequence. Not income, not way of salvation, not status,
not power over other people, but the technical processes themselves are gratifying.

Neither of these views, however—the secularized gospel of
work as compulsion, nor the humanist view of work as craftsmanship—now has great influence among modern populations.
For most employees, work has a generally unpleasant quality. If
there is little Calvinist compulsion to work among propertyless
factory workers and file clerks, there is also little Renaissance
exuberance in the work of the insurance clerk, freight handler,
or department-store saleslady. If the shoe salesman or the tex-
tile executive gives little thought to the religious meaning of his
labor, certainly few telephone operators or receptionists or schoolteachers experience from their work any Ruskinesque inner calm.
Such joy as creative work may carry is more and more limited
to a small minority. For the white-collar masses, as for wage
earners generally, work seems to serve neither God nor whatever they may experience as divine in themselves. In them there
is no taut will-to-work, and few positive gratifications from their
daily round.

The gospel of work has been central to the historic tradition
of America, to its image of itself, and to the images the rest of
the world has of America. The crisis and decline of that gospel
are of wide and deep meaning. On every hand, we hear, in the
words of Wade Shortleff for example, that 'the aggressiveness
and enthusiasm which marked other generations is withering,
and in its stead we find the philosophy that attaining and holding a job is not a challenge but a necessary evil. When work becomes just work, activity undertaken only for reason of subsistence, the spirit which fired our nation to its present greatness
has died to a spark. An ominous apathy cloaks the smoldering
discontent and restlessness of the management men of to-
morrow.'

To understand the significance of this gospel and its decline,
we must understand the very spirit of twentieth-century America.
That the historical work ethic of the old middle-class entrepreneurs has not deeply gripped the people of the new society is
one of the most crucial psychological implications of the struc-

tural decline of the old middle classes. The new middle class, despite the old middle-class origin of many of its members, has never been deeply involved in the older work ethic, and on this point has been from the beginning non-bourgeois in mentality.

At the same time, the second historically important model of meaningful work and gratification—craftsmanship—has never belonged to the new middle classes, either by tradition or by the nature of their work. Nevertheless, the model of craftsmanship lies, however vaguely, back of most serious studies of worker dissatisfaction today, of most positive statements of worker gratification, from Ruskin and Tolstoy to Bergson and Sorel. Therefore, it is worth considering in some detail, in order that we may then gauge in just what respects its realization is impossible for the modern white-collar worker.

2. The Ideal of Craftsmanship

Craftsmanship as a fully idealized model of work gratification involves six major features: There is no ulterior motive in work other than the product being made and the processes of its creation. The details of daily work are meaningful because they are not detached in the worker's mind from the product of the work. The worker is free to control his own working action. The craftsman is thus able to learn from his work; and to use and develop his capacities and skills in its prosecution. There is no split of work and play, or work and culture. The craftsman's way of livelihood determines and infuses his entire mode of living.

i. The hope in good work, William Morris remarked, is hope of product and hope of pleasure in the work itself; the supreme concern, the whole attention, is with the quality of the product and the skill of its making. There is an inner relation between the craftsman and the thing he makes, from the image he first forms of it through its completion, which goes beyond the mere legal relations of property and makes the craftsman's will-to-work spontaneous and even exuberant.

Other motives and results—money or reputation or salvation—are subordinate. It is not essential to the practice of the craft ethic that one necessarily improves one's status either in the re-

ligious community or in the community in general. Work gratification is such that a man may live in a kind of quiet passion 'for
his work alone.'

II. In most statements of craftsmanship, there is a confusion
between its technical and aesthetic conditions and the legal
(property) organization of the worker and the product. What is
actually necessary for work-as-craftsmanship, however, is that
the tie between the product and the producer be psychologically
possible; if the producer does not legally own the product he
must own it psychologically in the sense that he knows what
goes into it by way of skill, sweat, and material and that his own
skill and sweat are visible to him. Of course, if legal conditions
are such that the tie between the work and the worker's material
advantage is transparent, this is a further gratification, but it is
subordinate to that workmanship which would continue of its
own will even if not paid for.

The craftsman has an image of the completed product, and
even though he does not make it all, he sees the place of his part
in the whole, and thus understands the meaning of his exertion
in terms of that whole. The satisfaction he has in the result infuses the means of achieving it, and in this way his work is not
only meaningful to him but also partakes of the consummatory
satisfaction he has in the product. If work, in some of its phases,
has the taint of travail and vexation and mechanical drudgery,
still the craftsman is carried over these junctures by keen an-
ticipation. He may even gain positive satisfaction from encoun-
tering a resistance and conquering it, feeling his work and will
as powerfully victorious over the recalcitrance of materials and
the malice of things. Indeed, without this resistance he would
gain less satisfaction in being finally victorious over that which
at first obstinately resists his will.

George Mead has stated this kind of aesthetic experience as
involving the power 'to catch the enjoyment that belongs to the
consummation, the outcome, of an undertaking and to give to
the implements, the objects that are instrumental in the undertaking, and to the acts that compose it something of the joy and
satisfaction that suffuse its successful accomplishment.'

III. The workman is free to begin his work according to his own plan and, during the activity by which it is shaped, he is free to modify its form and the manner of its creation. In both these senses, Henri De Man observed, 'plan and performance are one,' and the craftsman is master of the activity and of himself in the process. This continual joining of plan and activity brings even more firmly together the consummation of work and its instrumental activities, infusing the latter with the joy of the former. It also means that his sphere of independent action is large and rational to him. He is responsible for its outcome and free to assume that responsibility. His problems and difficulties must be solved by him, in terms of the shape he wants the final outcome to assume.

IV. The craftsman's work is thus a means of developing his skill, as well as a means of developing himself as a man. It is not that self-development is an ulterior goal, but that such development is the cumulative result obtained by devotion to and practice of his skills. As he gives it the quality of his own mind and skill, he is also further developing his own nature; in this simple sense, he lives in and through his work, which confesses and reveals him to the world.

V. In the craftsman pattern there is no split of work and play, of work and culture. If play is supposed to be an activity, exercised for its own sake, having no aim other than gratifying the actor, then work is supposed to be an activity performed to create economic value or for some other ulterior result. Play is something you do to be happily occupied, but if work occupies you happily, it is also play, although it is also serious, just as play is to the child. 'Really free work, the work of a composer, for example,' Marx once wrote of Fourier's notions of work and play, 'is damned serious work, intense strain.' The simple self-expression of play and the creation of ulterior value of work are combined in work-as-craftsmanship. The craftsman or artist expresses himself at the same time and in the same act as he creates value. His work is a poem in action. He is at work and at play in the same act.

'Work' and 'culture' are not, as Gentile has held, separate spheres, the first dealing with means, the second with ends in themselves; as Tilgher, Sorel, and others have indicated, either work or culture may be an end in itself, a means, or may contain segments of both ends and means. In the craft model of activity, 'consumption' and 'production' are blended in the same act; active craftsmanship, which is both play and work, is the medium of culture; and for the craftsman there is no split between the worlds of culture and work.

vi. The craftsman's work is the mainspring of the only life he knows; he does not flee from work into a separate sphere of leisure; he brings to his non-working hours the values and qualities developed and employed in his working time. His idle conversation is shop talk; his friends follow the same lines of work as he, and share a kinship of feeling and thought. The leisure William Morris called for was 'leisure to think about our work, that faithful daily companion. . .'

In order to give his work the freshness of creativity, the craftsman must at times open himself up to those influences that only affect us when our attentions are relaxed. Thus for the craftsman, apart from mere animal rest, leisure may occur in such intermittent periods as are necessary for individuality in his work. As he brings to his leisure the capacity and problems of his work, so he brings back into work those sensitivities he would not gain in periods of high, sustained tension necessary for solid work.

'The world of art,' wrote Paul Bourget, speaking of America, 'requires less self-consciousness—an impulse of life which forgets itself, the alternation of dreamy idleness with fervid execution.' The same point is made by Henry James, in his essay on Balzac, who remarks that we have practically lost the faculty of attention, meaning . . . 'that unstrenuous, brooding sort of attention required to produce or appreciate works of art.' Even rest, which is not so directly connected with work itself as a condition of creativity, is animal rest, made secure and freed from anxiety by virtue of work done—in Tilgher's words, 'a sense of peace and calm which flows from all well-regulated, disciplined work done with a quiet and contented mind.'

In constructing this model of craftsmanship, we do not mean to imply that there ever was a community in which work carried all these meanings. Whether the medieval artisan approximated the model as closely as some writers seem to assume, we do not know; but we entertain serious doubts that this is so; we lack enough psychological knowledge of medieval populations properly to judge. At any rate, for our purposes it is enough to know that at different times and in different occupations, the work men do has carried one or more features of craftsmanship.

With such a model in mind, a glance at the occupational world of the modern worker is enough to make clear that practically none of these aspects are now relevant to modern work experience. The model of craftsmanship has become an anachronism. We use the model as an explicit ideal in terms of which we can summarize the working conditions and the personal meaning work has in modern work-worlds, and especially to white-collar people.

3. The Conditions of Modern Work

As practice, craftsmanship has largely been trivialized into 'hobbies,' part of leisure not of work; or if work—a marketable activity—it is the work of scattered mechanics in handicraft trades, and of professionals who manage to remain free. As ethic, craftsmanship is confined to minuscule groups of privileged professionals and intellectuals.

The entire shift from the rural world of the small entrepreneur to the urban society of the dependent employee has instituted the property conditions of alienation from product and processes of work. Of course, dependent occupations vary in the extent of initiative they allow and invite, and many self-employed enterprisers are neither as independent nor as enterprising as commonly supposed. Nevertheless, in almost any job, the employee sells a degree of his independence; his working life is within the domain of others; the level of his skills that are used and the areas in which he may exercise independent decisions are subject to management by others. Probably at least ten or twelve million people worked during the 'thirties at tasks below the skill level of which they were easily capable; and, as school attendance increases and more jobs are routinized, the number of people who must work below their capacities will increase.

There is considerable truth in the statement that those who find free expression of self in their work are those who securely own the property with which they work, or those whose work-freedom does not entail the ownership of property. 'Those who have no money work sloppily under the name of sabotage,' writes Charles Péguy, 'and those who have money work sloppily, a counter and different sloppiness, under the name of luxury. And thus culture no longer has any medium through which it might infiltrate. There no longer exists that marvelous unity true of all ancient societies, where he who produced and he who bought equally loved and knew culture.'

The objective alienation of man from the product and the process of work is entailed by the legal framework of modern capitalism and the modern division of labor. The worker does not own the product or the tools of his production. In the labor contract he sells his time, energy, and skill into the power of others. To understand self-alienation we need not accept the metaphysical view that man's self is most crucially expressed in work-activity. In all work involving the personality market, as we have seen, one's personality and personal traits become part of the means of production. In this sense a person instrumentalizes and externalizes intimate features of his person and disposition. In certain white-collar areas, the rise of personality markets has carried self and social alienation to explicit extremes.

Thoreau, who spoke for the small entrepreneur, objected, in the middle of the nineteenth century, 'to the division of labor since it divided the worker, not merely the work, reduced him from a man to an operative, and enriched the few at the expense of the many.' 'It destroyed,' wrote F. O. Matthiessen, 'the potential balance of his [Thoreau's] agrarian world, one of the main ideals of which was the union of labor and culture.'

The detailed division of labor means, of course, that the individual does not carry through the whole process of work to its final product; but it also means that under many modern conditions the process itself is invisible to him. The product as the goal of his work is legally and psychologically detached from him, and this detachment cuts the nerve of meaning which work might otherwise gain from its technical processes. Even on the professional levels of white-collar work, not to speak of wage-work and the lower white-collar tasks, the chance to develop and use individual rationality is often destroyed by the centralization of decision and the formal rationality that bureaucracy entails. The expropriation which modern work organization has carried through thus goes far beyond the expropriation of ownership; rationality itself has been expropriated from work and any total view and understanding of its process. No longer free to plan his work, much less to modify the plan to which he is subordinated, the individual is to a great extent managed and manipulated in his work.

The world market, of which Marx spoke as the alien power over men, has in many areas been replaced by the bureaucratized enterprise. Not the market as such but centralized administrative decisions determine when men work and how fast. Yet the more and the harder men work, the more they build up that which dominates their work as an alien force, the commodity; so also, the more and the harder the white-collar man works, the more he builds up the enterprise outside himself, which is, as we have seen, duly made a fetish and thus indirectly justified. The enterprise is not the institutional shadow of great men, as perhaps it seemed under the old captain of industry; nor is it the instrument through which men realize themselves in work, as in small-scale production. The enterprise is an impersonal and alien Name, and the more that is placed in it, the less is placed in man.

As tool becomes machine, man is estranged from the intellectual potentialities and aspects of work; and each individual is routinized in the name of increased and cheaper per unit productivity. The whole unit and meaning of time is modified; man's 'life-time,' wrote Marx, is transformed into 'working-time.' In tying down individuals to particular tasks and jobs, the division of labor 'lays the foundation of that all-engrossing system of specializing and sorting men, that development in a man of one single faculty at the expense of all other faculties, which caused A. Ferguson, the master of Adam Smith, to exclaim: "We make a nation of Helots, and have no free citizens." '

The introduction of office machinery and sales devices has been mechanizing the office and the salesroom, the two big locales of white-collar work. Since the 'twenties it has increased the division of white-collar labor, recomposed personnel, and lowered skill levels. Routine operations in minutely subdivided organizations have replaced the bustling interest of work in well-known groups. Even on managerial and professional levels, the growth of rational bureaucracies has made work more like factory production. The managerial demiurge is constantly furthering all these trends: mechanization, more minute division of labor, the use of less skilled and less expensive workers.

In its early stages, a new division of labor may specialize men in such a way as to increase their levels of skill; but later, especially when whole operations are split and mechanized, such division develops certain faculties at the expense of others and narrows all of them. And as it comes more fully under mechanization and centralized management, it levels men off again as automatons. Then there are a few specialists and a mass of automatons; both integrated by the authority which makes them interdependent and keeps each in his own routine. Thus, in the division of labor, the open development and free exercise of skills are managed and closed.

The alienating conditions of modern work now include the salaried employees as well as the wage-workers. There are few, if any, features of wage-work (except heavy toil—which is decreasingly a factor in wage-work) that do not also characterize at least some white-collar work. For here, too, the human traits of the individual, from his physique to his psychic disposition, become units in the functionally rational calculation of managers. None of the features of work as craftsmanship is prevalent in office and salesroom, and, in addition, some features of white-collar work, such as the personality market, go well beyond the alienating conditions of wage-work.

Yet, as Henri De Man has pointed out, we cannot assume that the employee makes comparisons between the ideal of work as craftsmanship and his own working experience. We cannot compare the idealized portrait of the craftsman with that of the auto worker and on that basis impute any psychological state to the auto worker. We cannot fruitfully compare the psychological condition of the old merchant's assistant with the modern saleslady, or the old-fashioned bookkeeper with the IBM machine attendant. For the historical destruction of craftsmanship and of the old office does not enter the consciousness of the modern wage-worker or white-collar employee; much less is their absence felt by him as a crisis, as it might have been if, in the course of the last generation, his father or mother had been in the craft condition—but, statistically speaking, they have not been. It is slow historical fact, long gone by in any dramatic consequence and not of psychological relevance to the present generation. Only the psychological imagination of the historian makes it possible to write of such comparisons as if they were of psychological import. The craft life would be immediately available as a fact of their consciousness only if in the lifetime of the modern employees they had experienced a shift from the one condition to the other, which they have not; or if they had grasped it as an ideal meaning of work, which they have not.

But if the work white-collar people do is not connected with its resultant product, and if there is no intrinsic connection between work and the rest of their life, then they must accept their work as meaningless in itself, perform it with more or less disgruntlement, and seek meanings elsewhere. Of their work, as of all of our lives, it can truly be said, in Henri Bergson's words, that: 'The greater part of our time we live outside ourselves, hardly perceiving anything of ourselves but our own ghost, a colourless shadow. . . Hence we live for the external world rather than for ourselves; we speak rather than think; we are acted rather than act ourselves. To act freely is to recover possession of oneself. . .'

If white-collar people are not free to control their working actions they, in time, habitually submit to the orders of others and, in so far as they try to act freely, do so in other spheres. If they do not learn from their work or develop themselves in doing it, in time, they cease trying to do so, often having no interest in self-development even in other areas. If there is a split between their work and play, and their work and culture, they admit that split as a common-sense fact of existence. If their way of earning a living does not infuse their mode of living, they try to build their real life outside their work. Work becomes a sacrifice of time, necessary to building a life outside of it.

4. Frames of Acceptance

Underneath virtually all experience of work today, there is a fatalistic feeling that work *per se* is unpleasant. One type of work, or one particular job, is contrasted with another type, experienced or imagined, within the present world of work; judgments are rarely made about the world of work as presently organized as against some other way of organizing it; so also, satisfaction from work is felt in comparison with the satisfactions of other jobs.

We do not know what proportions of the U.S. white-collar strata are 'satisfied' by their work and, more important, we do not know what being satisfied means to them. But it is possible to speculate fruitfully about such questions.

We do have the results of some questions, necessarily crude, regarding feelings about present jobs. As in almost every other area, when sponge questions are asked of a national cross-section, white-collar people, meaning here clerical and sales employees, are in the middle zones. They stand close to the national average (64 per cent asserting they find their work interesting and enjoyable 'all the time'), while more of the professionals and executives claim interest and enjoyment (85 per cent), and fewer of the factory workers (41 per cent) do so.

Within the white-collar hierarchy, job satisfaction seems to follow the hierarchical levels; in one study, for example, 86 per cent of the professionals, 74 per cent of the managerial, 42 per cent of the commercial employees, stated general satisfaction. This is also true of wage-worker levels of skill: 56 per cent of the skilled, but 48 per cent of the semi-skilled, are satisfied.

Such figures tell us very little, since we do not know what the questions mean to the people who answer them, or whether they mean the same thing to different strata. However, work satisfaction is related to income and, if we had measures, we might find that it is also related to status as well as to power. What such questions probably measure are invidious judgments of the individual's standing with reference to other individuals. And the aspects of work, the terms of such comparisons, must be made clear.

Under modern conditions, the direct technical processes of work have been declining in meaning for the mass of employees, but other features of work—income, power, status—have come to the fore. Apart from the technical operations and the skills involved, work is a source of income; the amount, level, and security of pay, and what one's income history has been are part of work's meaning. Work is also a means of gaining status, at the place of work, and in the general community. Different types of work and different occupational levels carry differential status values. These again are part of the meaning of the job. And also work carries various sorts of power, over materials and tools and machines, but, more crucially now, over other people.

I. *Income:* The economic motives for work are now its only firm rationale. Work now has no other legitimating symbols, although certainly other gratifications and discontents are associated with it. The division of labor and the routinization of many job areas are reducing work to a commodity, of which money has become the only common denominator. To the worker who cannot receive technical gratifications from his work, its market value is all there is to it. The only significant occupational movement in the United States, the trade unions, have the pure and simple ideology of alienated work: more and more money for less and less work. There are, of course, other demands, but they can be only 'fixed up' to lessen the cry for more money. The sharp focus upon money is part and parcel of the lack of intrinsic meaning that work has come to have.

Underlying the modern approach to work there seems to be some vague feeling that 'one should earn one's own living,' a kind of Protestant undertow, attenuated into a secular convention. 'When work goes,' as H. A. Overstreet, a job psychologist writing of the slump, puts it, 'we know that the tragedy is more than economic. It is psychological. It strikes at the center of our personality. It takes from us something that rightly belongs to every self-respecting human being.' But income security—the fear of unemployment or under-employment—is more important. An undertow of anxiety about sickness, accident, or old age must support eagerness for work, and gratification may be based on the compulsion to relieve anxiety by working hard. Widespread unemployment, or fear of it, may even make an employee happily thankful for any job, contented to be at any kind of work when all around there are many workless, worried people. If satisfaction rests on relative status, there is here an invidious element that increases it. It is across this ground tone of convention and fear, built around work as a source of income, that other motives to work and other factors of satisfaction are available.

II. *Status:* Income and income security lead to other things, among them, status. With the decline of technical gratification, the employee often tries to center such meaning as he finds in work on other features of the job. Satisfaction in work often rests upon status satisfactions from work associations. As a social role played in relation to other people, work may become a source of self-esteem, on the job, among co-workers, superiors, subordinates, and customers, if any; and off the job, among friends, family, and community at large. The fact of doing one kind of job rather than another and doing one's job with skill and dispatch may be a source of self-esteem. For the man or woman lonely in the city, the mere fact of meeting people at the place of work may be a positive thing. Even anonymous work contacts in large enterprises may be highly esteemed by those who feel too closely bound by family and neighborhood. There is a gratification from working downtown in the city, uptown in the smaller urban center; there is the glamour of being attached to certain firms.

It is the status conferred on the exercise of given skills and on given income levels that is often the prime source of gratification or humiliation. The psychological effect of a detailed division of labor depends upon whether or not the worker has been downgraded, and upon whether or not his associates have also been downgraded. Pride in skill is relative to the skills he has exercised in the past and to the skills others exercise, and thus to the evaluation of his skills by other people whose opinions count. In like manner, the amount of money he receives may be seen by the employee and by others as the best gauge of his worth.

This may be all the more true when relations are increasingly 'objectified' and do not require intimate knowledge. For then there may be anxiety to keep secret the amount of money earned, and even to suggest to others that one earns more. 'Who earns the most?' asks Erich Engelhard. 'That is the important question, that is the gauge of all differentiations and the yardstick of the moneyed classes. We do not wish to show how we work, for in most cases others will soon have learned our tricks. This explains all the bragging. "The work I have to do!" exclaims one employee when he has only three letters to write. . . This boastfulness can be explained by a drive which impels certain people to evaluate their occupations very low in comparison with their intellectual aspirations but very high compared with the occupations of others.'

III. *Power:* Power over the technical aspects of work has been stripped from the individual, first, by the development of the market, which determines how and when he works, and second, by the bureaucratization of the work sphere, which subjects work operations to discipline. By virtue of these two alien forces the individual has lost power over the technical operations of his own work life.

But the exercise of power over other people has been elaborated. In so far as modern organizations of work are large scale, they are hierarchies of power, into which various occupations are fitted. The fact that one takes orders as well as gives them does not necessarily decrease the positive gratification achieved through the exercise of power on the job.

Status and power, as features of work gratification, are often blended; self-esteem may be based on the social power exercised in the course of work; victory over the will of another may greatly expand one's self-estimation. But the very opposite may also be true: in an almost masochistic way, people may be gratified by subordination on the job. We have already seen how office women in lower positions of authority are liable to identify with men in higher authority, transferring from prior family connections or projecting to future family relations.

All four aspects of occupation—skill, power, income, and status—must be taken into account to understand the meaning of work and the sources of its gratification. Any one of them may become the foremost aspect of the job, and in various combinations each is usually in the consciousness of the employee. To achieve and to exercise the power and status that higher income entails may be the very definition of satisfaction in work, and this satisfaction may have nothing whatsoever to do with the craft experience as the inherent need and full development of human activity.

5. The Morale of the Cheerful Robots

The institutions in which modern work is organized have come about by drift—many little schemes adding up to unexpected results—and by plan—efforts paying off as expected. The alienation of the individual from the product and the process of his work came about, in the first instance, as a result of the drift of modern capitalism. Then, Frederick Taylor, and other scientific managers, raised the division of labor to the level of planful management. By centralizing plans, as well as introducing further divisions of skill, they further routinized work; by consciously building upon the drift, in factory and in office, they have carried further certain of its efficient features.

Twenty years ago, H. Dubreuil, a foreign observer of U.S. industry, could write that Taylor's 'insufficiency' shows up when he comes to approach 'the inner forces contained in the worker's soul. . .' That is no longer true. The new (social) scientific management begins precisely where Taylor left off or was incomplete; students of 'human relations in industry' have studied not lighting and clean toilets, but social cliques and good morale. For in so far as human factors are involved in efficient and untroubled production, the managerial demiurge must bring them under control. So, in factory and in office, the world to be managed increasingly includes the social setting, the human affairs, and the personality of man as a worker.

Management effort to create job enthusiasm reflects the unhappy unwillingness of employees to work spontaneously at their routinized tasks; it indicates recognition of the lack of spontaneous will to work for the ulterior ends available; it also indicates that it is more difficult to have happy employees when the chances to climb the skill and social hierarchies are slim. These are underlying reasons why the Protestant ethic, a work compulsion, is replaced by the conscious efforts of Personnel Departments to create morale. But the present-day concern with employee morale and work enthusiasm has other sources than the meaningless character of much modern work. It is also a response to several decisive shifts in American society, particularly in its higher business circles: the enormous scale and complexity of modern business, its obviously vast and concentrated power; the rise of successfully competing centers of loyalty—the unions—over the past dozen years, with their inevitable focus upon power relations on the job; the enlargement of the liberal administrative state at the hands of politically successful New and Fair Deals; and the hostile atmosphere surrounding business during the big slump.

These developments have caused a shift in the outlook of certain sections of the business world, which in *The New Men of Power* I have called the shift from practical to sophisticated conservatism. The need to develop new justifications, and the fact that increased power has not yet been publicly justified, give rise to a groping for more telling symbols of justification among the more sophisticated business spokesmen, who have felt themselves to be a small island in a politically hostile sea of propertyless employees. Studies of 'human relations in industry' are an ideological part of this groping. The managers are interested in such studies because of the hope of lowering production costs, of easing tensions inside their plants, of finding new symbols to justify the concentrated power they exercise in modern society.

To secure and increase the will to work, a new ethic that endows work with more than an economic incentive is needed. During war, managers have appealed to nationalism; they have appealed in the name of the firm or branch of the office or factory, seeking to tap the animistic identifications of worker with work-place and tools in an effort to strengthen his identification with the company. They have repeatedly written that 'job enthusiasm is good business,' that 'job enthusiasm is a hallmark of the American Way.' But they have not yet found a really sound ideology.

What they are after is 'something in the employee' outwardly manifested in a 'mail must go through' attitude, 'the "we" attitude,' 'spontaneous discipline,' 'employees smiling and cheerful.'

They want, for example, to point out to banking employees 'their importance to banking and banking's importance to the general economy.' In conferences of management associations (1947) one hears: 'There is one thing more that is wonderful about the human body. Make the chemical in the vial a little different and you have a person who is loyal. He likes you, and when mishaps come he takes a lot from you and the company, because you have been so good to him; you have changed the structure of his blood. You have to put into his work and environment the things that change the chemical that stimulates the action, so that he is loyal and productive. . . Somebody working under us won't know why, but . . . when they are asked where they work and why, they say "I work with this company. I like it there and my boss is really one to work with." '

The over-all formula of advice that the new ideology of 'human relations in business' contains runs to this effect: to make the worker happy, efficient, and co-operative, you must make the managers intelligent, rational, knowledgeable. It is the perspective of a managerial elite, disguised in the pseudo-objective language of engineers. It is advice to the personnel manager to relax his authoritative manner and widen his manipulative grip over the employees by understanding them better and countering their informal solidarities against management and exploiting these solidarities for smoother and less troublesome managerial efficiency.

Current managerial attempts to create job enthusiasm, to paraphrase Marx's comment on Proudhon, are attempts to conquer work alienation within the bounds of work alienation. In the meantime, whatever satisfaction alienated men gain from work occurs within the framework of alienation; whatever satisfaction they gain from life occurs outside the boundaries of work; work and life are sharply split.

6. The Big Split

Only in the last half century has leisure been widely available to the weary masses of the big city. Before then, there was leisure only for those few who were socially trained to use and enjoy it; the rest of the populace was left on lower and bleaker levels of sensibility, taste, and feeling. Then as the sphere of leisure was won for more and more of the people, the techniques of mass production were applied to amusement as they had been to the sphere of work. The most ostensible feature of American social life today, and one of the most frenzied, is its mass leisure activities. The most important characteristic of all these activities is that they astonish, excite, and distract but they do not enlarge reason or feeling, or allow spontaneous dispositions to unfold creatively.

What is psychologically important in this shift to mass leisure is that the old middle-class work ethic—the gospel of work—has been replaced in the society of employees by a leisure ethic, and this replacement has involved a sharp, almost absolute split between work and leisure. Now work itself is judged in terms of leisure values. The sphere of leisure provides the standards by which work is judged; it lends to work such meanings as work has.

Alienation in work means that the most alert hours of one's life are sacrificed to the making of money with which to 'live.' Alienation means boredom and the frustration of potentially creative effort, of the productive sides of personality. It means that while men must seek all values that matter to them outside of work, they must be serious during work: they may not laugh or sing or even talk, they must follow the rules and not violate the fetish of 'the enterprise.' In short, they must be serious and steady about something that does not mean anything to them, and moreover during the best hours of their day, the best hours of their life. Leisure time thus comes to mean an unserious freedom from the authoritarian seriousness of the job.

The split of work from leisure and the greater importance of leisure in the striving consciousness of modern man run through the whole fabric of twentieth-century America, affect the meaningful experiences of work, and set popular goals and daydreams. Over the last forty years, Leo Lowenthal has shown, as the 'idols of work' have declined, the 'idols of leisure' have arisen. Now the selection of heroes for popular biography appearing in mass magazines has shifted from business, professional, and political figures—successful in the sphere of production—to those successful in entertainment, leisure, and consumption. The movie star and the baseball player have replaced the industrial magnate and the political man. Today, the displayed characteristics of popular idols 'can all be integrated around the concept of the consumer.' And the faculties of reflection, imagination, dream, and desire, so far as they exist, do not now move in the sphere of concrete, practical work experience.

Work is split from the rest of life, especially from the spheres of conscious enjoyment; nevertheless, most men and many women must work. So work is an unsatisfactory means to ulterior ends lying somewhere in the sphere of leisure. The necessity to work and the alienation from it make up its grind, and the more grind there is, the more need to find relief in the jumpy or dreamy models available in modern leisure. Leisure contains all good things and all goals dreamed of and actively pursued. The dreariest part of life, R. H. Tawney remarks, is where and when you work, the gayest where and when you consume.

Each day men sell little pieces of themselves in order to try to buy them back each night and week end with the coin of 'fun.' With amusement, with love, with movies, with vicarious intimacy, they pull themselves into some sort of whole again, and now they are different men. Thus, the cycle of work and leisure gives rise to two quite different images of self: the everyday image, based upon work, and the holiday image, based upon leisure. The holiday image is often heavily tinged with aspired-to and dreamed-of features and is, of course, fed by mass-media personalities and happenings. 'The rhythm of the week end, with its birth, its planned gaieties, and its announced end,' Scott Fitzgerald wrote, 'followed the rhythm of life and was a substitute for it.' The week end, having nothing in common with the working week, lifts men and women out of the gray level tone of everyday work life, and forms a standard with which the working life is contrasted.

As the work sphere declines in meaning and gives no inner direction and rhythm to life, so have community and kinship circles declined as ways of 'fixing man into society.' In the old craft model, work sphere and family coincided; before the Industrial Revolution, the home and the workshop were one. Today, this is so only in certain smaller-bourgeois families, and there it is often seen by the young as repression. One result of the division of labor is to take the breadwinner out of the home, segregating work life and home life. This has often meant that work becomes the means for the maintenance of the home, and the home the means for refitting the worker to go back to work. But with the decline of the home as the center of psychological life and the lowering of the hours of work, the sphere of leisure and amusement takes over the home's functions.

No longer is the framework within which a man lives fixed by traditional institutions. Mass communications replace tradition as a framework of life. Being thus afloat, the metropolitan man finds a new anchorage in the spectator sports, the idols of the mass media, and other machineries of amusement.

So the leisure sphere—and the machinery of amusement in terms of which it is now organized—becomes the center of character-forming influences, of identification models: it is what one man has in common with another; it is a continuous interest. The machinery of amusement, Henry Durant remarks, focuses attention and desires upon 'those aspects of our life which are divorced from work and on people who are significant, not in terms of what they have achieved, but in terms of having money and time to spend.'

The amusement of hollow people rests on their own hollowness and does not fill it up; it does not calm or relax them, as old middle-class frolics and jollification may have done; it does not re-create their spontaneity in work, as in the craftsman model. Their leisure diverts them from the restless grind of their work by the absorbing grind of passive enjoyment of glamour and thrills. To modern man leisure is the way to spend money, work is the way to make it. When the two compete, leisure wins hands down.

11

The Status Panic

Prestige involves at least two persons: one to claim it and another to honor the claim. The bases on which various people raise prestige claims, and the reasons others honor these claims, include property and birth, occupation and education, income and power—in fact almost anything that may invidiously distinguish one person from another. In the status system of a society these claims are organized as rules and expectations which regulate who successfully claims prestige, from whom, in what ways, and on what basis. The level of self-esteem enjoyed by given individuals is more or less set by this status system.

The extent to which claims for prestige are honored, and by whom they are honored, may vary widely. Some of those from whom an individual claims prestige may honor his claims, others may not; some deferences that are given may express genuine feelings of esteem; others may be expedient strategies for ulterior ends. A society may, in fact, contain many hierarchies of prestige, each with its own typical bases and areas of bestowal, or one hierarchy in which everyone uniformly 'knows his place' and is always in it. It is in the latter that prestige groups are most likely to be uniform and continuous.

Imagine a society in which everyone's prestige is absolutely set and unambivalent; every man's claims for prestige are balanced by the prestige he receives, and both his expression of claims and the ways these claims are honored by others are set forth in understood stereotypes. Moreover, the bases of the claims coincide with the reasons they are honored: those who claim

239

prestige on the specific basis of property or birth are honored because of their property or birth. So the exact volume and types of deference expected between any two individuals are always known, expected, and given; and each individual's level and type of self-esteem are steady features of his inner life.

Now imagine the opposite society, in which prestige is highly unstable and ambivalent: the individual's claims are not usually honored by others. The way claims are expressed are not understood or acknowledged by those from whom deference is expected, and when others do bestow prestige, they do so unclearly. One man claims prestige on the basis of his income, but even if he is given prestige, it is not because of his income but rather, for example, his education or appearance. All the controlling devices by which the volume and type of deference might be directed are out of joint or simply do not exist. So the prestige system is no system, but a maze of misunderstanding, of sudden frustration and sudden indulgence, and the individual, as his self-esteem fluctuates, is under strain and full of anxiety.

American society in the middle of the twentieth century does not fit either of these projections absolutely, but it seems fairly clear that it is closer to the unstable and ambivalent model. This is not to say that there is no prestige system in the United States; given occupational levels, however caught in status ambivalence, do enjoy typical levels of prestige. It is to say, however, that the enjoyment of prestige is often disturbed and uneasy, that the bases of prestige, the expressions of prestige claims, and the ways these claims are honored, are now subject to great strain, a strain which often puts men and women in a virtual status panic.

1. White-Collar Prestige

The prestige position of white-collar employees has been one of the most arguable points about them as strata, the major point to be explained by those who would locate them in modern social structures. Although no one dimension of stratification can be adequate, the social esteem white-collar employees have successfully claimed is one of their important defining characteristics. In fact, their psychology can often be understood as the psychology of prestige striving. That it is often taken as their signal attribute probably reflects the effort, which we accept, to overcome the exclusively economic view of stratification; it also reflects the desire, which we reject, to encompass the entire group with a single slogan.

White-collar people's claims to prestige are expressed, as their label implies, by their style of appearance. Their occupations enable and require them to wear street clothes at work. Although they may be expected to dress somewhat somberly, still, their working attire is not a uniform, or distinct from clothing generally suitable for street wear. The standardization and mass production of fashionable clothing have wiped out many distinctions that were important up to the twentieth century, but they have not eliminated the distinctions still typical between white-collar and wage-worker. The wage-worker may wear standardized street clothes off the job, but the white-collar worker wears them on the job as well. This difference is revealed by the clothing budgets of wage-workers and white-collar people, especially of girls and women. After later adolescence, women working as clerks, compared with wage-working women of similar income, spend a good deal more on clothes; and the same is true of men, although to a lesser extent.

The class position of employed people depends on their chances in the labor market; their status position depends on their chances in the commodity market. Claims for prestige are raised on the basis of consumption; but since consumption is limited by income, class position and status position intersect. At this intersection, clothing expenditure is, of course, merely an index, although a very important one, to the style of appearance and the life-ways displayed by the white-collar strata.

Claims for prestige, however expressed, must be honored by others, and, in the end, must rest upon more or less widely acknowledged bases, which distinguish the people of one social stratum from others. The prestige of any stratum, of course, is based upon its mutually recognized relations with other strata. The 'middle position' of white-collar people between independent employers and wage-workers, 'a negative characteristic—rather than definite technical functions,' Emil Lederer wrote in 1912, 'is the social mark of the salaried employees and establishes their social character in their own consciousness and in the estimation of the community.' *

Salaried employees have been associated with entrepreneurs, and later with higher-ups in the managerial cadre, and they have borrowed prestige from both. In the latter nineteenth century, the foreman, the salesclerk, and the office man were widely viewed, and viewed themselves, as apprentices or assistants to old middle-class people. Drawing upon their future hopes to join these ranks, they were able to borrow the prestige of the people for whom they worked, and with whom they were in close, often personal, contact. White-collar people intermarried with members of the old middle class and enjoyed common social activities; in many cases the salaried man represented the entrepreneur to the public and was recruited from the same social levels—mainly, the old rural middle class. All this—descent, association, and expectation—made it possible for earlier salaried employees to borrow status from the old middle class.

Today, in big city as well as small town, white-collar workers continue to borrow such prestige. It is true that in larger concerns personal contacts with old middle-class entrepreneurs have been superseded by impersonal contacts with the lower rungs of the new managerial cadre. Still, all white-collar people do not lack personal contact with employers; not all of them are employed in the big lay-out, which, in many areas, is as yet the model of the future more than of present reality. The general images of the white-collar people, in terms of which they are often able to cash in claims for prestige, are drawn from present reality. Moreover, even in the big hierarchies, white-collar people often have more contact—and usually feel that they do—with higher-ups than do factory workers.

The prestige cleavage between 'the shop' and 'the front office' often seems to exist quite independently of the low income and routine character of many front-office jobs and the high pay and skills of jobs in the shop. For orders and pay checks come from

* According to a recent National Opinion Research rating, on a scale running from 90.8 for government officials and 80.6 for professionals and semi-professionals (both free and salaried) to 45.8 for non-farm laborers, the whole group of 'clerical, sales, and kindred workers' stand at 68.2, about on a par with the 'craftsmen, foremen, and kindred workers.'

the office and are associated with it; and those who are somehow of it are endowed with some of the prestige that attends its function in the life of the wage-worker. The tendency of white-collar people to borrow status from higher elements is so strong that it has carried over to all social contacts and features of the workplace.

Salespeople in department stores, as we have already seen, frequently attempt, although often unsuccessfully, to borrow prestige from their contact with customers, and to cash it in among work colleagues as well as friends off the job. In the big city the girl who works on 34th Street cannot successfully claim as much prestige as the one who works on Fifth Avenue or 57th Street. Writes one observer: 'A salesgirl in Bonwit Teller's . . . will act and feel different from a salesgirl at Macy's. She will be more gracious, more helpful, more charming . . . but at the same time she will have an air of dignity and distance about her, an air of distinction, that implies, "I am more important than you because my customers come from Park Avenue." '

It is usually possible to know the prestige of salespeople in department stores in terms of the commodities they handle, ranked according to the 'expensiveness' of the people who typically buy them. Prestige may be borrowed directly from the commodities themselves, although this is not as likely as borrowing from the type of customer.

If white-collar relations with supervisors and higher-ups, with customers or clients, become so impersonal as seriously to limit borrowing prestige from them, prestige is then often borrowed from the firm or the company itself. The fetishism of the enterprise, and identification with the firm, are often as relevant for the white-collar hirelings as for the managers. This identification may be implemented by the fact that the work itself, as a set of activities, offers little chance for external prestige claims and internal self-esteem. So the work one does is buried in the name of the firm. The typist or the salesgirl does not think of herself in terms of what she does, but as being 'with Saks' or 'working at *Time*.' A $38-a-week clerk in a chrome and mahogany setting in Radio City will often successfully raise higher claims for prestige than a $50-a-week stenographer in a small, dingy office on Seventh Avenue. Help-Wanted ads ('Beautifully Furnished Office in Rockefeller Center,' 'Large Nation-wide Concern,' 'Offices located on 32nd floor of Empire State Building') reveal conscious appeal to the status striving of the office worker. Such positions are often easier to fill, not because of higher salary and more rapid promotion, but because of the prestige of the firm's name or location.

In identifying with a firm, the young executive can sometimes line up his career expectations with it, and so identify his own future with that of the firm's. But lower down the ranks, the identification has more to do with security and prestige than with expectations of success. In either case, of course, such feelings can be exploited in the interests of business loyalties.

In the impersonal white-collar hierarchies, employees often attempt to personalize their surroundings in order to identify with them more closely and draw prestige therefrom. In the personnel literature, there are many illustrations of an often pathetic striving for a sense of importance—for example, when a girl's chair is taken from her and she is given one thought more convenient for her work, her production drops. When questioned, she asks, 'Why are you picking on me?' and explains that she had used the old chair for five years and it had her name plate on it. When the name plate is transferred to the new chair, it is explained, her attitude changes, and her production comes up to normal. Similar observations have been made in connection with the arrangement of desks in an office, in which, unknown to management, the old pattern had been in terms of seniority. Women are probably more alert to these prestige borrowings than men. The first consideration of one large group of women seeking employment had to do with 'the office environment,' the state of the equipment, the appearance of the place, the 'class of people' working there. Periodical salary increases and initial salary were both ranked below such considerations. Of course, such prestige matters often involve the desire to be available on a market for more marriageable males, yet the material signs of the status environment are in themselves crucial to the white-collar sense of importance.

That white-collar work requires more mental capacity and less muscular effort than wage work has been a standard, historical basis for prestige claims. In the office, as we have seen, white-collar technology and social rationalization have definitely lessened technical differences between white-collar and factory work. Many white-collar people now operate light machinery at a pace and under conditions that are quite similar to those of light industrial operations, even if they do so while wearing street clothes rather than overalls. Still, the variety of operations and the degree of autonomous decision are taken as bases of white-collar prestige. And it is true that in thousands of offices and salesrooms, the receptionist, the salesgirl, the general secretary, and even the typist seems to perform a wide variety of different operations at her own pace and according to her own decisions.

The time required to learn white-collar skills and how they are learned has been an important basis of their prestige, even though as white-collar work is rationalized the time needed to acquire the necessary skills decreases. Some 80 per cent of the people at work, it is frequently estimated, now perform work that can be learned in less than three months. Accompanying this rationalization of the work process, a stratum of highly skilled experts has arisen. Over the whole society, this stratum is popularly, even if erroneously, associated with 'white-collar' work, while the semi-skilled is associated with wage work. So those white-collar workers who are in fact quite unskilled and routinized still borrow from the prestige of the skills.

More crucially, perhaps, than type of skill is the fact that many white-collar skills are still acquired at school rather than on the job. The two ways of learning working skills that carry most prestige have been combined in many white-collar areas, whereas neither is now prevalent among wage-workers. Apprenticeship, involving close contact with entrepreneurs or managerial levels, continued in white-collar occupations after they had ceased to exist in wage work; then, formal education, in high school and 'business college,' became the typical white-collar way.

The shift from small independent property to dependent occupations greatly increases the weight of formal education in determining life conditions. For the new middle class, education has replaced property as the insurance of social position. The saving and sacrifice of the new middle class to insure a 'good education' for the child replace the saving and sacrifice of the old middle class to insure that the child may inherit 'the good property' with which to earn his livelihood. The inheritance of occupational ambition, and of the education that is its condition, replaces the inheritance of property.

To acquire some white-collar skills requires twenty years of formal and expensive education; others may be learned in one day, and are more efficiently performed by those with little education. For some white-collar jobs, people above the grammar-school level are not wanted, for fear boredom would lead to slow-down by frustration; for others, only the Ph.D. is allowed to go to work. But the educational center around which the white-collar worlds revolve is the high school.

In 1890, only 7 out of every 100 boys and girls between 14 and 17 were enrolled in high schools; by 1940, 73 out of every 100 were. During these fifty years, the number of children of this age increased some 82 per cent, the number of high-school enroll-ments, 1,888 per cent. The white-collar people, the great deposi-tory of the High-School Culture implanted in U.S. youth, have completed an average of 12.4 years of school, compared with the free enterprisers' 8.4 and the wage-workers' 8.2 years.* On every occupational level, white-collar men and women are better edu-cated, except for the single one of independent professionals, who, of course, lead educationally with 16.4 years of schooling. Many a clerk in a small office has a less educated, although more experienced, boss; many a salesclerk in a small store is super-vised by a higher-up not so well educated as she. Of course, the higher educational level of the white-collar people in part reflects their youthfulness; being younger, they have had more oppor-tunities for education. But they have availed themselves of it; for in the white-collar pyramids education has 'paid off'; it has been a source of cash and a means of ascent. Here 'knowledge,' although not power, has been a basis for prestige.†

* The breakdown by detailed groups (median years of school com-pleted, 1940): farmers, 7.6 years; businessmen, 9.9; free professionals, 16.4; managers, 10.8; salaried professionals, 14.9; salespeople, 12.1; office workers, 12.3; skilled workers, 8.5; semi-skilled, 8.4; unskilled, 8.2; rural workers, 7.3.

† No doubt some prestige accrues to white-collar people because of their youthfulness, first because if they are young they may, in the American ethos, still be hopefully seen as having more to win; and sec-

Even today, white-collar occupations contain the highest general average of educated people; but twenty-five years ago this was much more strongly the case; in large part, white-collar people monopolized intermediate and higher education. Twenty-five years ahead it will not necessarily be the case; in fact, all trends point to the continued narrowing of the educational gap between white-collar and wage-worker.

Fifty years ago the general labor market was almost entirely composed of grade-school graduates; today of high-school graduates; by the early 'fifties 9½ million college-educated youth will be in the labor market. Most of them will reach for the white-collar job, and many of them will not find routinized white-collar jobs a challenge, for, as H. K. Tootle has estimated for an office-management association, 'educated youth is being channeled into business faster than job satisfactions can be developed for it. . . As there are not enough stimulating jobs for the hordes of college graduates we see descending upon us in the years to come like swarms of hungry locusts, they will have to take jobs that satisfy, or perhaps even now do not satisfy, the high-school graduate.'

As the general educational level rises, the level of education required or advisable for many white-collar jobs falls. In the early 'twenties, personnel men said: 'I think it has become a principle with the majority of our progressive offices that they will not take into the office any person or candidate who has not had the benefit of at least a high-school education.' But soon they began to say that too much education was not advisable for many white-collar jobs. In fact, the educated intelligence has become penalized in routinized work, where the search is for those who are less easily bored and hence more cheerfully efficient. 'When you employ 2600 clerks,' says one personnel supervisor, 'you don't want all college people. I much prefer the young fellow who is fresh from high school, or graduated from normal school, and who is full of pep and ambition, and wants to get ahead. We could not use college men in many of our positions.' Education, in short, comes to be viewed as a sort of frustrating trap.

The rationalization of office and store undermines the special skills based on experience and education. It makes the employee

ondly, because youth itself often carries prestige, a prestige that is much advertised by displayed models and expected efficiency.

easy to replace by shortening the training he needs; it weakens not only his bargaining power but his prestige. It opens white-collar positions to people with less education, thus destroying the educational prestige of white-collar work, for there is no inherent prestige attached to the nature of any work; it is, Hans Speier remarks, the esteem the people doing it enjoy that often lends prestige to the work itself. In so far as white-collar workers base their claims for external prestige and their own self-esteem upon educated skills, they open themselves to a precarious psychological life.

In the United States, white-collar people have been able to claim higher prestige than wage-workers because of racial, but to a greater extent and in a more direct way, national origin.

The number of Negroes in white-collar jobs is negligible, but especially since World War I, considerable numbers have worked in unskilled and semi-skilled factory jobs. The new middle class contains a greater proportion of white people than any other occupational stratum: in 1940, some 99.5 per cent of the white-collar, compared with 90 per cent of free enterprisers, 87 per cent of urban wage-workers, and 74 per cent of rural workers.

Nativity and immigration differences between white-collar and wage-work are probably more direct bases of white-collar prestige. When the 'race peril' literature was popular, the textbook myth about the lowly character of newer immigrants was also widespread. Most of the major American historians of the period between 1875 and 1925 belligerently declared the superiority of 'Anglo-Saxon' stock, concludes Edward Saveth. Being of old stock themselves, their 'conception of the immigrant reflected, in some degree, their feeling that the newcomer somehow constituted a threat to what they hold dear, ideologically and materially. . .' Mass as well as academic publicity reflected and spread the fact of prestige distinctions between immigrant and native.

If the 'American' stature of a group may be judged by the proportion of its native-born members, white-collar workers have been the most American of all occupational strata. In 1930, after mass immigration had been stopped, only 9 per cent of the white population of the new middle class were foreign-born, compared to 16 per cent of the free enterprisers and 21 per cent of the wage-workers. But now there is no bulk immigration: soon, virtually all Americans will be American-born of American-born parents. Time will not automatically erase the prestige cleavages based on descent, but, for most white-collar- and wage-workers. as they become more similar in origin, it probably will. In the meantime, nativity differences still underlie the prestige claims of white-collar groups.

Every basis on which the prestige claims of the bulk of the white-collar employees have historically rested has been declining in firmness and stability: the rationalization and down-grading of the work operations themselves and hence the lessening importance of education and experience in acquiring white-collar skills; the leveling down of white-collar and the raising of wage-worker incomes, so that the differences between them are decidedly less than they once were; the increased size of the white-collar labor market, as more people from lower ranks receive high-school educations, so that any monopoly of formal training adequate to these jobs is no longer possible; the decline in the proportion of people of immigrant origin and the consequent narrowing of nativity differences between white-collar and wage-worker; the increased participation of white-collar people, along with wage-workers, in unemployment; and the increased economic and public power of wage-workers because of their union strength, as compared with that of white-collar workers.

All these tendencies for white-collar occupations to sink in prestige rest upon the numerical enlargement of the white-collar strata and the increase in prestige which the wage-workers have enjoyed. If everybody belongs to the fraternity, nobody gets any prestige from belonging. As the white-collar strata have expanded they have included more offspring of wage-worker origin; moreover, in so far as their prestige has rested upon their sharing the authority of those in charge of the enterprise, that authority has itself lost much of its prestige, having been successfully challenged at many points by unionized wage-workers.

Although trends should not be confused with accomplished facts, it is clear that many trends point to a 'status proletarianization' of white-collar strata.

2. The Smaller City

To understand the prestige of white-collar people we must examine the kinds of people among whom they successfully raise claims for prestige. For different groups do not honor white-collar claims to the same extent; in fact, their estimates often clash, and there is much ambivalence about white-collar prestige.

White-collar workers are city people; in the smaller cities, they live on the right side of the tracks and work 'uptown'; in the larger cities they often live in suburbs and work 'downtown.' The city is their milieu and they are shaped by its mass ways. As the city has expanded, more and more of its inhabitants have been white-collar people. And it is in cities of differing size that they must raise their claims for prestige.

In the smaller cities, lower classes sometimes use the term 'white collar' to refer to everyone above themselves. Sometimes their attitude is that white-collar people are 'pencil pushers' who 'sit around and don't work and figure out ways of keeping wages cheap'; and sometimes it is that 'the clerks are very essential. They are the ones who keep the ball rolling for the other guy. We would be lost if we didn't have the clerks.' The upper classes, on the other hand, never acknowledge white-collar people as of the upper levels and sometimes even place them with 'the laborers.' An upper-class man in a city of 60,000, for instance, says: 'Next after retailers, I would put the policemen, firemen, the average factory worker and the white-collar clerks. . . I've lived in this town all my life and come to the bank every day but Sunday and I can't name five clerks downtown I know.'

This situation of white-collar prestige in the smaller city is in part due to the fact that white-collar occupations are divided into higher and lower, in terms of almost every basis on which prestige claims might be made: social origin, occupational history, income, education. Now, the images held of the white-collar people by upper-class groups seem to be derived, by and large, from the lower groups of these occupations, the 'clerk' and the 'salesperson.' When upper-class individuals do focus upon higher-income salesmen, or professional and managerial employees, they think of them as part of 'business' rather than as part of 'white collar.' Members of lower classes, on the other hand, tend to blend white collar, both higher and lower, into business and to make little distinction between them.

The ambiguous prestige of the smaller businessman in these smaller cities is explained, in part, by the 'power' ascribed to him by lower groups but denied to him by the upper. In so far as power is concerned, the ambiguous status position of the white-collar worker rests less upon complications in his power position than upon his lack of any power. White-collar employees have no leaders active as their representatives in civic efforts; they are not represented as a stratum in the councils; they have no autonomous organizations through which to strive for political and civic ends; they are seldom, if ever, in the publicity spotlight. No articulate leaders appeal directly to them, or draw strength from their support. In the organized power of the middle-sized city, there is no autonomous white-collar unit.

The few organizations in which white-collar employees are sometimes predominant—the Business and Professional Women's Clubs, the Junior Chamber of Commerce, and the YWCA—are so tied in with business groups that they have little or no autonomy. Socially, the lower white-collar people are usually on 'the Elk level,' the higher in the No. 2 or 3 social club; in both they are part of a 'middle-class mingling' pattern. They are 'led,' if at all, by higher-income salesmen and other 'contact people,' who are themselves identified with 'business,' and whose activities thus lend prestige to businessmen rather than to white-collar people.

Even in the smaller cities, then, there is no homogeneous social arena in which white-collar prestige is uniformly honored; in the big city this fact is the key to the character of white-collar prestige.

3. The Metropolis

The rise of the big city has modified the prestige structure of modern society: it has greatly enlarged the social areas with reference to which prestige is claimed; it has split the individual from easily identifiable groups in which he might claim prestige and in which his claims might be acknowledged; it has given rise to many diverse, segregated areas in each of which the individual may advance claims; and it has made these areas impersonal. The prestige market of the big city is often a market of strangers, a milieu where contacts having relevance to prestige are often transitory and fleeting.

The neighbors of the small-town man know much of what is to be known about him. The metropolitan man is a temporary focus of heterogeneous circles of casual acquaintances, rather than a fixed center of a few well-known groups. So personal snoopiness is replaced by formal indifference; one has contacts, rather than relations, and these contacts are shorter-lived and more superficial. 'The more people one knows the easier it becomes to replace them.'

The metropolitan man's biography is often unknown, his past apparent only to very limited groups, so the basis of his status is often hidden and ambivalent, revealed only in the fast-changing appearances of his mobile, anonymous existence. Intimacy and the personal touch, no longer intrinsic to his way of life, are often contrived devices of impersonal manipulation. Rather than cohesion there is uniformity, rather than descent or tradition, interests. Physically close, but socially distant, human relations become at once intense and impersonal—and in every detail, pecuniary.

Apart from educational opportunities, the status of most middle- and working-class people becomes individualized, one generation cut off from the other. Among the propertyless, status must be won anew by each generation. The small businessman's sons or the farmer's might look forward to the inheritance of a more or less secure property as a basis for their status; the floor-walker's sons or the assistant manager's cannot expect to inherit such family position.

The more transparent lives of people in smaller cities permit status bases, such as social origin, to be more readily transferred to various occupational levels. The nature of the opaque contacts characteristic of big city life make this difficult: members of one occupational level may see or even contact members of others, but usually in a stereotyped rather than in a personal manner. They meet on impersonal terms and then retire into their socially insulated personal lives. In smaller cities and smaller enterprises, the status lines between white-collar and wage-worker are, per-haps, drawn most clearly. In metropolitan areas white-collar people seldom contact wage-workers; the physical lay-out of the city, the segregation of routes of travel for different occupations often restrict people to separate circles of acquaintances.

The mass media, primarily movies and radio, have further en-larged the whole prestige area and the means of status expres-sion. In the media the life styles of the top levels are displayed to the bottom in a way and to an extent not previously the case.

Some communication system is needed to cover any prestige area, and in modern times, with the enlargement of prestige areas, 'being seen' in the formal media is taken as a basis of status claims as well as a cashing of them. When national prestige was focused in local society, local newspapers used to be the princi-pal media involved in the prestige of local society matrons. But since the 1920's, radio and especially motion pictures and TV have supplemented newspapers and have created a national status market in which the movie star, a status type who sud-denly acquires liquid assets and a lavish style of life has re-placed the local society matron. The deciders and originators in matters of the highest fashion and style of life have definitely passed from the old families of Boston, Philadelphia, Baltimore, and Newport to the stars of Hollywood and Radio City.

'In Newport, and on Fifth Avenue,' Lloyd Morris has observed, 'wealth had been a weapon indispensable to those who fought to win social power. In Hollywood, social prestige was an instru-ment essential to those determined to win wealth.' The society reporters of all the eastern cities combined cannot compete with the several hundred journalists who cover Hollywood. Two dozen magazines are devoted to the film center; Louella Parsons reaches thirty million readers. Eighteen thousand movie houses are vis-ited by ninety million people each week. The heterogeneous public appears avid for intimate details of the Hollywood elite. And the movies, which made them an elite, are set up to supply new images of them continuously. Not the society matron, but the movie star becomes the model for the office girl.

The rich of previous eras could not so readily be known by the public, the way they lived being known only by hearsay and glimpses through curtained windows. But by the 1920's in America a democracy of status vision had come about; the area of prestige was truly national; now the bottom could see the top —at least that version of it that was put on display. It did not matter if this top was sometimes contrived and often a cloak. It did not matter if the real top was even more secluded and unseen than before. For those on the bottom, the top presented was real and it was dazzling.

The enlargement and animation, the anonymity and the transitoriness, the faster turnover and the increased visibility of the top, filling the individual's vision with a series of big close-ups— these changes have been paralleled by less noticed but equally intense changes in the prestige dynamics of the middle and lower strata.

4. The Status Panic

The historic bases of white-collar prestige are now infirm; the areas in which white-collar people must seek to have their claims honored are agitated. Both sides of the situation in which they are caught impel them to emphasize prestige and often to engage in a great striving for its symbols. In this, three mechanisms seem to be operating:

1. In the white-collar hierarchies, as we have seen, individuals are often segregated by minute gradations of rank, and, at the same time, subject to a fragmentation of skill. This bureaucratization often breaks up the occupational bases of their prestige. Since the individual may seize upon minute distinctions as bases for status, these distinctions operate against any status solidarity among the mass of employees, often lead to status estrangement from work associates, and to increased status competition. The employees are thus further alienated from work, for, in striving for the next rank, they come to anticipate identification with it, so that now they are not *really* in their places. Like money, status that is exterior to one's present work does not lead to intrinsic work gratification. Only if present work leads to the anticipated goal by a progression of skills, and is thus given meaning, will status aspirations not alienate the worker. Status ascent within

the hierarchy is a kind of illusionary success, for it does not necessarily increase income or the chance to learn superior skills. Above all, the hierarchy is often accompanied by a delirium for status merely because of its authoritarian shape: as Karl Mannheim has observed, people who are dependent for everything, including images of themselves, upon place in an authoritarian hierarchy, will all the more frantically cling to claims of status.

The sharp split of residence from work place, characteristic of urban life since the Industrial Revolution, is most clearly manifested in the big city suburb, where work associates are formally segregated from neighbors. This means that the subordinate may compete in two status worlds, that of work place in the big city and that of residence in the suburb.

At the work place, it is difficult, even in large enterprises, to inflate real occupational status, although great status tensions are likely to be lodged there. But actual job position is not so well known to those whom one meets away from work. It may be that to the extent that status aspirations and claims are frustrated at work, there is a more intense striving to realize them off the job. If the status struggle within the job hierarchy is lost, the status struggle outside the job area shifts its ground: one hides his exact job, claims prestige from his title or firm, or makes up job, title, or firm. Among anonymous metropolitan throngs, one can make claims about one's job, as well as about other bases of prestige, which minimize or override actual occupational status.

The place of residence, which is a signal of income and style of life, limits this inflation of status; for neighbors, like job associates, will not readily cash in higher claims. But there are other areas. Anonymous and the just-known strangers, who cannot so readily 'place' one, may cash in one's claims. Among them, the first, often the only, impression one makes may permit a brief success in status claiming, sometimes as a sort of mutual deal.

II. 'Under modern conditions,' Thorstein Veblen wrote, 'the struggle for existence has, in a very appreciable degree, been transformed into a struggle to keep up appearance.' Personal worth and integrity may count for something but 'one's reputation for excellence in this direction does not penetrate far enough into the very wide environment to which a person is exposed in

modern society to satisfy even a very modest craving for respectability. To sustain one's dignity—and to sustain one's self-respect—
under the eyes of people who are not socially one's immediate
neighbors, it is necessary to display the token of economic worth,
which practically coincides . . . with economic success.'

The leisure of many middle-class people is entirely taken up
by attempts to gratify their status claims. Just as work is made
empty by the processes of alienation, so leisure is made hollow
by status snobbery and the demands of emulative consumption.
It takes money to do something nice in one's off time—when
there is an absence of inner resources and a status avoidance of
cheaper or even costless forms of entertainment. With the urban
breakdown of compact social groups in smaller communities, the
prestige relations become impersonal; in the metropolis, when
the job becomes an insecure basis or even a negative one, then
the sphere of leisure and appearance become more crucial for
status.

'One does not "make much of a showing" in the eyes of the
large majority of the people whom one meets with,' Veblen continued, 'except by unremitting demonstration of ability to pay.
That is practically the only means which the average of us have
of impressing our respectability on the many to whom we are
personally unknown, but whose transient good opinion we would
so gladly enjoy. So it comes about that the appearance of success
is very much to be desired, and is even in many cases preferred
to the substance . . . the modern industrial organization of society has practically narrowed the scope of emulation to this one
line; and at the same time it has made the means of sustenance
and comfort so much easier to obtain as very materially to widen
the margin of human exertion that can be devoted to purposes
of emulation.'

Of an eighteenth-century nobility, Dickens could say that 'dress
was the one unfailing talisman and charm used for keeping all
things in their places,' but in a mass society without a stable
system of status, with quick, cheap imitations, dress is often no
talisman. The clerk who sees beautifully gowned women in the
movies and on the streets may wear imitations if she works hard
and, skipping the spiced ham sandwich, has only cokes for lunch.
Her imitations are easily found out, but that is not to say they

do not please her. Self-respectability is not the same as self-respect. On the personality markets, emotions become ceremonial gestures by which status is claimed, alienated from the inner feelings they supposedly express. Self-estrangement is thus inherent in the fetishism of appearance.

III. The prestige enjoyed by individual white-collar workers is not continuously fixed by large forces, for their prestige is not continuously the same. Many are involved in status cycles, which, as Tom Harrison has observed, often occur in a sort of rhythmic pattern. These cycles allow people in a lower class and status level to act like persons on higher levels and temporarily to get away with it.

During weekdays the white-collar employee receives a given volume of deference from a given set of people, work associates, friends, family members, and from the transient glimpses of strangers on transport lines and street. But over the week end, or perhaps a week end once a month. one can by plan raise oneself to higher status: clothing changes, the restaurant or type of food eaten changes, the best theater seats are had. One cannot well change one's residence over the week end, but in the big city one can get away from it, and in the small town one can travel to the near-by city. Expressed claims of status may be raised, and more importantly those among whom one claims status may vary—even if these others are other strangers in different locales. And every white-collar girl knows the value of a strict segregation of regular boy friends, who might drop around the apartment any night of the week, from the special date for whom she always dresses and with whom she always goes out.

There may also be a more dramatic yearly status cycle, involving the vacation as its high point. Urban masses look forward to vacations not 'just for the change,' and not only for a 'rest from work'—the meaning behind such phrases is often a lift in successful status claims. For on vacation, one can *buy* the feeling, even if only for a short time, of higher status. The expensive resort, where one is not known, the swank hotel, even if for three days and nights, the cruise first class—for a week. Much vacation apparatus is geared to these status cycles; the staffs as well as clientele play-act the whole set-up as if mutually consenting to be part of the successful illusion. For such experiences once a year, sacrifices are often made in long stretches of gray weekdays. The bright two weeks feed the dream life of the dull pull.

Psychologically, status cycles provide, for brief periods of time, a holiday image of self, which contrasts sharply with the self-image of everyday reality. They provide a temporary satisfaction of the person's prized image of self, thus permitting him to cling to a false consciousness of his status position. They are among the forces that rationalize and make life more bearable, compensate for economic inferiority by allowing temporary satisfaction of the ambition to consume.

Socially, status cycles blur the realities of class and prestige differences by offering respite from them. Talk of the 'status fluidity of American life' often refers merely to status cycles, even though socially these cycles of higher display and holiday gratification do not modify the long-run reality of more fixed positions.

Status cycles further the tendency of economic ambition to be fragmented, made trivial, and temporarily satisfied in terms of commodities and their ostentatious display. The whole ebb and flow of saving and spending, of working and consuming, may be geared to them. Like those natives who starve until whales are tossed upon the beach, and then gorge, white-collar workers may suffer long privation of status until the month-end or year-end, and then splurge in an orgy of prestige gratification and consumption.

Between the high points of the status cycle and the machinery of amusement there is a coincidence: the holiday image of self derives from both. In the movie the white-collar girl vicariously plays the roles she thinks she would like to play, cashes in her claims for esteem. At the peak of her status cycle she crudely play-acts the higher levels, as she believes she would like to always. The machinery of amusement and the status cycle sustain the illusionary world in which many white-collar people now live.

12

Success

'SUCCESS' in America has been a widespread fact, an engaging image, a driving motive, and a way of life. In the middle of the twentieth century, it has become less widespread as fact, more confused as image, often dubious as motive, and soured as a way of life.

No other domestic change is so pivotal for the tang and feel of society in America, or more ambiguous for the inner life of the individual, and none has been so intricately involved in the transformation of the old into the new middle classes. Other strata have certainly been affected, but the middle classes have been most grievously modified by the newer meanings of success and the increased chances of failure.

To understand the meaning of this shift we must understand the major patterns of American success and the ideologies characteristic of each of them; the changing role of the educational system as an occupational elevator; and the long-run forces, as well as the effects of the slump-war-boom cycle, which lift or lower the rate of upward movement.

1. Patterns and Ideologies

During booms, success for the American individual has seemed as sure as social progress, and just as surely to rest on and to exemplify personal virtue. The American gospel of success has been a kind of individual specification of the middle-class gospel of progress: in the big, self-made men, rising after the Civil War, progress seemed to pervade the whole society. The ambitious springs of success were unambiguous, its money target clear and visible, and its paths, if rugged, well marked out; there was a surefootedness about the way middle-class men went about their lives.

The idea of the successful individual was linked with the liberal ideology of expanding capitalism. Liberal sociology, assuming a gradation of ranks in which everyone is rewarded according to his ability and effort, has paid less attention to the fate of groups or classes than to the solitary individual, naked of all save personal merit. The entrepreneur, making his way across the open market, most clearly displayed success in these terms.

The way up, according to the classic style of liberalism, was to establish a small enterprise and to expand it by competition with other enterprises. The worker became a foreman and then an industrialist; the clerk became a bookkeeper or a drummer and then a merchant on his own. The farmer's son took up land in his own right and, long before his old age, came into profits and independence. The competition and effort involved in these ways up formed the cradle of a self-reliant personality and the guarantee of economic and political democracy itself.

Success was bound up with the expansible possession rather than the forward-looking job. It was with reference to property that young men were spoken of as having great or small 'expectations.' Yet in this image success rested less on inheritances than on new beginnings from the bottom; for, it was thought, 'business long ago ceased to be a matter of inheritance, and became the property of brains and persistence.'

According to the old entrepreneur's ideology, success is always linked with the sober personal virtues of will power and thrift, habits of order, neatness, and the constitutional inability to say Yes to the easy road.* These virtues are at once a condition and a sign of success. Without them, success is not possible; with them, all is possible; and, as is clear from the legends of their

* The statement of success ideologies in this section is based on thematic analyses of some twenty books, selected at random from files of the New York Public Library, ranging from 1856—Freeman Hunt's *Worth and Wealth* (New York, Stringer & Howard)—to 1947—Loire Brophy's *There's Plenty of Room at the Top* (New York, Simon & Schuster).

lives, all successful men have practiced these virtues with great, driving will, for 'the temple of Fortune is accessible only by a steep, rugged and difficult path, up which you must drag yourself.'

The man bent on success will be upright, exactly punctual, and high-minded; he will soberly refrain from liquor, tobacco, gambling, and loose women. 'Laughter, when it is too hearty, weakens the power of mind; avoid it.' He will never be in a hurry, will always carefully finish up 'each separate undertaking,' and so 'keep everything under control.' He will know 'that Method makes Time,' and will 'promptly improve small opportunities' by diligent attention to detail. He will gain an ease and confidence of endeavor, for self-reliance in all things will insure a moral presence of mind. Also, 'a man's self-respect, and the respect of his wife and children for him and themselves, will increase continually as his savings augment.'

To honesty, he will add 'a great degree of caution and prudence'; then honesty, besides being rewarded in the hereafter, will here and now, be 'the surest way to worldly thrift and prosperity.' He will come to understand that 'religion and business . . . are both right and may essentially serve each other'; that 'religion is a mighty ally of economy. . . Vices cost more than Virtues. . . Many a young smoker burns up in advance a fifty-thousand-dollar business'; and more broadly, that religion fortifies the 'integrity which is a man's best "reserve stock."'

This inspirational ideology does not often concern itself with the impersonal structure of opportunity, the limits the economy sets to the practice of personal virtues; and when it does, personal virtues still win through: 'The men who are made by circumstances are unmade by trifling misfortunes; while they who conquer circumstances snap their fingers at luck.' Yet in relating the detailed means of success, this literature also reveals a good deal about its social conditions. It seems to have been directed to rural and small-town boys. If city boys have better education, country boys have greater 'physical and moral pre-eminence.' In providing instruction in 'polish,' it indicates in detail how the rural 'bumpkin' must conduct himself in country town and larger city to avoid being laughed at by city slickers. The aspiring boy is cautioned never to be 'boisterous' nor have 'free and easy manners. . . The manners of a gentleman are a sure passport to success.' The city, in this literature, is imagined as a goal, but more importantly, there is a Jeffersonian warning about the evils of the city and the practical admonition that 'Businessmen . . . are not accidental outcroppings from the great army of smooth-haired nice young clerks who would rather starve in the city than be independent in the country.'

Occupationally, the legendary road runs from clerk and then bookkeeper in the country retail store, then to drummer or traveling salesman, and finally, to business for oneself, usually as a merchant. 'He who seeks for the merchant of the future will find him in the clerk of today,' but the intermediate step is very important and much desired. To the clerk, the drummer is a source of advice about promising locations and opportunities for new stores; the drummer can inspect opportunities for himself and learn about a wide variety of commodity 'lines.' He also learns to judge others quickly and shrewdly 'so that in making a statement he could follow in his hearer's mind its effects, and be prepared to stop or to go on at the right moment.' In fact: 'All that goes towards making a man a good merchant is needed on the road by a traveling salesman.'

The legendary fork in the road is often 'a business career' versus farm life or life in a factory. But whatever its occupational content, it is identified with a moral choice: 'Keeping on the right side' versus 'being lost.' He who fails, who remains a clerk, is 'lost,' 'destroyed,' 'ruined.' That end can be met by going either too slow or too fast, and the 'easy success' of a few prominent men should not 'dazzle other men to destruction.'

The entrepreneurial pattern of success and its inspirational ideology rested upon an economy of many small proprietorships. Under a centralized enterprise system, the pattern of success becomes a pattern of the climb within and between prearranged hierarchies. Whatever the level of opportunity may be, the way up does not now typically include the acquisition of independent property. Only those who already have property can now achieve success based upon it.

The shift from a liberal capitalism of small properties to a corporate system of monopoly capitalism is the basis for the shift in the path and in the content of success. In the older pattern, the white-collar job was merely one step on the grand road to independent entrepreneurship; in the new pattern, the white-collar way involves promotions within a bureaucratic hierarchy. When only one-fifth of the population are free enterprisers (and not that many securely so), independent entrepreneurship cannot very well be the major end of individual economic life. The inspirational literature of entrepreneurial success has been an assurance for the individual and an apology for the system. Now it is more apologetic, less assuring.

For some three-fourths of the urban middle class, the salaried employees, the occupational climb replaces heroic tactics in the open competitive market. Although salaried employees may compete with one another, their field of competition is so hedged in by bureaucratic regulation that their competition is likely to be seen as grubbing and backbiting. The main chance now becomes a series of small calculations, stretched over the working lifetime of the individual: a bureaucracy is no testing field for heroes.

The success literature has shifted with the success pattern. It is still focused upon personal virtues, but they are not the sober virtues once imputed to successful entrepreneurs. Now the stress is on agility rather than ability, on 'getting along' in a context of associates, superiors, and rules, rather than 'getting ahead' across an open market; on who you know rather than what you know; on techniques of self-display and the generalized knack of handling people, rather than on moral integrity, substantive accomplishments, and solidity of person; on loyalty to, or even identity with, one's own firm, rather than entrepreneurial virtuosity. The best bet is the style of the efficient executive, rather than the drive of the entrepreneur.

'Circumstances, personality, temperament, accident,' as well as hard work and patience, now appear as key factors governing success or failure. One should strive for 'experience and responsibility within one's chosen field,' with 'little or no thought of money.' Special skills and 'executive ability,' preferably native, are the ways up from routine work. But the most important single factor is 'personality,' which '. . . commands attention . . . by charm . . . force of character, or . . . demeanor. . . Accomplishment without . . . personality is unfortunate. . . Personality . . . without industry is . . . undesirable.'

To be courteous 'will help you to get ahead . . . you will have much more fun . . . will be much less fatigued at night . . . will be more popular, have more friends.' So, 'Train yourself to smile. . . Express physical and mental alertness. . . Radiate self-confidence. . . Smile often and sincerely.' 'Everything you say, everything you do, creates impressions upon other people . . . from the cradle to the grave, you've got to get along with other people. Use sound sales principles and you'll do better in "selling" your merchandise, your ideas, and yourself.'

The prime meaning of opportunity in a society of employees is to serve the big firm beyond the line of a job's duty and hence to bring oneself to the attention of the higher-ups who control upward movement. This entails dependability and enthusiasm in handling the little job in a big way. 'Character . . . includes . . . innate loyalty in little things and enthusiastic interest in the job at hand. . . In a word, thoroughly dependable and generally with an optimistic, helpful attitude.'

'Getting ahead' becomes 'a continual selling job. . . Whether you are seeking a new position or are aiming at the job just ahead. In either case you must sell yourself and keep on selling. . . You have a product and that product is yourself.' The skillful personal maneuver and the politic approach in inter-organizational contacts, the planful impressing of the business superior become a kind of Machiavellism for the little man, a turning of oneself into an instrument by which to use others for the end of success. 'Become genuinely interested in other people. . . Smile. . . Be a good listener. . . Talk in terms of the other man's interest. . . Make the other person feel important—and do it sincerely. . . I am talking,' says Dale Carnegie, 'about a new way of life.'

The heraldry of American success has been the greenback; even when inspirational writers are most inspirational, the big money is always there. Both entrepreneurial and white-collar patterns involve the remaking of personality for pecuniary ends, but in the entrepreneurial pattern money-success involved the acquisition of virtues good in themselves: the money is always to be used for good works, for virtue and good works justify riches. In the white-collar pattern, there is no such moral sanctifying of the means of success; one is merely prodded to become an instrument of success, to acquire tactics not virtues; money success is assumed to be an obviously good thing for which no sacrifice is too great.

The entrepreneurial and white-collar ways of success, although emerging in historical sequence, are not clear-cut phases through which American aspiration and endeavor have passed. They now co-exist, and each has varying relevance in different economic areas and phases of the economic cycle. Each has also come up against its own kinds of difficulty, which limit its use as a prod to striving. In a society of employees in large-scale enterprises, only a limited number can attempt to follow the entrepreneurial pattern; in a society that has turned itself into a great salesroom, the salesman's ways of success are likely to be severely competitive, and, at the same time, rationalized out of existence; in a society in which the educational level of the lower ranks is constantly rising and jobs are continually rationalized, the white-collar route to the top is likely to come up against competition it never knew in more educationally restricted situations.

2. The Educational Elevator

The American belief in the value of universal education has been a salient feature of democratic ideology; in fact, since the Jacksonian era, education for all has often been virtually identified with the operation of a truly democratic society. Moreover, the hope for more education has slowly been realized. Eighty years ago a little over half, but today over four-fifths of the children of appropriate age are enrolled in public elementary and secondary schools.

This massive rise in enrollment has strengthened the feeling of status equality, especially in those smaller cities where all the children, regardless of social or occupational rank, are likely to attend the same high school. It has aided immensely in Americanizing the immigrant. And it has spread and generally strengthened old middle-class ideologies, for teachers represent and reinforce middle-class attitudes and values, manners and skills.

Yet, in spite of this reinforcing of old middle-class mores, mass education has also been one of the major social mechanisms of the rise of the new middle-class occupations, for these occupations require those skills that have been provided by the educational system.

In performing these functions, especially the last, American education has shifted toward a more explicit vocational emphasis, functioning as a link in occupational mobility between generations. High schools, as well as colleges and universities, have been reshaped for the personnel needs of business and government. In their desire for serviceable practicality, the schools have adapted themselves to changing demands, and the public has seemed glad to have its children trained for the available jobs.

The most fundamental question to ask of any educational system is what kind of a product do its administrators expect to turn out? And for what kind of society? In the nineteenth century, the answer was 'the good citizen' in a 'democratic republic.' In the middle of the twentieth century, it is 'the successful man' in a 'society of specialists with secure jobs.'

In the world of small entrepreneurs, little or no educational preparation was needed for success, much less to get along: one was stubborn, or courageous, had common sense and worked hard. Education may have been viewed as a main road to social equality and political freedom, and as a help in meeting opportunity so that ability and talent might be appropriately rewarded. But education was not the big avenue of economic advancement for the masses of the populace.

In the new society, the meaning of education has shifted from status and political spheres to economic and occupational areas. In the white-collar life and its patterns of success, the educational segment of the individual's career becomes a key to his entire occupational fate.

Formal requirements for entry into different jobs and expectations of ascent tend to become fixed by educational levels. On the higher levels, college is the cradle of the professions and semi-professions, as well as a necessary status-mark for higher positions. As the virtues and talents of the entrepreneur are replaced by the skills and prestige of the educated expert, formal education becomes central to social and economic success. Sons who are better educated than their fathers are more likely to occupy higher occupational positions: in one sample of urban males, studied by Richard Centers, some 46 per cent of the sons who were better educated than their fathers reached higher positions, whereas only 16 per cent of those whose education was poorer did. The educational link was specifically important in the U.S. Army during World War II: 64 per cent of the officers, but only 11 per cent of the enlisted men, had been to college.

The aim of college men today, especially in elite colleges, is a forward-looking job in a large corporation. Such a job involves training not only in vocational skills, but also in social mannerisms. Harold Taylor, president of Sarah Lawrence, writes: 'The ideal graduate in the present employment market of industrial executives is a fraternity man with a declared disinterest in political or social affairs, gentile, white, a member of the football team, a student with a record of A in each course, a man popular with everyone and well known on the campus, with many memberships in social clubs—a man who can be imagined in twenty years as a subject for a Calvert advertisement. The large successful universities have confirmed this stereotype by the plans they make for the campus social life of the students and by the value system implicit in its organization. . . Even the liberal arts colleges seem bent upon becoming training schools for conservative industrial executives.'

Although the middle-class monopoly on high-school education has been broken, equality of educational opportunity has not been reached; many young people are unable to complete their secondary school education because of economic restrictions. 'Generally speaking,' Walter Kotschnig concludes, 'the children of large families in the lowest income brackets have little chance of graduating from high school. They have to leave school early to help their families. Most of them will never be anything but poorly paid unskilled workers for the simple reason that . . . education has become the main avenue to economic and social success. The situation on the college level is even worse. . .' The most careful study available reveals that in many cases the father's income rather than the boy's brains determines who shall be college trained.

The parent's class position is also reflected in the type of curriculum taken. Students of law, medicine, or liberal arts generally come from families having twice the yearly income of students in nursing, teaching, or commercial work. 'Of the 580 boys and girls in a thousand who reach the third year of high school,' Lloyd Warner and his associates write, 'about half are taking a course which leads to college. One hundred and fifty enter college, and 70 graduate. These are average figures for the country as a whole . . . an average of some two hundred out of every thousand young people fail to achieve the goal toward which they started in high school.'

The major occupational shift in college education has been from old middle-class parents to new middle-class children; the major shift via high-school education has been from skilled-worker parents to new middle-class children. Colleges and universities have been social elevators carrying the children of small businessmen and farmers to the lower order of the professions. At the University of Chicago, for example, between 1893 and 1931, about 4 out of 10 of the fathers of graduates (bachelor degrees) were in business, commercial, or proprietary occupations. Only about one-fourth of these fathers were in professional service, but 62 per cent of the sons and 73 per cent of the daughters entered such service.

Mobility between generations probably increases from old to new middle classes during depressions, as, especially in the upper-middle brackets, parents seek to secure their children from the effects of the market. Rather than carry on his father's business, many a boy has been trained, at his parents' sacrifice, to help man some unit of the big-business system that has destroyed his father's business.

As the old middle classes have come to be distressed and insecure about their small-propertied existence, they have become uneasy about their ability to get their children into positions equal to or better than their own. At the same time, wage-workers have aspired to have their children attain higher levels. Both classes have emphatically demanded 'educational opportunity' and both have sacrificed in order to give children better (more) education.

Thirty-five years ago John Corbin cried in the name of the educated white-collar people that education was as much a contribution to the nation's wealth as property, that education *was* the white-collar employee's 'capital,' the major basis of his claim to prestige, and the means by which he should close up his ranks. Yet, as a type of 'capital,' education carries a limitation that farms and businesses do not: its exercise is dependent upon those who control and manage jobs. Today, according to a *Fortune* survey, the idea of going into business for oneself 'is so seldom expressed among college graduates as to seem an anachronism.'

On the one hand, there is a demand for 'equal educational opportunities' for all, which once unambiguously meant better and more secure positions for all. On the other hand, there are now strong tendencies, which in all probability will continue, for the educational requirements of many white-collar positions to decline, and, moreover, for the competition for even these positions to increase. As a result, the belief in universal education as a sacrosanct fetish has come to be questioned. This questioning, which began about the time of World War I, became more widespread during the 'thirties and came to sharp focus after World War II, represents, in Perry Miller's phrase, the 'dislocation in a basic tradition.'

Democratic ideologists now point out that almost 80 per cent of fifth-grade students, who are mentally capable of college education, never reach college, so millions of citizens, according to E. J. McGrath, U.S. Commissioner of Education, 'go through life functioning below the level of their potential.' This is undoubtedly true, but statisticians, occupational forecasters, and an increasing number of educational officials raise the question whether or not the occupational structure can possibly provide the jobs that are expected by college graduates.

During the last half century, college graduates, increasing four times as much as the general population, were involved in the expansion of higher white-collar occupations. So education paid off: ten years ago, college graduates earned one-third more than the U.S. average. Today, however, college graduates earn only one-tenth more than the U.S. average, and, according to an informed prediction by Seymour E. Harris, in twenty years 'it won't pay to be educated.' By then, instead of 3 million living college graduates as in 1930, there will be between 10 and 14 million. In order to meet their expectations, the professions would have to absorb between 8 and 11 million of them, yet between 1910 and 1940 professions expanded less than 2 million. There are warning cries among educational ideologists, recalling the contributions made by 'disappointed intellectuals to the rise of fascism in Europe,' and there are maneuvers and proclamations among school officials which reflect shifts in the role of education in the American success story.

Chancellor William J. Wallin of the New York State Board of Regents has decried higher education for all, declaring 'that the country might produce "surplus graduates" who, embittered with their frustration, would "turn upon society and the government, more effective and better armed in their destructive wrath by the education we have given them." ' 'Equality of opportunity,' Harvard President Conant has recently said, 'is one of the cardinal principles of this country. . . Yet at the same time, no young man or woman should be encouraged or enticed into taking the kinds of advanced educational training which are going to lead to a frustrated economic life.' 'For a large majority of young Americans, a four-year college education was not only "needlessly expensive," but "socially undesirable." '

One of the most popular solutions now being proposed is the establishment of several educational ladders, each reaching to different levels of the occupational hierarchy. Such ideas are now rather widely, although informally, being put into practice in U.S. high schools. The principal of one high school says: 'This educational system is a terrific waste of money and time to the city, since so few people can by any chance become members of the white-collar class and so many must follow some vocational line. . . It is surprising how many people in 8C want the prestige of a white-collar job. So I point out how poor the pay is and endeavor to point out how hard it is to fit oneself for such a job and to make a success of it; the majority of them are unfitted for any such work. . . I am giving all the groups A, B, and C a talking to, explaining the disadvantages of the white-collar job to all of them.' 'There is clear evidence,' comments sociologist Lloyd Warner, who gathered these quotations, 'that our educational system is now permitting too many to use high school and college for the purpose of attaining unavailable professional and managerial positions, with resultant failure and frustration and loss of social solidarity.'

Education will work as a means of success only so long as the occupational needs of a society continue to demand education. The recognition that they might not has led to the idea, in Kotchnig's words, of giving 'the masses of young people a general and special education in keeping with their abilities, while preparing leaders for the "several *élites*," thus breaking down the one-sided emphasis on the intellectual careers.' Confronted with such ideas, 'Progressive' educational theorists add to them the assumption that tests, measurements, placement services, and vocational guidance can at early ages select those who should go on, via education, to higher positions and those who should terminate their education, and hence their occupational chances, at lower levels.

We have thus come a long way from the simple faith in 'equal educational opportunity' as part of the American pattern of success. First, with education a highly specialized channel for elites with high class chances, the major avenues of advancement do not involve education: independent men, who are 'making themselves,' compete on the open market and find their own levels.

Second, with the democratization of education as political demand and economic need, the occupational structures require literacy and some skills, and bring about a period of success via education. The single ladder is not questioned, the ideology of equal opportunity means that all top positions are competed for by all those with the ability to climb the educational ladder.

Third, almost all occupational mobility requires education, but as supply exceeds demand, education is stratified bureaucratically, by sorting out the young through tests and measurements. There are increased tendencies to manage the education-occupation structure and steer it; and magical notions of the environment are given up. As demand for educated people falls behind supply, as educated occupations are divided and rationalized, as enrollments continue to rise, the income and prestige differences between the more-educated and the less-educated masses decrease. Among those who are not allowed to use the educated skills they have acquired, boredom increases, hope for success collapses into disappointment, and the sacrifices that don't pay off lead to disillusionment.

3. Origins and Mobilities

In both entrepreneurial and white-collar patterns of success, movement upward has been subject to rather severe counter-tendencies during the course of the twentieth century. No one knows precisely whether the rate of upward mobility—the proportion of people who rise from one occupational level to another —has remained constant, declined, or gone up. That rate, however, depends upon a set of factors that at any given time determine the chances of those on each level to rise, fall, or hold their own.

In the past, certain well-known trends supported upward mobility in the entrepreneurial pattern. The most obvious of these were: the total economic expansion of a society of decentralized property; the physical spread of markets and the rise in volumes of production; the industrialization, which rested upon a private exploitation of unexampled natural resources in a steadily rising market. In short: the American nineteenth century, when the entrepreneurial pattern of success seemed almost automatic.

By the 'nineties, however, and increasingly during the twentieth century, the centralization of property worked to decrease the chances of those lower on the scale to rise to entrepreneurship, to retain and to expand their holdings. Resources were less accessible to men of small means, access to the higher capital requirements of enterprise more difficult; many markets were monopolized, and as a national whole the market began to have a lower rate of increase, as birth rates and immigration dropped.

Yet, even as the entrepreneurial was declining as a mass way of success, the white-collar pattern was opening up. What happened between the 'nineties and the middle 'thirties is easy to understand from a few general figures.

The chance to rise is, of course, affected by the ratio of upper positions to lower aspirants. The wage-worker strata level off and the white-collar strata expand, so the chance to rise from wage-worker to white-collar standing increases. Between 1870 and 1930, Eldridge Sibley has calculated, an average of about 150,-000 workers and farmers per year 'ascended' into white-collar ranks. But the entrepreneurial stratum declined sharply as a proportion of the total at work. Therefore, we may suppose white-collar employees to have been recruited from both old middle class and wage-workers. Of course we can never know the intricate individual patterns of job-shifting within and between the last two or three American generations that have resulted in the present division of occupations. We have only fragmentary snapshots, most of them recent, of the occupational distances sons and daughters have moved from the stations of their fathers.

Most of the white-collar workers of the present generation—the office workers and salespeople—seem to be rather evenly split in origin between old middle classes and wage-worker strata; about 4 out of 10 have fathers who were free enterprisers, and another 4, urban wage-workers. Over the past three generations, lower white-collar workers have probably shifted in origin to include greater proportions of wage-worker children.* The new middle class itself has expanded so recently that only a small proportion of the present white-collar generation could be expected to be of white-collar origin.

The higher white-collar people, salaried professionals and managerial employees, are less likely to derive from wage-workers and more likely to come from higher levels, or from their own ranks.†

As white-collar strata have expanded, they have fallen into line with the over-all historical pattern of occupational structure: the upper strata became more rigid in the presence of upward

* In a small California town, studied in the middle 'thirties by Percy Davidson and Dewey Anderson, 46 per cent of the clerks had fathers who were proprietors, 41 per cent wage-workers. But 55 per cent of the fathers who were themselves clerks were the sons of proprietors and only 29 per cent, wage-workers. Of course, such figures probably reflect over-all occupational changes as well as shifts in the origins of white-collar workers.

† In one middle-sized middle-western city in 1945, for example, we found that 43 per cent of such people, but only 36 per cent of lower white collar—salespeople and office workers—had fathers who were free enterprisers. Origins from wage-worker strata of these two groups were 37 and 46 per cent respectively.

mobility among the middle and lower. In fact, the rise of white-collar occupations has allowed for the historical continuance of American mobility. For while the rise of men from wage-worker origins into top business positions was definitely curtailed by the beginning of the twentieth century, the formation of new white-collar hierarchies allowed for the upward mobility of the wage-workers to continue.

Even as the new replaces the old middle class, the top levels of each are being replaced from among its own strata: over one-third of the business, managerial, and professional people today derive from the same occupational categories. This rigidity may be stronger than appears from tables of the origin of the present labor force, for the statistical snapshot only catches the daughter of a big businessman as an office worker; it does not show her as a young girl in a middle or small-sized city, working as the secretary or receptionist to a friend of her father, leaving in a year to marry the rising manager of one of the town's largest corporations, quite different from the carpenter's daughter clerking in the bargain basement of the town's department store, glancing up at the floorwalker who passes twice each day. Yet upward mobility is still prevalent today among the sons of wage-workers who move into white-collar or business positions. Probably about one-third of today's small businessmen are sons of wage earners.

Upward mobility between generations has often been accounted for by the low fertility rate of higher social classes. This difference in fertility is due largely to the later age of marriage, and the greater use and effectiveness of birth-control measures among higher-income groups. Now, with rising standards of living and broader access to methods of birth control, it is an open question how long upward mobility based on differing fertility rates can continue. Also, with the importance of the educational link in the pattern of success, the father's position is crucial to the child's. And when, as we have seen, the educational link becomes insecure, a consciousness of something wrong in middle-class life becomes more widespread.

Within the individual's lifetime, the chance to rise has been affected by the shape-up of white-collar jobs. Their concentration into larger units and their specialization have made for many blind alleys, lessened the opportunity to learn about 'other departments,' or the business as a whole. The rationalization of white-collar work means that as the number of replaceable positions expands more than the number of higher positions, the chances of climbing decrease. Also, as higher positions become more technical, they are often more likely to be filled by people from outside the hierarchy. So the ideology of promotion—the expectation of a step-by-step ascent, no longer seems a sure thing. As many as 80 per cent of one large sample of clerical workers, reported the War Manpower Commission, expected no promotion.

Yet there is one fact—heavy turnover at the bottom—which still allows ascent within many large white-collar hierarchies. The personnel manager of one insurance company, employing some 14,000 clerks, says: 'To tell you the truth our turnover is just about as I like it. Turnover of course is relative to the times and to what goes on in other companies. But our file clerks, which is the lowest level of clerical work, well, you couldn't find one here who had worked more than a year at that job. We get them right from high school. The young girl is what we want, and in a year they are either promoted or they have gone away. On the other hand, you can't find any secretaries who have been here only two or three years; all those better jobs are held by people who are six to eight years here.' Most of those who stick rise, a fact made possible by the heavy turnover at the bottom: the proportion of higher positions to those who compete for them is relatively favorable for advancement.

If anyone is to rise into the white-collar ranks, it must be from wage-worker levels. What, then, are the chances for the wage-worker to rise to white-collar status? Suppose we consider an unskilled worker making about $500 a year in a slump, who loses his paltry job, can't find other work, and goes on relief. There were many in this situation; in the middle 'thirties, at least one-third of the unskilled were out of work.

The chances that this man will become ill are 57 per cent greater than those of a higher white-collar man making $3000 a year; moreover, according to the national health survey, his illness will last about 63 per cent longer. If the white-collar man did become ill, he would get 46 per cent more medical attention than the unskilled worker.

Suppose this worker gets his old job back or another comparable one, and his wife has a child. Robert Woodbury has calculated that there are almost three times as many chances that this child will die before he is one year old than is the case for a white-collar man making only a little better than $1250 a year. But if the worker's child does live, and the worker remains an unskilled laborer, what are the child's chances to rise?

Many working-class parents want their children to rise above manual labor, but few know anything about the variety of jobs in higher spheres or the preparation required for them. The child himself usually has few convictions about the value of school, which to him is merely something he must pass through before he grows up; he also needs more spending money than his parents can give him. His chance to rise out of manual labor is in fact very slim if he does not at least finish high school, but he doesn't know that or think much about it.*

The son of an unskilled laborer has 6 chances in 100 of ever getting into a college; the son of a professional man has better than a 50-50 chance. But only 10 per cent of the whole adult population in 1940 had gone to college. What is the chance of the worker's son to get above the eighth grade? During the 'thirties it was less than 14 out of 100.

The wage-worker's children leave school because of the financial need of the family, because they finish high school or trade school, or because they simply 'dislike school.' Probably half have no specific occupational plan or ambition, nor do many parents' aspirations go beyond the vague desire to see the children 'get ahead' or get as much schooling as possible. They usually find out about their first job by random applications at work-places or through acquaintances and relatives. The only thing they are likely to know about these jobs before beginning work is the starting wage, and the majority of jobs, perhaps two-thirds, are blind alleys.

* For the following account, I have drawn extensively on L. G. Reynold's and Joseph Shister's *Job Horizons* (New York: Harper, 1949).

When that first job ends, or the workers quit, they are simply on the market again, with lower chances of obtaining an education and hence lower chances of getting a better job. In San Jose, California, the unskilled worker's son, in 58 cases out of 100, will become an unskilled or a semi-skilled laborer. Most workers probably leave one job before they have a new one lined up, and they do not have the opportunity to compare jobs, but only the choice at any given time of accepting this job or of waiting to see if a better one turns up.

The wage-worker gets married early, so he must earn, and cannot think seriously of training for skilled work during the first crucial years of his occupational life. By the time he is twenty-five, 'the orbit in which he will move for the rest of his life is firmly established.' He is interested in an 'agreeable life on the job' as well as the money earned; moreover, his judgment of his income is made in a frame of comparison with the wages of other workers around him. The status value of the work is in his mind when he considers his income, but the money becomes more important as he acquires more dependent children. He comes to understand that the good job is scarce and he develops a technique for hunting such jobs by depending on his friends for 'tips.' To him, a change of jobs does not mean a job advancement, as it probably does to more secure middle-class people; it is as likely to mean the personal disaster of layoff or unemployment.

Roughly one-third of the wage-workers prefer to remain in their present jobs; as many as one-fourth want and expect to move up in their present hierarchy; others who would like to move up, don't expect to: they see no vacancies in sight, believe they lack the necessary competence, or feel themselves too old. In their daydreams about the kind of work they would really like, workers are concerned about the variety of work, the using of skills, and contact with other people; as many want white-collar jobs as want skilled labor; less than a fifth have in mind small businesses. We have already seen what is likely to happen to the 0.2 per cent of the adult population who try to start small businesses and be their own bosses, and we know that farming is now an economically over-crowded business. Both are risky dreams, which now affect only small portions of the population.

Workers do not aim at the foreman's job, supposedly their

classic ambition. They often believe that gaining such a job would 'upset their friendly relations with other workers.' 'If you're a foreman, you've got to get so much work out of men; if you know a man is holding out, you've got to push him along. When you do that that makes you a no-good guy with the other men.' 'The supervisors have no friends.' Others don't aspire to a foreman position because it 'would entail too much responsibility'; or wouldn't 'offer enough job interest.' 'Foremen today aren't what they used to be forty years ago.'

The ladder for workmen today is not the lower end of one general ladder leading to white-collar levels; it is a shortened ladder that does not extend above the wage-worker level. But that does not mean that working men act and feel as their inability to follow the precepts of 'getting ahead' might lead the academic and inexperienced to expect. The wage-worker comes to limit his aspirations, and to make them more specific: to get more money for this job, to have the union change this detail or that condition, to change shifts next week. In the meantime, hope of high rates of upward mobility must be largely confined to those who begin above the wage-worker level.

4. Hard Times

Some of the factors that make for upward mobility or for its decline are long-run, but many are geared to the ups and downs of the economic cycle. The old ideology of success assumed that the structure of opportunity was always expanding: the heights to be gained and the chances of gaining them seemed to increase from one generation to the next and within the lifetime of a man. Moreover, these opportunities were not felt to be threatened by cyclical ups and downs. Virtually everyone could feel lifted upward, both in income and status, because real income generally rose, and because each new immigrant group coming in at the bottom lifted the prestige and jobs of many who had arrived before them. The new ideology of success assumes that the structure of opportunity waxes and wanes within a slump-war-boom economy. Depressions have left heavy traces, noticeable even during war and boom when opportunities to rise become more available.

The shift from an economy behaving according to a theory of linear progress to an economy behaving according to theories of cyclical movement has affected the white-collar strata in two direct economic ways: (I) their income levels, especially in relation to those of wage-workers; and (II) their security of employment, again in relation to wage-workers.

I. In 1890, as we have already noted, the average income of the salaried employee was roughly double that of the average wage-worker. From then until the First World War the salaried employees' incomes steadily climbed, whereas the climb of wage-workers' earnings was slowed by the depression which closed the nineteenth century and which affected wages until the First World War. Thus, in the early twentieth century the salaried employee's advantage over the wage-worker was solidly based on economic facts. The white-collar worlds were just beginning to expand, so new and wider employment opportunities were continually being made available to the white-collar employees who held a monopoly on high-school education. There were no masses of white-collar workers, who, as a stratum, thus occupied a select educational and occupational position.

World War I boosted the incomes of both wage- and salary-workers; but the wage-workers, perhaps being closer to war production, being unionized, and reaping the benefits of overtime pay, had greater increases in income than did salaried employees. By 1920, the gap between wages and salaries had narrowed: salaried workers in manufacturing were receiving incomes that were only 65 per cent higher than those of wage-workers, compared to the 140 per cent advantage of 1900.

The economic dip of 1921—the lowest year of employment before the 'thirties—hit wage-workers more than salaried employees. Average wages in manufacturing dropped 13 per cent; salaries dropped less than three-tenths of one per cent. The favorable employment and income situation of the white-collar workers was still in effect, and the average salaries in manufacturing again rose quickly, by 1924 overtaking their 1920 level. The incomes of wage-workers, however, throughout the 'twenties never regained their 1920 level. Hence, salaried workers gained over wage-workers, although their advantage was not so great as in the early twentieth century.

Between 1929 and 1933, average wages in selected industries dropped 33 per cent, salaries dropped 20 per cent. The slump hit the wage-workers harder than the white-collar employees, the income differences between the two increasing slightly. The salaries that were 82 per cent higher than wages in 1929 were 118 per cent higher in 1933. But the threat of slump, the stigma of unemployment, and the anxieties surrounding it definitely invaded the white-collar ranks. And the salary advantage held by the white-collar employees at the peak unemployment did not last.

World War II benefited wage-workers more than salaried employees, the difference between their average earnings being reduced. But the end of the war, which meant no more overtime in factories, benefited salaried more than wage-workers. Figures for 1939 and 1948 are interesting, because they suggest long-term changes affected by the war, but not due to temporary dislocations of war-time conditions. In each of these years, the income of the white-collar mass—the office and sales people—was lower than that of the skilled urban wage-workers. These lower white-collar workers, however, held a margin of advantage over the semi-skilled, although it had definitely decreased.* The white-collar income margin over wage-workers has become less, and whatever margin they still have as a group will most likely be further decreased in the coming decade. For it is during inflated periods, when salaries seem more rigid than wages, that white-collar leveling is most likely to occur.

II. Historical information on unemployment in the United States is fragmentary, contradictory, and hard to come by, but it seems likely that before the 'thirties, with the possible exception

* Office-men in 1939, for example, received incomes 40 per cent higher than those of semi-skilled male workers; in 1948, only 9.5 per cent higher. Salesmen's incomes in 1939 were 19 per cent higher than those of semi-skilled male workers; in 1948, only 4 per cent. Among women, the advantage of office employees over semi-skilled workers was 68 per cent in 1939 but only 22 per cent in 1948; saleswomen, however, saw their incomes drop below the level of women semi-skilled workers in 1948.

of 1921, unemployment had involved considerably less than 10 per cent of the total labor force. Employment was at its lowest point in 1933, when 12.8 million workers, or 25 per cent of the labor force, were out of work or on relief. By 1936, 17 per cent of the labor force was still unemployed, and unemployment stayed near this level until the onset of World War II. Then, unemployment declined sharply each year until it hit its war-time low of less than 1 per cent of the labor force in 1944.

White-collar employees are no longer as immune to crises of unemployment as they once were, but so far unemployment has been heavier among wage-workers. In 1930 probably 4 per cent of the new middle class were unemployed, compared with over 10 per cent of the skilled and semi-skilled and about 13 per cent of the urban unskilled workers. These figures reveal only the beginnings of the slump; by 1937 the worst was over,* but in that year about 11 per cent of the office and sales people were out of work or on public emergency work, compared with from 16 to 27 per cent of the urban wage-workers. So the white-collar margin of job security was probably narrowed during the ten years before World War II.

Yet, historically, white-collar employees have been more protected than wage-workers from unemployment. In large part this may be due to the special character of white-collar work: 'The volume of paper work doesn't shrink automatically when production falls off,' the editors of *Business Week* observe. 'Sometimes it even increases—because the company puts on more selling pressure to round up new orders.' Nevertheless, many of the factors that have protected the white-collar workers are probably weakening in force. During the 'thirties white-collar offices and salesrooms were less mechanized than now; as offices have been enlarged, they have become 'an increased cost' of the business enterprise. In future depressions, therefore, the incentive to cut down office costs by increased mechanization and white-collar layoffs will be greater than in the past. Furthermore, many white-collar jobs have required more training than they do now, and employers have been reluctant to let trained personnel go. In the future, however, as more white-collar jobs are routinized, and

* No reliable nation-wide figures for 1933 and 1934 are available.

the people in them are more easily replaceable, this reluctance will be minimized. The general educational requirements for white-collar work are also becoming more widely available. Thus there are more people available to perform easier tasks, and the possibility of unemployment increases. Present conditions within the white-collar world, continuing and emphasizing the historical trend, thus point to a lesser margin of employment security between wage-workers and white-collar employees.

5. The Tarnished Image

In the last twenty years, a new style in inspirational literature, relevant to a new style of aspiration, has risen in the United States. This literature does not provide its large readership with techniques for cultivating the old middle-class virtues, nor the techniques for selling oneself, although, like other inspirational material, it is concerned with the individual rather than society. It emphasizes peace of mind and various physical and spiritual ways of relaxation, rather than internal frenzy in the service of external and known ambitions. As a literature of resignation, it strives to control goals and ways of life by lowering the level of ambition, and by replacing the older goals with more satisfying internal goals.

This is accomplished, negatively, by tarnishing the old images of success. In *The Hucksters, The Gilded Hearse, Death of a Salesman, The Big Wheel,* the externally successful are portrayed as internal failures, as obnoxious, guilt-ridden, ulcerated people of uneasy conscience, at war with all the peaceful virtues of the old life and, above all, miserably at war with their tormented selves. 'I tried to tell myself to snap out of it,' says a James M. Cain hero, in *The Moth,* 'that I had everything I had ever wanted, a dream job, big dough, the respect of the business I was in. I had a car, a Packard that just floated. I had an apartment looking right over the ocean. . . I had a woman with every kind of looks there was . . . And yet, if it was what I had been thirsty for, it never came clear, really to quench thirst, but had bubbles in it, like . . . champagne. . . I felt like life was nothing but one long string of Christmas afternoons. . . I felt big and cruel and cold, a thick, heavy-shouldered bunch of whatever it takes to be success.'

Positively, the new literature of inspiration holds out internal virtues, in line with a relaxed consumer's life rather than a tense producer's. It is the spiritual value, even of material poverty, available to everyone, which a *Reader's Digest* or a *Peace of Mind* philosophy exemplifies. These are not the old sober virtues of thrift and industry, nor the drive and style of the displayed personality, nor the educated skills of the bureaucratic professions. These are virtues which go with resignation, and the literature of resignation justifies the lowering of ambition and the slackening of the old frenzy.

If men are responsible for their success, they are also responsible for their failure; if success is an individual specification of social progress, failure is an individual specification of declining opportunities. But regardless of its true source, failure in the literature of success is seen as willful, is imputed to the individual, and is often internalized by him as guilt, as a competitive dissatisfaction. The imperative to keep trying, not to slacken off, results in anxiety. But in the literature of resignation, such anxieties are relieved, not by an external success which is considered to lead to personal unhappiness, but by an internalization of the goals of success themselves. 'We write successful stories about unsuccessful people,' says soap-opera producer Frank Hummert. 'This means that our characters are simply unsuccessful in the material things of life, but highly successful spiritually.'

The literature of the peace of the inner man fits in with the alienating process that has shifted men from a focus upon production to a focus upon consumption. The old success models indicated the opportunities open to everyone, were intended to prompt the will to action, and paid attention to all sorts of personal means to their end. If they held out the end-image of *Acres of Diamonds*, they also made those acres seem a natural result of hard, productive work, or, later, of guileful tricks: at any rate, of something the individual could do or some change he could make in himself. But now, as the ambition of many people solidifies into the unreasoning conscientiousness of the good employee or becomes lost in consumer dreams, ambition is often displayed in movies and novels as a drive polluting men and leading them to bad choices. Success entails cash, clothes, cars, and lush women with couch voices, but it also inevitably means a loss of integrity and, in the extreme, insanity. For there is a furor about the ambitious man, the man dead-bent on success. Increasingly we are shown The Successful ending up broken, in at least some internal way. Success is the dead end of an easy street. And when we are shown the means of success they are as likely to be frankly miraculous as the result of personal effort or sacrifice; as likely to be due to a magical stroke of luck, which suddenly turns the blind alley into an open prairie, as to personal virtue or intelligence.

Just as the 'lucky stroke' magically bolsters hope in an increasingly limited structure of opportunity, so the idea of the 'bad break' softens feelings of individual failure. Life as a game, as a sort of lottery brotherhood out of which the main chance will come—these correspond to the tightening up of stratification and the increased difficulty of climbing up the ladder for those born under the lower rungs. Success for many has 'become an accidental and irrational event,' and as a goal has become so dazzling that the individual is absorbed in contemplating it, enjoying it vicariously.

'The distance between what an average individual may do and the forces and powers that determine his life and death has become so unbridgeable that identification with normalcy, even with Philistine boredom, becomes a readily grasped empire of refuge and escape,' observes Leo Lowenthal. 'It is some comfort for the little man who has become expelled from the Horatio Alger dream, who despairs of penetrating the thicket of grand strategy in politics and business, to see his heroes as a lot of guys who like or dislike highballs, cigarettes, tomato juice, golf and social gatherings—just like himself. He knows how to converse in the sphere of consumption and here he can make no mistakes.'

Before capitalism, men found their occupational level by tradition and inheritance; jobs were passed on from father to son, by means of caste rank; or, as in feudalism or peasant societies, each man did nearly identical work. Under liberal capitalism, men found their places in the division of labor by competing on an open market. They put their skills and efforts on the market, to

acquire enterprises or jobs, and there were no formal or traditional bounds to the extent of their rise. Now, the market begins
to close, and men to come under restrictions and guidance. Economic rigidities limit ascent, property inheritance or educational
training become necessary to occupational success. Increasingly,
there are attempts to guide by test and counsel, and various occupational markets are closed up by professional associations,
unions, state licensing systems.

The vocational guide studies individuals and jobs, aiming to fit
the one into the other. To the extent that he succeeds, vocational choice rests upon his studies and consequent advice, rather
than upon the random wishes or 'uninformed' desires of the individual. Where ambition and initiative are stressed and yet so
many people must work below their capacities, the problem of
frustration becomes very large. For the goals to which men aspire
can be reached by only a few. Educators and those who run educational institutions become concerned: they must help children
to construct 'valid ambitions,' they must put the brakes on ambition, regulate the plans of youth in accordance with what is
possible within the present society—practice a more careful, a
more centralized management of ambition.

There is a curious contradiction about the ethos of success in
America today. On the one hand, there are still compulsions to
struggle, to 'amount to something'; on the other, there is a poverty of desire, a souring of the image of success.

The literature of resignation, of the peace of the inner man,
fits in with all those institutional changes involving the goal of
security and collective ways of achieving it. As insecurities become widespread and their sources beyond the individual's control, as they become collective insecurities, the population has
groped for collective means of regaining individual security. The
most dramatic means has been the labor union, but demands on
government have resulted in social security, and increasingly the
government intervenes to shape the structure of opportunity.
The governmental pension is clearly of another type of society
than the standard American dream. The old end was an independent prosperity, happily surrounded by one's grandchildren;
the end now envisioned is a pensioned security independent of
one's grandchildren. When men fight for pensions, they assume

that security must be guaranteed by group provision. No longer can the $5000-a-year man work twenty-five years and retire independently on $3000.

Of course, governments have always guaranteed and modified class chances, by the laws of property, by land policies and tariffs; but now the tendency of New Deals and Welfare States is to modify the class chances of lower groups upward, and of higher groups downward, by minimum-wage laws, graduated income tax, social security; and, except during wars, to guarantee minimum life chances, regardless of class level. Thus do governments intervene to keep men more equal.

FOUR

13

The New Middle Class, II

Ever since the new middle class began numerically to displace the old, its political role has been an object of query and debate. The political question has been closely linked with another—that of the position of new middle-class occupations in modern stratification.

This linkage of politics and stratification was all the more to be expected inasmuch as the white-collar man as a sociological creature was first discovered by Marxian theoreticians in search of recruits for the proletarian movement. They expected that society would be polarized into class-conscious proletariat and bourgeoisie, that in their general decline the in-between layers would choose one side or the other—or at least keep out of the way of the major protagonists. Neither of these expectations, however, had been realized when socialist theoreticians and party bureaucrats began at the opening of the present century to tinker with the classic perspective.

In trying to line up the new population into those who could and those who could not be relied upon to support their struggle, party statisticians ran squarely into the numerical upsurge of the white-collar salariat. The rise of these groups as a problem for Marxists signalized a shift from the simple property versus no-property dichotomy to differentiations within the no-property groups. It focused attention upon occupational structure. Moreover, in examining white-collar groups, along with the persistent small entrepreneurs of farm and city, they came upon the further fact that although the new middle class was propertyless, and the smaller entrepreneurs often suffered economic downgrading, members of these strata did not readily take to the socialist ideology. Their political attachments did not coincide with their economic position, and certainly not with their imminently expected position. They represented a numerical upthrust of falsely conscious people, and they were an obstacle to the scheduled course of the revolution.

1. Theories and Difficulties

To relate in detail all the theories that followed upon these discoveries and speculations would be more monotonous than fruitful; the range of theory had been fairly well laid out by the middle 'twenties, and nothing really new has since been added. Various writers have come upon further detail, some of it crucial, or have variously combined the major positions, some of which have had stronger support than others. But the political directions that can be inferred from the existence of the new middle class may be sorted out into four major possibilities.

I. The new middle class, in whole or in some crucial segment, will continue to grow in numbers and in power; in due course it will develop into a politically independent class. Displacing other classes in performance of the pivotal functions required to run modern society, it is slated to be the next ruling class. The accent will be upon the new middle class; the next epoch will be theirs.

II. The new middle classes will continue to grow in numbers and power, and although they will not become a force that will rise to independent power, they will be a major force for stability in the general balance of the different classes. As important elements in the class balance, they will make for the continuance of liberal capitalist society. Their spread checks the creeping proletarianization; they act as a buffer between labor and capital. Taking over certain functions of the old middle class, but having connections with the wage-workers, they will be able to co-operate with them too; thus they bridge class contrasts and mitigate class conflicts. They are the balance wheel of class interests, the stabilizers, the social harmonizers. They are intermediaries of the new social solidarity that will put an end to class bickering. That is why they are catered to by any camp or movement that is on its way to electoral power, or, for that matter, attempted revolution.

III. Members of the new middle class, by their social character and political outlook, are really bourgeoisie and they will remain that. This is particularly apparent in the tendency of these groups to become status groups rather than mere economic classes. They will form, as in Nazi Germany, prime human materials for conservative, for reactionary, and even for fascist, movements. They are natural allies and shock troops of the larger capitalist drive.

IV. The new middle class will follow the classic Marxian scheme: in due course, it will become homogeneous in all important respects with the proletariat and will come over to their socialist policy. In the meantime, it represents—for various reasons, which will be washed away in crises and decline—a case of delayed reaction. For in historical reality, the 'new middle class' is merely a peculiar sort of new proletariat, having the same basic interests. With the intensification of the class struggle between the real classes of capitalist society, it will be swept into the proletarian ranks. A thin, upper layer may go over to the bourgeoisie, but it will not count in numbers or in power.

These various arguments are difficult to compare, first of all because they do not all include the same occupations under the catchword 'new middle class.' When we consider the vague boundary lines of the white-collar world, we can easily understand why such an occupational salad invites so many conflicting theories and why general images of it are likely to differ. There is no one accepted word for them; white collar, salaried employee, new middle class are used interchangeably. During the historical span covered by different theories, the occupational groups composing these strata have changed; and at given times, different theorists in pursuit of bolstering data have spotlighted one or the other groups composing the total. So contrasting images of the political role of the white-collar people can readily exist side by side (and perhaps even both be correct). Those, for instance, who believe that as the vanguard stratum of modern society they are slated to be the next ruling class do not think of them as ten-cent store clerks, insurance-agents, and stenographers, but rather as higher technicians and staff engineers, as salaried managers of business cartels and big officials of the Federal Government. On the other hand, those who hold that they are being proletarianized do focus upon the mass of clerklings and sales people, while those who see their role as in-between mediators are most likely to include both upper and lower ranges. At any rate, in descriptions in Part Two, we have split the stratum as a whole into at least four sub-strata or pyramids, and we must pay attention to this split as we try to place white-collar people in our political expectations.

Most of the work that has been done on the new middle class and its political role involves more general theories of the course of capitalist development. That is why it is difficult to sort out in a simple and yet systematic way what given writers really think of the white-collar people. Their views are based not on an examination of this stratum as much as on, first, the political program they happen to be following; second, the doctrinal position, as regards the political line-up of classes, they have previously accepted; and third, their judgment in regard to the main course of twentieth-century industrial society.

Proletarian purists would disavow white-collar people; United Fronters would link at least segments of them with workers in a fight over specific issues, while carefully preserving organizational and, above all, doctrinal independence; People's Fronters would cater to them by modifying wage-worker ideology and program in order to unite the two; liberals of 'Populist' inclination, in a sort of dogmatic pluralism, would call upon them along with small businessmen, small farmers, and all grades of wage-workers to coalesce. And each camp, if it prevailed long enough for its intellectuals to get into production, would evolve theories about the character of the white-collar people and the role they are capable of playing.

As for political doctrines, the very definition of the white-collar problem has usually assumed as given a more or less rigid frame-

work of fated classes. The belief that in any future struggle between big business and labor, the weight of the white-collar
workers will be decisive assumes that there is going to be a
future struggle, in the open, between business and labor. The
question of whether they will be either proletariat or bourgeoisie,
thus in either case giving up whatever identity they may already
have, or go their independent way, assumes that there are these
other sides and that their struggle will, in fact if not in consciousness, make up the real political arena. Yet, at the same
time, the theories to which the rise of the new middle class has
given birth distinguish various, independent sectors of the proletariat and of the bourgeoisie, suggesting that the unit of analysis has been overformalized. The problem of the new middle
class must now be raised in a context that does not merely
assume homogeneous blocs of classes.

The political argument over white-collar workers has gone on
over an international scale. Although modern nations do have
many trends in common—among them certainly the statistical
increase of the white-collar workers—they also have unique features. In posing the question of the political role of white-collar
people in the United States, we must learn all we can from dis-
cussions of them in other countries, the Weimar Republic especially, but in doing so, we must take everything hypothetically
and test it against U.S. facts and trends.

The time-span of various theories and expectations, as we have
noted, has in most of the arguments not been closely specified.
Those who hold the view that white-collar workers are really
only an odd sort of proletariat and will, in due course, begin to
behave accordingly, or the view that the new middle class is
slated to be the next ruling class have worked with flexible and
often conflicting schedules.

What has been at issue in these theories is the objective position of the new middle classes within and between the various
strata of modern society, and the political content and direction
of their mentality. Questions concerning either of these issues
can be stated in such a way as to allow, and in fact demand,
observational answers only if adequate conceptions of stratification and of political mentality are clearly set forth.

2. Mentalities

It is frequently asserted, in theories of the white-collar people, that there are no classes in the United States because 'psychology is of the essence of classes' or, as Alfred Bingham has put it, that 'class groupings are always nebulous, and in the last analysis only the vague thing called class-consciousness counts.' It is said that people in the United States are not aware of themselves as members of classes, do not identify themselves with their appropriate economic level, do not often organize in terms of these brackets or vote along the lines they provide. America, in this reasoning, is a sandheap of 'middle-class individuals.'

But this is to confuse psychological feelings with other kinds of social and economic reality. Because men are not 'class conscious' at all times and in all places does not mean that 'there are no classes' or that 'in America everybody is middle class.' The economic and social facts are one thing; psychological feelings may or may not be associated with them in expected ways. Both are important, and if psychological feelings and political outlooks do not correspond to economic class, we must try to find out why, rather than throw out the economic baby with the psychological bath, and so fail to understand how either fits into the national tub. No matter what people believe, class structure as an economic arrangement influences their life chances according to their positions in it. If they do not grasp the causes of their conduct this does not mean that the social analyst must ignore or deny them.

If political mentalities are not in line with objectively defined strata, that lack of correspondence is a problem to be explained; in fact, it is the grand problem of the psychology of social strata. The general problem of stratification and political mentality has to do with the extent to which the members of objectively defined strata are homogeneous in their political alertness, outlook, and allegiances, and with the degree to which their political mentality and actions are in line with the interests demanded by the juxtaposition of their objective position and their accepted values.

To understand the occupation, class, and status positions of a set of people is not necessarily to know whether or not they

(1) will become class-conscious, feeling that they belong together or that they can best realize their rational interests by
combining; (2) will organize themselves, or be open to organization by others, into associations, movements, or political parties; (3) will have 'collective attitudes' of any sort, including
those toward themselves, their common situation; or (4) will
become hostile toward other strata and struggle against them.
These social, political, and psychological characteristics may
or may not occur on the basis of similar objective situations. In
any given case, such possibilities must be explored, and 'subjective' attributes must not be used as criteria for class inclusion,
but rather, as Max Weber has made clear, stated as probabilities
on the basis of objectively defined situations.

Implicit in this way of stating the issues of stratification lies
a model of social movements and political dynamics. The important differences among people are differences that shape their
biographies and ideas; within any given stratum, of course, individuals differ, but if their stratum has been adequately understood, we can expect certain psychological traits to recur. The
probability that people will have a similar mentality and ideology, and that they will join together for action, is increased the
more homogeneous they are with respect to class, occupation,
and prestige. Other factors do, of course, affect the probability
that ideology, organization, and consciousness will occur among
those in objectively similar strata. But psychological factors are
likely to be associated with *strata*, which consist of people who
are characterized by an intersection of the *several* dimensions
we have been using: class, occupation, status, and power. The
task is to sort out these dimensions of stratification in a systematic way, paying attention to each separately and then to its
relation to each of the other dimensions.

The question whether the white-collar workers are a 'new
middle class,' or a 'new working class,' or what not, is not entirely
one of definition, but its empirical solution is made possible only
by clarified definitions. The meaning of the term 'proletarianized,'
around which the major theories have revolved, is by no means
clear. In the definitions we have used, however, proletarianization
might refer to shifts of middle-class occupations toward wage-

workers in terms of: income, property, skill, prestige or power, irrespective of whether or not the people involved are aware of these changes. Or, the meaning may be in terms of changes in consciousness, outlook, or organized activity. It would be possible, for example, for a segment of the white-collar people to become virtually identical with wage-workers in income, property, and skill, but to resist being like them in prestige claims and to anchor their whole consciousness upon illusory prestige factors. Only by keeping objective position and ideological consciousness separate in analysis can the problem be stated with precision and without unjustifiable assumptions about wage-workers, white-collar workers, and the general psychology of social classes.

When the Marxist, Anton Pannekoek for example, refuses to include propertyless people of lower income than skilled workers in the proletariat, he refers to ideological and prestige factors. He does not go on to refer to the same factors as they operate among the 'proletariat,' because he holds to what can only be called a metaphysical belief that the proletariat is *destined* to win through to a certain consciousness. Those who see white-collar groups as composing an independent 'class,' *sui generis,* often use prestige or status as their defining criterion rather than economic level. The Marxian assertion, for example L. B. Boudin's, that salaried employees 'are in reality just as much a part of the proletariat as the merest day-laborer,' obviously rests on economic criteria, as is generally recognized when his statement is countered by the assertion that he ignores 'important psychological factors.'

The Marxist in his expectation assumes, first, that wage-workers, or at least large sections of them, do in fact, or will at any moment, have a socialist consciousness of their revolutionary role in modern history. He assumes, secondly, that the middle classes, or large sections of them, are acquiring this consciousness, and in this respect are becoming like the wage-workers or like what wage-workers are assumed to be. Third, he rests his contention primarily upon the assumption that the economic dimension, especially property, of stratification is the key one, and that it is in this dimension that the middle classes are becoming like wage-workers.

But the fact that propertyless employees (both wage-workers and salaried employees) have not automatically assumed a socialist posture clearly means that propertylessness is not the only factor, or even the crucial one, determining inner-consciousness or political will.

Neither white-collar people nor wage-workers have been or are preoccupied with questions of property. The concentration of property during the last century has been a slow process rather than a sharp break inside the life span of one generation; even the sons and daughters of farmers—among whom the most obvious 'expropriation' has gone on—have had their attentions focused on the urban lure rather than on urban propertylessness. As jobholders, moreover, salaried employees have generally, with the rest of the population, experienced a secular rise in standards of living: propertylessness has certainly not necessarily coincided with pauperization. So the centralization of property, with consequent expropriation, has not been widely experienced as 'agony' or reacted to by proletarianization, in any psychological sense that may be given these terms.

Objectively, we have seen that the structural position of the white-collar mass is becoming more and more similar to that of the wage-workers. Both are, of course, propertyless, and their incomes draw closer and closer together. All the factors of their status position, which have enabled white-collar workers to set themselves apart from wage-workers, are now subject to definite decline. Increased rationalization is lowering the skill levels and making their work more and more factory-like. As high-school education becomes more universal among wage-workers, and the skills required for many white-collar tasks become simpler, it is clear that the white-collar job market will include more wage-worker children.

In the course of the next generation, a 'social class' between lower white-collar and wage-workers will probably be formed, which means, in Weber's terms, that between the two positions there will be a typical job mobility. This will not, of course, involve the professional strata or the higher managerial employees, but it will include the bulk of the workers in salesroom and office. These shifts in the occupational worlds of the propertyless are

more important to them than the existing fact of their propertylessness.

3. Organizations

The assumption that political supremacy follows from functional, economic indispensability underlies all those theories that
see the new middle class or any of its sections slated to be the
next ruling class. For it is assumed the class that is indispensable in fulfilling the major functions of the social order will
be the next in the sequence of ruling classes. Max Weber in his
essay on bureaucracy has made short shrift of this idea: 'The
ever-increasing "indispensability" of the officialdom, swollen to
millions, is no more decisive for this question [of power] than is
the view of some representatives of the proletarian movement
that the economic indispensability of the proletarians is decisive
for the measure of their social and political power position. If
"indispensability" were decisive, then where slave labor prevailed
and where freemen usually abhor work as a dishonor, the "indispensable" slaves ought to have held the positions of power,
for they were at least as indispensable as officials and proletarians
are today. Whether the power . . . as such increases cannot be
decided *a priori* from such reasons.'

Yet the assumption that it can runs all through the white-collar
literature. Just as Marx, seeing the parasitical nature of the capitalist's endeavor, and the real function of work performed by
the workers, predicted the workers' rise to power, so James Burn-
ham (and before him Harold Lasswell, and before him John
Corbin) assumes that since the new middle class is the carrier of
those skills upon which modern society more and more depends,
it will inevitably, in the course of time, assume political power.
Technical and managerial indispensability is thus confused with
the facts of power struggle, and overrides all other sources of
power. The deficiency of such arguments must be realized positively: we need to develop and to use a more open and flexible
model of the relations of political power and stratification.

Increasingly, class and status situations have been removed
from free market forces and the persistence of tradition, and
been subject to more formal rules. A government management

of the class structure has become a major means of alleviating inequalities and insuring the risks of those in lower-income classes. Not so much free labor markets as the powers of pressure groups now shape the class positions and privileges of various strata in the United States. Hours and wages, vacations, income security through periods of sickness, accidents, unemployment, and old age—these are now subject to many intentional pressures, and, along with tax policies, transfer payments, tariffs, subsidies, price ceilings, wage freezes, et cetera, make up the content of 'class fights' in the objective meaning of the phrase.

The 'Welfare State' attempts to manage class chances without modifying basic class structure; in its several meanings and types, it favors economic policies designed to redistribute life-risks and life-chances in favor of those in the more exposed class situations, who have the power or threaten to accumulate the power, to do something about their case.

Labor union, farm bloc, and trade association dominate the political scene of the Welfare State as well as of the permanent war economy; contests within and between these blocs increasingly determine the position of various groups. The state, as a descriptive fact, is at the balanced intersection of such pressures, and increasingly the privileges and securities of various occupational strata depend upon the bold means of organized power.

It is often by these means that the objective position of white-collar and wage-worker becomes similar. The greatest difficulty with the Marxist expectation of proletarianization is that many changes pointing that way have not come about by a lowering of the white-collar position, but often more crucially by a raising of the wage-worker position.

The salary, as contrasted with the wage, has been a traditional hall-mark of white-collar employment. Although still of prestige value to many white-collar positions, the salary must now be taken as a tendency in most white-collar strata rather than a water-tight boundary of the white-collar worlds. The contrast has rested on differences in the time-span of payment, and thus in security of tenure, and in the possibilities to plan because of more secure expectations of income over longer periods of time. But, increasingly, companies put salaried workers, whose salary for some time in many places has been reduced for absences, on an hourly basis. And manual workers, represented by unions, are demanding and getting precisely the type of privileges once granted only white-collar people.

All along the line, it is from the side of the wage-workers that the contrast in privileges has been most obviously breaking down. It was the mass-production union of steel workers, not salaried employees, that precipitated a national economic debate over the issue of regularized employment; and white-collar people must often now fight for what is sometimes assumed to be their inherited privilege: a union of professionals, The Newspaper Guild, has to insist upon dismissal pay as a clause in its contracts.

Whatever past differences between white-collar and wage-workers with respect to income security, sick benefits, paid vacations, and working conditions, the major trend is now for these same advantages to be made available to factory workers. Pensions, especially since World War II, have been a major idea in collective bargaining, and it has been the wage-worker that has had bargaining power. Social insurance to cover work injuries and occupational diseases has gradually been replacing the common law of a century ago, which held the employee at personal fault for work injury and the employer's liability had to be proved in court by a damage suit. In so far as such laws exist, they legally shape the class chances of the manual worker up to a par with or above other strata. Both privileges and income level have been increasingly subject to the power pressures of unions and government, and there is every reason to believe that in the future this will be even more the case.

The accumulation of power by any stratum is dependent on a triangle of factors: will and know-how, objective opportunity, and organization. The opportunity is limited by the group's structural position; the will is dependent upon the group's consciousness of its interests and ways of realizing them. And both structural position and consciousness interplay with organizations, which strengthen consciousness and are made politically relevant by structural position.

14

White-Collar Unionism

Flint, Mich., 18 December 1945. Only 25 to 30 pickets were on duty this morning when the police, under the leadership of Capt. Gus Hawkins, drove parallel lines through the midst of the strikers. About 500 white collar workers went into the plant through the police corridor. There was no disorder, the workers giving way as they hissed and booed the salaried and clerical personnel of the plant. Then the police withdrew to permit an orderly resumption of orderly picketing. Declaring that he would have 10,000 men on hand in the morning, Jack F. Holt, regional director of the U.A.W., said: 'We'll see if they can get through 10,000 men.'

The best chance to organize the white collar people, said the expert organizer with 30 years practical experience, is to get them where they see how the workers have made gains, and how powerful the workers are when they mass pickets and go on strike. In my long experience wherever there's strong wage worker unions they'll all come into the union in those places. . .

In a letter to Mr. Kirby, president of the NAM, Mr. Emery, counsel for the NAM, wrote in 1912: The time is at hand when the Sixteenth Amendment will provide for the possession of a union card for the president [of the United States].

Flint, Mich., 19 December 1945. After standing about in near zero weather for nearly two hours, 500 office workers who walked into the plant through a corridor formed by police yesterday, when only a token picket line was on duty, dispersed.

New York City, 30 March 1948. At 8:55 this morning violence broke out in Wall Street. Massed pickets from local 205 of the United Financial Employees union, supported by members of an AFL seamen's union, knocked over four policemen at the entrance to the stock exchange and lay down on the sidewalk in front of the doors. One hundred police officers swarmed up and, in several knots of furious club-swinging, 12 people were hurt, 45 seized and arrested. The outbreak was over in 30 minutes, but most of the day, 1200 massed pickets surrounded the stock exchange building and shouted epithets at those who entered the building. . .

Show me two white collar workers on a picket line, said Mr. Samuel Gompers, president of the AFL, and I'll organize the entire working class.

IN the minds of the white-collar workers a struggle has been going on between economic reality and anti-union feeling. Whatever their aspirations, white-collar people have been pushed by twentieth-century facts toward the wage-worker kind of organized economic life, and slowly their illusions have been moving into closer harmony with the terms of their existence. They are becoming aware that the world of the old middle class, the community of entrepreneurs, has given way to a new society in which they, the white-collar workers, are part of a world of dependent employees. Now alongside unions of steel workers and coal miners, there are unions of office workers and musicians, salesgirls and insurance men.

What is the extent of white-collar unionism? What causes white-collar workers to accept or reject unionism, and what is its meaning to them? What bearing do white-collar unions have on the shape of American labor unions as a whole? On the possibilities of a democratic political economy in the United States?

1. The Extent Organized

By the opening of the twentieth century, 8.2 per cent of the wage-workers and 2.5 per cent of the white-collar employees were in unions. Here are the proportions organized for selected years since then:

	White Collar	Wage-Worker	Total
1900	2.5%	8.2%	6.5%
1920	8.1%	21.5%	17.9%
1935	5.0%	12.1%	9.6%
1948	16.2%	44.1%	34.5%

After 1915, with profitable business, growing labor scarcity, and an easier Federal Government attitude, the proportions of wage-workers and white-collar people in unions nearly doubled; by 1920 some 8.1 per cent of the white-collar and 21.5 per cent of the wage-workers were in unions, a total of nearly five million people. Contrary to the general rule, the prosperity of the 'twenties did not bring a union boom, for technical advances were so great they created labor surpluses even in boom time; industries benefiting most from the boom were not unionized, while the boom in unionized industries was not so great; and the prevailing craft-type unions were not in harmony with the mass-production techniques which were rapidly coming to the fore.

With the slump, the unions lost heavily: by 1935 only 5.0 per cent of the white-collar and 12.1 per cent of the wage-workers were in unions: a total of 3.4 millions. But that year the tide turned. Legislation establishing the right to unionize; a favorable sequence of court decisions; an atmosphere of official friend-liness and of worker receptivity; the wider advent of industrial unionism; and finally, implementing all these, the war boom with its tight labor market—these developments in labor's decade brought the 1948 proportion of organized wage-workers to 44.1 per cent and of white-collar workers to 16.2 per cent. Unions for wage-workers grew more, if for no other reason than that the great organizing drives were centered in them. In comparing the proportion of wage-workers with white-collar employees in unions we must also keep in mind that white-collar unionism has faced an uphill fight: in the first 48 years of this century the number of potential white-collar unionists increased 406 per cent (from 3.7 to 14.7 million), while potential wage-worker unionists increased only 320 per cent (from 9.1 to 29 million).

White-collar unionism is now beyond the position of wage-workers' in the middle 'thirties, when 12.1 per cent of the wage-workers were organized. Today, with 16.2 per cent of the white-collar workers already in unions, and the 'white-collar mass in-dustries' practically untouched, American labor unions are in a much better position to undertake white-collar unionization. The law is favorable and perhaps soon will be more so; the unions have money to put into it; they have more skilled and experi-enced organizers; there is general prosperity, yet some still fear slump; the unions are working in a friendly political atmos-phere, and moreover one created, as they see it, to a great extent by their power—power which, over the last decade and a half, has given the unions much greater prestige. With all these as-sets, there is no doubt that, given the will and the intelligence, organizing drives among unorganized white-collar workers could be successfully carried through. Yet as of now, 84 per cent of white-collar workers are still not in unions.

The historical centers of white-collar unionism have been rail-roading, government, and entertainment. Before World War I, these three fields together accounted for between 64 and 77 per cent, and during the 'twenties and early 'thirties, for over 85 per cent, of all unionized white-collar people. Only with the or-ganizing drives of the latter 'thirties did they lose their relative ascendency, although even today they contain 58 per cent of all white-collar unionists.

One might suppose that white-collar unions would be strong in areas where wage-worker unions flourish, but this is the case only in certain industries, such as railroads. During the first third of the century, labor unions meant largely unions in coal mining, railroading, and building trades. During the First World War, clothing, shipbuilding, and the metal trades entered the union world. None of these industries, except railroading, contains concentrations of white-collar workers. So the industries in which unionism has centered preclude a clear historical test of the idea that white-collar unions flourish when they supplement wage-worker unions.

Today, the industries in which substantial numbers of white-collar employees are organized include transportation, communication, entertainment, and one branch of the Federal Government, the Postal Service. In all other areas, including manufacturing and retail trade, the proportion organized is never more than 10 per cent, seldom more than 4 or 5.

2. Acceptance and Rejection

The acceptance or rejection of unions depends upon employees' awareness of their objective problems and recognition of unions as means for meeting them. For people to accept unions obviously requires that unions be available to them, and moreover, that they view unions as instruments for achieving desired aims rather than in terms of the illusions about unions so often current in white-collar circles.

Objective circumstances of the work situation influence the white-collar employees' psychology when they are confronted with the idea of joining a union. By and large, these are not different from those affecting the organizability of wage-workers, and include: strategic position in the technological or marketing processes of an industry, which conditions bargaining power; unfair treatment by employers, which creates a high state of grievance; a helpful legal framework, which protects the right to organize; a profitable business but one in which labor costs form a small proportion of the cost of production, which means that higher wages will not severely affect total costs; relative permanency of employment and of labor force, so that organization may be stable.

The relation to the 'boss' is an often crucial and usually complicated matter. On the one hand, the technological and educational similarity of white-collar work to the work of the boss; the physical nearness to him; the prestige borrowed from him; the rejection of wage-worker types of organization for prestige reasons; the greater privileges and securities; the hope of ascent—all these, when they exist, predispose the white-collar employee to identify with the boss. On the other hand, there is fear and even hatred of the boss. In fact, loyalty to management, advanced by white-collar employees, is often, unknown even to them, an insecure cover-up for fear of reprisal. In one office, for example, during a union drive, ten old employees held out firmly: 'We're perfectly happy in our jobs. We like to work here. We make enough to live on, maybe as much as we're worth. And besides, our boss, who is a real gentleman, is doing all he can afford to do for us.' The company's attitude toward the union was outspokenly bitter; but soon, because of pressure from the already organized sales force, it shifted to acquiescence. Then, almost overnight, the attitude of the ten old-line employees also shifted; they began to spill grievances, their one great fear now being that they might not be allowed to join the union. They expressed their intimately felt disapproval of the boss's ways, and one of them even reported daydreams of heavy ledgers dropping from tall filing cases on the boss's head.

Although acceptance of unions does involve some sense of the separateness of one's economic interest from that of the boss and the company, the attitude to management is not an explicit, simple key to the psychology of white-collar unionism. The white-collar organizer finds other psychological circumstances lying deeper and variously reflected by the white-collar man or woman he approaches. Three general indices to these circumstances, each involving a whole complex of accompanying feelings and opinions, are involved in 'white-collar' appraisals of unions:

1. One major reason white-collar employees often reject unions is that unions have not been available to them. An immensely

greater effort over a longer period of time has been given to wage-worker unionism. For most white-collar employees to join or not to join a union has never been a live question, for no union has been available, or, if it has, was not energetically urging affiliation. For these employees, the question has been to organize or not to organize a union, which is a very different proposition from joining or not joining an available union.

Moreover, unless they are themselves unionized, white-collar workers usually have relatively little personal contact with union personnel or with friends or relatives who are union members. Being personally in contact with union leaders and union members, however, is a decisive factor in one's union attitude. In the absence of such contact and given the general hostile atmosphere that prevails in many white-collar circles, an anti-union attitude often results. Personal exposure to unions not only reveals their benefits, but sometimes creates a social situation in which those who don't belong feel socially ostracized. More generally, contacts with union people tend to discount anti-unionism; in fact, they seem to be the most single important antidote.

II. The political party affiliations of white-collar employees and their families buttress their union feelings. Although some white-collar groups have tended to shift from their parents' Democratic or Republican tradition to an independent position, generally stated as voting for 'the best man,' but frequently coming to mean Republican, most remain in the same party as their parents. People generally come into contact with party rhetoric before they do union rhetoric, and this affects their receptivity to union proposals. Party identifications are closely associated with union attitude: third-party and Democratic people tend to be more pro-union than Independents or Republicans. The New Deal, and especially the personality of President Roosevelt, did more for unions than create an encouraging legal framework; it raised the prestige value of unions, and for many middle-class groups, it did much to neutralize the prestige depreciation which joining had entailed. It made the union a more respectable feature of American life, and since the New Deal, the union's public success and increased power have further supported its increased respectability.

III. Not job dissatisfaction in general, but a specific kind of job dissatisfaction—the feeling that as an individual he cannot get ahead in his work—is the job factor that predisposes the white-collar employee to go pro-union. This opinion is more important in the conscious psychology of white-collar unionism than the good or bad will of the company, the degree of job routinization, et cetera. There is a close association between the feeling that one *cannot* get ahead, regardless of the reason, and a pro-union attitude: 'I don't think there are any chances . . . only a few can get promotion . . . I would join a union . . . we are exploited. . .' But others say: 'I think there's a good chance to get ahead. It's entirely up to you. An assistant to the boss is going to leave. I've got the opportunity to step in there. . . Maybe with more training I can be the boss. . . If I don't make good it's my own fault. . . I really don't see what you gain from belonging. . .'

Personal exposure to unions, political party affiliation, and feelings about individual chances to climb—these three factors predispose white-collar people to accept unions.* And each of these predisposing factors is generally moving in the direction of pro-unionism: despite some counter-tendencies during the war, individual ascent chances and hopes will probably continue to decline for white-collar people. The 1948 Democratic victory further increased the respectability of the 'liberal' political column and hence the numbers in it. And if, as labor grows, white-collar drives get underway, more and more white-collar people will be exposed, directly or indirectly, to unionism.

The white-collar worker may accept or reject unions (1) in terms of their *instrumental value,* seeing them as ways to realize

---

* Among a small group (128) of white-collar people intensively studied, 85 per cent of those with strong predisposition (all three factors positive), 53 per cent of the intermediate (1 or 2 factors), and none of the weakly predisposed felt favorable to unions. At the other end of the scale, none of the strongly predisposed, 16 per cent of the intermediate, and 75 per cent of the weakly predisposed were anti-union.

People who have experienced only one or two, but not all, of these three factors turn out to be on-the-fence about unionization, for they have been under contradictory influences: their hope of ascent is dim but they have not been personally exposed to unions; or their politics are against unions but they have been favorably exposed to unions; or, if they are liberals, perhaps they see a good chance of ascent.

economic and job benefits; or in terms of *principle,* seeing them as good or bad in themselves with no concern over their immediate effects on his life; (2) in terms of *himself* and his own job situation, or in terms of *'other people'* and their job situations.

In the mass media of communication, unions are more likely to be presented ideologically than as helpful instrumentalities. 'Union news' is seldom presented 'up close,' in such a way that members of the public could easily identify with unions as practical means to their own practical ends. So some ideological counter-force is often needed if unions are to be accepted on principle, or, as is more usual, if principled rejection is to be by-passed and the instrumental benefits of unions understood. That ideological counter-force is often summed up in political-party identification. Unless the non-unionized white-collar worker has been influenced by liberal political-party rhetoric, there is little chance that he will accept unions for himself on principle.

Given the generally hostile atmosphere, still carried by the mass media, there is undoubtedly more principled rejection than principled acceptance of the unions. Pro-union ideology serves primarily to clear away principled objections in order that an instrumental view may come to the fore. One reason personal contact with union members weighs so heavily in pro-unionism is that such contact frequently results in a more instrumental type of judgment. Then various interest factors, notably feelings about ascent chances, can become decisive.

Unions are usually accepted as something to be used, rather than as something in which to believe. They are understood as having to do strictly with the job and are valued for their help on the job. They rest upon, and perhaps carry further, the alienated split of 'job' from 'life.' Acceptance of them does not seem to lead to new identifications in other areas of living.

3. Individual Involvement

One might suppose that pro-unionism would involve greater feelings of solidarity among co-workers, and greater antagonism toward the higher-ups or the company. But this is not necessarily the case: those white-collar workers who are in unions or who are pro-union in outlook do not always display more co-worker

solidarity than those not in unions or who are anti-union in feeling. Equal proportions on either side are competitively oriented
toward co-workers, see co-workers off the job, are friendly with
them, have a feeling of belonging to the work-group rather than
just happening to be there, and feel estranged from the company
or the higher-ups.

In the union or out of it, for it, against it, or on the fence, the
white-collar employee usually remains psychologically the little
individual scrambling to get to the top, instead of a dependent
employee experiencing unions and accepting union affiliation as
collective means of collective ascent. This lack of effect of unions
is of course linked with the reasons white-collar people join
them: to most members, the union is an impersonal economic
instrument rather than a springboard to new personal, social, or
political ways of life.

The main connection between union and individual member is
the fatter pay check, a fact which is in line with the general
American accent on individual pecuniary success, as well as the
huckstering animus of many union organizers. Unions, 'instru-
mentally' accepted, are alternatives to the traditional individu-
alistic means of obtaining the traditional goals of success. They
are collective instruments for pursuing individual goals; belonging to them does not modify the goals, although it may make the
member feel more urgently about these goals. Union organizers
are salesmen of the idea, as one organizing pamphlet for white-
collar employees puts it, that 'You can get it, too!' and 'Union
organization is the modern way to go places.' The prevailing
strategy is to by-pass the status, the ideology, and the politics
and to stress economic realities and benefits. The only status appeal, a kind of hard-boiled 'keeping up' tactic, is still focused on
the pay lag between white-collar and wage-worker: 'If you are
not organized, the world is passing you by!'

Yet, despite the dominant ways unions are sold and accepted,
there are indications that they often mean more to white-collar
people: 'I feel I have somebody at the back of me.' 'I have a feeling that we are all together and strong—you are not a ball at
the feet of the company.' 'The union, it's my protection.' 'You
feel you are not being pushed around.' These apparently simple
and straightforward feelings in reality rest upon complex factors

of prestige claims and economic security and upon certain intervals of exciting powerfulness which the union has brought into
the routine and often dreary white-collar life. In such intervals,
the union appears as a social force on the job with which employees can identify positively; and with this, the company and
its higher-ups appear as counter-forces about which the employee feels ambiguous or negative.

The fact that union affairs can be exciting during times of
struggle must not be underestimated in the union's appeal to the
white-collar people. Generally it is only then that the union,
rather than an unattended instrument, becomes a social norm—
'When you work with people and they belong, you feel you
should belong too'—as well as a welcome variation from normal
work routines: 'During the strike we had a couple of months ago
we talked a lot . . . we were out two days and got an increase
of $2.00 . . . we had a meeting about a week before the strike.
That was probably the most exciting thing that happened at
work. It made it sort of exciting to go to work. Everybody was
talking about it. It was something different from every other day.
I felt I had a part in it. . .'

Resentment, slowly produced by the routine of dull work, finds
an outlet in strong anti-company and strong pro-union loyalties,
but to hold these loyalties, unions, like any other institution, must
operate dramatically as well as in the obvious interests of the
members. Perhaps nothing is so exciting to the employee, apart
from a strike, as the union's 'investigating the company.' 'They
said that that was the reason—they couldn't afford it. But they
have paid off a million-dollar loan and still have a million in the
bank. They have it. The union had them investigated. You should
have seen the head's face when he found out.'

In all this, white-collar unionism does not differ markedly from
those wage-worker unions we have had occasion to study. The
UAW member in Detroit, for example, does not differ in his
union attitude very markedly from members of New York City
white-collar unions. Both are after, in the first instance, better
conditions of work, especially more pay and more secure pay,
and both consciously get 'protection' out of unions. More systematically, the union performs four functions in the employee's
life:

I. Economically, unions mean economic advances and protection against arbitrary wage action. The fruits of increased productivity, brought about by the rationalization of white-collar work, are not automatically passed on to the employee: only by organizations that force bargaining and concessions can white-collar workers make economic gains. They cannot continue indefinitely to benefit from wage-workers' organizations—as they have undoubtedly been doing in many industries—and not shoulder part of the risk and the work involved.

Differences in what various unions fight for reflect differences in employer policy more than differences in union philosophy. The trend in white-collar unions seems to be to line up salaries and conditions with those of other organized white-collar workers rather than with the pattern prevailing in the same industry among production workers. Yet the plain economic struggle of white-collar workers will continue, whether or not they have unions, to be part of the fight of labor as a whole, of carpenters and auto workers and coal diggers. It will not have any autonomy, as the economic struggle of a separated group, because of any economically peculiar position white-collar people may think they occupy. Although, as more white-collar people are unionized, their share in deciding the terms of the struggle may become greater, their economic struggle is not different from that of the wage-workers.

The privileges that white-collar employees have traditionally enjoyed are being formalized in the union contracts they secure; and, as National Industrial Conference Board studies have shown, it is in this area of 'fringe benefits' that their contracts differ most from wage-workers'. White-collar contracts are usually much more likely than those of production workers' to contain welfare clauses: personal leaves, paid sick leaves, severance pay, holiday and vacation rules. Yet the formalization of such privileges, in white-collar contracts, comes at a time when wage-worker unions are also seriously beginning to fight for them, as well as for the more solid privileges of medical and pension plans.

II. If the unions raise the level and security of the employees' income, at the same time they may lower the level and security of prestige. For in so far as white-collar claims for prestige rest upon differences between themselves and wage-workers, and in so far as the organizations they join are publicly associated with worker organizations, one of the bases of white-collar prestige is done away with. White-collar people are often quite aware of this: 'It is not possible that a union would start in my business, but if it did I do not think I would join because . . . people think less of you. Management unconsciously thinks that people who belong to a union have not enough sense to talk for themselves.'

The status psychology of white-collar employees is part of a 'principled' rejection of unionism, although it often has instrumental content as well: the hope of being judged by management as different from wage-workers, and so of climbing by traditional individual means. Apart from this, the prestige claims are purely invidious and principled; and usually are overcome only when the employee, by personal contact, comes to see the union as an instrument, is exposed to more liberal political rhetoric, and, above all, has lost his hope of ascent by individual means.

However widespread the prestige resistances to unions may now be, solid, long-run factors are acting to reduce them, for these are the same factors we saw affecting general white-collar prestige: lack of differences between wage-worker and white-collar income; white-collar unemployment, as during the 'thirties; the breakdown of the white-collar monopoly on high-school education; the inevitable reduction of the claims of white-collar people for prestige based on their not being 'foreign-born, like workers'; the concentration of white-collar workers into big work places and their down-grading and routinization; the mere increase in the total numbers of white-collar people—all these factors and trends are tearing away the foundations of the white-collar rejection of unions on the basis of prestige.

Today white-collar workers and their organizations use many dodges to avoid identification with wage-workers and yet secure the benefits of unionism. They call their unions 'guilds' or 'associations'; they have a permanent no-strike policy, et cetera. In the end all this is nonsense so far as the central economic purpose of unions is concerned; yet, although their sacrifice of prestige is the sacrifice of a fading value, this value is still real to white-collar employees, often more so than their low incomes. In his appeal the union organizer has to balance the prestige loss against the economic gains: in the short run, the loss is greatly softened by the strictly instrumental way unionism is accepted; in the long run, objective forces will destroy the bases of such claims for higher prestige.

III. Unionism objectively means a declaration of collective independence, and, correspondingly, a tacit acceptance of individual dependence. We have seen how closely the feeling that one has no individual chance to rise is related to a pro-union attitude. White-collar unions, like those of wage-workers', are in part a consequence of a rationalization of the work process. For only an organization can talk back and exert power over the conditions of such work and over the work-life itself. In their quest for occupational justice—equal conditions and equal pay for equal grades of work—the unions further rationalization of work, while at the same time shaping it more to the interests of the work group as a whole. Regardless of the union's ideology, the task of the job-description committee, soon at work in many union drives, is to reorganize the personnel hierarchy of the company, incidentally wiping out many prestige distinctions without economic content cultivated by management or allowed to encrust on the hierarchy by usage. Sometimes this creates active resentment among employees: 'I'm not sure I'd want to join. . . My friend says they brow-beat them in her office. They walk up and down the office and watch what people are doing, and if a file girl types even a label, they threaten to have her fired.'

The employees' modern choice is not between individual independence and individual dependence on the employer. Unions are devices by which collections of people get done what the employer is in a position to do for himself, and what in a simpler age of more kindly exploitation employees were in a position to do for themselves individually. As the union lessens the employees' dependence upon the employer, it substitutes dependence upon the union, an organization expected to act more in accordance with their interests. In many industries, the union is an additional bureaucracy, seeking to influence the way employees are geared into the larger bureaucracy of the business. Within the company, the unionized white-collar worker associates himself with a new sort of personnel organization, one having his interests in mind; to the extent that his union is internally democratic, he gains a collective voice with which he shouts to the top of the company about his specific job and his individual grievances. Inside the office and salesroom and up in the front of the plant, unions increase the collective power of the white-collar employee over the conditions and the security of his work-life.

iv. The power of the union, white-collar or otherwise, is also exerted in the political economy, where, to the extent that they are members of effective national unions, the power of the white-collar employees increases. For, as union members, they are represented by organized pressure groups that are increasingly effective in the politics of economic bargaining.

4. The Shape of Unionism

Since at least the 'thirties the organization of white-collar workers has been a standard item on the liberal-labor agenda, but the political meaning of such organization is not often seriously discussed. Suppose that 8 or 9 million of the 12.3 million unorganized white-collar people were in the unions—what would it mean for the political character and direction of U.S. labor?

To answer this question we must consider: i, whether white-collar unionism has or is likely to develop a mentality and direction of its own; ii, whether white-collar unions tend to display more or less militancy than wage-worker unions; and iii, whether or not, and in what sense, an enlargement of white-collar unions might constitute 'labor's link to the middle class.'

i. Throughout the present century, the AFL has remained dominant in the white-collar field. In 1900, white-collar unionists were evenly divided between AFL and independent unions; since then the AFL proportion has grown and by 1935 contained two-thirds of all unionized white-collar workers. The rise of the CIO has only slightly weakened AFL dominance in the white-collar field; for the big CIO organizing drives were in mass industrial rather than white-collar areas. As of 1948, 62 per cent of all un-

ionized white-collar employees were in the AFL, 22 per cent
in independent unions, and 16 per cent in the CIO. If we turn
these figures around, and compute the white-collar proportions
within each union bloc, 21 per cent of all independent unionists
were white-collar workers, 19 per cent of all AFL members, and
only 8 per cent of all CIO union members.

If more white-collar workers are organized, they will most
likely, under present conditions, be organized by existing labor
organizations. In the fall of 1948, CIO heads did announce a
white-collar drive, and since then various moves have been made
to get it under way. In so far as they were serious about it, they
were probably impelled, in addition to the standard motive of
protecting these workers' interests, by certain political considerations. Within the CIO, 'the white-collar drive' was a drive against
certain highly vocal Communist elements, which top CIO men
wished to be rid of. The way to upset as well as to gain union
power is to organize and counter-organize. They also desired, in
the current political phase, to overtake and surpass AFL unions
in the numbers of enrolled members. The white-collar fields are
new frontiers, which involve a minimum of jurisdictional tangle.

Many CIO leaders are young, ambitious men who have already
organized their initially chosen fields; a white-collar drive offers
an outlet for their energies; organizing drives are power accumu-
lators for leaders no less than for workers. Also some older leaders, recently risen to top power in their middle age, might wish to
make their own marks; in trade-union circles, this means to organize. Labor leaders, in and out of the CIO, probably think that
white-collar organizing will increase their political pull in the
'middle-class' area, and thus improve the unions' public relations.
In so far as they are contenders for power and influence in one
or the other of the standard political parties, they look upon inclusion of white-collar people in their unions as a winning card
in contests within and between party and state.

The chance for a freewheeling bloc of white-collar unions separate from the existing blocs seems very slight, in part because
of the existing union set-up, and in part because white-collar
employees, and potential leaders among them, have no firm ideological or practical reasons to wish to play an independent part.

In the existing union world, wage-worker unions have the priority of organization; their base is so large and firm that in our time white-collar people, even if completely organized, would not be able to achieve dominance. Organization requires money; in the modern accounting system of unionism, so much a head is required; in a world of big business, big government, and big unions, small unions without funds fall behind or are swallowed by larger ones.

White-collar organization in the 'fifties is less likely to be spontaneous or to come from the bottom up than was the case in the 'thirties. Organizations are likely to be initiated from the top by existing union powers, for when unionization is quasi-spontaneous, new and more militant leaders have better chances to come to the top. The CIO organizing drives of the 'thirties split the old union world and, largely in response to worker demands, gave rise to new men of power, who for a historical moment seemed free to choose new union alternatives.

But that happened when only 3.4 million workers were organized; now 15.4 million are members. Labor is so big, and the legal requirements so much more complex, that the chance for new types of leaders to emerge in connection with organizing drives is rather limited. Of course, techniques and tactics of organizing may appropriately differ, and leaders possessing a rhetoric more congenial to white-collar employees may arise, but in the natural course of affairs, older men already in power will select and encourage types of men not too different from themselves.

Established powers at established headquarters, and the men they favor, will run the drives and probably manage any new unions that are formed. New leaders will rise and old ones will fall, but there is not much chance for white-collar unions to emerge as a new type of organization or for new types of white-collar leaders to gain great power.

II. The psychology of white-collar unionism, as we have seen, is not different from that of wage-workers; in both cases it is expedient and instrumental, rather than principled or ideological. Of course, unions of carpenters differ in shape and policy from unions of auto workers or insurance salesmen or clerks. But the common denominators of unionism are not divided according to white-collar and wage-worker types.

A few speculations on either side of the issue, however, need to be made. It can be argued that white-collar unionists will turn out to be more cautious and less militant because the style of life of white-collar people, as contrasted with that of workers in the mass-production fields, throws them into contact with the general (middle-class) culture, routines of information, and dominant values. They have more chances to belong to other organizations, so unionism will mean even less in their political and social lives than it has meant in the lives of steel, auto, or coal workers. Because of their cleaner, more prestigeful work, and their consciousness of the blue-shirted masses below them, they will feel that they have more to lose from militant unionism that might fail. Since many of them are of middle-class origin, their biographical ties with entrepreneurial elements will restrain them. Furthermore, since other white-collar employees are of wage-worker origin and connection, the white-collar mass will be divided in allegiance and hence waver in policy and action.

There is some truth in each of these points. But it is also possible to argue, with a measure of truth, that white-collar unions will be *more* militant than wage-worker unions, because they will be young at power bargaining and hence, at least for a while, a taste of power will prod them to less disciplined and more spontaneous movement. Having claims to higher prestige than the wage-worker, having more links with the older middle class, they will not 'take it' so readily, will be more likely to stand up higher and fight harder. Since many of them have been dependent upon their employers, once they break that allegiance and go pro-union, their reaction against employers is likely to be stronger and more aggressive. Since they are more highly educated, once they get the union slant, they will have a greater capacity to generalize it, will be more politically and ideologically oriented in their unionism.

These points, too, have elements of truth. Yet neither view stands up very well. Many of the factors in support of the idea that white-collar unions will be more militant than wage-worker unions rest upon the relative smallness and youth of white-collar unionism. But compared with wage-worker unions of the same size and age, they do not differ from them. Many of the factors in support of the idea that white-collar unions will be less militant than wage-worker unions rest upon differences that, in the course of historical development, will quite likely be washed away.

The lesson from the historical experience of unionism in the United States, which of course need not be a dogmatic lesson, is that wage-workers and white-collar employees in due course form the same types of unions, and that there is nothing peculiar or distinctive about white-collar unionism; that variations in terms of militancy among wage-worker unions and among white-collar unions are just as slight as any other variations between the two.

Trade unions, after all, are the most reliable instruments to date for taming and channeling lower-class aspirations, for lining up the workers without internal violence during time of war, and for controlling their insurgency during times of peace and depression. There are no reasons why unions should not perform the same services among white-collar groups.

One historical fact, however, must be noticed: during the 'thirties and early 'forties, larger proportions of white-collar than of wage-worker unionists were in CIO unions controlled by Communist party cliques. In the CIO, during 1948 about 4 out of 10 white-collar members were in CP controlled unions, whereas only about 2 out of 10 wage-workers were. But that was only within the CIO, which contains vastly more wage-workers than white-collar employees. If we base our calculations on the union world as a whole (including AFL and independents, as well as CIO), we find that CP factions controlled about 6 per cent of unionized white-collar workers and about 7 per cent of unionized wage-workers.

That CP factions have controlled so many white-collar unions within the CIO is more a historical accident of the CIO's development than a sign that unionized white-collar workers are 'more political' than wage-workers. It so happens that these white-collar unions were mainly in larger cities, especially New York, which has been the stronghold of the Communist Party in America. Moreover, it is probably true that this party has appealed quite strongly to the petty bourgeois mentality represented by many sectors of New York's white-collar world.

III. The old radical faith that the mere enlargement of unions is good because it brings more workers into 'organizing centers' is now naive, as is the belief that winning the white-collar people to unionism is necessarily 'a link to the middle class.' Both ideas depend on the kinds of unions that prevail and what their political potential may be. Both ideas have assumed that unions are, or will be when they are big enough, engines of radical social change, that they will conduct themselves with militant intelligence and intelligent militancy.

The question whether or not the unionization of white-collar workers will mean that labor has a link to the middle classes depends upon the definition of 'middle class' and of 'labor.' The question is inherited from the rhetoric of Socialist movements, in which 'labor' means proletariat—a politically conscious group separated from the rest of society, and assumed to be the motor of all historic change—and in which 'middle class' means 'strata with entrepreneurial ideology.'

But American labor, as expressed in unions, is now politically a set of pressure groups, and white-collar workers, especially when they join unions, increasingly assume the pressure-group kind of labor mentality.

The question whether white-collar workers form 'a new middle class' or 'a new proletariat' is being answered, as we have seen, by changes in both classes, as well as by changes in the kind of organizations U.S. labor unions have become. Economically, the white-collar strata are less 'middle class' than has been supposed; socially and ideologically, the wage-workers are more 'middle class' than has been supposed. In the bureaucratic scene in which social change now occurs, organizations, not spontaneously alerted classes, often monopolize the chances for action. And in the world of organizations and interest groups, the white-collar and wage-worker strata come together in a kind of lower middle-class pressure bloc.

Politically, the presence of more white-collar workers in labor unions will give liberal and labor spokesmen a chance more truthfully to identify 'the interests of labor' with those of the community as a whole. The mass base of labor as a pressure group will be further extended, and labor spokesmen will inevitably be involved in more far-reaching bargains over the national political economy.

5. Unions and Politics

No matter what unionism may mean to the individual white-collar worker, organizationally it brings the white-collar strata into labor as an interest group. Unless white-collar unions develop a distinctive program of their own—and there seems to be no tendency in that direction—or unless the meaning of unionism to them becomes politically distinctive—and it apparently does not—white-collar unionism will carry the same meaning as wage-worker unionism. Therefore, what white-collar unions mean for America depends on what U.S. unions in general mean.

So far, that meaning has been felt mainly in the economic sphere, and there is no doubt that unions for white-collar workers will increase their chance to have a voice in their conditions of work and levels of pay. But the larger meaning of unionism involves the question of democracy and labor unions, that is, the question of whether the unions are to become a movement, or whether they are going to become another vested interest, an agency of political regulation at an economic price. Or, in the words of Lionel Trilling, whether 'the conflict of capital and labor is a contest for the possession of the goods of a single way of life' or a 'culture struggle.'

For a long time the unions, considered nationally, were a set of largely 'un-invested' organizations. Up to the middle 'thirties, they were thought to be able to go either way: as a free movement, they would grow bigger and yet retain their freedom to act, and they would strive to act in a way that would re-order U.S. society in the image of a libertarian and secure society; or as a set of interests, they would attempt to vest themselves within the framework of capitalist society and the administrative state.

Along this last road, unions might take stands on broader issues, but only in bargaining with other vested interests. Their spokesmen might talk of responsibility, but only in this meaning: those to whom I say I am responsible are those whom I seek to manage. The 'responsibility' of those who in gaining power have become hampered in their action is often a responsibility to regulate the discontent of the underlying strata, in order that, as responsible spokesmen at the top, they may deal in a more intelligent and practical way with other spokesmen.

The question of democracy and unionism is a question whether in protecting the employees' economic position by an adroit struggle among organized interest blocs, the unions will be forced to become 'watchdogs' over the working of the economy as a whole. And there is a second question: whether in being watchdogs over the economy, as against being merely an interest group within it, the unions will be *forced* to take on a larger cultural and political struggle. We say 'forced' because present labor leadership does not encourage us to believe that labor leaders as a general rule will do so from any sort of conviction, much less any vision of the need.

Historical experience, as well as the character of present-day labor leadership, says No to these questions, but neither presents a conclusive argument. Labor leadership changes, although change is likely to be more difficult in the future than in the past; and historical experience must be countered, in a balanced judgment, by the mid-century facts of the social structure.

In the main drift of this structure, the point to watch is the type and the extent of labor's involvement with business corporations and with the administrative state. How much free action, just what kind, in what spheres, for approximately what ends—these are the questions we must be asking ourselves about U.S. labor in the coming decade. The main drift now involves four coinciding trends:

(1) Economically practical conservatism, expressed by such men as Robert Taft, is being overtaken and supplanted by politically sophisticated conservatism—a conservatism that is aware of the political conditions of modern profit working and economic power, and of the kind of softening co-operation with unions that is needed to control them. (2) Liberalism, now almost a common denominator of U.S. politics, becomes administrative liberalism, a powerful and more absorptive state framework, within which open political struggles are being translated into administrative

procedures and pressures. (3) The labor interest, coinciding with sophisticated conservatism, is being vested within this administrative state and is in fact becoming one of its major supporting pillars; labor is committed to the support of this state, and, in turn, draws much of its strength from it. (4) All these developments are going on within the building of a total war economy during an era with no treaty-structured peace in Europe or Asia.

U.S. labor, like U.S. small business, seems to be trying to follow the route of the U.S. farmer. Once this farmer was a source of insurgency of a kind; in the recent past, labor has seemed to be such. Now the farmer is often a fat unit in an organized farm bloc, firmly entrenched within and pressuring the welfare state. Despite its greater objective antagonism to capitalism as a wage system, labor seems to be trying to go the same way; its leaders, following the policy of success, would apparently model the political role of their organizations upon those of the farmer. Talk of farm-labor unity, which used to rest upon a unity of insurgents, now seems to rest upon attempted bargains between two pressure groups.

Unlike farmers, and unlike wage-workers, white-collar employees were born too late to have even a brief day of autonomy; their structural position and available strategy make them rearguarders rather than movers and shakers of historic change. Their unionization is a unionization into the main drift and serves to incorporate them as part of the newest interest to be vested in the liberal state.

The story of labor in the Franklin Roosevelt era encouraged hope because labor was then emerging for the first time on any American scale; it had little need of any sense of direction other than to 'organize the unorganized.' But in Truman's Fair Deal this is not the case: not the mandate of the slump, but the farmer's fear that his enormous prosperity might be taken away from him; not millions of unemployed, but labor's fear that Taft-Hartley acts will be used against existing unions are the underpinnings of this administration. Then thought of war was not dominant, and men of power could pay serious attention to the distribution of domestic power; now fear of war hangs over all political speculation and deadens the political will for new domestic beginnings.

There are counter-tendencies to the main drift, and there are possible crises in the increasingly rigid structure that would unite and allow these tendencies to assert themselves as historical forces. But in the meantime, if the future of democracy in America is imperiled, it is not by any labor *movement*, but by its absence, and the substitution for it of a new set of vested interests. If these new interests often seem of particular peril to democratic social structure, it is because they are so large and yet so hesitant. Their business may well become the regulation of insurgent tendencies among those groups and strata that might reorganize American society out of its frenzied order of slump and boom and war, and stop its main drift toward a society in which men are the managed personnel of a garrison state.

15

The Politics of the Rearguard

THE political psychology of any social stratum is influenced by every relation its members have, or fail to have, with other strata; all the objective and subjective factors to which they are exposed play into their political psychology. Composed as they are of a wide range of in-between occupational groups, the new middle classes are especially open to many cross-pressures, as well as to all those larger forces that more or less define the structure and atmosphere of modern society.

To understand the political form and content of white-collar mentality, we must first understand what political consciousness, as well as lack of it, means; to understand how it has been shaped, we must explore the effects on it of the mass media of communication, of the social-historical structure, and of the political institutions and traditions that have prevailed in the United States.

1. Models of Consciousness

Our most familiar model of political consciousness is liberalism, which in focusing upon the individual citizen has tried to enlarge his political rights, his formal opportunities to act politically and to be political. It has assumed that once given the rights, the individual citizen would naturally become politically alerted and act on his political interests. It might be that he would require more education, but education was one of the rights that liberalism sought to make universal.

The difficulties of liberalism's assumption of the alert citizen were well stated by Walter Lippmann in the early 'twenties. His point was that the citizen was unable to know what was going on politically, to think about it straight, or to act upon it intelligently. There was a great gap between individual men, on the one hand, and events and decisions of power, on the other; this gap was filled by the media of communication, which, in their necessity to compress the volume of communication into shorthand slogans, created a pseudo-environment of stereotypes that stood for the unseen political world and to which the citizen reacted. In the great society, the citizen had no time to study things out, his politically fruitful contact with others as well as with the media of communications being limited to fifteen or twenty minutes a day. These facts, in addition to those of artificial censorship and the fear of facing realities that might disturb routine, added up to this, that the political alertness required of the citizen by liberal theory was based on a woefully utopian, rational psychology, which might make sense in a simpler democratic set-up but was impossible in modern society. No one of liberal persuasion has refuted Lippmann's analysis.

The other familiar model of political-consciousness, Marxism, has focused upon the class rather than the individual. It is an ingenious model which reaches from gross material conditions, anchored in property, into the inner consciousness of men of similar class positions. Class-consciousness has always been understood as a political consciousness of one's own rational class interests and their opposition to the interests of other classes. Economic potentiality becomes politically realized: a 'class in itself' becomes a 'class for itself.' Thus for class consciousness, there must be (1) a rational awareness and identification with one's own class interests; (2) an awareness of and rejection of other class interests as illegitimate; and (3) an awareness of and a readiness to use collective political means to the collective political end of realizing one's interests.

These three requirements interact in various ways, depending upon the phase of the movement and the branch of Marxism one examines. Lenin and Trotsky, for instance, placed more emphasis than leaders before them on the party militants, who articulate rational awareness, as a key to the development of mass political consciousness. Yet, underlying the general Marxian model there is always, in Louis Clair's words, the political psychology of 'becoming conscious of inherent potentialities.' This idea is just as rationalist as liberalism in its psychological assumptions. For the struggle that occurs proceeds on the rational recognition by competing classes of incompatible material interests; reflection links material fact and interested consciousness by a calculus of advantage. As Veblen correctly pointed out, the idea is utilitarian, and more closely related to Bentham than Hegel.

Marx, of course, allowed for 'false consciousness,' by which he meant an untrue calculation of interests. He explained it as a rationalist error, due to ignorance or, in more willful moods, to a lack of correct proletarian propaganda. False consciousness, a mental lag from previous eras, is no longer in line with present interests; it is an incorrect interpretation which hides the real world rather than reveals it in a manner adequate for effective action.

Both Marxism and liberalism make the same rationalist assumption that men, given the opportunity, will naturally come to political consciousness of interests, of self or of class. Each in its own way has been more concerned with enlarging the opportunities for men to play political roles than with any psychological unwillingness or inability on their part to do so. Since one or the other of these models of consciousness usually underlies questions and answers about the politics of various social strata, current theories do not usually allow for the view that a stratum may have no political direction, but be politically passive. Yet such indifference is the major sign of both the impasse of liberalism and the collapse of socialist hopes. It is also at the heart of the political malaise of our time.

To be politically indifferent is to be a stranger to all political symbols, to be alienated from politics as a sphere of loyalties, demands, and hopes. The politically indifferent are detached from prevailing political symbols but have no new attachments to counter-symbols. Whatever insecurities and demands and hopes they may have are not focused politically, their personal desires and anxieties being segregated from political symbols and authorities. Neither objective events nor internal stresses count politically in their consciousness.

Political indifference does not necessarily involve a collapse of political expectation; it is not necessarily the end of a scale: hopeful, resigned, despairing, apathetic; that is only one route to it, and one of its meanings. Nor is political indifference necessarily irrational; in fact, it may be a reasoned cynicism, which distrusts and debunks all available political loyalties and hopes as lack of sophistication. Or it may be the product of an extra-rational consideration of the opportunities available to men, who, with Max Weber, assert that they can live without belief in a political world gone meaningless, but in which detached intellectual work is still possible. For men less burdened with insight and enjoying less secure class positions, indifference frequently co-exists with a minimum sacrifice of time and self to some meaningless work, and for the rest, a private pursuit of activities that find their meanings in the immediate gratification of animal thrill, sensation, and fun.

To be politically conscious, either in loyalty or insurgency, is to see a political meaning in one's own insecurities and desires, to see oneself as a demanding political force, which, no matter how small, increases one's hopes that expectations will come off. To be politically indifferent is to see no political meaning in one's life or in the world in which one lives, to avoid any political disappointments or gratifications. So political symbols have lost their effectiveness as motives for action and as justifications for institutions.

2. Political Indifference

In the United States in the middle of the twentieth century, there are, of course, people who approximate the liberal view of the citizen, especially among the educated upper middle class; there are also people who are class-conscious in a Marxian sense, especially among the upper ranks and, in a derived way, among intellectuals. There are also people who display all the necessary qualifications for political loyalty, and some who fulfil the requirements for the insurgent.

But the most decisive comment that can be made about the state of U.S. politics concerns the facts of widespread public indifference, which today overshadow in significance both those of loyalty and those of insurgency.

In our political literature, we do not have many attempts to explain the facts of political indifference, perhaps because neither liberalism nor Marxism raises the question to a central position. Yet, we are now in a situation in which many who are disengaged from prevailing allegiances have not acquired new ones, and so are distracted from and inattentive to political concerns of any kind. They are strangers to politics. They are not radical, not liberal, not conservative, not reactionary; they are inactionary; they are out of it. If we accept the Greek's definition of the idiot as a privatized man, then we must conclude that the U.S. citizenry is now largely composed of idiots.

Our knowledge of this is firmer than any strict proof available to us. It rests, first of all, upon our awareness, as politically conscious men ourselves, of the discrepancy between the meaning and stature of public events and what people seem most interested in.

The Second World War was understood by most sensitive observers as a curiously unreal business. Men went away and fought, all over the world; women did whatever was expected of women during war; people worked hard and long and bought war bonds; everybody believed in America and in her cause; there was no rebellion. Yet it all seemed a purposeless kind of efficiency. Some sort of numbness seemed to prohibit any awareness of the magnitude and depth of what was happening; it was without dream and so without nightmare, and if there was anger and fear and hatred, and there was, still no chords of feeling and conviction were deeply touched. People sat in the movies between production shifts, watching with aloofness and even visible indifference, as children were 'saturation bombed' in the narrow cellars of European cities. Man had become an object; and in so far as those for whom he was an object felt about the spectacle at all, they felt powerless, in the grip of larger forces, having no part in these affairs that lay beyond their immediate areas of daily demand and gratification. It was a time of somnambulance.

It was not that people were insensitive clods with no complaints, but that in all the matter-of-fact efficiency, no mainspring of feeling was let loose in despair or furor; that no complaints were focused rebelliously upon the political meanings of the universal sacrifice and brutality. It was not that people in the United States were apathetically dulled; on the contrary, they were often brightly hopeful, but never politically so, and what used to be called the deepest convictions seemed fluid as water.

It was as if the expert angle of the camera and the carefully nurtured, pompous voice of the commentator had expropriated the chance to 'take it big.' It was as if the ear had become a sensitive soundtrack, the eye a precision camera, experience an exactly timed collaboration between microphone and lens, the machines thus taking unto themselves the capacity for experience. And as the world of this mechanically vivified experience was expanded a hundredfold, the individual became a spectator of everything, rather than an experiencer of what he earned by virtue of what he was becoming. There were no plain targets of revolt; and the cold metropolitan manner had so entered the soul of overpowered men that they were made completely private and blasé, down deep and for good.

Many observers have noted the decline of confidence in the future that had prevailed in the United States fifty years ago, and its replacement by apprehensiveness, pessimism, tension, 'spiritual disillusionment' with the social order. Some time after World War I, American democracy, no longer a widespread confidence and an authentic social feeling, became an objective for official propaganda. It became official and conventional. Over the last half century, Lloyd Morris has remarked, Americans have become a people whose 'freedom, power, material advantages and way of life are widely envied throughout the world; but whose confidence, and faith in their future, have signally diminished.' There has been a parallel development of mighty progress and weak disenchantment.

The fact of formal democracy is not widely questioned, but the way it has been drifting is. An anonymous comment on an Auden poem concludes: 'All the committees and commissions . . . in the

Federal Executive Departments and Agencies, all the employees of all the states, counties, municipalities, townships, and villages, are our employees and they manage our affairs with our consent. All the judges, all the police, are delegated by us to administer a justice that they do not invent or improvise but that we have invented over the centuries. . . We have our managers and they . . . do not push us off the sidewalks. And they cannot forget us because we can see to it that they lose their jobs. . . We have the best system in the world, to be sure, but often we get to thinking that we are no more than spectators at a play—with the right to watch the actors (the managers) come and go, the right to applaud and hiss, and even to put on other actors. But not the right to put on another script. For the play seems to be written once and for all—and not by us.'

'What appalls us is that it is not written by the managers either . . . it is not that [the two wars] came to us against our will; it is that they came to us from some zone that was altogether outside the possibility of being affected by our will. The wars came neither by or against our will. Our appointed managers were at their posts; the wars enveloped them like fog drifting in from sea. . . The agonizing question is, What do our managers control? Without them, there is anarchy. With them there is sometimes the feeling, not that they are remote from us, but that the matter they handle—the matter of life and death—is remote from them.'

It might be thought that our inherited standard of political alertness is too high, that only in crises can it be achieved. But this does not confront the problem at its true level, and lacks an adequate conception of 'crisis.' Crises have involved the publicity of alternatives, usually forced alternatives. But what if the authorities face and choose alternatives without publicity? In a system of power as centralized as ours, 'crises' in the old-fashioned sense occur only when something slips, when there is a leak; and in the meantime, decisions of vital consequence are made behind our backs. The meaning of crisis has to be made clear before it can be hopefully asserted that political alienation will be replaced by alertness only in crises. For today there are crises not publicized for popular political decision but which carry much larger consequences than many publicized crises of the past.

It is a sense of our general condition that lies back of our conviction that political estrangement in America is widespread and decisive. There are, of course, shallower even though more precise indicators, for instance, the meaning and extent of the vote. To vote is not necessarily to be politically involved; nor failure to vote to be politically alienated. Perhaps as high as 80 per cent of those who do vote feel they owe it to their families' tradition of voting one way or the other. In the majority of cases the vote indicates a traditional loyalty not to a set of principles or even to a consistent party position, but to a family traditionally attached to one or another party label. Voting does not typically involve political expectations of great moment, and such demands as it entails are formalized and not often connected with personal troubles. Only a little over half of the people eligible to vote do so, which means that the United States is a government by default as much as by positive election: it is the 50 million who do not vote who determine the outcomes as much as those who do.

The upsurge of trade unionism, involving as it does about one-third of the people at work, might be taken as an indication of a rudimentary form of political insurgency. But trade unionism, as we have seen, does not typically question prevailing symbols, has not typically involved counter-symbols. Its usual demands are for a larger slice of the going yield, and its conscious expectations are short-run expectations of immediate material improvements, not of any change in the system of work and life.

So, in their present shape and motives, neither patronage parties nor trade unions are tokens of widespread political consciousness, either of deeper loyalty or alerted insurgency.

The white-collar people are probably no more or no less politically alienated than other large strata; in fact, judging from the indices available, they seem to be in-between. Thus, 41 per cent of them, as against 59 per cent of the business and professional and 33 per cent of the wage-workers, said they had given 'much thought' rather than 'little thought' to the election for presidency in 1948. In this, the white-collar proportion was the same as the national average. The same is true with respect to participation in voting; every indication available reveals them as exactly average, between business and labor.*

When it was believed, correctly or not, that the workers formed an identifiable camp, it could be asserted that the white-collar man was spiritually powerless because he could not find his way to the workers at a time when the house of middle-class concepts and feelings had collapsed. But whatever house the workers might have been thought to be building has not been built. Now there are no centers of firm and uniform identification. Political alienation and spiritual homelessness are widespread.

How has this political indifference come about? What are the factors that regulate the state of political alienation in America today? We cannot understand the political role of the new middle class until we have explained why in the United States today people of all classes are more or less politically indifferent. In trying to explain it, we shall pay attention, first, to the political contents and function of the mass media of communication; second, to certain features of the social-historical structure of the United States which have formed the character of its political sphere; and third, to the salient characteristics of U.S. political institutions themselves.

3. The Mass Media

To believe that 'the ideology wherein men become conscious of class conflict and fight it out' is determined solely by 'material contradictions' is to overlook the positive role of the mass media of communications. If the consciousness of men does not determine their existence, neither does their material existence determine their consciousness. Between consciousness and existence

* Somewhat more than one-third of the white-collar people, polled in the late 'forties, felt the Republican party best served their interests, about one-third that the Democratic party did; the rest believed that there was no difference between the parties on this point or had no opinion. The 1948 poll vote by occupation is not considered reliable. Analysis of the 1936, 1940, and 1944 presidential elections reveals in each case that the white-collar vote was intermediate between the extremes of business and unskilled labor. In 1936 (proportions for Roosevelt): business, 47; white collar, 61; unskilled labor, 81. In 1940: business, 34; white collar, 48; unskilled labor, 69. In 1944: business, 35; white collar, 49; unskilled labor, 59.

stand communications, which influence such consciousness as men have of their existence. Men do 'enter into definite, necessary relations which are independent of their will,' but communications enter to slant the meanings of these relations for those variously involved in them. The forms of political consciousness may, in the end, be relative to the means of production, but, in the beginning, they are relative to the contents of the communication media.

In Marx's day there was no radio, no movies, no television; there was only printed matter, which, as he demonstrated several times, was in such shape that it was possible for an enterprising individual to start up a newspaper or magazine. It was easier to overlook the role of mass media or to underplay it, when they were not so persuasive in effect and yet were more widely accessible and, despite political censorship, more widely competitive.

What Edward Ross said of custom also applies to the mass media today: their main prop is 'the dread of self-mutilation. For to give up the customary [or the mass-media routine] is to alienate portions of one's self, to tear away the sheath that protects our substance.' Commercial jazz, soap opera, pulp fiction, comic strips, the movies set the images, mannerisms, standards, and aims of the urban masses. In one way or another, everyone is equal before these cultural machines; like technology itself, the mass media are nearly universal in their incidence and appeal. They are a kind of common denominator, a kind of scheme for pre-scheduled, mass emotions.

In these mass arts, instead of form there is formula; they lead 'to no final revelation,' but exhaust themselves immediately as they appear. As Milton Klonsky has observed, 'it is the great indistinction of both the mass arts and contemporary life that they reflect one another so closely, feature by feature, it is almost impossible to tell the image from its source. Both collaborate to form a common myth. . . The fictive heroes of this myth are the archetypes to which the masses try to conform, and the dies from which they stamp their own behavior.' We are so submerged in the pictures created by mass media that we no longer really see them, much less the objects they supposedly represent. The truth is, as the media are now organized, they expropriate our vision.

There is the eventful scene itself, the pictures of the scene, and the response to it. Between scene and response is the picture, given by the mass media. Events outside the narrow scene of the weekly routine have little meaning and in fact are mostly not known except as they are omitted, refracted, or reported in the mass media. The mass-communication system of the United States is not autonomous: it reflects society, but selectively; it reinforces certain features by generalizing them, and out of its selections and reinforcements creates a world. In so far as people live beyond their immediate range of contacts, it is in this world they must live.

The forms and contents of political consciousness, or their absence, cannot be understood without reference to the world created and sustained by these media. The deprivations and insecurities arising from structural positions and historic changes are not likely to be politically symbolized if these media do not take them up in appropriate contexts, and thus lend generalized, communicable meaning to them. Class-consciousness or its absence, for example, involves not merely the individual's experience in and of some objective class-situation, but the communications to which he is exposed. What he comes to believe about the whole range of issues is in some way a function of his experienced situation, plus his first-hand contact with other people, plus his exposure to mass media. And it is often the latter which gives him his standard of reality, his standard of experience.

The contents of the mass media are now a sort of common denominator of American experience, feeling, belief, and aspiration. They extend across the diversified material and social environments, and, reaching lower into the age hierarchy, are received long before the age of consent, without explicit awareness. Contents of the mass media seep into our images of self, becoming that which is taken for granted, so imperceptibly and so surely that to modify them drastically, over a generation or two, would be to change profoundly modern man's experience and character.

The world created by the mass media contains very little discussion of political meanings, not to speak of their dramatization, or sharp demands and expectations. Instead, on the explicitly tagged political level, the media display, the short news flash, and the headlined column or snippet, the few round-tables and editorials. In these, the mass media plug for ruling political symbols and personalities; but in their attempts to enforce conventional attachment to them, they standardize and reiterate until these symbols and personalities become completely banal, and men are attached to them only, as to a brand of clothes, by convention-alized reaction. The whole marketing animus is put behind pre-vailing clichés; politics is squeezed into formulas which are re-peated and repeated; in the words of the advertising manual, you 'make contact, arouse interest, create preference, make specific proposals, close the order.' 'Ad drives' are set up 'to sell the U.S. system,' with an 'agency task force' whose number one job is to 'stress the free enterprise aim' and 'point out to the American people that management, labor and all other groups are agreed that the American system should work towards the basic objec-tive of better living . . .' and so on. The prevailing symbols are presented in such a contrived and pompous civics-book manner, or in such a falsely human light, as to preclude lively involve-ments and deep-felt loyalties.

At the same time, the mass media do not display counter-loyal-ties and demands to the ruling loyalties and demands which they make banal. They are polite, disguising indifference as tolerance and broadmindedness; and they further buttress the disfavor in which those who are 'against things' are held. They trivialize issues into personal squabbles, rather than humanize them by asserting their meanings for you and for me. They formalize ad-herence to prevailing symbols by pious standardization of worn-out phrases, and when they are 'serious,' they merely get detailed about more of the same, rather than give big close-ups of the human meanings of political events and decisions. Their detailed coverage is probably not attended to except by those already in-terested, the slanted material only by those already in agreement with the slant. They reinforce interest and slant, but do not arouse interest by exposing genuine clash. The ruling symbols are so inflated in the mass media, the ideological speed-up is so great, that such symbols, in their increased volume, intensifica-tion, and persuasion, are worn out and distrusted. The mass media hold a monopoly of the ideologically dead; they spin records of political emptiness. To banalize prevailing sym-bols and omit counter-symbols, but above all, to divert from the

explicitly political, and by contrast with other interests to make
'politics' dull and threadbare—that is the political situation of the
mass media, which reflect and reinforce the political situation of
the nation.

The explicit political content of the mass media is, after all,
a very small portion of their managed time and space. This
badly handled content must compete with a whole machinery
of amusement, within a marketing context of distrust. The most
skilled media men and the highest paid talent are devoted to the
glamorous worlds of sport and leisure. These competing worlds,
which in their modern scale are only 30 years old, divert attention from politics by providing a set of continuing interests in
mythical figures and fast-moving stereotypes. The old-fashioned
political rally, to which men traveled in the world of the small
entrepreneur, when politics were not crucial, is replaced by an
elaboration of dazzling alternatives to which men in the new
society, when politics are objectively crucial, can turn without
movement of body or mind.

The attention absorbed by the images on the screen's rectangle
dominates the darkened public; the sonorous, the erotic, the mysterious, the funny voice of the radio talks to you; the thrill of the
easy murder relaxes you. In our life-situation, they simply fasci-
nate. And their effects run deep: popular culture is not tagged as
'propaganda' but as entertainment; people are often exposed to
it when most relaxed of mind and tired of body; and its characters offer easy targets of identification, easy answers to stereotyped personal problems.

The image of success and its individuated psychology are the
most lively aspects of popular culture and the greatest diversion
from politics. Virtually all the images of popular culture are concerned with individuals, and more, with particular kinds of individuals succeeding by individual ways to individual goals. Fiction and non-fiction, movies and radio—indeed almost every
aspect of contemporary mass communication—accentuate *individual* success. Whatever is done is done by individual effort, and
if a group is involved, it strings along after the extraordinary
leader. There is displayed no upward climb of and by collective
action to political goals, but individuals succeeding, by strictly

personal efforts in a hostile environment, to personal economic and erotic goals.

Dramatization in popular art has always involved the personalities of social life, even though an adequate picture of opportunities can be had only by statistically reliable portraits. It is the individual exception rather than the mass facts, however, which is seized upon, diffused, and generalized by the mass media as a model criterion. The Horatio Alger stories of the newsboy who 'made it' by reason of personal virtues may seem merely corny to victims of impersonal depression, yet Mickey Mouse and Superman are followed with zeal by millions, and there is a clear line of connection between Horatio and Mickey. Both are 'little men' who knife their way to the top by paying strict attention to No. One—they are totem-like individuals who are seen in the miraculous ritual of personal success, luckily winning out over tremendous obstacles. Latter-day heroes of success, however, have become sharper in their practices; they win by tricks and often by stabs in the back; the fights they wage are dirtier than Horatio's.

The cowboy and the detective, standard popular culture types, are also out for No. One, although it is often necessary to sanctify their violent methods by linking their motives to wider ends. But they are autonomous men: 'I want to be my own man,' they say, 'I want to do as I please.'

The easy identification with private success finds its obverse side, Gunnar Myrdal has observed, in 'the remarkable lack of a self-generating, self-disciplined, organized people's movement in America.' Not collective adventures, nor even self-centered fantasy, but other people's private success is often at the center of popular-media attention. This generous romanticism of success, resting upon an easy identification with those who succeed, undoubtedly lessens the psychological pressure of economic inequality, which otherwise might find collective outlet in political action aimed at the social ideal of more equality of wealth and power.

Only a few of the major characters appearing in the movies pursue any social goals, the majority are engaged by ends lying within their immediate circles. 'The interest in individuals,' Leo Lowenthal comments more generally, 'has become a kind of mass gossip.' This interest and the way it is satisfied and produced are not, however, of the same type as in the novels of the eighteenth and nineteenth centuries. The subjects chosen for popular biographies are no longer models in terms of which people may cultivate themselves for serious individual endeavor; on the contrary, they are idols of leisure and of consumption, the concern being with their private lives, valuable friends, hobbies, style of consumption—on 'the psychological gadgets' with which they are equipped for success. In their presentation, Lowenthal concludes, 'the language of promotion has replaced the language of evaluation. Only the price tag is missing.' They are pseudo-individuals displayed in an un-serious sphere of life. Their 'problems' arise and are solved individually, by means of their own vices and virtues, and such envy as they evoke is focused individually rather than in terms of position in a social structure. Not individual envy or collective resentment, but respect and awe adhere to the glamour of individual success.

The contents of the mass media are frequently blamed on the political ignorance of the public. It is true that only 21 per cent of the public has 'a reasonably accurate idea of what the Bill of Rights is'; that only about half claim to know what a lobbyist is, and that many of these cannot recall any group who they believe hire lobbyists, et cetera. Yet, in the past, the highly educated have not held a monopoly on political alertness, much less on insurgency. Moreover, in connection with the political world of the mass media, one must ask why is it that people are so ignorant, given the tremendous volume of mass communication and the increase in school populations.

The educational system is most appropriately seen as another mass medium, a parochial one with an assured public of younger age groups. In their most liberal endeavors, the political content of educational institutions is often unimaginative and serves to lay the basis for the successful diversion by other mass media, for the trivialization, fragmentation, and confusion of politics as a sphere of life. With their ideological dead-matter and intricately boring citizenship courses, the schools cannot compete with popular culture and its dazzling idols. And when, realizing this, they imitate such popular culture and its manner of presentation, they too merely trivialize their subject, without making it much less dull. The mass educated are perhaps the most politically uninterested, for they have been most exposed to politics in civics-book detail. They have been dulled by being stuffed with the conventional idols of U.S. politics. Popular culture pervades all classes of the American population, but perhaps, if only because of the age and sex differences, it grips the white-collar girl and the black-coated man most firmly. They are at the center of the high-school culture at which the mass media are targeted, and as a new lower middle class, they form an eager market for the gross output.

Yet, why do mass-communication agencies contain such persistently non-political or false political content? These agencies are of course owned and directed by a small group of people, to whose interest it is to present individual success stories and other divertissement rather than the facts of collective sucesses and tragedies.

But the fact that they are vested interests is not a sufficient explanation for their content. Although it is not true that consumers' tastes and feelings 'direct' their output, it is true that if enough individuals felt able to boycott such programs, the movie makers, the advertisers, and the personnel departments would in some way seek to change their policies. It is also true that just as many isolated, impoverished people do not have a conception of adequate housing because they have never seen it, so most movie-goers and radio listeners do not know what movies and radio could be. People put up with their present content and like it because they are not aware of any other possibility; they are strongly predisposed to see, hear, and read what they have been trained to see, hear, and read. Yet we cannot overlook the social bases of their fascinated receptivity.

To understand the continued enthusiasm for present media content, we must look beyond the psychology of apathetic and uninformed individuals, and the vested interests of the agencies of mass communication. The media do create, but they also reinforce existing tendencies, cater to existing want. They do facilitate and focus impulses and needs there before them. There is a close interplay between media and public, as wants are inculcated as well as satisfied. To understand the bases of public receptivity as well as the contents of the media, we must go beyond the media as such, and examine the social-historical setting of the U.S. political world itself.

4. The Social Structure

Explanations of a theme running as deep as political alienation must be made in terms of factors that extend over several generations. For it arises from the very shaping of the total society, and must be understood in terms of shifts over a period of time which it helps to define as an epoch.

Many of the psychological trends we have examined in connection with the transformation of the middle classes implement indifference as a prevailing political tone. One of the characteristic psychological features of the American social structure today is its systematic creation and maintenance of estrangement from society and from selfhood. Only against this broad background can we hope to understand the specific factors that have focused these trends in the political sphere.

The United States has been historically characterized by a progressive boom of real income, broken only once on a wide scale—the slump of the 'thirties—and climbing out of that to new heights in World War II. At first a frontier expansion and later a gigantic industrial elaboration fed this trend. As for wars, the United States has been lucky to a degree that is unimaginable to most Europeans. People experiencing such a history of increasing and uninterrupted material contentment are not likely to develop economic resentments that would turn their political institutions into means of ideological conflict, or turn their minds into political forums.

The discrepancy between want and satisfaction has not been so wide and prolonged for any group as to affect vitally the general tone of U.S. life. The possibilities for climbing have been real for at least a visible minority, and political demands of lower-income and occupational ranks have thus been minimized by economic and social mobility. As small entrepreneurship began to close, the white-collar opportunities opened up, which even if they led to little more income were seen as above mere farm and wage work. These facts have made for an acceptance of stratification, which has not been experienced as a permanent or oppressive arrangement, but as somehow natural and fair. If, as Karl Mannheim has noted, the expectations of an inevitable class struggle merely reflect an era of scarcity, in the United States such ideas have not taken hold by virtue of the long era of abundance.

To the economic facts of abundance, the rise in real standards of living, and the upward mobility, there was added a relatively fluid system of deference in a rising status market. Entering the social structure at or near the bottom, each wave of the 35 million immigrants who poured into the United States in the decades before 1920 took on for a while at least the difficult jobs and the lowest esteem, thus lifting all the layers above themselves. Those who had come before had somebody to look down upon. Moreover, the expectations of these immigrants, used in gauging their satisfactions and discontents, were not of the top of U.S. society, but rather U.S. society versus the homeland; their standards were inter-national rather than inter-class. And their homelands were lower in standard than the United States: for millions from Europe, America remained the great land of promise, no matter how low they were in the United States. Besides, given the volume of migration, it was not long before they, too, could find newer or different immigrants to look down upon as competitive menaces. The entire force of nationalism was thus behind the idea and the image of individual ascent and against notions of class equality. The Americanization struggle rather than the class struggle was the central psychological fact. And the increased chance for education, resting upon free institutions and changes in occupational structure, was seen as an American cultural lift, and nourished the feelings of status equality.

Immigrants added to a geographically immense and scattered country the further heterogeneities of language, culture, religion. And among the lower ranks such differences often seemed more important than their common class and occupational levels. This was a major blow at psychological, not to speak of political, cohesiveness of lower classes. To it, again, must be added the extreme mobility between regions, industries, and jobs that has been so extensive in America. The contrasts in occupational environments and the movement from one to another diversify and even fragment the material conditions, and hence the bases of potential solidarity. Consciousness of position and political will, observes Edmund Wilson, have been more likely to be local and sporadic than a 'social split that runs through the whole people like a fissure. . .'

The rapidity of change, resting on technological progress in a large open space, has made for extreme diversity and mobility. The people have not been 'settled' or fixed by tradition, and so from their social birth they have been alienated. The status panic and the salesmanship aegis have undoubtedly furthered this un-settling process and further distracted the individual from politi-cal demand and action as well as from himself. For the problem of political apathy, viewed sociologically, is part of the larger problem of self-alienation and social meaninglessness. It rests on an absence of firm legitimations, and hence of accepted, du-rable premiums for roles played—and yet on the continued, even the compulsive, enactment of these roles.

Many of the historical factors and trends may now be at their historical turning point or even end, but mentalities do not usually keep in lock-step with history. Moreover, the political order itself has not encouraged, and does not encourage, a politi-cal mentality alert to new realities.

5. U.S. Politics

Political consciousness is most immediately determined by po-litically available means and symbols. It is the political sphere itself, its institutions and traditions, its rhetoric and practices, its place in a total social structure, that must, after all, be in the forefront of an explanation of political indifference. For these are what political consciousness is about. In fact, all other factors in the mass media and the historic social structure play into the political sphere and there interact as a complex of causes.

Economic rather than political institutions have undoubtedly been of greater importance to life endeavor in the United States. Politics, in fact, has been widely understood as a means for gain-ing and protecting economic ends and practices. The whole lais-

sez-faire tradition, so unevenly applied but so persistently asserted, has been the anchor and expression of this view. However inflated by rhetoric, 'political fights' have been less over
political principles than over economic and regional interests.
This political order has given rise to the patronage machine,
rather than the ideological party, to the trade union rather than
the 'worker's movement.' Party contests have been contests between varied types and sizes of property, rather than between
property and propertylessness, and unions have taken their place
within and alongside the dominant parties, rather than in opposition to them.

In short: U.S. politics has rarely been an autonomous force.
It has been anchored in the economic sphere, its men using political means to gain and secure limited economic ends. So interest in it has seldom been an interest in political ends, has seldom involved more than immediate material profits and losses.

If greater American statesmen on the national level, as Matthew Josephson has asserted, have been concerned to adjust
larger business interests with the whole community, lesser politicians on the local levels have often been concerned to realize
smaller but more directly lucrative business ends. And sometimes this local bent has manifested itself on higher levels. National scandals about the private morality of public men have
not done much to heighten the level of public sensibility or
deepen the image of political life to make it central, urgent, and
worth while.

Locally, as Robert and Helen Lynd have shown, there has been
a tendency for a political participation to alternate with indifference and even with repugnance. 'The ward heeler' gets control and many people are disgusted and withdraw—which gives
the ward heeler his chance. In due course, a clean-up is made,
in an attempt to detach politics from more immediate and local
business grafts. Often this clean-up is more 'moral' than fundamental: politics is seen as made up of good people and bad
people, in terms of the morality and status of individuals rather
than of an institutional system that selects and forms individuals.
So gradually the old machine or another like it moves in and the
cycle of 'alternating exasperation and cynical apathy' continues.

The distrust and the ambivalent status afforded the American politician has been rooted in the balloting system, which with its long list of unknown names allows the party machine to select loyal men of little or no worth to the community. Many of these party workers are pay-offs, who have 'got things done' without publicity or formal sanction; others are selected precisely because they are 'weak sisters' and thus controllable as 'dummies' of the boss. The need of the boss and his machine for funds means that offices have often been sold and bought. Also, decentralized party control has made for 'a premium on parochialism' in national leaders: men, usually governors, who have carefully refrained from committing themselves on national and international issues are pumped up during the campaign to a national status they have by no means earned. The dominance and the near sacrosanct character of the business system have meant that when things go wrong in the political economy, blame is displaced from the businessman to the politician. The successful candidate, therefore, tends to be selected from among the uncommitted and the mediocre.

Brighter men have found more suitable careers outside politics and the people have become uninterested in politics. The exception to both has probably occurred only in situations in which the politician has been forced to act—as in slump or war. Lincoln, Wilson, and Franklin Roosevelt found themselves in such situations, and the general status impugnment of politicians has not touched them with its usual force.

In our day, muckraking, despite the glaring need for it, is properly seen as 'an integral part of an era, an era that ended with the soggy public response to the Teapot Dome disclosures.' No longer can a Lincoln Steffens command attention by detailed proof that 'in a country where business is dominant, businessmen will corrupt a government which can pass laws to hinder or help business.' That, as Walter Shannon puts it, is now 'old stuff,' which is to say, that people cynically accept it rather than revolt against it.

Conflicts within the social structure have not been fully articulated in the political sphere; great changes have occurred without benefit of any political struggle. The U.S. political order has been continuous for more than a century and a half, and for this continuity it has paid the price of many internal compromises and adjustments without explicit reformulations of principle or symbol. Its institutions have been greatly adaptive; its traditions, expedient; its great figures, inveterate opportunists.

The American political order has never known deeply situated movements, or parties with the will and the chance to change the whole political structure. For a hundred and sixty years parties have argued over symbols and issues concerned with who got what within the prevailing system. There has been no relatively successful 'third party' which questioned that system, and so no indigenous political theory which might proceed with such a movement. American politics has bred the opportunistic politician in the compromised party in the two-party state.

Each of the two parties must appeal to diverse interests and variegated strata and therefore may articulate only generalized, widely accepted issues. Neither can afford to articulate explicit views or the interests of specific groups; and their competition leads to universal appeals and hence to many broken pledges, to a universal rhetoric of vacuity rather than conflicting ideologies of particular strata. The more variegated the public to which the patronage party must appeal for support, the more empty of decisive, antagonistic content its programs will be. It blunts the issues it reflects, attenuates the desires it serves. In its fear of alarming anyone, it talks while managing to say nothing. So lively issues, closely connected with everyday reality, are not presented in the controversies of the parties. Trotsky, in quite another context, once wrote: 'A party for whom everybody votes except that minority who know what they are voting for, is no more a party, than the tongue in which babies in all countries babble is a national language.'

Political selection, for the electorate, comment the Lynds, 'becomes a matter of lining up on one side or the other of an either-or situation. The issues involved in supporting the eithers or the ors have become somewhat more blurred since the 'nineties. . .' And because of this artificial party situation, 'elections are no longer the lively centers of public interest they were in the 'nineties. In 1890 Middletown gave itself over for weeks be-

fore each election to the bitter, hilarious joy of conflict. . . Today torchlight processions and horns no longer blast out the
voters or usher in the newly elected officials, and, although
speeches persist with something of their old vigor, new inven-
tions offering a variety of alternate interests are pressing upon
politics as upon lodges, unions, and churches.'

The compromises in the two-party state tend to occur within
the party formations; when they do occur between the parties,
they often take the form of non-publicized, even non-publiciz-
able, deals. So popular will is less effective than the pressure of
organized minorities; where power is already distributed in extremely disproportionate ways, the principle of hidden compromise is likely to work for the already powerful.

The *compromising* party means, ideally at least, that two
groups, each representing definite, antagonistic interests, integrate policy as best they can in order to realize all the existent
interests possible. How well they can succeed in this depends in
large part upon how deep the antagonisms are. The *compromised* party, on the other hand, refers to a party in which there
has been so much expediency and compromise going on *within*
it that its leaders really can't do anything decisive or stand up
and say No to anybody. Party managers minimize the public
discussion of fundamental issues; politicians solve them by means
of the personal contact and the private integration. The compromised party is everybody's friend.

There is usually very little real difference between the two
major U.S. parties, yet together they virtually monopolize the
chances at political organization and political propaganda on a
large scale. This party system is ideal for a people that is largely
contented, which is to say that such a people need not be interested in politics as a struggle for the power to solve real issues.

Such political contentment as has prevailed is no doubt aided
by the general fact of occupational, pecuniary, and social ascent,
but more specifically, the potential leaders of the lower ranks
have had, in each generation, available channels of upward mobility. In this way, as Gunnar Myrdal has shown, they have been
drained off as opposition leaders. In the two-party system probably 'the best men' go into the dominant and long-established

local party. The latest channel, open in this way, has been the big labor unions that came out of the great depression. These unions have quickly been bureaucratized, in many ways tamed; but they have provided new ways up, to higher income, prestige, and power, for many 'militant' young men, working-class boys who could adapt their views to the organizational practices of the unions. In so far as organizers and articulate spokesmen of definite interests might increase general political alertness, this draining of talent from the lower circles has decreased their chances to become alert.

Most political decisions of consequence have been moved from local to state to federal establishment. The issues of local politics, to which the individual might be supposed most alert, have become in some part a matter of deals between federal powers and local authorities. 'During the 'twenties,' says a liberal organization's leader, 'you could get together local pressures to squeeze Congress. During the 'thirties, you didn't need it so much. It was there at the center, and we got dependent on it. Then the war stymied political efforts. . . Now, just a while ago, we wanted wide support for a bill, but we couldn't find any. There just aren't any local organizations or local fire any more. They've withered away.'

The distance between the individual and centers of power has become greater, and the individual has come to feel powerless. Between political hope and political realization there are the two parties and the federal bureaucracy, which, as means of political action, often seem to cut the nerve of direct political interest. Indifference may thus be seen as an understandable response to a condition of powerlessness. In Barbara Wootton's words, ' "Political apathy" may be the expression of a sort of horse-sense. It may be the indifference not so much of those who can, but will not, as of those who realize when they cannot—a refusal, in fact, to attempt a response to demands that are recognized to be impossible.' There is a felt lack of power between the individual's everyday life and what is going on in the distant worlds of politics.

The issues of politics, it is often said, are now so technical and intricate that the individual cannot be expected to under-

stand them or be alert to their consequences. And it is undoubtedly true, as Jefferson made clear, that participation is more possible, politics more engaging, when the issues to be settled are
within the everyday experience of those to whom they are ad-
dressed. But it would be more accurate to say that the political
organs now existing, and the politicians in charge of them, are
not willing to think through such issues. In fact, they are incapable of doing so, of tying their various solutions to readily understood ideas, of using the mass media to spell out in dramatic,
accurate ways what is involved; in short, of exercising leadership
responsibly by translating intricate issues into their human and
political consequences for specific sets of people. And to tell them
about it. The idea that the issues are too intricate for a people's
decision is a curious blend of bureaucratic perspectives (which
transform political issues into administrative problems) and a
simplistic notion of democracy (which would equate the public
with the executive organs of the government, rather than with
effective intervention in general decisions of general consequence).

The more decentralized rule of the old spoils system brought
government closer to at least certain opinion-leader circles of the
populace. Bureaucracy, with its trained staff, often seems far
removed; the official, not being dependent for his job upon the
opinions of constituents and bosses, does not develop and exploit
the personal touch. Thus Jackson believed (as did Lenin) that
official duties could be made 'so plain and simple that men of
intelligence may readily qualify themselves for their performance.' The 'good side' of the spoils system was that it brought
more people into the sphere of governmental participation; the
state was no longer to be 'an engine for the support of the few
at the expense of the many.' What has happened in parties, and
especially in the executive organs of the state, is that bureaucratization has contracted the areas open to political decision and expanded those subject to administrative rule.

In pre-capitalist societies, power was known and personal. The
individual could see who was powerful, and he could understand
the means of his power. His responses, of obedience and fear,
were explicit and concrete; and if he was in revolt, the targets

of that revolt were also explicit and concrete. Comments H. D. Lasswell, 'Once your eye lights on the Indian who lies in wait behind a tree, you know you are being ambushed. But you may see a modern financier at his desk for hours a day for years and catch no clue to the nature of the security structure which he has set up to ambush investors.' Or, when a man owns land with water on it, and others need water for their cattle, they can see the power of property; but when the price-wage-profit ratio is manipulated to lower their standard of living, they cannot find out who is to blame.

In an impersonalized and more anonymous system of control, explicit responses are not so possible: anxiety is likely to replace fear; insecurity to replace worry. The problem is who really has power, for often the tangled and hidden system seems a complex yet organized irresponsibility. When power is delegated from a distant center, the one immediately over the individual is not so different from the individual himself; he does not decide either, he too is part of the network by means of which individuals are controlled. Targets for revolt, given the will to revolt, are not readily available. Symbols in terms of which to challenge power are not available—in fact, there are no explicit symbols of authority to challenge.

As political power has been centralized, the issues professionalized and compromised by the two-party state, a sort of impersonal manipulation has replaced authority. For authority, there is a need of justifications in order to secure loyalties; for manipulation, there is exercise of power without explicit justifications, for decisions are hidden. Manipulation, as we have suggested, arises when there is a centralization of power that is not publicly justified and those who have it don't believe they could justify it. Manipulation feeds upon and is fed by mass indifference. For in the narrowed range of assertion and counter-assertion no target of demand, no symbols or principles are argued over and debated in public. If the areas of assertion and of counter-assertion are narrow in the mass media, it is in some part because politics is monopolized by the two major parties, and the economic-political arena of struggle, monopolized by the labor-union-corporation battle. In all three—communications, unions, political parties—there is a narrowed range of assertion and counter-assertion. And so insecurity and striving are not attached to political symbols, but are drained off by the distractions of amusement, the frenzied search for commodities, or turned in upon the self as busy little frustrations. There is no organized effort to develop common consciousness of common interests, and men feel distanced from events and without the power to order them.

By virtue of their increased and centralized power, political institutions become more objectively important to the course of American history, but because of mass alienation, less and less of subjective interest to the population at large. On the one hand, politics is bureaucratized, and on the other, there is mass indifference. These are the decisive aspects of U.S. politics today. Because of them, political expression is banalized, political theory is barren administrative detail, history is made behind men's backs. Such is the political situation in which the new middle classes enact their passive role.

6. The Rearguarders

Politics, no matter how important, is only one sphere in the social order, which by no means needs to be tied together by political loyalties. It may even be that political indifference should be taken as an expected psychological fact about a society so dominated by such individuated, pecuniary standards and activities as the United States. This is a bureaucratized society of privatized men, and it may very well go along in this condition for a long time to come.

The decline of the old middle classes does not mean that the U.S. framework of capitalist democracy is broken. But it does mean that the old legitimations of that system no longer move men, and that the institutions under which we live, the framework of our existence, are without enthusiasm. Again, this does not mean that we are in a situation without norms, a situation of anomy, although it is fairly clear that ours is an era of wide moral distress. But moral or ideological consensus is not the only basis for a social order. A network of expediences and conventions, in a framework of power not entirely or firmly legitimated, can hold together a society with high material standards of comfort.

Still, it must be recognized that this is not the idea of democracy (based upon the old middle classes) we have known; that there is a struggle over men's minds even if there is no struggle in them; that our bureaucratized society has its own contradictions and crises, in which the payoffs that have kept the United States going ahead may become much harder to organize and deliver.

The transformation of the middle classes has split them in such a way that no 'middle-class policy' seems possible, even if the power and the opportunity for it to become a movement existed. A political movement seeks to promote the interests of the groups that it involves; in this sense, there is no distinctly middle-class movement on the United States political scene. For these classes are diversified in social form, contradictory in material interest, dissimilar in ideological illusion; there is no homogeneity of base among them for common political movement.

Farmers want higher protective tariffs and higher price supports; white-collar clerks, cheap consumer's prices. Government employees want higher salaries; small shopkeepers, lower taxes. In matters of wages and social policies, new middle-class people increasingly have the attitude of those who are given work; old middle-class people still have the attitude of those who give it. If the old middle classes have, from time to time, fought monopoly corporations, in the name of small property, the new middle classes have been dependent upon monopoly corporations for secure jobs and have revealed the fact psychologically by loyalties to the firm. Small businessmen, especially retailers, fight 'chain stores,' government, and unions—under the wing of big business. White-collar workers, in so far as they are organized in the fight at all, are organized in unions which in all essentials are under the wage-workers. Thus both old and new middle classes become shock troops for other more powerful and articulate pressure blocs in the political scene.

No common symbols of loyalty, demand, or hope are available to the middle classes as a whole, or to either of its wings. Various segments join already existing blocs to compete by pressure within party and state. The major instruments are not differentiated in such a way as to allow, much less to encourage them, to take upon themselves any specific political struggle.

Nothing in their direct occupational experiences propels the white-collar people toward autonomous political organizations. The social springs for such movements, should they occur, will not occur among these strata. Lenin's remark that the political consciousness of a stratum cannot be aroused within 'the sphere of relations between workers and employers' holds doubly true for white-collar employees. Their occupational ideology is politically passive; they are not engaged in any economic struggle, except in the most scattered and fragmentary sense; they lack even a rudimentary awareness of their economic and political interests: they do not feel any sharp crisis specific to their stratum. Such problems as the relations of party, trade union, and class cannot be posed for them, for they are not a homogeneous class; they are not heavily in trade unions; neither major party caters specifically to them; and there is no thought of their forming an independent party.

In so far as political strength rests upon organized economic power, the white-collar workers can only derive their strength from 'business' or from 'labor.' Within the whole structure of power, they are dependent variables. Estimates of their political tendencies, therefore, must rest upon larger predictions of the manner and outcome of the struggles of business and labor. Only when 'labor' rather obviously 'wins out,' if then, will the lower white-collar employees go all out for unions; if labor leaders are included in compromised committees, stemming from big-business circles, then white-collar groups will be even more so.

Theories of the rise to power of white-collar people are generally inferred from the facts of their numerical growth and their indispensability in the bureaucratic and distributive operations of mass society. But only if one assumes a pure and automatic democracy of numbers does the mere growth of a stratum mean increased power for it. And only if one assumes a magic leap from occupational function to political power does technical indispensability mean power for a stratum.

When such large questions are translated into the terms of American life, one sees clearly that the jump from numerical growth and importance of function to increased political power requires, at a minimum, political awareness and political organization. The white-collar workers do not have either to any appreciable extent. Moreover, their advance to increased stature in American society could not result in increased freedom and rationality. For white-collar people carry less rationality than illusion and less desire for freedom than the misery of modern anxieties. Their socially bleak ways of life writ large would not mean freedom or rationality for the individual or for society.

Such speculations, however, are academic; there is no probability of the new middle classes' forming or inaugurating or leading any political movement. They have no steady discontent or responsible struggle with the conditions of their lives. For discontent of this sort requires imagination, even a little vision; and responsible struggle requires leadership.

The political question of the new middle classes is, Of what bloc or movement will they be most likely to stay at the tail? And the answer is, The bloc or movement that most obviously seems to be winning.

They will not go politically 'proletarian,' if for no other reason than the absence of any political proletariat in America. They will not go politically 'middle class,' if for no other reason than the absence of middle-class policy or formation, and because they will not be economically able to maintain such a status. They will not go political as an independent bloc or party, if for no other reason than their lack of either the unity or the opportunity. They will not become a political balance-wheel, if for no other reason than their lack of will to choose one bloc or another before it has already shown itself in the ascendant; they will 'choose' only after their 'choice' has won.

Since they have no public position, their private positions as individuals determine in what direction each of them goes; but, as individuals, they do not know where to go. So now they waver. They hesitate, confused and vacillating in their opinions, unfocused and discontinuous in their actions. They are worried and distrustful but, like so many others, they have no targets on which to focus their worry and distrust. They may be politically irritable, but they have no political passion. They are a chorus, too afraid to grumble, too hysterical in their applause. They are rearguarders. In the shorter run, they will follow the panicky ways of prestige; in the longer run, they will follow the ways of power, for, in the end, prestige is determined by power. In the meantime, on the political market-place of American society, the new middle classes are up for sale; whoever seems respectable enough, strong enough, can probably have them. So far, nobody has made a serious bid.

Acknowledgments and Sources

I wish to thank the John Simon Guggenheim Foundation, which, by a Fellowship, gave me time for work; and the Social Science Research Council of Columbia University, which provided funds. Whenever in this book, I have written 'we' I mean my wife, Ruth Harper, and myself: during the last three years, her assistance in careful research and creative editing has often amounted to collaboration. As with other writings, so with this: my friends and colleagues William Miller and Hans Gerth have given generously of their time, ideas, and skill.

Irving Sanes read the manuscript and gave me much astute criticism; Richard Morris criticized Chapter 1; Bernhard Stern, the materials on the medical world. Beatrice Kevitt's editing of a large portion of an earlier draft was of great help. Honey Toda, who was my assistant for several years at the University of Maryland and later at Columbia University, patiently compiled many occupational statistics that appear in the book, as well as many others which stand behind it.

At the galley stage, much invaluable advice was kindly given by Quentin Anderson, Charles Frankel, Richard Hofstadter, Harvey Swados, and Lionel Trilling. I am very grateful to them for their generosity and indulgence.

II

Several of my previous publications have been drawn upon for this work, in fact, some are more properly seen as technical by-products of it. I wish to thank the editors of the publications in which they appeared for allowing me to draw upon them here: 'A Marx For the Managers' (written with H. H. Gerth), *Ethics: An International Journal of Legal, Political & Social Thought*, January 1942; 'The Powerless People: The Role of the Intellectual in Society,'

Politics, April 1944; 'The American Business Elite,' *The Tasks of Economic History*, Supplement v to the *Journal of Economic History*, December 1945; 'The Middle Classes in Middle-Sized Cities,' *American Sociological Review*, October 1946; 'The Competitive Personality,' *Partisan Review*, September-October 1946; 'Small Business and Civic Welfare,' Senate Document No. 135, 79th Congress, 2nd Session, Washington, D.C., 1946; 'Doctors and Workers,' a report to the United Automobile Workers, CIO, March 1948 (unpublished); 'The Contribution of Sociology to Studies of Industrial Relations,' *First Annual Proceedings of the Industrial Relations Research Association*, Cleveland, Ohio, 30 December 1948; 'White Collar Unionism,' *Labor and Nation*, March-April 1949 and May-June 1949.

III

The administrative generosity of Paul F. Lazarsfeld made it possible for me to obtain 128 intensive interviews with white-collar workers in New York City during the fall of 1946. Jeannette Green supervised this work and personally performed several important interviews; I am indebted to Zena Smith for a preliminary analysis of these materials in connection with unions. In a later volume on qualitative method, I hope to present these materials, used here only as a source of quotations and an informal limit to psychological statements, in full. I am indebted to James B. Gale, Marjorie Fiske, and Helen Powell for information based on close-up experience in department stores, which I could have got in no other way. To Mr. Gale, who, while attending the University of Maryland, prepared a memorandum of types of salesgirls with supporting documentation, I am especially grateful.

I have also drawn, directly and indirectly, upon several more formal field experiences. In 1945 I examined the stratification and power structure of six middle-sized cities in the Middle-West and New England for the Smaller War Plants Corporation in preparation for a Senate hearing. That same year and later, I did a more intensive study of one middle-western city of 60,000 population, in connection with a research project undertaken for the Bureau of Applied Social Research (to be published by Harper & Bros. in 1952). In 1946 I had an opportunity for a close-up look at the New York State Department of Labor; in 1947, at Puerto Rican problems in Spanish Harlem, Manhattan; in 1948 I undertook a survey of union members in Detroit for the United Automobile Workers, CIO. In all these jobs, I kept my eyes open for 'white-collar material.' I am grateful to John Blair, who was Research Director of the Smaller War Plants Corporation and Nat Weinberg, Research Director of the UAW, for their leniency in this matter.

IV

The technical vocabulary used, and hence in many ways the general perspective of this volume, is derived from Max Weber. Such concepts as class, occupation, status, power, authority, manipulation, bureaucracy, profession are basically his. Back of Weber, of course, stands Karl Marx, and I cannot fail, especially in these times when his work is on the one side ignored and vulgarized, and on the other ignored and maligned, to acknowledge my general debt, especially to his earlier productions.

Literature in this tradition, or influenced by it, which I have found especially useful or suggestive in connection with various themes and problems includes the following. Although by no means complete, these works will be found especially rewarding to those who would explore the problems of this book further.

Eduard Bernstein, *Socialisme Théorique et social-démocratie practique*, tr. d'Alexandre Cohen (Paris, 1900); Alfred M. Bingham, *Insurgent America* (New York: Harper, 1935); G. D. H. Cole, *What Marx Really Meant* (New York: Knopf, 1937); Lewis Corey, *The Crisis of the Middle Class* (New York: Covici-Friede, 1935); Erich Fromm, *Escape from Freedom* (New York: Farrar & Rinehart, 1941); Henry Durant, *The Problem of Leisure* (London: George Routledge, 1938); Daniel Guérin, *Fascism and Big Business* (New York: Pioneer Publishers, 1939); Karl Kautsky, *Le Marxisme et son critique Bernstein*, tr. de Martin-Leray (Paris: 1900); Harold D. Lasswell, 'The Moral Vocation of the Middle-Income Skill Group, *International Journal of Ethics*, vol. XLV, no. 2, January 1935, and *World Politics and Personal Insecurity* (New York: McGraw-Hill, 1935); Emil Lederer, *The Problem of the Modern Salaried Employee: Its Theoretical and Statistical Basis* (chapters II and III of *Die Privatangestellten in der Modernen Wirtschaftsentwicklung*, Tubingen, 1912), WPA Project No. 165-6999-6027; Emil Lederer and Jacob Marschak, *The New Middle Class* ('Der neue Mittelstand,' *Grundriss der Sozialökonomik*, IX Abteilung I, 1926; WPA Project No. 165-97-6999-6027, New York, 1937); Leo Lowenthal, 'Biographies in Popular Magazines,' *Radio Research* 1942-3 (New York: Duell, Sloan and Pearce, 1944); Karl Mannheim, *Ideology and Utopia* (New York: Harcourt, Brace, 1936), and *Man and Society in an Age of Reconstruction* (New York: Harcourt, Brace, 1940); Herbert Marcuse, *Reason and Revolution* (New York: Oxford, 1941); Alfred Meusel, 'Middle Class,' *Encyclopedia of the Social Sciences*, vol. X; Arthur Salz, 'Occupations,' *Encyclopedia of the Social Sciences*, vol. XI; Edward Shils and Herbert Goldhammer, 'Types of Power and Status,' *American Journal of Sociology*, September 1939; Werner Sombart, *The Quintessence of Capitalism* (New York: Dutton, 1915), and 'Capitalism: the Capitalist

Enterprise,' *Encyclopedia of the Social Sciences,* vol. III; Hans Speier, *The Salaried Employee in German Society* (WPA Project No. 465-970391, New York, 1939), and 'The Salaried Employee in Modern Society,' *Social Research,* February 1934; Thorstein Veblen, *Absentee Ownership* (New York: Viking, 1938); Graham Wallas, *The Great Society* (New York: Macmillan, 1936); William E. Walling, *Progressivism and After* (New York: Macmillan, 1914).

V

The statistics in this volume have been reworked, predominantly from U.S. Government sources: the Department of Commerce, especially its Bureau of the Census; the U.S. Department of Agriculture's Bureau of Agricultural Economics; the Department of Labor's Bureau of Labor Statistics. Many of these figures are readily available in the Bureau of the Census, *Historical Statistics of the United States, 1789-1945,* the *Statistical Abstract of the United States* for appropriate years, and technical journals such as the *Journal of Farm Economics, Federal Reserve Bulletin,* and the *Survey of Current Business.* The monographs of the Temporary National Economic Committee's Investigation of Concentration of Economic Power in the U.S. are invaluable for anyone who would understand the American economy, as are many publications of the Smaller War Plants Corporation. I have also taken much factual material and opinion from publications of the American Management Association and the National Association of Office Managers. I wish to thank the libraries of these several agencies for their courtesies.

These government and business sources are not the only materials used in constructing this book. I have not burdened the text with specific citations to facts and figures. The complete documentation, which is unfortunately lengthy, has not been printed here, but is available privately to interested scholars. There are, however, four topics, my statistics for which have involved rather elaborate reclassification and about which brief comment should be made: the occupational categories used, and their cross-tabulation by income, unemployment, and union membership.

1. The historical occupational tables are based upon a reclassification of census data as presented in detailed breakdowns by Alba Edwards (Bureau of the Census, *Comparative Occupational Statistics for the U.S., 1870-1940,* pp. 105-12). The difficulties of any historical comparison of occupational data have been immensely aided by Edwards' painstaking work. Another important work, which I have found especially useful for industrial classifications as well as commentaries on specific occupations, is H. Dewey Anderson and Percy E. Davidson, *Occupational Trends in the United States* (Stanford, California: Stanford University Press, 1940). See also Victor Perlo's

1939 attempt and remarks thereupon in Spurgeon Bell, *Productivity, Wages and National Income* (Washington, D.C.: Brookings Institution, 1940, pp. 210-32).

In my reclassification, the 'free enterprisers' were isolated by ascertaining whether or not each occupation listed by Edwards mainly received payments through profits, entrepreneurial withdrawal, rents, or royalties. This was mainly determined by projecting 1940 information in regard to 'class of work' (primarily the distinction between 'employers and own-account workers' and 'wage and salary workers') to earlier years. (See 16th *Census of the U.S.* 1940. *Population.* The Labor Force [Sample Statistics] Occupational Characteristics, pp. 119-33). The question of 'class of work' was carried on the population schedule as far back as 1910, but was not tabulated until 1940. 'The question did serve a very useful purpose, however, as an aid in the occupational classification. . . It would not be possible to make the cross-tabulation you want for some earlier census. . .' (Letter to the author from Philip M. Hauser, Deputy Director, Bureau of the Census, 27 March 1947.) 'Class of work' as of 1940, of course, does not always hold back through the years; each case was examined and individual decisions made about it. The distinction between white-collar and wage-worker was based in part on the 'non-commodity-producing' character of white-collar work. The Labor Economics Staff of the Bureau of Labor Statistics ('White-Collar Workers: The Problem of Definition,' unpublished) uses, along with 'fixed payment by the day, week, or month,' two other criteria which I found helpful: 'A well-groomed appearance' and 'the wearing of street clothes at work.' The broad occupational groups included within the category of 'white-collar workers' by the Labor Economics Staff are quite similar to my four categories, except they omit salaried managerial employees.

Owing to the negative definition of the occupational function of the new middle class as 'non-commodity producing,' the group as a whole is quite heterogeneous, and continues to be so even when subdivided into the four sub-categories I have used. To combine these heterogeneous elements into one group and call them the 'New Middle Class' would seem hazardous if it were not for the fact that by their very nature, given the census classifications with which we must work, they are residual groups, and further that 'other classes . . . likewise exhibit considerable lateral extensions: the entrepreneur class takes in the small manufacturer and the commercial entrepreneur, as well as the industrial magnate. The manual laborer's class includes the unskilled proletarians of the lowest strata . . . as well as the skilled, regularly employed and well-paid male wage earners.' The white-collar group can be 'comprehended as an entity only in contradistinction to the other classes.' (Lederer and Marschak, op. cit. p. 6.) This point becomes important when we realize that in a good number of cases we do not have any criteria for placing a given occupation *in* the new middle class, but we have many criteria for *not placing* it in the free enterpriser or the wage-worker.

The occupational classification was applied to cross-tabulations in the 1940 census volumes of *detailed* occupation by age, sex, education, et cetera. The nature of all existing national occupational figures, except in the broadest terms, suggests that they can be considered accurate only to within 3 or 4 per cent.

2. Definitive historical information on income by occupation does not exist for the United States. Even in the simplest historical series of income by occupation four major difficulties make historical comparisons of absolute incomes unreliable: (1) The scope of the studies—many are confined to only one city or locality, to certain industries, types of industries, or only to certain occupations. (2) Occupational classifications—variations in the way the occupations are classified often prohibit regrouping data into other occupational categories, thus obviating comparisons between studies. Such comparisons of occupational groups that are possible usually include occupations having such a wide spread in income that important income variations within the groups are obscured. For instance, we cannot always separate office and sales employees from the higher-paid managerial and professional employees; nor can we always separate unskilled wage-workers from the skilled or semi-skilled. (3) The type of recipient whose income is measured often varies; one study covers family income; another, each member of the labor force; another, 'spending units.' Also, the sex composition of the recipients is only rarely available. (4) Types of income—sometimes income is only money derived from work; sometimes it is all forms of income, including or excluding income-in-kind.

Therefore, we cannot provide a complete income history of the new middle class in America. From existing data, we can only patch together certain limited comparisons with wage workers. I wish to thank Norman Kaplan for his assistance in connection with my income tabulations.

For the earlier figures, especially wages and salaries in manufacturing industries, see Paul H. Douglas, *Real Wages in the United States*, 1890-1926 (New York: Houghton Mifflin, 1930). For data on wages and salaries in manufacturing between 1929 and 1939, see U.S. Bureau of the Census, *Biennial Census of Manufacturers,* Washington, D.C., 1939. The Department of Commerce compiled a yearly series from 1929 to 1939 of wages and salaries in three selected industries, which is available in the *Statistical Abstract of the United States,* 1940. For an early series based on four selected industries, see W. I. King, *The National Income and Its Purchasing Power* (New York: National Bureau of Economic Research, 1930); and for the early 'thirties, Robert F. Martin, *National Income and Its Elements* (New York: National Industrial Conference Board, 1936).

For 1935-6 there is nation-wide income data for non-relief families in eight occupational groups from a study by the National Resources Committee, *Consumer Incomes in the United States: Their Distribution in 1935-6* (U.S. Government Printing Office, Washington, D.C., 1938). For 1939, the 16th Census of the U.S. 1940 Population, vol. III, The Labor Force, part I, U.S. Summary, pp. 120ff gives wages and salaries. For 1946 and 1948, see the Bureau of the Census, *Current Population Reports: Consumer Income,* Series P-60, no. 3, 3 June 1948, 'Income of Non-Farm Families and Individuals, 1946,' and Series P-60, 6, 14 February 1950, 'Income of Families and Persons in the U.S., 1948.' These four studies are the only ones that may readily be discussed in terms of my broad occupational categories, and the last three are the only ones that distinguish the sex of the employee.

See also, for the later 'forties, Department of Agriculture, Bureau of Agricultural Economics, Division of Program Surveys, 'National Survey of Liquid Asset Holdings, Spending, and Saving,' Part Two; and the yearly studies since 1946 of the Board of Governors of the Federal Reserve System, 'Survey of Consumer Finances,' reprinted in issues of the *Federal Reserve Bulletin.* These studies deal with 'spending units' rather than individual earners, and their occupational classifications are not entirely comparable with ours, but they do provide an indication of rough shifts in income over these years.

3. On the difficulties of determining unemployment, see W. S. Woytinsky, 'Controversial Aspects of Unemployment,' *Review of Economic Statistics,* May 1941. In addition to the U.S. censuses of 1890, 1900, 1930, 1937, and 1940, and various state and local censuses during the 'thirties, unemployment series have been compiled over the years by such agencies as the labor unions, the National Industrial Conference Board, the Bureau of Labor Statistics. Before 1929, reliable unemployment data exists only for certain industrial groups. For the best discussion and estimates, see Paul H. Douglas, op. cit. pp. 409-60. From 1929 to date unemployment information on the total labor force is more reliable; the Bureau of Labor Statistics has recently eliminated much of the confusion between conflicting reports by releasing its revised estimates of the size of the labor force and unemployment since 1929 (*Monthly Labor Review,* July 1948, pp. 50-53).

If estimates of general unemployment are often difficult, those for specific occupational groups are often impossible. In the best, there is an element of plain guess. Nation-wide unemployment data by occupation exists only for 1930, 1937, and 1940, which are not the years of worst unemployment. We have computed the proportions of unemployment by occupation for these years from W. S. Woytinsky, *Labor in the United States: Basic Statistics for Social Security* (Washington, D.C.: Committee on Social Security, Social Science Research Council, 1938), pp. 312-15; *Census of Partial Employment, Unem-*

ployment and Occupations: 1937, *Final Report on Total & Partial Unemployment,* vol. I, p. 5, table 4, interpolating the employable labor force for 1937 from 1930 and 1940 census data; and from unemployment revealed in the 1940 census as presented in the *Statistical Abstract of the United States:* 1948, pp. 179-87. For 1930, see also Woytinsky, *Three Aspects of Labor Dynamics* (Washington, D.C.: Committee on Social Security, Social Science Research Council, 1942), p. 153. The value of many local and state-wide studies of unemployment made between 1932 and 1934 is of course limited, and their occupational classifications vary, but they do serve as guide-posts to general statements and often give added insight to various aspects of the incidence of unemployment. Especially helpful to our work in this connection were the Massachusetts Department of Labor and Industries, Division of Statistics, Report on the Census of Unemployment in Massachusetts as of 2 January 1934; Pennsylvania State Emergency Relief Administration, Harrisburg, Pa., *Census of Employable Workers in Urban & Rural Non-Farm Areas of Pa.,* 1934; and various studies reported in the *Monthly Labor Review,* October 1933, p. 811, April 1934, p. 792, and September 1934, p. 643.

4. Union membership figures for 1948 were taken from the Bureau of Labor Statistics, 'Directory of Labor Unions in the U.S., June 1948,' *Bulletin No.* 937. Membership in directly affiliated locals is not included by BLS nor in our estimations. In certain cases where the BLS gave no membership figure for a union, we have used the reported membership given by other sources; if such alternative figures could not be found for a given union, we have substituted the 1944 membership figures in Florence Peterson, *American Labor Unions* (New York: Harper, 1945). Each of the 194 unions listed in the BLS directory was classified in regard to whether it was com-posed primarily of wage-workers or white-collar employees; and all unions were isolated into one of three types: (1) BLS, *Bulletin No.* 745, June 1943, lists 35 unions as 'unions, most of all of whose members are engaged in what are commonly considered to be white-collar occupations.' This list was brought up to date in consultation with various union officials, thereby adding 11 unions—making the total number of primarily white-collar unions 46. (2) Personal letters to the author by various union officials, and data reported in *Business Week,* 7 February 1948, p. 92, allowed us to classify 13 production unions in the CIO as 'mixed' unions, containing substantial propor-tions of white-collar workers. For most of these unions, certainly the most important, the estimated numbers of white-collar workers in-volved were given by the sources cited above. (3) All other unions were considered to be primarily composed of wage-workers.

Figures on the proportions of white-collar workers unionized in each industrial group can only be approximations. Each type of union mentioned above was classified according to its industrial group; as no information about the precise proportions of white-collar workers working in each industrial group (potential union members) exists for 1948, we had to project the proportions of white-collar workers in each industrial group as of 1940 to the numbers of 'wage and salary' workers in each industry as of 1948 given in the *Monthly Labor Review,* July 1948. For earlier figures on union membership and proportions organized, see Leo Wolman, *Ebb and Flow in Trade Unionism* (New York: National Bureau of Economic Research, 1936). I am especially grateful to Professor Wolman for allowing me access to his unpublished data on membership figures for 1935.

C. WRIGHT MILLS

New York City
1 May 1951

Index

A

Absentee owner, 21
Academic man, types of, 132
Accountants, x, 139
Adams, H., 145
Advertising
  employment in, 67
  salesmanship and, 181
Agricultural ladder, 20
Agriculture, increase in output of,
    18; *see also* Farmer
Alger, H., xi, 284, 337
Alice Adams, xviii; office girl,
    201-2
Alienation, cult of, among intel-
    lectuals, 159-60
  political, 327-32
  self and personality market,
    187-8
  from work, 224-8
American Bar Association, 121
American Federation of Labor;
    dominance in white-collar
    unionism, 314-15
American gospel of work, 219-20
American Medical Association,
    119, 120
Anderson, D., 273, 358
Anderson, Q., 355
Anomy, 350
Architect, 139
Authority, as basis of prestige
    claims, 241-3, 249
  coercion, manipulation and,
    109-11

Authority (Cont.)
  decline in foreman, 87, 89-91
  distribution of, in early 19th-
    century U.S., 9-12; change
    in, 69
  intellectuals and, 143
  political indifference and, 348-
    50
  see also Manipulation, Power

B

Balzac, H. de, 28, 30, 91, 192,
    223; on social climber, 95
Beard, C., xx
Bell, S., 358
Bendix, R., on social origins of
    government officials, 83
Bennett, H. H., on farmers, 29
Bentham, 326
Bergson, H., 220, 228
Berle, A. A., Jr., 123
Bernstein, E., 357
Big Business, effects on smaller
    city, 48-51
  lawyer and, 126
  occupational structure of, **68-9**
  power of managers in, 100-106
Big city, social psychology of,
    251-4
Biggest bazaar in the world, 166-9
Bingham, A. F., 357; on class
    consciousness, 294
Blair, J., 356

Intellectuals (Cont.)
  technicians contrasted with,
    156-60

J

Jackson, A., 348
James, H., on Balzac, 223
Jefferson, T., 3, 9, 55, 56, 348
Job satisfaction, income and, 229,
    230-31
  power and, 229, 230, 232-3
  status and, 229, 230, 231-2
  white-collar unionism and, 307-
    8
Jones, L. W., 115
Josephson, M., 56, 157, 343
Journalist, 131

K

Kafka, F., xvi; on bureaucracy,
    106
Kaplan, N., 360
Kautsky, K., 357
Kevitt, B., 355
Kierkegaard, S., 148
King, W. I., 360
Kirchheimer, O., on Nazism, 53
Kitty Foyle, xi, xviii, 200
Klonsky, M., 333
Kotschnig, W., 271; on educa-
    tional opportunities, 267
Krout, J., 7

L

Labor unions, *see* Unions, Union-
    ism
LaFollette, R., 56, 57
Laski, H., 138
Lasswell, H. D., 32, 298, 349, 357
Lawyers, x, 113, 114, 130, 133,
    138, 140
  big business and, 126
  bureaucratic organization of,
    124-6
  income of, 122
  loss of monopolies, 128-9
  politics and, 127-8
  prestige of, 121
  skills of, 121, 123, 127

Lazarsfeld, P. F., 356
Lecky, W. E. H., 32
Lederer, E., 357, 360; on salaried
    employees, 241
Leffingwell, H. W., on office, 192
Leisure, mass media focus on,
    336, 338
  psychology of contemporary,
    235-8
  status panic and, 256
  work and, in craftsman ideal,
    223; modern, 224
Leonardo da Vinci, 217
Lenin, 146, 325, 348, 352
Lewis, S., on the office, 198, 200
Liberalism, era of classic, 9-12
  as model of political conscious-
    ness, 324-5
Lincoln, A., 55, 344; on property,
    8
Lippmann, W., 325
Literature of resignation, 282-4,
    285
'Live-Wires,' bureaucratic per-
    sonality type, 93, 94
Llewellyn, K., 125
Locke, on work, 217
Lowenthal, L., 284, 338, 357; on
    work, 236
Luce, H., 149, 157
Lukacs, G., 156
Lumpen-bourgeoisie, 28-33
  composition and proportion of,
    28-9
  psychic security among, 30-33
Lundberg, F., 124
Luther, M., meaning of work to,
    216
Lynd, H. and R., 343, 345

M

Macdonald, D., 147
McGrath, E. J., 269
MacLeish, A., 147
MacMahon, A. W., 84
Macy's, 166-9
Man, H. de, 141, 222, 227
Managerial demiurge, ch. 5
  bureaucracy and, 78-81
  case of the foreman, 87-91

Galaxy Books

HISTORY

PHILOSOPHY

POLITICAL SCIENCE

SOCIOLOGY AND ANTHROPOLOGY